P9-ARZ-060

WE EAT THE MINES AND THE MINES EAT US
Dependency and Exploitation in Bolivian Tin Mines

WE EAT THE MINES
AND
THE MINES EAT US

dependency and exploitation in bolivian tin mines

JUNE NASH

WITH A NEW PREFACE BY THE AUTHOR

COLUMBIA UNIVERSITY PRESS
New York

Columbia University Press
New York   Chichester, West Sussex
Copyright © 1993 Columbia University Press
All rights reserved

Library of Congress Cataloging-in-Publication Data

Nash, June C., 1927–
We eat the mines and the mines eat us : dependency and
exploitation in Bolivian tin mines / June Nash ; with a new preface
by the author.
p.   cm.
Originally published: 1979. With new introduction.
Includes bibliographical references and index.
ISBN 978–0–231–08051–4 (pbk.)
1. Tin miners—Bolivia.   2. Tin mines and mining—Bolivia.
3. Trade-unions—Tin miners—Bolivia.   4. Bolivia—Social life and
customs.   I. Title.
HD8039.M72B65   1993
331.7'6223453'0984—dc20
92-35964
CIP

Casebound editions of Columbia University Press books are printed on permanent
and durable acid-free paper.
Printed in the United States of America
p 10 9 8 7 6

*For
Herbert, Eric,
and
Laura*

Contents

Preface

◆DURING ONE of the many rituals in the mines that I attended when I worked in the mining community of Oruro in 1970, a miner said, "We eat the mines and the mines eat us. For that reason, we have to give these rituals to the spirit of the hills so that he will continue to reveal the veins of metal to us and so that we can live." The occasion was the sacrifice of a llama as an offering to Supay, the hill spirit who controls the wealth of the mines. It followed an accident that took the lives of three young miners. The miners blamed the deaths on the failure of management to permit them to carry out the regular rituals of sacrifice that fed the spirit of the hills and satisfied his appetite so that he would not eat the workers.

His statement seemed to sum up the sense miners have of their dependency on the mines in order to make a living and their sense of exploitation, both in the loss of health from lung disease and in the low returns for their labor. It is at the root of the contradiction in their consciousness: the sense of dependency on the mines and those who control them makes for conformity to the conditions of work imposed upon them. At the same time, their outrage at those conditions leads to the militant actions that have characterized their history since the beginning of industrial mining. How they deal with this contradiction is the central focus of this book.

This consciousness of an indigenous proletariat contrasts with that of the Mnong gar as described by Georges Condominas in his monograph, *Nous avons mangé la forêt*. His title, drawn from the Mnong gar expression for marking the passage of time in the succession of the brush burning for the cultivation of their crops, parallels the first part of the miner's phrase, "We eat the mines. . . ." However, as horticulturalists not yet caught up in the world market, they have not yet experienced the exploitation that industrial workers express in the final clause, ". . . and the mines eat us."

My research was made possible by the Social Science Research Council, which financed my summer field trip in 1969, and by the Fulbright-Hayes Title V grant that I received for twelve months of field work in 1970. A Guggenheim fellowship in 1971 enabled me to pull together the material for two autobiographies which have been published in Spanish: *He agotado mi vida en la mina*, by Juan Rojas and June Nash (Buenos Aires: Nueva Visión 1976), and *Dos mujeres indigenas' Basilia* (Mexico: Instituto Indigenista Interamericano 1976). I am indebted to those granting institutions for enabling me to complete that work.

I hope this book will satisfy the men and women who work in the mines and gave of their time and support to make it possible. I have not mentioned their names because of possible reprisals in the fluctuating political environment in which they live. I want to give particular thanks to those of my *comadres* and *compadres* who had faith in me when I was attacked as a counterinsurgency agent and urged me to continue with the work. To the scholars in Oruro who have supported the rich folklore traditions of the city, I owe an intellectual debt for giving me insight into a meaningful tradition which has resisted the erosion of modernization and industrialization. Among these are Eduardo Ibañez, who shared his artist's vision of the mines with me and who took some of the photographs included in the book, and Josermo Murillo, whose insightful article on carnival I have quoted. Like every scholar of the labor movement in Bolivia, I owe a great debt to Guillermo Lora, whose books, articles and lectures have provided basic understandings of historical trends.

My stay in the field was brightened by the presence of my daughter, Laura, and a visit from my son, Eric. Doris Widerkehr and Annette Thorne, students who joined me during my stay in Oruro in 1969 and 1970, as well as Andrew Weiss, who got his first field experience in Bolivia before undertaking his research in Cochabamba in 1970, helped me in the preliminary survey of the mining compound as well as in sharing with me their impressions and knowledge of the mining community. My colleagues Judith Marie Buechler and Hans Buechler made many suggestions which improved an earlier version of the book. Billie Jean Isbell and her students made astute observations which helped to sharpen the chapter on religious ritual. Jorge Dandler and Ernest Feder contributed to a broadening of the context in which the field observations are set. I hope that I have remained faithful to the vision which the miners shared with me of the world they live in and the life they lead. It is with the hope of sharing their understandings with other workers throughout the world that I have tried to reflect that reality and relate it to problems that all workers face.

In retrospect, I can see that the sixteen months I spent in Bolivia coincided with an extraordinary opening up of the political forces in the country. The dynamic energies of people who have endured the most extreme forms of economic exploitation and political repression on the South American continent is revealed by the fact that both President Ovando in the first few months of his year of office from September 1969 to September 1970, and President Torres, who succeeded him in October and served as president until the military coup in August 1971, found it necessary to seek support from the workers and peasants. The seven years of extreme repression under Colonel Hugo Banzer, who seized power in August 1971,[1] did not succeed in putting an end to the resistance of the people. Intermittent protest action brought about the murder of over a hundred peasants in the Cochabamba Valley in 1974 and scores of miners in 1976. The extraordinary breakthrough of their latent resistance came in January 1978.

The step-by-step process by which Banzer turned back the populist movement from the coup in 1971 is summarized in several documents which I shall briefly summarize. The first is a report by the Justice and Peace Commission (1974) entitled "The Massacre of the Valley," which recounts the January 1974 massacre of peasants and workers in Cochabamba. The second is the report of the Bolivian Workers Center (Central Obrera Boliviana; COB 1976) on the

---

[1] In the annual "Report to the Congress: Bolivia—an Assessment of U.S. Policies and Programs," by the Comptroller General of the United States, January 30, 1975, credit is taken for the Banzer coup by virtue of the loans, grants, and use of U.S. military advisers.

suppression of trade unions. The third is the letter drafted by a group of American citizens living in Bolivia which was presented to the State Department representative, Terence Todman, when he visited Bolivia in April 1977. (Anonymous 1977) The fourth is a document drafted by the Anti-Slavery Society of Great Britain, (1977) entitled "Report on a Visit to Investigate Allegations of Slavery" based on the findings of a representative who went to Bolivia in 1977. Data on the conditions of peasants in this report are supplemented by another report by representatives of the British Mineworkers Union (1977) on Bolivian miners after their trip in 1977. Finally there are two reports by the International Work Group for Indigenous Affairs (1978) on the Indian Liberation and Social Rights Movement and the colonization program for white African settlers. I shall summarize the events from 1971 to the present as reported in the documents cited.

Bolivia has lived under military regimes varying in the degree of repression since General René Barrientos' coup in 1964. A law of internal security giving the armed forces almost unlimited rights to arrest and interrogate citizens has been on the books since that time. A brief interim during the first few months of General Ovando's period as president and the nine months of General Juan José Torres' presidency permitted an opening for democracy. This was ended by the Banzer coup in August 1971. Hundreds of people were murdered in the three-day coup, and in the days that followed, students, workers, labor leaders, and political opponents of the Banzer regime were imprisoned, held without trial, and tortured. Over five thousand have gone into exile where they remained, often without official papers. All universities were closed for over a year in 1971–72 and for several months in 1974. Concentration camps were set up, sometimes in universities closed because of student protest. The Gabriel René Moreno University in the state of Santa Cruz is one of these. The Women's Prison in Obrajes, La Paz, became another camp, along with the Panoptico Nacional in the Plaza de San Pedro, another in Chonchocoro, 25 kilometers from La Paz, and Puesto "E" in Viacha.

Economic assistance and military loans were immediately forthcoming from the United States and Brazil to support the regime. American economic assistance included immediate gifts of $10.6

million and $4.5 million for special programs—refurbishing of the market place and leveling of a hill outside of Miraflor barracks in La Paz that provided easy access for anti-military demonstrators.

In October 1971 the Bolivian peso was devalued from 12 per U.S. dollar to 20. Small increases in the wages of mine workers have not made up for the inflationary pressures created by this artificial change in the exchange rate when the dollar was losing value throughout the world. Price increases affecting imported goods did not, however, assist the peasants, whose subsistence crops were kept at artificially low prices. At the same time that there was a 100 percent increase in the prices of sugar, rice, macaroni, and oil, the government set controls on local products. This resulted in the uprising of peasants, who set up a blockade on the highways leading out of the valley of Cochabamba in January 1974.

The effectiveness of this nonviolent action, supported by factory workers and miners who called a strike at their centers of production, resulted in a confrontation with Banzer's troops. Promising to meet with the peasant leaders, Banzer sent troops and armored cars, massacring over one hundred of the unarmed demonstrators. This wanton destruction, reported at length in the Catholic church's Justice and Peace Commission report, "The Massacre of the Valley," gave impetus to the Indian Liberation and Social Rights Movement for Indigenous Affairs. Their reaction to the genocidal threat in a massacre in which the army used machine guns and bazookas to kill children as well as men and women massed in a peaceful protest was combined with a general awareness that life could not be sustained and reproduced at the standard of living to which Indian and cholo peasants and workers had been reduced. That reduction persisted to the present. According to a report of the Bolivian Ministry of Health, published in *Presencia* on January 5, 1977, the average lifetime of a Bolivian peasant is less than thirty-five years. Only 9 percent of the peasantry had access to a nearby regular source of water. The average consumption of calories, 1870 calories a day in 1962, a level 16 percent below the generally accepted minimum, declined to 1,834 calories a day in 1970. When Banzer's government maintained strict price controls on the products grown by small farmers during a time of rising inflation following his deflation of the Bolivian currency, diets reached starvation levels. This was the cause for the protest and blocking the highways in the Cochabamba Valley area. When Banzer rejected their demands with such massive force, they became fully conscious of the threat to life. One of the positive results was the rejection of the Military Pact which peasant leaders had signed with General Barrientos in 1965 and a realliance with other workers who had been the target of the military in the intervening years.

By November 1974 all political activity was suspended with the passage of Decreto 11947. In this decree, the Bolivian Workers Center (COB) was declared illegal, along with all the member federations, and all unions were prohibited. Strikes and other worker actions were prohibited. The same decree established an Obligatory Civil Service through which the state could require any Bolivian over the age of 21 to serve the state for an undetermined period of time, without exception and under penalty of two years' imprisonment or indefinite exile. Decreto Supremo 11952, passed on November 12, 1974, established compulsory nomination of *coordinadores laborales* to replace trade union leaders with stooges of the mining and industrial enterprises. The articles of the decree indicate that the purpose was to destroy the economic as well as political position of all labor organizations. The directors of the Federation of Bolivian Mine Workers Unions (FSTMB), Victor Lopez Arias, Oscar Salas Moya, Irineo Pimentel, and others were imprisoned when they rejected nomination as coordinadores.

The militant miners persisted in organizing a congress in Corocoro in May 1976. The workers demanded an increase of wages from B $1.50 to B $4.00 a day and demanded the repatriation of the body of President Torres, who had been slain while in exile in Argentina. Their wages had sunk to one-third those of agricultural workers in Beni cattle ranches, where a laborer earned B $3.00 a day plus food and drink as well as housing. Even migrant cotton workers earned B $2.50 a day. The mine centers of Oruro and Potosí were declared military zones, and the army entered them, and have remained stationed there ever since. Fifty mineworkers were exiled to Chile and others were imprisoned. The government put a complete halt to the constitutional rights of free association and voluntary work. The Anti-Slavery Society reported that arrests in the mine centers were a daily occurrence (1977).

In addition to the harrassment of miners, the Anti-Slavery Society reported that peasants were consistently subjected to arrest for failure to join the official trade unions. Approximately seven hundred peasants had been deceived into working on road construction in eastern Cochabamba in return for land grants, only to learn that a military official, Captain Galindo, was taking over the best lands there.

Bolivia enjoyed a favored position as one of the biggest beneficiaries of military aid from the United States to South America throughout the Banzer regime. In 1971 Bolivia received $14.3 million in grants and loans, $2.6 million of which was for military programs. In 1972 this jumped to $66.2 million, of which $6.2 million was for the military. It dropped to $32.4 million in loans and grants in 1973, of which $5.1 million was for the military, but rose again in 1974 to $54.9 million, of which $7.9 million was for the military. In 1975 $33.2 million was given, with $7.4 million for the military (Wilkie and Reich 1977: Table 3100). The total loans from independent sources were $19 million from 1962 to 1971, while in the Banzer regime (1972–76) Bolivia received $47 million, over twice as much in half the time. Investments went up from a total of $37 million in the decade 1960–69 to $46.5 million in 1971, $82.3 million in 1972, $28 million in 1973, and $41.9 million in 1974. (Wilkie and Reich 1977: Table 3006, p. 417).

These grants and loans did not reach the people. The death rate for children between one and four years was 16.8 in 1960–62 and rose to 27.6 in 1970, with only Haiti and Guatemala higher (Wilkie and Reich 1977: 31). Wages, which had risen 4 percent over the previous year in 1971 as a result of some of the changes President Torres had made, dropped 0.8 percent in 1972, 19.5 percent in 1973, and reached a new low of 35.0 percent less in 1974 (Wilkie and Reich 1977: Table 1412). Only Chile had as big a percentage drop, with 33.6 percent lower wages in 1973.

Journalists who printed news of the regime's violations of civil rights were imprisoned or exiled. In 1977 there were fifty-eight Bolivian journalists in exile and two in prison. What radio stations were permitted to broadcast were directed largely by government officials. The transmitters of the church were destroyed. Radio "Pio XII," which was one of the few stations broadcasting news of the repression of miners throughout General Barrientos' presidency from 1964 to 1969, no longer could operate. No journalists were allowed in the mining centers, and neither the Red Cross nor International Amnesty visited Bolivia from 1974 to the present time.

These violations of human rights were stated in a letter drafted by American citizens living in Bolivia and presented to Terence Todman on his official visit to La Paz in April 1977. They specifically rejected the embassy report on human rights for its inconsistency and ambiguous tone. They objected to the embassy statement that there were "occasional" violations of human rights, asserting that they witnessed repression of the most brutal sort as a daily occurrence affecting the lives of most Bolivian workers, peasants, and professionals. Assassinations, imprisonments without trial, torture of prisoners, entry of private homes without warrants, and theft of personal goods—these were the standard operating procedures they had observed in the conduct of the Banzer government. They urged their State Department representative to carry this report back to President Carter, who had stated his concern with human rights in the atmosphere of taking office.

Along with this report by American witnesses is that of the British Mineworkers Union (1977) representatives, who visited La Paz and the mining center of Siglo XX in April 1977. They found an impoverished work force earning only two-thirds of what is calculated as minimal wages for a family of five. With an inflation rate of 159 percent over the last six years, the basic wage was decreased, and even with "incentives" in bonuses given for perfect attendance, did not reach the level paid during the Torres presidency. Pensions averaging B $30 dollars a month for workers retired because of silicosis or old age were found below what was needed for food alone. The trade union leaders were able to talk with Bolivian labor leaders operating underground, who indicated that the union representatives sent in as coordinators by the government operated more as a police force than as union agents. The British miners looked at the houses, which they described as concentration camps, and they talked with Domitila Chungara, leader of the housewives' association of Siglo XX. An outspoken critic of the military regimes since President Barrientos' days in office, she had spent many months in jail and her husband had been fired from the company.

She told them of the malnutrition of children and the starvation rations on which they barely survived.

As a result of their report, combined with that of the Anti-Slavery Society, the British mineworkers succeeded in blocking a loan of £19 million that the British government was considering for capital improvements in the mines. The mineworkers' union urged the government to withhold any loans until the Bolivian government withdrew troops from the mines, freed imprisoned miners, returned the radio stations, and discussed wages with the Bolivian miners' own representatives.

By 1977 the Banzer regime's program for development of the unsettled agricultural lands was revealed by Dr. Guido Strauss, under secretary for immigration. The government intended to encourage the entry into Bolivia of large numbers of white immigrants from Namibia, Zimbabwe Rhodesia, and South Africa. *Presencia* reported that the government expected some 150,000 whites would be accommodated, with funds amounting to US $150 million offered by the Federal German Republic. Over 800,000 hectares would be turned over to the immigrants free of charge. Dr. Strauss's plan did not include any mention of the forty-one Indian tribes with a total population of about 120,000 recorded as living in the zone specified for colonization in eastern Bolivia. The International Work Group on Indigenous Affairs (1978) published the report of English correspondant Norman Lewis as Document 31 of their series. When Lewis questioned Strauss about the disposition of the Indians, he was referred to Summer Institute of Linguistics missionaries. In an interview with one of the missionaries, Mr. Victor Halterman, the nature of the institute's intervention on the part of the Indians became clear: the missionaries rounded up Indians living in the tract and assigned them to local farms where they worked without pay, living in abysmal conditions. Mr. Lewis also learned from Jurgen Riester, an anthropologist working in eastern Bolivia, about the conditions on the estates in Santa Cruz where Indians were brought from the altiplano under false promises of land and wages. The Chiriguano Indians working on the sugar estates of Abapo Izozog, one of the principal areas for the planned white settlement, cut cane for fifteen hours a day every day except Sunday, when they worked thirteen hours. Although their contracts stipulated that water, firewood, and medicines would be provided free, there was no wood, only muddy water from wells, and nothing more than aspirin to treat the enteritis, tuberculosis, and snakebite from which they suffered. Dr. Strauss's only expressed concern about the Indians was that the white immigrants "will certainly find our Indians no more stupid or lazy than their own blacks." Indians from the altiplano were considered more amenable to the working conditions on the plantations than the "non-integrated" Indians from the jungle area. Ayoreo Indians resisted the recruitment into what Bolivian journalists themselves described as "slave camps" (*Excelsior,* June 23, 1977). The major protest against the treatment of the workers came from Catholic priests, who have worked unstintingly despite severe harrassment to bring these conditions to international attention.

In 1977 Bolivia did not seem to rank with the more flagrant violators of human rights, such as Chile, Brazil, or Argentina. However, the appearance of political peace during the Banzer regime was won at the cost of total repression of protest both within and outside the country. When former President Torres was assassinated in Argentina in July 1976, it was apparent that the regime was not only afraid of Communist opposition, but of center and even right-wing opposition. Colonel Selich, one of the co-conspirators with Banzer in the coup of August 1971, died three years after the victory while undergoing "interrogation" by Banzer's police. Political leaders of all parties, labor, and professional organizations were forced into exile. These included not only labor and left exiles such as Juan Lechín Oquendo, but also Víctor Paz Estenssoro, president (1952–56 and 1960–64), and Hernán Siles Zuazo, president from 1956 to 1960; Benjamin Miguel, leader of the Democratic Christian Party; and numerous ex-ministers of the populist movement such as Marcelo Quiroga Santa Cruz of the Socialist Party.

As a result of President Carter's call for recognition of human rights in the hemisphere, Banzer proclaimed amnesty for political prisoners and exiles on the Day of Miners, December 21, 1977. He did nothing to assure guarantees for those people in exile nor did he release the prisoners. However the heroic action of a half-dozen women and their children, wives of tin miners who were jailed in the protest action in the mines in 1976, brought about a true amnesty. These women started a hunger strike in the mining communities but came to La Paz, where they took refuge in the archdiocese of the Catholic church and the newspaper offices of *Presencia*. They were joined by hundreds more as the demand for amnesty of political prisoners and the return of exiles attracted support by leaders such as Hernán Siles Zuazo and the cardinal of La Paz. The demands included the legalization of trade unions, return of the radios taken from mining camps, and removal of the military from the mines. By mid-January the number of hunger strikers reached 1,283, and symbolic hunger strikes were carried out by Bolivian exiles throughout Europe and Latin America by their supporters. On January 16 thousands of miners, defying military occupation, walked out on a two-day strike. Factory workers at Manaco, the Bata shoe factory, laid down their tools for a twenty-four-hour strike. Banzer responded with a police raid on the centers of the hunger strike, then being staged at the university, the offices of *Presencia*, the FAO offices, and the archdiocese. This succeeded in provoking further protests on the part of the newspapers and the radio stations, and the largest textile mill in the country launched a twenty-four-hour strike.

Given the magnitude of the protest, Banzer was forced to give in to the demands of the hunger strikers. Following the amnesty, many exiled leaders returned to engage in the campaign for the elections that Banzer promised would take place in July 1978. The Unión Democratica Popular, with their leader, Hernán Siles Zuazo, and the Christian Democrat candidate, General René Bernal, were the leading contenders opposed to Banzer's hand-picked successor, General Juan Pereda Asbún. Pereda had served as minister of the interior under Banzer and had proven his loyalty throughout the regime. Because he represented a relatively weak segment of the armed forces as general of the air force, Banzer is said to have considered him a person he could continue to manipulate.

The elections took place as scheduled on July 9. When over half the votes were counted, Pereda was ahead with 513,653 votes against 283,824 for Hernán Siles Zuazo. However, witnesses, including two members of an international team of observers—the British representative, Lord Avebury, and an American lawyer, Robert Goldman—claimed that ballot boxes were stuffed by Banzer's supporters, and peasants and workers were threatened if they did not vote for Pereda (Latin American Political Report, July 21, 1978). Pereda himself halted the election counts and then installed himself as president. Whatever the voting did or failed to do in deciding the winner, all informed observers agreed that peasants were mobilized to support Siles Zuazo. Delegations of peasants were observed carrying in votes from rural areas to avoid their being stuffed by the military, and these proved to be predominantly orange, the color for Siles Zuazo. While it was expected that miners, factory workers, and the urban poor would rally for Siles, the peasant vote surprised many.

Following the coup, the Russian ambassador was the first to recognize the new government, while the United States, because of its declared concern for human rights and its stand for democratic elections, wavered. Ten days later, it did recognize Pereda's government. It has been rumored that Pereda has had a falling out with Banzer because of the failure of the latter to support him in the coup. After a meeting between the two on August 24, Banzer stated that his form of nationalism had come to an end (*Latin American Political Report*, September 1, 1978). The vulnerability of his regime was shown in its rapid demise in November 1978 when General Padilla seized control. In the months since the elections there has been another opening for democratic mobilization in Bolivia. Neither Pereda nor Padilla has as yet used the armed forces against the people. Some of the more repressive rulings of Banzer have been repealed: the internal security law giving unlimited power to the armed forces and the civil service law. In response to the university students' protest against the Banzer-appointed rector, elections for a new rector took place in October 1978. The unions have reorganized and Juan Lechín Oquendo is again leader of the Federation of Mine Workers' Unions (FSTMB) and the COB. Pereda gained the support of the four groups that opposed his predecessor—the *Unión Democrática Popular*, the *Alianza Democrática Revolucionaria*, and the Christian Democrat and Socialist parties—when he agreed to set the date for the new elections in 1979 rather than delaying it (*Latin American Political Report*, September 1, 1978.)

The North American response to the situation is disappointing to observers concerned with human rights within and outside ot Bolivia. Shortly after the breakthrough in human rights gains in January

1978, a bill was put before the U.S. Congress allowing the government to contribute 5,000 long tons of tin to the International Tin Agreement buffer stock. If passed, this "dumping" of such quantities of tin would have caused a drop in prices that would aggravate the economic crisis, estimated by some to mean a loss of $60 million. At the same time, the bill provided that the money released from these sales would have been used to buy Chilean copper. Thus we can see the rewards offered to the Pinochet regime for carrying out an election that effectively denied any democratic mobilization and the punishment for Bolivia where, despite the confusion, real democratic processes are again at work.

This book recounts the story of the people in their struggle to maintain their way of life. Given this background of massacres, resistance, and protest, the courage they show in this current situation is remarkable. It should be an inspiration for those who maintain that progress can be made only when the rank and file of workers are the architects of the institutions in which they work and live, just as it is a refutation of those who reject the primary role of workers in bringing about such a future.

Preface to the Centennial Edition

◇ IN THE TWENTY years since I did fieldwork in the mining centers of Bolivia, the hopes for a better future engendered by the revolution of 1952 have been defeated.[1] Conditions of work and life had declined from bad to abysmal when I returned to the mining centers of Oruro and Siglo XX–Catavi in 1985. In July of that year the voters reelected Victor Paz Estenssoro—who had ushered in the era of nationalist progress in 1952—only to see him reverse many of the decrees made in his earlier term of office. Chief among these reversals were his declaration of the New Economic Policies decreeing the closing of the nationalized mines and his imposition of a tax on farmers. Both provisions, dictated by International Monetary Fund adviser Jeffrey Sachs, denied the spirit of the revolution that called for the nationalization of the riches of the mines, the institution of land reform, and the safeguarding of the economic position of small farmers. Advances made in education, social welfare, and health benefits were reversed as government funding was withdrawn. Thousands were laid off in the mines, and in the Chapare miners were joining poor farmers in cultivating coca, the principal plant ingredient in the production of cocaine.

What distinguished this episode in Bolivia's long history as the poorest country in South America was the extraordinary dislocation

[1] My fieldwork in the summer of 1969 was financed by the Social Science Research Council and the year's stay in 1970 was done with a grant from the National Defense and Education Fund. I am grateful to both sources for allowing me to carry out this work. I am indebted to Maria Lagos and Carmen Medeira for their careful reading of the introduction, which helped clarify some of the points I tried to make.

of families and communities that took place. Throughout the hundreds of years of labor abuse in the colonial and independence periods, Bolivia's indigenous population had managed to reconstruct family units and communities torn apart by migrations forced upon them by the *mita*.[2] With more than twenty thousand laid off from the mines and thousands more left without employment in agriculture or the factories, the destruction was far greater than anything experienced in the past. With little of the subsistence economy left intact, rural and urban populations were left without food, shelter, or clothing. Social services were nearly defunct, with many rural schools closed and teachers throughout the country leaving their posts. Hospitals and medical services that had always been limited were now virtually unavailable to the vast majority of the people.

The impact on the mining communities and families of the changes brought about by the New Economic Policies was visible within a year. In June and July of 1985 I lived in the household of Juan and Petrona Rojas, the pseudonymous couple whose life histories I had recorded in Spanish during my first stay (Nash and Rojas 1976). Their house was in Barrio Minero "Santa Fe," in the mining compound of San José, Oruro, built by the National Housing Commission (CONAVI) in the heyday of the Revolution of 1952. Juan and Petrona had expanded it during the 1970s to include a two-story annex that was rented to two families. Their house contained the amenities derived from four decades of work in the mines—a red plastic upholstered sofa with a matching armchair and dining room set, a television, and a sewing machine.

I was impressed with the continued unity of the family after a decade of military rule and overwhelming economic disruption. Their eldest son, Filemón, clerked in the mine commissary at a job that the Rojases considered an "inheritance" by virtue of Juan's having "left his lungs in the mines." Filemón lived nearby with his wife and five children. Juan's eldest daughter, María, lived only three blocks away with her husband, Guido, and their three children. Guido, whose

---

[2] Ann Zulowski (1990:100–102) emphasizes that in the late sixteenth and early seventeenth centuries most Indians migrated in family groups or as couples, even those forced by the colonial state to leave their homes and serve in the Potosí *mita*. Women maintained their husbands and even hauled metal out of the mines and sorted it according to mineral content.

family came from Santa Fe where Juan had worked in the mines most of his life, was employed by the national oil company. Another son, Aníbal, worked as a temporary employee in the San José mines where Juan ended his mining career working as a nightwatchman. Aníbal lived in Barrio Minero "Santa Fe" with his wife's parents, who had returned from Sweden where her father had been exiled as a militant mine union organizer during the years of Banzer's rule. Their daughter Elena, now the mother of a five-year-old boy, still lived with her parents and her younger siblings: Anita, who was still in school; Juan Manuel, the fifteen-year-old who had run away from the army just before I showed up; and the youngest son, Victor Hugo, born in 1971. This close-knit family had endured the ten-year military rule, survived numerous massacres, and experienced the erosion of their income when the economic disasters of the 1980s began to hit home; yet they were able to remain together.

I returned in August of the following year and found Anita alone in the house waiting for tenants to move in. The furniture was piled up in one room to be shipped off to Cochabamba where her parents had moved with Victor Hugo, because of Juan's worsening health. Elena, who had joined them with her son, was working in a Chinese restaurant in that city. Filemón and María had moved with their respective families to Santa Cruz in the hope of finding jobs in that more prosperous area. Aníbal had gone to Sweden with his wife. Juan Manuel was back in the army. I found Anita packing up the furniture piled up in one room of their house, which had been rented out to other families. She was waiting the visit of two Mormon missionaries who were proselytizing in the mining camp. When the two blond youths in their navy blazers, white shirts, and ties appeared, I left, overcome by a feeling of alienation in a house that had been so full of life. I doubted that the family could ever reunite in the community where they had lived their lives as workers in the mines.

Their story, which was originally published in Spanish as *He agotado mi vida en la mina,* is now translated into English as *I Spent My Life in the Mines: The Story of Juan Rojas, Bolivian Tin Miner* (Columbia University Press, 1992), with new chapters on the fifteen-year period after my first encounter with them in 1970. The family's history replicates the history of thousands of mining families that have experienced the changes brought about by the New Economic Policies.

In August of 1986 I joined the marchers from Oruro and other mining centers—more than ten thousand miners, housewives, and civil employees—converging on La Paz to protest the closing of the mines and other provisions of the New Economic Policies. It was the last desperate attempt to mobilize the communities in the industrial mining centers, where they had lived for generations, in order to protect their livelihood. When the march was intercepted by thousands of soldiers and the participants were forced to return to their homes, I visited the mining sites where hundreds of workers and their family members were conducting a hunger strike to protest the shutting down of the mines. I observed a despair unlike anything I had ever before seen, even in the days when I first visited Bolivia shortly after the June 1967 Massacre of San Juan, when more than a hundred members of the Siglo XX–Catavi mining community were killed.

Some of those on the hunger strike had even entered the mines, in which poisonous gases were accumulating in tunnels where the ventilation had been shut off, to stage this final and possibly fatal protest. Mothers surrounded by their children joined those who were fasting, ready to die rather than abandon their homes and communities. The government seemed to have accomplished the goal of policymakers responding to international financial advisors—the breaking up of the most organized sector of the working class in mining communities.[3]

I went with a Bolivian colleague, Rosario Leon—now director of the Center for the Study of Economic and Social Issues (CERES)—to the USAID office in La Paz to try to get financing for a cooperative to stimulate artisan production by the women left behind by men who quit the mining centers in search of work in Argentina, Brazil, and the pioneer agricultural areas of Bolivia. We were told that the policy of the United States was to discourage people from remaining in the mining areas; they were, in fact, lending AID funds to the Bolivian government to pay the workers indemnity in order to hasten the demobilization of the mines. The complex and rare metals the work-

---

[3] Only after the thousands of laid-off workers had abandoned the mines did U.S. AID finance some artisan cooperatives. Janet Page (1991) critiques the capitalist principles that inspired this project, which competed with and finally destroyed some of the grass-roots movements that had flourished in the interim.

ers might discover could have kept the mines open if geological explorations to retrieve them had been carried out as the miners had pleaded. Instead the mines that contained these valuable metals were to be sold to foreign private mining companies that did not have to contend with a militant labor force in nationalized mines. A brightly colored brochure distributed by the Bolivian consul in the United States advertises the mining properties for sale to foreign investors.

In the twenty years since I carried out the basic fieldwork for *We Eat the Mines and the Mines Eat Us*, the discipline of anthropology has shifted from a focus on the ways of people in vastly different societies to an involuted concern with what is called the "anthropological critique." The customary techniques of anthropological research—participant-observation, reflexivity, dialogical and interpretive approaches—have often been translated into narrowly conceived textual analyses; practitioners turn to past texts, thus avoiding the field research experience. Reflexivity, always a concern of anthropologists who wished to explore their relations as outside observers of distinct cultures, sometimes turns into fetishized concerns about the "self," thereby ignoring the "other." Dialogical encounters, the wellspring of discovery in most anthropology, past and present, devolve into internal dialogues with Freudian, Marxian, or hermeneutic paradigms drawn from literary criticism. Discourse analysis departs from a concern with power in society to the dissection of texts examined out of context.

I have not been averse to these approaches in my own work in Bolivia and elsewhere, but rather to the attempt to make them the goal itself. While I was still engaged in writing *We Eat the Mines and the Mines Eat Us*, I reflected on my own field experiences in a paper I presented at the 1973 International Congress of Ethnological and Anthropological Sciences (Nash 1976). I wrote about my fear of exposing the identities of union leaders who were subject to imprisonment and torture, of concerns I had for the safety of my daughter when Garcia Mesa's first[4] attempted coup in September 1970 left the country without a legitimate government for five days, and of my constant anxiety concerning my ability to maintain rapport with key

---

[4] General García Mesa initiated his first coup against President Ovando in September 1970, but his attempt was rejected by the army itself. Juan José Torres received the backing of the workers, along with other moderate groups of the center.

informants, because of the growing hatred of North Americans. In what might now be called the decentering of the authoritarian voice of the outsider, I tried to capture in the book as much as possible the workers' own statements of their condition. I hoped to convey to the reader the historical consciousness of workers in formation, bypassing the metatheories of Marx, Lukács, Althuser, and the rising numbers of neo-Marxists in the United States who were pouring over nineteenth-century texts to find out how proletarians ought to think and behave. In 1976, when I finished writing the first draft, I felt the book criticized some propositions central to Marxism at the same time that it reinforced others.

In the early weeks of my research in 1970 I met Guillermo Lora—a leading Trotskyist leader, an organizer of the Revolutionary Party of Workers (POR), and a historian of the Bolivian mining economy (1977)—who advised me that I would be radically transformed by my association with the mining community. Although I thought then that I had a good working knowledge of Marxism, I soon realized that the members of the mining community were developing in me a new awareness of the interpenetration of the work site and the home that sharpened the dialectic of the class struggle. With little formal education but with a life experience that enabled them to understand their conditions in a global context, miners always emphasized women's participation in the historic confrontations of the mining communities when they tried to explain to me how and why they organized to defend their interests as a working class. Women, too, continually expressed their sense of involvement in the operation of the mines and referred to themselves as "we miners." Their explanation for the old saying that "miners did not countenance the presence of women in the mines" was that the men did not want their wives to see their suffering.

The managers used this adage to try to keep me out of the mines, but the miners approved of my entering the mines with them to see what conditions were really like, and even made the arrangements over the objections of the superintendent. One day, as I approached the mines to enter with the 7 A.M. shift, I realized that an altercation was occurring between the work crew and the superintendent of mines. When I arrived, the superintendent began to yell at me, asking who had advised me of the protest and why was I always showing up when there was trouble. I was tempted to respond that there always was trouble because of the way the mines were managed. Before I could answer, one of the leaders in the union stepped up, greeting me as his *comadre* (I had just participated in a Mass for the confirmation of his daughter), and three members of the soccer team intervened, greeting me as *madrina* since I had acquired the title after donating socks for the team. The astonished superintendent simply left the scene, and we proceeded to enter the shaft.

I felt that the magic of participant observation in the months of my living (along with my daughter, Laura) in the mining community was the reason why they accepted me. Because of the U.S. intervention in the stabilization plan of 1956 that cut their wages and limited worker self-participation and the conviction that General Barrientos had been backed by the CIA in the 1964 coup, union leaders expressed extreme hatred for North Americans. Our direct and continuous participation in everyday life and the many dinners we shared with mining families both at my house and theirs was, undoubtedly, important. But, as I learned later, they had independent sources of information. One of my *compadres* told me that the woman who operated a small shop across from my house, who was the wife of one of the exiled union leaders, was keeping a constant check on who came and left my house. Much later, when I returned clandestinely in 1973, I learned that people opened their doors to me because they had learned from students who had contact with the government and police force that the CIA had ordered a security check to try to find out what I was doing there; this convinced the people not only that I was not working for the CIA but also that I probably did not share the politics of my government.

In writing about what I saw and heard, I tried to capture the sense of solidarity that men and women of the mining communities shared. Domitila Barrios de Chungara, whom I met at the Congress of the Federation of Mine Workers Unions of Bolivia (FSTMB) in Siglo XX–Catavi in September 1970, revealed the essence of this shared experience in a talk she gave at the Congress and, later, in interviews I had with her in her tiny house in the compound. She confirmed what the men and women had been telling me, that the genesis of all the militant actions that had taken place in the mining communities were based in the home, as women and children participated in the class struggle at the point of consumption. She reiterated accounts of strikes that had begun in the waiting lines of the *pulpería*, or company store, and the fact that women always headed the marches demonstrating the needs of workers to the administrators. From my informants I borrowed books by Trotsky, Luxemburg, and Kautsky that I had never read, because of my more academic (or maybe Leninist) entry into Marxist literature. Men who had had no more than two or three years of schooling discussed these books knowledgeably and were quite happy to educate me.

Participating in rituals of the *ch'alla* offerings to the Pachamama and Supay (the lord of the hills), in the celebrations of life-crisis events, and in union meetings, I learned that consciousness, though it may find expression through the shared experience of exploitation as workers, embraces many distinct sources of inspiration, including pre-conquest beliefs, Catholic theology, and narratives of ancestors kept alive in oral traditions. In the dialogical spirit I often countered their interpretations, only to find mine wanting. When I pointed to what I perceived as a contradiction between their offerings to the Tío and their belief in Jesus and the saints, they indicated that they never recognized them in the same setting—i.e., below and above ground, respectively—and that they scheduled the rituals for each on distinct days of the week. With this segmentation in time and place, they could expand their reference system to include all the powerful figures required to encompass their multicultural history.

Yet with all this coexistent and apparently contradictory cultural accumulation of beliefs and rituals related to power, there was no confusion as to who were the class enemies and who were friends. This was the fundamental lesson that they taught me. I fully realized how distinct it was from the "American" experience of the world only when a Maryknoll priest tried to convoke a meeting of the "Left" to overcome the divisive political scene in the wake of Barrientos's repression. Among those invited were leaders and followers of the POR (Lora's leftist party following the line of the Fourth International), the National Revolutionary Movement (MNR)—already split into the right-wing National Authentic Revolutionary party (PRA) and the left-wing Revolutionary Left Nationalist party [PRIN]—the Communist party (both the Moscow and the Beijing lines), the Socialist Workers party (PSO), and the Falange Socialista Boliviana.

Although I was not present at the occasion, which was a first for Bolivians, even accustomed as they were to the contradictions of political life, those who attended told me that the priest must have been working for the CIA. No one in his right mind, they told me, could expect to get unity from a congregation of parties that were at each others' throats, a meeting of people who had been tortured with those who had tortured. Yet, with whatever I retained of the naive political views I formed in the McCarthy period of my country, I realized that this priest was operating with the logic of a polarized Right and Left, and that, in dedicating himself to getting the Left together, he had made none of the distinctions that were the essence of Bolivia's conflictful political life.

When I finished the first year of my fieldwork, I started writing the "texts" I had compounded from all these sources, beginning with the life history of Juan and Petrona (Rojas and Nash, 1976), then that of Basilia (Nash and Roca 1976) and, finally, that of a union leader whose life story remains unpublished. Juan, a rank-and-file worker who had been engaged as a follower, not a leader, in all the major upheavals of the mining community from his entry into the work-force at the age of eight, synthesized these apparently distinct and often contradictory streams of consciousness in an integrated belief system in a way that transcends the bounded categories of theoreticians and leaders in the labor movement. His wife Petrona kept the family grounded in the day-to-day reality that required compromise and occasional capitulation to political pressures in order to ensure the survival of themselves and their children.

After I published the life history of Juan and Petrona, I set to work editing the much briefer narrative of Basilia Jimenez, a woman who had worked in the mines from the time of the Chaco War until her forced retirement at the age of fifty-seven when U.S.-financed concentration machines replaced the women. They were forced out of the mines and onto the slagpiles, picking over the ore that had been rejected in earlier years when they were of too low a metal content to process economically.

Born fifteen years earlier and coming of age during the Chaco War, Basilia represented an older generation than Juan. She was caught between the era of the paternalistic but extremely exploitative operation of the mines under the tin barons, and the era of the nationalized Mining Company of Bolivia (COMIBOL). She was forced to work in the mines during the Chaco War with Paraguay in the place of a deceased brother whom the army had "drafted." Her parents had buried the child—who died soon after birth—without purchasing a death certificate, since they were so poor. Assuming that the son had run away to avoid the draft, the Bolivian military demanded that the family give a child, even a daughter, to work in the mines. Basilia entered the mines, sometimes dancing on top of the elevator that lowered her and her girlfriends into the "bowels of the earth." There she made herself at home with her spirit lamp and teapot, fending off the harassment of male co-workers and the blame for accidents, which were often attributed to the women on the work teams. When the men returned from the war, she worked in the concentration plant. When, as a result of the Triangular Plan, COMIBOL got the loan from U.S., German, and English financiers, her work and that of the other women in the concentration of metal by hand was replaced with the mechanized "Sink and Float" processing system that employed only men. Basilia was fired along with the other women; their pleas for compensation were ignored by the unions and the government administrators alike. Living on the pittance of a social security pension and the rent from her CONAVI house in which she occupied a small back room, Basilia raged against the betrayal of the revolution in which she had fought while still working in Siglo XX. Though she lacks the noble principles of Domitila (Barrios de Chungara and Viezzar 1977) who sacrificed self-interest in the class struggle, her story nevertheless revealed the paradoxes of the compromises made in the National Revolutionary Movement (Nash and Roca 1976) and the failure to incorporate women in a meaningful way (Gueiler 1973).

Only after I finished these publications did I feel ready to write my monograph on life in the Bolivian mining community. I wanted the interpretations of members of the community to take precedence over the views I offered to my community of reference—students of anthropology and colleagues. The first draft took three years, what with teaching three courses a semester and developing a conference and publication on women in Latin America. I tried to avoid the twin dangers of appropriating informants' insights as my own (Sanjek 1989) and of imposing my ethnocentric paradigms on their lives. Yet

I am very aware that "my" central "discovery" in the book—that the consciousness of class is generated in the home and community and derives its force from the interpenetration of social reproduction and industrial production—comes from what they told me. This "discovered" lesson has, since the 1980s when feminist scholarship provided increasing evidence for it, become central to an understanding of the linkages between production and social and biological reproduction.

After completing the first draft in 1976, I turned to the study of an industrial community in the U.S. that was experiencing another aspect of the constriction in the world economy. Although it was not an explicit comparison of First World workers to Third World workers, some of the questions I formulated were drawn from my experience in Bolivia. Why did U.S. workers, often with more years of education than Bolivian miners, have a far more limited view of their relation to the global economy? Why were they so complacent in the face of monumental forces beginning to affect their lives, eroding the advantageous position they once occupied? How had corporate capitalist enterprise constructed the hegemonic controls that stifled workers' initiatives in the work site and in public life? This study gave me some perspective on the Bolivian miners. I realized, even more forcefully than when I worked in Bolivia, that the immediacy of the class struggle and the miners' acute awareness of the global dimensions of their struggle came precisely from their peripheral position in the international exchange setting. If Marx had learned that lesson earlier, he might have predicted the coming of the revolution in Russia rather than in England. It is a reminder to us now to look for revolutionary change in the marginal populations rather than the vanguard sectors of the proletariat.

Absorbed in the life and literature regarding the strange and exotic life of corporate America, I paid little attention to the reinterpretations of what I had published on Bolivia. When I completed the first draft of the monograph on Pittsfield, Massachusetts, *From Tank Town to High Tech; The Clash of Community and Industrial Cycles*, I decided to return to Bolivia in the summer of 1985, and I took the time to read some of these works. I was amused to find that one anthropologist, whose major fieldwork was done with peasants in Potosí, decided that the title, *We Eat the Mines and the Mines Eat Us*, was a misnomer. It should have been called, Platt (1984) reasoned,

"We Feed the Mines and the Mines Feed Us," following the logic of Aymara ritual offerings to the hill spirits. Never mind that the title was a direct quotation of a miner, who was fully cognizant of his cultural heritage but was playing with the aphorism to show how entry into capitalist mining enterprises had changed the terms of the relationship. Platt had missed the Brechtian humor displayed by members of the mining community, a striking example of which was the quotation I used as the title of the book. It was not the first time I had seen anthropologists prefer a more "traditional" stance wherein their subjects replicate the cultural idiom without irony or playfulness. The cultural relativism fostered in our discipline often gets in the way of a sharper awareness of how "they" enter into the dialogue with "us" in just as sophisticated, or even more highly cultivated, terms.

Like Platt, Godoy (1985) confuses the "emic" accounts of informants with my own analysis when he states that I had a simple functionalist approach to the interpretation of the rituals in the mine. I had included a very lyrical statement by Manuel, a leading trade unionist, about the moment of the ch'alla being the "moment . . . when we talk about our work problems, and there is born a generation so revolutionary that the workers begin thinking of making structural change." (Nash 1979:159) I used to joke with Manuel about how he outdid Bronislaw Malinowski in his functionalism, explaining what that term meant in the history of anthropology. He was fully aware of how these moments could become the basis for moving workers to action, and he was adept at identifying and using them. This he was able to do in the fields of Cala Cala, when the miners fought with dynamite sticks fired from slingshots against General Barrientos' well-armed takeover of the mines. The solidarity cultivated in the intimate moments of rituals carried out inside the mines could not be denied as an element in the class struggle. My "etic" analysis is derived from a historical materialist approach where I tried to connect the imagery and ritual practices related to the lord of the hills to distinct systems of labor control. Supay—sometimes referred to as Huari, or the owner of the hills, and endearingly as Tío (or uncle)—is termed "the Devil" mainly to simplify things for the outsider. The miners use the term among themselves in the context of the specific contracts made by individuals who seek selfish gain and individual rewards for their work in the mines. "Devil" was only one of these terms, a vestige of the colonial period when there were greater opportunities for individual gain in the *pirkiñero* contract system. Under this system, the entire group shared the profit or loss for the exploitation of a tunnel. Anyone who stayed behind in the tunnels was suspected of seeking selfish gains, of selling metal on the side in his contract with the "Devil." The industrial mining system introduced "gringo" supervisors and the Tío appeared in the imagination of some miners as a ruddy cowboy. With the nationalization of the mines the rituals, no longer co-opted by the owners of the mines, were available for reinterpretation. During this period the "Devil's" image, particularly in the niches where the miners took their coca breaks, was that of an ordinary miner, with helmet, boots, and a modest pair of horns sprouting from either side of his helmet. The images varied greatly, from one level to another in the same mine, and from the more public areas near the elevator shafts— where they were larger and gaudier—to those in the coca niches— where they were often dressed in Carnival dance costumes with elaborate plaster-of-paris devil's heads. None of these representations is entirely relegated to the past; they are evoked in dance costumes, masks, or simply imagined in the dark passages underground when miners are alone. Functionalist explanations of what happens in these cultural experiences, such as those expressed by Manuel, capture a truth that those who are a part of them realize. Yet what I tried to indicate was that the very same ritual could change from the expression of the solidarity of a small pirkiñero in-group, in competition with other such work gangs, to the entire work force of Patiño's major mining complex of Siglo XX-Catavi, when industrial mining of tin superceded the colonial extraction of silver. Yet it could also relate to the compromise in the class struggle when mine owners participated in the ritual. Patiño was aware of this and donated the llamas that were slaughtered during the major *k'araku* offerings celebrated at Carnival and on the last day of July. He joined the miners in these celebrations, giving each one of the men a shirt, the women a skirt, and then dancing with them at the height of the ceremony when the miners ritually handed over to him a solid block of metal. When the major mines were nationalized in the post-revolutionary period, the ritual "function" of the ch'alla again changed, this time from the paternalism cultivated in the prerevolutionary period of industrial mining to an attempt by union organizers to forge an industry-wide solidarity. Shortly after the revolution the superintendent of Santa Fe mines asked Juan what he thought they could do to raise productivity. Juan suggested that they have a ch'alla to the Tío, the familiar term for Huari. His logic was that Huari, as owner of the mines and "uncle" to the workers would be more likely to yield the riches he controlled if he was honored in this way. Miners like Juan were able to convince some of the national supervisors (who replaced the gringos of the private industrial mining period) that only with a proper k'araku would they be able to find the riches that the hill owner possessed. Whether these *mestizo* leaders—cut off from their own cultural roots as they were—believed in this magical connection, or whether they simply wanted to gain the support of miners who knew (and often hid their knowledge) of where the richer veins were, they went along with the miners' demands that the ritual take place. Manuel was able to give a rich and evocative expression to this, since he had honed his argument with other leaders who felt it should be left behind along with other "irrational" aspects of the past.

When the army seized control of the mines in 1964, General Barrientos prohibited the rituals, but they were still held clandestinely. The supervisor of San José mine explained the prohibition on the basis that the miners were turning the tunnels into saloons for drinking and carousing, but the miners claimed that the managers prohibited the rituals because they feared the group solidarity these sessions might provoke. In these arguments over the functional value of the rituals I could not take sides, since I felt that both captured an element of the wider truth. What I could discern was the class consciousness evoked in the context of the rituals when I participated in them. This emerged in the k'araku held in San José mine on the eve of the month of Huari in 1970, which occurred shortly after the death of three young miners in a cave-in. It was also evident in the celebration of the warming of the earth festival that I attended in Siglo XX–Catavi in 1967, where I saw miners commemorate the massacre of San Juan that occurred on June 24, 1967. But I could also comprehend Basilia Jimenez's desire to return to the paternalism of Patiño when she asserted that she would kneel down before him if he were to return to the mines. Fired from her regular job as a concentrator of mineral when the nationalized mines introduced the Sink-and-Float machinery, her appeals for reinstatement ignored by the union, she yearned for the personal connectedness Patiño had evoked as he danced with the miners.

The rich variety of symbols involved in the complex of rituals in the mines cannot possibly be interpreted in a single theory, as Taussig (1980) tries to do. Equating the "devil" narratives he encountered in Colombia with those of Bolivian miners, he attributes these beliefs to a resistance to commoditization by "precapitalist" peasants, personified in the contract with the devil. This imposition of a universalizing interpretation derived from an alien intellectual tradition to assess the phenomena associated in the ritual relations with the supernatural powers of the mines negates their many distinct manifestations: Huari, Supay, the *awichas,* and the Tío, who may even help the miners with his bull, which digs out the ore with its horns. The manifold contexts in which miners relate to these multiple images encompass several transformations as rural cultivators first became absorbed in the Inca empire, then in the colonial mines, and finally in the industrial mines of the twentieth century. Taussig's selection of a single representation of these powers as mediating "commodity fetishism" in the transition from "precapitalist" to "capitalist" defies a historically situated analysis in which rituals can be shown to mean very different things at different times, as well as encompassing several distinct and often contradictory meanings.

The k'araku is a celebration of life and the collective effort that maintains it. The "origin myth" of the ritual known to most residents of Oruro relates how miners overcame the threat of annihilation in pre-Hispanic times when Huari threatened three times to devour them, along with their Quechua conquerors, who had come to mine the riches of his hills without making the offerings that the farmers customarily rendered. Each time the people were saved by invoking the Ñusta, the princess of the pre-conquest period. They were able to ensure safety for themselves by carrying out the appropriate rituals—first in collective work teams at the work sites, then in the communitywide ceremonies at the mouth of the mines.

The imposition of devil narratives is apparently a post-conquest innovation, and the devil imagery coexists uneasily with Huari in the mines. According to these stories, miners could make a contract with the devil whereby they earned fabulous riches. But it was only those miners who approached the devil as individuals, in order to gain riches for themselves, who were bedeviled by his power, working themselves to death within three months of the encounter. All the wealth they accumulated would evaporate upon their death.

In contrast, Huari, or Supay, promised enduring wealth when the collective group offered the feast of the k'araku and the weekly ch'alla. The sense of success achieved by collective rituals to Huari is clarified in Juan Rojas's life story (Nash 1992) when he recounts how the miners persuaded the superintendent to have a gigantic k'araku, involving all the miners and their families, following the nationalization of the mines in 1952. This celebration enabled him, as an explorer-driller, to discover the vein that he named El Porvenir (The Future), which extended the life of the Santa Fe mine and the community that depended on it.

The demonic aspect of the Lord of the Hills, whether he is called Huari, Supay, or the devil, comes out in the rituals that I participated in after three men were killed in an accident in Itos mines (which occurred only a few days before the appropriate time for the ritual on July 31). Miners blamed their deaths on the failure of the management to carry out the appropriate ritual, and they would not consent to go back into the mines unless an offering was made to the "hill owners." When this was celebrated, with a black and a white llama donated by the management, the men were able to work without fear. By feeding the hill owner, the miners felt that his appetite would be satisfied and he would not eat them.

Overcoming alienation to capitalist intervention is only one reading of the rituals. In the weekly collective rituals of the ch'alla, the miners reenact their success in ensuring continued productivity of the mines, safety in the work setting, and collective enrichment. Miners' resistance to the capitalist enterprise in which they worked was not to "commodity fetishism," or the earnings or the wealth it represented; they opposed selfish pursuit of gain at the expense of other workers. They tried to draw near the wealth, personified in the devil images in the mines, and gain more of it through their collective action in the union. What they struggled against was the exploitation of their labor so that their earnings did not reflect their contribution to production. Through their weekly ch'alla and the semiannual k'araku they restored balance with the hill spirit and ensured the reproduction of the mines. In this sense the rituals follow a logic that is neither pre-capitalist nor capitalist; they entertain a wider vision of power and conflict that includes natural wealth before it has been appropriated by human agencies of any defined "class."

Anthropologists share with historians the frustration of trying to capture such processes in the structural categories provided by science (Thompson 1978), but those who deal seriously with the ethnographic data can hardly stuff the expressions of cultural behavior into a universalizing interpretation that assumes a unilineal evolutionary process from precapitalist to capitalist.

The ch'alla is thus the master key to the life of the mining communities. As miners pour their offering of chicha, the fermented corn drink favored in the mining communities, into the ground for the Pachamama, they say "To life!" Life is dependent on the wealth of the mines and the exploitation of minerals. The assertion of the right to life became the leitmotif of the struggle to keep the mines open after the New Economic Policies threatened to destroy a way of life that had generated the most militant sectors of the working class. The people recognize the threat and are arming themselves to resist the new forms of attack that conform to the policies of privatization and demobilization of people's movements. They lost the first round when their March for Life was halted by the army in August 1986 (Nash 1992). But the spirit they manifested in the many historic encounters with the army and a ruling class dominated by external forces will not easily be laid to rest.

July 1992

WE EAT THE MINES AND THE MINES EAT US
Dependency and Exploitation in Bolivian Tin Mines

Chapter 1

<>◇<>

Introduction

◆THE PARADOX of Bolivia is the root of the problems that plague all South American countries. The second country in world production of tin, with big deposits of iron and zinc as well as bauxite, lead, copper, magnesium, gold, and whatever silver was left by the Spaniards, it has the lowest indices in per capita income, literacy levels, and life span. The Spaniards took enough silver from its mines to build a transatlantic bridge to Madrid, but left nothing in the mining centers from which these riches came except the mint in Potosí and a few religious relics. The penetration of foreign capital in the twentieth century has fostered one of the most exploited working-class populations along with one of the richest millionaires of the century, Simon Patiño, a Bolivian Creole who worked with his wife to found the biggest tin-producing combine in the world. Its history of struggle since the uprising of Tupac Amaru and his ally Tupac Catari against the Spaniards in 1781 to the advent of the Che Guevara guerrilla movement in 1967 reveals its people to be among the most politically responsive to revolutionary ideology, while at the same time it seems most vulnerable to reactions against reform or fundamental change. Despite a century of overthrows of nonrepresentative governments and a major revolution in 1952, when peasants and workers initiated a structural change, it has for most of its history been governed by political opportunists and military leaders who respond to external dictates rather than internal demands.

The Bolivian paradox is the most extreme case in South America of nations incompletely integrated in a world market on which they have become completely dependent. Like the monocrop producers of Central America, reliance on mineral exports, particularly tin, increases the vulnerability of a nation dependent on external trade for survival. Locked in the heart of the southern cone, it is subject to control by its neighbors, who limit its access to the sea and leave it to manipulation by the carriers as well as the purchasing countries. Despite internal potential for growth in nearly uninhabited tropical and subtropical areas, capital generated in the mines has been directed into oil production in Santa Cruz that serves external interests or enterprises outside its borders. Instead of fostering subsidiary enterprise in the concentration and production of metal products, Bolivia's profits have been invested in British smelters and its crude minerals transported at great cost to distant ports.

Bolivian tin miners have the reputation of being the most revolutionary segment of the working class. They share a life experience that has given them a strong identity as a community and as a class. In the seventy years of industrial exploitation of the mines, they have transformed themselves from a peasant population with a localized world view to a proletariat aware of the world market in which the product of their labor is sold and from which they buy many of their consumption needs. Although they number only 28,000, or 2 percent of the work force, they have had a profound effect on the labor movement of the nation.

The cultural transformation is a continuation of the process of absorption in the labor force and in a national society that began with the conquest. From the time of national independence until the revolution of 1952, this meant acquiring some command of spoken Spanish and skills for dealing with modern industrial and urban enterprises which permitted limited participation in the national society as a *cholo* or *chola*. In Bolivia, chola is a cultural rather than a racial category, as in Peru and Chile. "Cholification" began with the movement of Indians into urban and industrial centers. The chola cultural stratum revealed resistance to, as well as selective acceptance of items in the dominant culture. The core of this resistance is the recognition of the *Pachamama*, or space/time concept of the pre-conquest, linked to a community that constantly reinforces the beliefs and rituals giving the people a distinct identity. Unlike the labor force of many industrial centers, the Quechua- and Aymara-speaking Indians who were drawn into the mines have not lost touch with their roots.

The strength of their identity with pre-conquest beliefs provides them with the basis for self-determination in the new class definition of their national status. Men differ from women in the rate and degree to which they can take advantage of the new opportunities in the post-revolutionary period, but the solidarity of the group, which has its roots in a community where women define the major style and motivation, stems from their continuity with the Indian culture. The transection of social consciousness based on indigenous roots by sophisticated class ideologies will be the core of this study.

Participation of cholos in national, political, and economic institutions is limited by poverty and lack of education. The attraction of the mines and the cities lay in the hope of overcoming both these limitations. Indians entered the new economic system based on mining as the most exploited segment of the working class. Since the Chaco War of 1930, many of the workers and peasants broke out of the insulation of chola culture to enter directly into national political activity. The populist movement of the MNR (Movimiento Nacional Revolucionario), in which cholos participated and became leaders in the forties and fifties, was the avenue for overcoming the illiteracy and poverty that previously had held them back. When Victor Paz Estenssoro, leader of the MNR, was prevented from being seated as president after his election, it was the cholo miners and factory workers who took to the streets, seized arms from the barracks, and won the revolution that brought him to power in April 1952. Leaders in the Federation of Mine Workers Unions of Bolivia (*Federación de Sindicatos de Trabajadores Mineros de Bolivia;* FSTMB) and in the newly formed peasant *sindicatos* became national senators and departmental representatives. However, the integration of cholo and Indian leaders ended as the movement became dominated by the commercial middle class geared to an external market. U.S. influence, particularly after 1957, and the imposition of the Stabilization Plan (chapter 8) upset the play of internal forces. By the early sixties, those leaders who continued to represent the interests of the workers were killed, exiled, or imprisoned while others were coopted into a new system of dependency supporting *los gobiernos de turno,* governments who were for the moment in power.

When I arrived in La Paz in July 1967, on my first visit to Bolivia, Che Guevara was still fighting in the tropics of Santa Cruz. One of the worst massacres in the long history of mining repression had just been carried out by Barrientos' troops in Siglo XX and Catavi, where over eighty-seven men, women, and children were killed on June 24, the eve of the celebration of San Juan.

I took a bus to the old mining center of Oruro, where I found the San José mine paralyzed because of the reorganization of work according to plans proposed by the Interamerican Development Bank (BID) when they loaned capital to the Nationalized Mining Corporation of Bolivia (COMIBOL). The mining corporation had just fired several hundred women who had worked in the concentration of metals and replaced them by man-operated machines in the new Sink and Float plant. I spoke to only a few people—a teacher in the mine school who sympathized with the workers and told me some of their problems, a woman in chola dress selling candy and fruit to idlers, and a gatekeeper who was no longer able to work inside the mines due to silicosis. All of them spoke bitterly of the government and the nationalized administration. I read the writing on the walls of all the company buildings calling for the "fight against imperialism" and "death to the military assassins and parasites" signed with the initials of the political parties and union federations: MNR, FSB, PRIN, PCB, MCB, COB, FSTMB. In large red letters, dripping from the hastily executed inscription, the word *"Liberación"* dominated the walls of the company store. It was as though the cry of the French revolution for Liberty, Equality, and Fraternity were reduced to its minimal demand: liberty to work out their own destiny. Later I saw an exhibition of paintings in the University of Oruro, the work of a son of a miner. The walls seemed to retreat into the mine shafts depicted, where the *Tío,* the devil spirit to whom the miners give offerings so that he will help them in their work, sat in his niche and where the beauty and mystery of the mines were captured in the stalactites and textured rock. I was determined to return to study in this center that revealed, even in such a short time, the turbulence of a society holding onto its traditions at the same time that it was trying to come to grips with an imposed system of exploitation.

I was able to return to Bolivia for a summer field session in June 1969, with a grant from the Social Science Research Council, to carry out a study of the ideology of tin miners. Barrientos had died in an air crash two months before. His vice president, Siles Salinas, lacked what American journalists termed "charisma" for holding the people under a repressive military subjugation. Many of the mines were running, as they had for several years, at a loss, decapitalized by inefficient management and the transfer of unaccounted earnings into military equipment. Pensioned workers were not receiving the subsistence checks that, even when forthcoming, could not cover their food costs. Government-employed teachers had not received their paychecks for months. Union leaders were still in hiding or exile, and "yellow" union agents were serving as spies for the mining administration. Mining police received more pay than the production workers to catch *jucos,* unemployed miners who entered deserted shafts at night and "stole" what they considered to be their national rights to the minerals left behind.

In that encounter, I sensed that Bolivia represented the nadir of an industrial development which, although it had nationalized some enterprises, was more concerned with the balance of payments than with the welfare of the producers. I returned in January 1970 to continue research on the process of decline that climaxed a century of industrial exploitation of the mines.

From the very beginning of industrial mining, the men and women who were drawn from the agricultural valleys of Cochabamba and the *ayllus* of the altiplano in the latter part of the nineteenth and early twentieth centuries endured extreme hardships in the working and living conditions they encountered in the mines. Whenever the workers joined in collective action to improve their lot, the army, quartered in barracks close to all the major mining centers, crushed their protest. The history of massacres and the murder and exile of their leaders has raised their consciousness of the need for political action in defense of their class interests. The imported ideologies of revolutionary action directed toward socialism have found receptive ground in the mines, where the thesis of the inevitability of class struggle and the ultimate victory of the proletariat are founded in their present misery and their utopian visions of the future. Bolivia is one of the increasingly numerous countries of the world where the once-repudiated Marxist thesis of the increasing misery of the working class can be measured in a real decline in subsistence levels, not just in a proportionate decline in earning power in relationship to capitalist expropriation.

In the ideology of capitalist production, the moral issues of labor exploitation are considered extraneous to rational market relationships since labor is treated simply as another factor of production comparable to capital or rent. However, morality of necessity enters into assessment of the labor market, since the wage determines whether human life can be sustained and regenerated at a level corresponding with minimal social values. Weber's equation of modern society with an outlook of rational expediency (Gerth and Mills 1946:56) and traditional society with affectual, value-loaded, and hence irrational sentiment negates the importance of the past in shaping human consciousness and provoking resistance to attrition in periods of rapid change.

The growing recognition that, in Singer's (1973:2) words, "the classical dichotomy of traditional and modern societies—was largely a definition of ideal type concepts and not a description of empirical realities" has brought about a rethinking of anthropological approaches to the study of change. Evidence from India (Singer 1973; Ames 1973), Japan (Abegglen 1958), and Indonesia (Peacock 1968) shows that the transformation of the traditional culture is not only not a necessary condition for modernization, but that retention of the traditional culture may well ease the transition.

In my study of the Bolivian mining community I was convinced that not only is the transition eased by retention of some traditional values, but that the opportunity to advance beyond the imposed model of modernization is heightened by virtue of retaining a basis of self-determination for adaptation along new and innovative lines that are not contained in the old paradigms. I found that contemporary ideologies of socialism and communism are combined with beliefs in primordial mythic forces such that the people are not alienated from their cultural roots. Unlike workers in most industrial centers, they have not lost their sense of personal worth and their faith in human potential.

When there is more than a single stream of cultural influences, as with the Indians of the altiplano, the roots of consciousness may appear dissonant to an outsider. Unless individuals are forced to make choices based on differing ideologies, they may be able to sustain totally contradictory modes of thought. Because the motivation to act derives from multiple and often contradictory sources of consciousness, each act becomes the resolution of an internal crisis. One of the basic dualisms in the miners' worldview is that of upper and lower worlds, with Christian deities active above ground and pre-conquest spirits operating below. These two worlds are in harmony. This ability to embrace apparently contradictory systems of belief is based not on the usual syncretism described for indigenous people of the New World, but rather on compartmentalization in time and space. Tuesday and Friday are the days for recognizing these indigenous forces, while Sunday and saints' days in the Catholic calendar are assigned to Christian deities. The ceremonies and symbols appropriate to each category are contained in the separate spheres. Miners cross themselves as they enter the mine and pray to the saint in the chapel at level zero, but once they enter the lift to go down into their work levels, they are in the domain of the Devil, or Tio, the Spanish term for the pre-conquest Supay or Huari. They cannot utter the names of the Christian saints or deities, nor can they bear any Christian symbols such as a cross, and they are even wary of working close to the veins of metal with a pick, which looks like a cross and might cause the Tío to withdraw the riches he has revealed.

Although many union and political leaders reject the spiritual beliefs of the past when they embrace the secular political ideologies, the rank-and-file miners sustain such beliefs and practices along with Marxist-Leninist programs, whether Maoist or Moscoworiented, without any sense of dissonance. Dissonance arises when choices are made between competitive ends. While the workers are not conscious of conflict between their rituals to the Pachamama or Tío and their observation of Christian ceremonies, secular leaders in political parties and trade unions reject other-worldly orientations as competition for their program of revolutionary action to achieve socialism, while sacred leaders oppose primordial belief systems that compete with Christian orthodoxy. The sense of dissonance is forced upon them by those who wish to maintain control over a group through a unifying ideology. In the past, the priesthood has pitted its program for salvation against that of the Marxist-Leninist ideology, but the new orders of missionary priests, who call themselves "priests of the Third World" and who have been working with the miners, have tried to find ways of synthesizing the efforts of the church with those of revolutionary movements. In their attempt to find a common meeting ground with those who espouse a revolutionary ideology for the oppressed, they have opened their minds to some of the indigenous beliefs of the workers, although they are still chary of the rituals that accompany them. Union leaders assert that the alliance with the church is a temporal one, since they still fear that the church will gain some of its old power by supernatural appeals.

This book is concerned with the ideology of miners both as a way of perceiving and interpreting experience and as it influences action. In some sense it might be more accurate to call the subject of this study "worldview," following anthropological tradition in the study of folk societies outlined by Robert Redfield (1947) and Sol Tax (1941). This has the advantage of avoiding the confusion caused by those who equate ideology with false consciousness, following Mannheim (1936:40), who accepted the Marxian critique of ideology as "the collective unconscious of certain groups [that] obscures the real conditions of society both in itself and others and thereby stabilizes it." However, if we include as ideology the value premises that influence all scientific investigation, then we can accept the view that ideologies are not just distortions of other peoples' thoughts but orientations that underlie all analyses. I prefer to use the term ideology when I refer to areas where there is a greater codification of thought leading to action, and the term world view when I discuss general perspectives. I remain within anthropological tradition in using ideology to refer not only to political orientations and action, but to social, economic, and supernatural spheres (Hobsbawm 1977). The question of how the workers put together the orientations they acquire in the family, in their work, in the union and federated workers' movement, and church and political parties, is basic to the problem of how ideology is related to action.

These basic orientations, raised to the level of consciousness within collective action-oriented groups, provide the origin from which ideological propositions arise. Action may be paralyzed by the underlying contradictions if the conflict is not recognized and made explicit, and somehow resolved. One such resolution is to impose a hierarchy of values that suggests priorities in the field of action. Another resolution is to forge hegemonies, so that the priorities of one social group are brought into alignment with those of another such as to form a partnership for some collective goal. For the tin miners, as well as many other workers, the class culture is at variance with class consciousness as promoted in worker organizations. The root of this is the cultural emphasis on individual striving, competition, and familial rather than collective goals. The more successful a worker is as a wage earner, the more likely he is to promote his children's ambitions to leave the ranks of the working class. Given this orientation, the working class loses those members who, because of their energy and ambition to improve their own lot, would be the most dedicated to improving the general welfare. Another contradiction lies in the workers' sense of exploitation on the job along with the awareness of their dependence on the job as the only means of making a living. The tendency has been to suppress or deny this variance rather than recognize the sources of it and come to grips with it.

The unions cultivate the understanding of exploitation through comparable wage figures or by pointing to the difference between the profit of the enterprise and the returns to the workers. It is the basis for mobilizing militant action. What is left out of the discourse in the syndicates is what every worker senses—without the job there would be no life. This cultivates a strategy of compromise, of seeking a patron to protect one's interest. The vulnerability of family life with a single wage earner sharpens this dependency, since the lives of all the members are at stake if the wage earner loses his job. The company is very aware of the effect of anxiety for the job and plays on the workers' fears whenever there is militant action. Thus the solidarity of the workers in the work site is at odds with the responsibility in the family unit. Until this is clearly recognized, the latent competitiveness of demands set in the home and those set on the job will be a counter to militant action.

The basic dialectic between individual opportunism and collective ideology emerges in the family. The family proposes a set of rules for getting along with others, for minimizing conflict, and for maximizing individual goals, but at the same time it demonstrates the need for cooperation and provides the minimal unit for realizing collective action. The chola culture of the miners provides a family form adapted to the shock of transition from an agricultural to an industrial setting. In form it is flexible, able to expand as economic prosperity permits or sudden death of a wage earner requires. It is expansible through the institution of *compadrazgo*, which permits the addition of allies or patrons through ritual godparenthood. It provides a complementarity of roles between men and women such that women are not so subordinated that they cannot support themselves and their children if the man should desert them or die.

Roles played out in the family dramatize the tension between individualism versus cooperation and dominance versus subordination. Sibling rivalry is constantly aggravated by parental display of favoritism. In an economy of scarcity, rivalry even for food is a means of displaying preferences. Such preferential treatment, especially in the distribution of educational opportunities, probably has a survival value in that it concentrates the limited resources of the family and enables one to succeed. This tends to reinforce the dominance relations in the wider society, especially since the values on which preferential choices are made—whiteness of complexion, maleness, and, as the child becomes further socialized, the ability to ingratiate oneself with superordinates—are those cultivated in the wider society.

At the same time, the family teaches the meaning of self-sacrifice of the older generation to give a better life to the younger. The great labor leaders of the past saw the magnitude of their parents' striving to give them life and hope for a better lot and were able to translate this sense of responsibility for others into a class allegiance. The old order of Catholic priests sentimentalized and reduced this primary unit to a vehicle for domesticating and pacifying the working class. The Holy Family, with its internal contradiction of a cuckolded father and a mother who became a passive agent for bearing a bastard, was the best model it could offer for these idealized roles. The workers of San José mines reject their patron saint with all the Brechtian humor of their class and respond to the vigorous sexual excitement that the independent chola, fictionalized in the *Chaskañawi* (Medinacelli 1935) and mythologized in the tales of La Viuda (see chapter 5), could give them to pique their interest in life.

Education is seen by miners as the primary means of climbing out of the working class. The essence of the educational philosophy from the colonial period up to the present is to denigrate indigenous culture and to exemplify the values and ideals of the dominant European culture. Education became a process of alienation from familial and cultural roots. Until recently, Spanish was the only language used in the schools. Foreign degrees were rated much more highly than any acquired in the country and became a commodity to bargain for inflated salaries for the technicians. The fact that the mines offer the miners an opportunity to educate their children gives them a high incentive to work there, and the one great hope that many of them express is to "buy" their children out of the mines with their own sacrifice. After the reorganization of the Federation of Mine Workers Unions of Bolivia (FSTMB) following the repression under General Barrientos, leaders of the union tried to gain control over the educational process by organizing institutes for technical training in the mining centers where their children could be trained to become technicians. Thus they hoped to free themselves from the alienated middle-class technicians, who they felt abused them more than the former foreign technicians. These plans and all the other aspirations of the working class were dashed by the Banzer coup of August 22, 1971.

Once, after giving a lecture on the mines, I was asked whether miners were alienated. I said no, and after thinking about the question a good deal since then, I am convinced that they are not alienated from the work situation nor from the community which has grown out of these working relations, but they are alienated from the system of exploitation on which it is predicated. In order to translate the desires and goals of the workers into a revolutionary movement, one must sharpen the sense of alienation against a system of exploitation without alienating the workers from the primary group loyalties that give them the spur to act collectively. As

Thompson (1963:54) has pointed out for the English working-class movement, the tensions among intellect, enthusiasm, and love complement each other in the revolutionary traditions of the proletariat. In order to feel love and to share collective goals, the workers cannot be totally alienated.

Action, whether directed toward revolutionary goals or merely the maintenance of self and family, depends on motivations that arise from self-respect and love for those included in the primary group. A totally alienated person is unable to meet his or her own physical or emotional needs and certainly not those of others in the social environment. Despite the exploitative wage system and poverty in the mining communities, I did not find alienated people. One reason for this is that there is a greater fulfillment of expressive needs—at least for the male population—than in other occupational groups. There is the excitement of the danger of the work itself, which adds a certain élan to the workers' self-image. Then there is the mystery and excitement of the mine, where it is easy to imagine oneself caught in the spell of the demons with which miners inhabit it in their imagination. When I asked one miner what fears he had when he entered the mine he said,

❖ I don't have any fears. I was born to be a miner! I like the mine. I like the excitement of putting myself in danger to prove my manhood and my capacity. I like it when, after working hard and sweating, I throw water on my head and feel the coolness and I imagine all sorts of power in me. I like the comradeship. I believe we all ought to live like brothers in a family, the way we workers feel inside the mine. Someday I hope to propose some solutions to the social problems we have in the union, but I have to gain the respect of the workers.

The solidarity with working companions that this miner expresses captures the effusion of shared experience that Marx speaks of as basic to class consciousness. In the mine, workers address each other as *ñaña,* brother; each one has a nickname that captures his characteristic qualities.

There is less opportunity for women to gain self-expression and the community endorsement for it. A married woman is subjected to the limitation of the house, to almost unrestricted childbearing, and to dominance by the man whose needs she must dedicate herself to serve. Women who work as *palliris,* pulverizing ore and selecting out the metal, have some of the satisfaction that comes with independence, but they have a harder time maintaining a satisfactory domestic relation with a man of respect in the community. The very fact that a woman works is a threat to an industrious worker whose reason for being is to support a family. Male and female roles are dichotomized in the mining community, and there is still a mystique about women not entering the mine. This did not prevent the recruitment of women as miners when the men were mobilized into the army during the War of the Chaco.

In the early decades of the twentieth century, when industrialized mining was in its infancy and extraction and concentration processes were labor intensive, women—and children—were an integral part of the labor force. Their work was lost when machines were installed in the flotation processes for sorting minerals in the sixties, when the National Revolutionary Movement (MNR) government agreed to the Triangular Plan to get capital to develop the mines. Later in the sixties, widows and women without male providers fought for the right to work. They were permitted to toil on the slag pile, selecting out the rock that contained some mineral, for which they were paid by the bag, on the average earning 80 cents (US) a day, with no right to hospitalization or other benefits.

The women's domain extends to the market, where they enter both as buyers and sellers. Goods, particularly perishable food products and home-produced clothing, are carried by cholas from low altitudes and sold in the high-altitude mining communities. In these spheres, the chola cultural traits of individualism, competitiveness, and cultivation of limited, dyadic relations flourish. These traits are in complementary opposition to the collective interests cultivated in the men's work and union spheres. Some of the interpersonal strategies cultivated in the chola culture are used by the men, especially those who seek opportunistically to use limited avenues of mobility to gain a better position in life. Paradoxically, it is in the union, which has become a stairway to self-promotion for some leaders, especially in the MNR period, that the tactics of patron-clientage and currying of favor from other union leaders as well as from the administration are combined with a rhetoric espousing collective morality and stressing egalitarianism and the advance of the working class.

The mines, from the point of view of the workers and their

families, are a giant storehouse of riches to which they have limited access. The main recipients are the banks and the bureaucrats, and the military governments that divert profits to the army. Next in line are the petty bureaucrats, who, in their role as bookkeepers and accountants, can divert some funds to their own use. Following them are the contract workers, especially drillers, who by exploiting their own labor in operating the machines, are able to make somewhat more money than petty clerks and schoolteachers working on the surface. Then come the workers who live on the base pay and have no margin to exploit other than by working every day of the month and thereby gaining a small incentive pay. These men are usually long-term workers who have expended their strength in their youth as drillers or blasters and who end their days working as carters, winch operators, or, when they are unable to enter the mine because of lung disease, as watchmen at level zero.

These are the regular core of workers who benefit from some of the social welfare provisions they have gained since the revolution of 1952. Peripheral to these are the men and women who work for private contractors who buy the rights to pan the metal coming from the streams flowing out of the hills, or who pick over the rocks in the slag pile, scratching a scant subsistence for themselves and their children. The margins of the mines are like a giant ant hill with a growing corps of desperate workers who each day receive a lowering marginal return for their efforts.

Statements about consciousness are reflections of those thoughts and attitudes people are willing to show to the investigator. The process of learning what is communally shared seems fortuitous when one works at gathering data. But like the key veins of a mine that seem to be discovered by luck, it is by consistently following the many clues that one arrives at the core of meaning. Alexandro, Basilia, Celso, Domingo, Efraim, Jorge, and Manuel are products of the mining experience, and each reflects a differing consciousness. Juan's oldest son once said of his father, "You are like a piece of ore; you are a part of the mine." This is true of all the men and women who work in the mine. In their shared experience they learn to appreciate their own strength as they pit it against the resistance of the rock that they penetrate. The impressive thing to me is that they have transformed their hard and often bitter experience into a meaningful and rewarding life.

This sense comes at odd moments in fieldwork. The first time I felt it was in the beginning of my field work during the celebration of the Feast of the Compadres. A twenty-four-hour continuous band announced the locale of the feast in a small house of the widow of a man who had taken on the burden of holding the fiesta. Shortly after he had made the promise to pay for the fiesta he was paralyzed by an accident in the mine and died during the year. *Chicha* was flowing and a meal was served shortly after I arrived. Following this the band struck up a lively *cueca*, and a small spidery man dressed in black and wearing a fedora seized the hand of his partner, a huge chola with sunglasses and derby, and led a snake dance out into the rain. As we danced across the mud-rutted bus terminal, the dancers leaping and twirling according to their individual fancy but never letting go of the hands of their partners, I felt the urgency of their claim, not just on life, but on self-expression.

I experienced that feeling many times that year—at a potato feast on Corpus Christi, during the sacrifice of a llama on July 31 after an accident that took the lives of three men, and on the Day of the Dead as I sat in the living room of a man who had died in the abortive October uprising. I could then see Carnival as the epitome of this experience. In the lavish costumes, the enormous expenditure of effort and wages that went into the magnificent display, they asserted a profound respect for their work and lives and a momentary denial of their impoverishment.

The mines are a synecdoche for the modern age of industrialization. Their history encompasses the rise of international expansion of capitalism that exported capital and machinery from the metropolitan centers to the farthest corners of the world, rapaciously absorbing labor and natural resources for the profit of a few, to the decline of interest in natural minerals as synthetics based on petroleum feedstock became the prime raw material. The concentration of military and economic power in mining centers from colonial times until the present prevented the wealth that was created from diffusing to more than a small privileged sector of the commercial bourgeoisie. As the needs and expectations of the workers in the extraction of primary resources have been growing, the resource base has been dwindling. Within the structure of a world market dominated by private capitalist exploitation there are no margins set aside for the worker in the transition from declining enterprises. The slag piles, which workers consider to be the resource base for an orderly phasing out of extraction when the interior veins are exhausted, were being leased to U.S. companies that were depleting even this fallback of the mining population.

The only solution the development ideology of modern capitalism offers for the future is more of the same process that threatens the very resource base on which it has thrived in the past. The mining communities are fast approaching that day of destruction envisioned in their pre-conquest myths, when the natural balance of the world was upset and primeval monsters were unleashed by the spirit of the hills to devour the people that had left a pastoral-agricultural life to work in the mines (chapter 2). Only a redefinition of the aim of the development process which will put people at the center of planning and reject the exploitation of natural riches for short-run gains will reverse the situation. Bolivia, like many dependent countries, cannot respond to the internal problems that beset the population because of the controls operating on it from beyond its borders.

Chapter 2

◈◆◈

The Miners' History

◈BOLIVIA'S ENTRY into world history begins with the mines. The miners' sense that history as the exploitation of national riches and their own physical forces for the enrichment of others. It is made up of myths received from the pre-conquest, the historic myths playing up nationalistic sentiments taught in the schools, and the memories related by their parents and experienced in their own lifetime. These are projected in a framework of national and international events communicated by radio, the press, and in meetings of the union and political parties. The selection of what is worth remembering comes from the impact of an event on their own lives as it is filtered through the main channels of communication: the family, the union, political parties, and the religious order. This mythic and memorized history shapes the view of current events and gives people the rationale for action in their own life.

I shall not attempt an objective reconstruction of the history of mining in Bolivia.[1] My task here is to put together the events that shaped the development of the mining industry with the impact these events—both the personally experienced and the socially transmitted—have had on the lives of miners and their families. My entry into these events is primarily through autobiographies. After

[1] Blanco published an account of mining in the colonial and independence period up to the first decade of the twentieth century in a book that is devoted more to advertising the advantages of investing capital in Bolivian mining than to summarizing historic fact (1910). Ibañez C. (1943) and Ruiz Gonzalez (1965) included later trends in economic histories of Bolivia. Hanke (1956) has summarized data bearing on Potosí and Klein has given many illuminating insights into mining in his history of politics prior to the 1952 revolution (1969). As yet, however, a comprehensive account remains to be done.

questioning several members of the mining community about their most memorable experiences, I interviewed twenty miners about those events which I had learned were significant, asking them what they were doing at the time each took place. This "event analysis" (Turner 1957) gives one not only an insight into the processes of change but also the sense of the political orientations formed in each generation (Mannheim 1936). The second source of information is myth—inherited from the past and generated in the process of the history in which each miner lived. Without equating myth with history, we can discover from myths those general persuasions that influenced peoples' interpretations of historical events. The third source was direct participation in some of the changes that took place during the period from June 1969 to December 1970, in which my study was conducted. This material is included in subsequent chapters. I learned to view events from the miners' perspective as I observed the reorganization of the labor movement and the events that led to two governmental coups and the formation of a third during a brief return trip in 1971.

Mythological Past

A myth surviving from the pre-conquest deals with the transition from an agricultural past to mining and incorporates the second transition from an Inca to a Spanish conquest. This version is a paraphrasing of Beltrán Herédia (1962).

> The community of Uru Uru [pre-Hispanic name for Oruro] was one of fishermen and pastoralists devoted to the worship of the Sun. Every day Huari [the spirit of the hills] was awakened by the first-born daughter of the Sun, Ñusta. He fell in love with her and pursued her with arms of smoke and volcanic fire. The father came to her aid and hid her in the caves. Huari swore that he would bring vengeance against the town by turning it against the true religion. He became the apostle of a new religion and preached against Pachacamac and his religious and social work. He thundered against Inti, the Sun God, and the old social hierarchy. He exalted in the superiority of material goods over spiritual, and of the labor of the mines over that of the field. The Urus resisted, but when Huari showed them gold and silver, they rebelled against their old beliefs and sacred authorities. Desirous of riches, they

abandoned the daily hard but healthy work in their fields. They stopped praying to Inti and turned to wild drinking and midnight revels with chicha, a liquor unknown before then. In their drunken state there came forth serpents, toads, lizards, and ants who, in the acts of the witches' sabbath, overwhelmed them. The inhabitants of the neighboring towns and even their friends and parents appropriated their goods. The people, abject with vice, were transformed into apathetic, silent and loveless beings.

The town would have disappeared because of internal fights had not Ñusta appeared on a rainbow one day after a heavy storm. Accompanying her were the chiefs and priests who had been exiled from the town when the people were perverted from their old ways. Little by little, men returned to what had been. They revived their traditions, costums, religion, and social order. They imposed Quechua on the Uru dialect. The fields would have recovered and even surpassed their fertility if Huari, in vengeance, had not sent four plagues on the repentant town: a serpent, a toad, a lizard, and ants. The monstrous serpent moved from the mountains of the south and devoured their fields and flocks. The Urus saw him and fled in terror, when suddenly someone shouted for Ñusta and the monster was divided in two by a sword. The other three plagues, advancing from the other compass points, were also killed by the intervention of Ñusta, who overwhelmed the vengeful Huari. Today a chapel stands on the hill where the giant lizard was killed. It is said that the lake [near Cala Cala] still turns red at dawn from the blood of the lizard that flowed into it. The ants were turned into sand dunes that can still be seen on the southern borders of the town. Peace returned to the town.

The myth dramatized the resolution of the crisis experienced by workers as they entered the unnatural and unfamiliar world which they believed to be inhabited by the male fertility god, Huari. The anxiety raised by entering the domain of the source and giver of agricultural wealth is resolved on two levels: First, Supay is reduced to manageable terms—endowed with human weaknesses of avarice and love of ostentation which make him vulnerable to propitiation. Second, the Inca maiden Ñusta is conjured up and evoked whenever danger threatens (she was later transformed into the Virgin of the Mineshaft). A myth tells of her miraculous appearance before an unemployed miner who had turned thief.

One night when Nena Nena went out as usual to steal from the homes of the rich, he was surprised by the houseowner and in the

scuffle that ensued was wounded with a knife. He managed to escape to his cave hollowed out in the hill Pie de Gallo. There he
pulled out the tiny picture of the Virgin of Candalaria, and, as was
his custom after all his exploits, he prayed to her with his dying
breath. Miraculously there appeared in the very rock walls of his
cave a full-life-size representation of the Virgin.

The Virgin is ensconced in a church built at the entrance to the first
major silver mine, now inactive, where she appeared before Nena
Nena. Decked in jewels and lit up with neon, she inclines her head
benignly toward her worshipers from her marble altar in the
Church of the Mineshaft. Ñusta has left only a footprint in a rock
called *Rumi Campana* (Stone Bell) because of the resounding tone
from its hollow interior when it is knocked. These are living myths,
enacted in rituals, dance, and drama, and available for reference
when daily suffering becomes unbearable.

Spanish chronicles relate that the mines were being operated
by the Inca when they arrived on the scene in 1535. Orureños can
point to the hill of San Pedro, where the Inca are said to have
emerged out of a tunnel which begins in Cuzco, the imperial center
in highland Peru. The tunnel entrance, or *Inka loq 'sina* (exit of the
Inca), as it is called, is blocked with rocks to prevent the exit of the
Devil and his assistants, who are believed to inhabit its recesses as
well as to prevent people from falling in. It is the site of sacrificial
rituals to the Devil and his son, Supay Saq' Wachasqan, and the
rocks blocking the exit are spattered with the blood of sacrificial
animals used to propitiate the spirits and gain favors from them.
Cocanis, those who sell coca in the market, are said to sacrifice their
first-born child to gain power with the Devil to make high profits in
their trade.

I first heard about the Inca invasion and the spirits that lived in
the hill of San Pedro when I climbed to the summit with a miner's
widow. She told me of their arrival:

❖ The Inca were rulers of the whole of South America, and the king
of the Inca was the authority for the whole continent. His palace
was in Cuzco, and the entrance from Cuzco was in Oruro through
this tunnel. Oruro was like an office for the Inca. They came out of
the hills dressed like the dancers in Carnival. And that is why Carnival is here in Oruro because it is the history of the arrival of the
Inca.

My companion on our hike up San Pedro believed fully in the powers of the hill spirits. She was *de vestido,* had traveled widely to the mines of Chile and Argentina, and had completed secondary school.[2]

My awareness that these beliefs were not limited to Indian *campesinos* was further confirmed when a family of five arrived: a woman carrying a baby, a man carrying a two-year-old who was holding a small dog, and a four-year-old boy carrying a baby lamb. In addition they carried bundles of faggots, a lunch bag, a bottle of tea, and some ceremonial objects. The first thing they did on arriving was feed the lamb with a nursing bottle of milk. Until that moment I thought they were going to sacrifice the lamb in the ritual called *wilancha,* but instead they discussed with us how hard it was to maintain the correct intake of food for the orphaned lamb, who, if left to itself, would overeat and kill itself. They showed me the dried fetus of a llama and other offerings they had brought and would burn in the wood fire as an offering to Huari. The man was a painting contractor in the city and had come to ask Huari for more business to come his way. He and his wife were de vestido and spoke Spanish. He had the same motivations as any independent contractor, but he appealed to ancient forces to stimulate demand for his trade.

As we chatted with this industrious young tradesman about how to increase his profits, occasionally gazing over the saucer-like plain that had been a prehistoric lake but now looked as though the tide had run out, leaving behind the Gulf Oil tanks, the chimney stacks of mud-brick factories, the rows on rows of new cooperative housing, and the festering lines of old company housing edging the slagpile of San José mine, I realized that the simple traditional/modern dichotomies were not going to explain much in this society. Present and past are fused in the struggle for survival, and the people maintain their alliances with old demons as they strive to strike a better bargain for the future.

[2] *De vestido* refers to those who have taken on eastern styles of dress. It is assumed that other aspects of being modernized, including knowing how to read and write as well as speak Spanish, are present. Members of the same family may dress differently and have different levels of education.

Colonial Period

The Uru Urus, who were the pre-Inca occupants of the present department of Oruro, are either merged with the Quechua population, who came as conquerors, discovered the mines, and forced the agricultural population to work for them, or they have been pushed to the margins of the agricultural and mining area (Beltrán Herédia 1962). In 1535, 570 Spaniards led by Diego de Almagro arrived, accompanied by 15,000 Indians from lower Peru. They founded the city of Paria where they worked a silver mine. A miner told me the following about the Spanish settlement:

❖ When the Spaniards arrived they took their position in the town of Paria. This was the first mining town to exploit silver. They used the rawhide helmets that the campesinos still use as armament in the t'inku (armed encounter) as a safety helmet to go into the mines, and they also made boots of rawhide called p'olkos.

The mine has been exhausted, but the nearly vacant town, whose baked adobe houses and skeletal spire of the partially destroyed church seem to grow out of the soil, is still a ceremonial center for the Indians of the surrounding countryside, who come to the church to carry out their religious fiestas and attend mass.

The miners view the Spanish conquest as an invasion by rapacious and corrupted convicts that left its mark on the present character of Bolivian leaders. My companion on the climb up San Pedro gave me the following account of their arrival:

❖ Columbus discovered America just by accident. He was looking for the East Indies and he came to this side to open up trade. They say he went seeking aid to navigate to the East Indies by ship. No one believed him. They thought he was crazy. Finally there was a priest who was very friendly with him and he went to Queen Isabella to ask her to help Columbus. She gave him money to set sail. Then she gave freedom to the prisoners in the jail if they would go find land with Columbus. She didn't believe that they were going to find land, but that they would perish on the way. But finally Columbus found land with these delinquents. He touched the island of San Salvador and said, "I have discovered the East Indies" and went to advise the queen. He didn't take into account the Indians whom he found there.
After they discovered the islands they were still looking for the route to the East Indies and that is how they came upon South

America. Vespucci gave Columbus a map. He was kicked out—
that is to say, he was not permitted to stay in his country—and he
was a vagabond who wandered everywhere. With this, Columbus
went on to discover South America. Then the Spaniards came to
see how the land was.

Columbus announced that there were three areas of high civilization, but that the greatest was that of the Inca. The vagabonds
and delinquents who followed Columbus came to rob the Inca.
They brought a great deal of corruption and taught their delin-
quent customs at least in Chile to the Araucanians. They left all
their drunkenness and vices to us.

This hatred of the Spanish heritage is acted out in the play presented during Carnival dramatizing the betrayal of Atahualpa by
Pizarro. Rejection of Spanish genes and the customs they brought is
combined with a respect for pre-conquest beliefs and practices even
by those who left the Indian culture.

The history of mining in the highlands of Bolivia began in the
middle of the fifteenth century when the Spaniards started operations in the silver mines opened by the Inca. According to Crespo's
account of the founding of the town of San Felipe de Austria, now
Oruro (1967), the first Spaniard to mine silver in the area was
Lorenzo de Aldana in 1557. After his death, the mines were abandoned until 1581, when other Spanish adventurers arrived on the
scene. A shortage of workers inhibited the growth of the mines
until Diego de Medrano secured a *mita*, or concession of involuntary workers assigned by the Crown, in 1605. The veins were easy
to work and rendered a high return. The town of San Felipe de Austria was established as a center for mining operations in the area in
1606. By 1607, when Diego de Portugal was sent by the Audiencia
de la Plata to reconnoiter the mines, he visited 207 mines where nine
hundred Indian workers, most of them voluntary laborers, mined
the silver. These early silver mines remained in operation until the
War of Independence. Some date the demise of colonial mining
back to the rebellion of 1781, when Indian and cholo uprisings
created a labor shortage (Aguirre Zeballos 1959).

Mining in Oruro followed the major trends affecting the industry throughout the nation. The first cycle of exploitation of silver
in the colonial period gave way during the republic as the lowering
of the mineral content of the silver ores led to a withdrawal from

mining and development of consumption-oriented handicrafts and agriculture as well as some commercial cropping of quinua in the east. The third cycle began in the latter part of the nineteenth century when industrial metals—tin, copper, zinc, lead, and antimony—were mined instead of the metals for conspicuous display and commerce desired by the Spaniards. In 1877 the small mines of the area were reorganized by the Companía Minera de Oruro (Aguirre Zeballos 1959). The first foreign capital to be invested in Bolivian mines in this period came from Chile. Capital from the Chilean mines of Chuquicamarca kept the mines in operation until Hochschild bought the mines. The Companía Minera de Oruro, managing three mine shafts, continued operating under the Hochschild administration until 1947, when activities were suspended because the metal content had declined from 3.55 to 1.69 and the cost of production had risen to US $2,708 per ton for silver valued at US $1,675 (Aguirre Zeballos 1959). The government took over the mine to avoid unemployment and operated it under the aegis of the Banco Minero de Bolivia until the nationalization of the mines in 1953.

In the history of industrial mining we can trace the increasing penetration of workers into world history. Generation, sex, and category of work within the mine are the parameters of historical consciousness. They set limits but do not determine the individual's mental or physical adjustment to the social setting. A collective consciousness arises in the shared historical experiences that give shape to each generation. Zeitlan and Petras (1968) have pointed to the significance of generational differences in the formation of political ideology in Cuba. Their thesis, which develops Karl Mannheim's general formulation that common experiences during youth create a common world view (1936:270), is that "the specific historical period in which succeeding generations of workers first became involved in the labor movement had significant consequences for the formation of their political outlooks" (Zeitlan and Petras 1968:52). This approach to the analysis of consciousness of Bolivian workers makes it possible to bring together the insights gained from particular experiences of individuals with the ideological perspectives they share.

In Bolivia there have been four major ideological orientations generated in the twentieth century. The first generation developed during early industrialization of the mines from 1880 until 1910. The second developed in the early decades of union organization that culminated in the Massacre of Uncía in 1923. The third generation was that of the War of the Chaco, which ended not only in a military defeat but a rejection of governments dominated by the tin and commercial oligarchy. The fourth generation was that of the National Revolutionary Movement (MNR), which had a taste of power in the Busch and Villarroel governments of the forties and rose to power in 1952. Its decline was heralded by the miners' strikes in 1957 and 1962 and its demise came when General René Barrientos, the military leader who claimed to be the inheritor of the revolution after his coup of 1964, carried out the worst massacre in mining history on the night of San Juan in 1967. A new generation is now in formation with an ideology shaped by the disillusionment with the nationalist populist leaders and sharpened by a revolutionary consciousness of the need for structural change. Whether its leadership, now in exile or operating underground, can find a positive core with which to generate a new movement is uncertain. Since these last two generations are the actors in the community today, their story is a part of subsequent chapters. The events that marked the national changes of these decades are analyzed in Almaraz Paz (1969), Lora (1964, 1965, 1967, 1969, 1970b), Klein (1969), Malloy (1970), and Patch (1960). What I shall do here is record workers' reaction to events that touched them personally and show how it shaped their consciousness of their role in history.

Early Industrialized
Mining Labor Organization, 1880–1929

Older informants, who received their first impressions of what life was like growing up in mining communities at the end of the last century or the first decade of the twentieth century, contrasted what had been in their parents' and grandparents' time with what they had experienced in their lifetime. Within this long span of history, they saw a trend toward improvement in the quality of their lives. Looking back over the decades of the twentieth century with wonder that they had survived the disasters they had seen—accidents and disease that took the lives of their comrades, a disastrous war that decimated families and communities, and a dozen violent changes of government—they still had a commitment to life and to the possibility of progress. The only two survivors of the nineties and first decade of the twenties whom I knew in San José, Alejandro and Efraim, had an Olympian sense of irony. They spoke with a tragi-comic sense of their own innocence in the early days of mining.

Alejandro, who was born in 1900, showed more humor but less ideological consciousness than Efraim, who was his senior by eight years. Our first interview was arranged by the assistant to the industrial relations manager in the first week of my field study. Alejandro wore a rubber collar and a tie under his suit jacket and vest, the symbols of affluence gained by forty years in the mine. He had worked for gringos of all nations, as an assistant in preparing samples of metal for the chemical plant. Usually he was frivolous, making jokes of himself, his fellow workers, the bosses, and even the devil, but once, when I visited him he spoke of the massacres that are the epitome of the miners' experience.

❖ In the time of my grandfather we lived like animals when the Spanish were here. They whipped us [Alejandro used the first person plural when referring to these times as though he had experienced it]. We dressed in *bayeta* [coarse, handwoven wool] and ate *charki* [jerked beef]. We lived in *p'utu,* houses made of straw in a round form. Formerly the Spanish did not let us be free. Now we travel to Chile and Argentina, but then we could not leave the mine. During the time of the Spaniards, when a man died, he was buried right there where he was, inside the mine, like an animal, a beast of burden. When people got sick, they died without the mass. They had poor food—charki, toasted broad beans, *maíz mote* [stewed corn], flour, and water. My grandfather told me this. He died in 1880 after working all his life in the Coro Coro mines.

After Independence, there was more liberty. There was no slavery. It was a different generation. My father was in Coro Coro in the *arsenate* in 1850. There was a great deal of injustice in the mines. My grandfather's brother was called by the police. He and others were fired and some were killed. Many wanted to leave the mines. They would say, "Let's go from this city to another. Where to? To Oruro? To La Paz? Not to La Paz, not to Cochbamba. To Potosí, to the beautiful hill of Potosí!"

Many went to Potosí; some died on the way. In Potosí they lived in very cold houses without any facilities, called *choquia*. These were round houses made of adobe and with a straw roof. Some were made of stone. In this land there was better living. My grandfather earned two reales a day, but things were cheap: five centavos for *pata*, 10 centavos for *p'isu*, 20 centavos for *tumina*, a one-peso *billete* could buy anything you wanted. My grandmother worked at the mouth of the mine and helped with expenses.

In those days, men crawled into the mine. They had patches of cowhide on the seat of their pants, at their knees, at their elbows. They wore sheepskin in hats and fur in shoes. It was very deep inside the Potosi mine—four hundred to five hundred meters, like a *ch'allado* [offering place]. There was boiling water down there.

I worked in Potosí a year and then went to the army because there was no more work. I was in the army two years.

[Was there any fighting?" I asked.]

In 1920 they [the Republican forces] wanted to make a revolution. They wanted to kill the president, José Gutiérrez Guerra. They took the plaza Murillo in La Paz. We took it back. [However, the government of the Liberals under President Gutiérrez fell on July 12, 1920.] Afterward I went to the Pulacayo mine in Uyuni, then to Chuquicamarca in Chile where there is a copper mine. Many people worked there. I was a watchman in the Casa Verde for the Chile Exploitation Company, in the San Luis mine. They put the copper in acid, bathed it, and liquified it. From this tank of water they put it in a tank with poles of lead and into each section of the tank they ran an electric current. The copper, liquified by the acid, circulated there and then the electric current began to produce copper. We had a round of three guards watching the metal plates. I worked there for two years.

Then I came to Patiño mines and worked in Siglo XX with *el señor* Tole, Johnny Pang, Mister Malkinson, Douglas from Texas, Lloyd Downy, and Nelson. They were geologists; they taught me to read maps of the mines. I worked inside and learned how to find the veins. I knew all the shafts and tunnels. I earned two and a half pesos a day. This was enough for all I needed. Now everything is very high: the bread we paid five centavos for then now costs two pesos. Chicken was thirty centavos and now it is eighteen to twenty-five pesos, and an *arroba* [twenty-five pounds] of potatoes was thirty centavos, now eighteen pesos.

In 1929 I was sent to the concentration plant in the mine of Siete Suyos. There were people from Argentina working there. Señor Anglo, a real gentleman, was there. I had a great deal of love for him. People spoke Quechua. The *ch'alla* [ritual of offering] is the same, but there they drank wine.

In 1933 I was sent to the Chaco to the army. I thought I would

never return to my land. But on the third of June there was demobilization, the Day of San Antonio. I was sent to Sucre Hospital
with a gun-shot wound in my leg. When I got out, I went to the
Patiño mines.

Alejandro was a third-generation miner. His grandfather's
memories, which he incorporated into his own recollections,
spanned the colonial, independence, and contemporary mining industry. For him the decade of the twenties was the period of greatest prosperity when prices were low and he was at the peak of his
earning power. The fact that he found a patron in the foreign technicians softened his attitude toward the company.

This acceptance of paternalism was not true of his peer, Efraim,
a 78-year-old retired miner, who was more critical of the mine
owners from the Independence to the present. I recorded by hand
the recollections of Efraim, since my tape recorder was not sensitive
enough to record his narration because of the sibilations from his
few remaining teeth and the hoarse rasping of his silicosis-affected
lungs. He had entered the mine near his village of Charaña on the
Chilean border before the turn of the twentieth century. It was a
silver mine with only forty workers. His father came from Arica to
work in the interior and his mother worked in the concentration
shed as a palliri to make ends meet. As Efraim spoke of the past, he
continually made comparisons with the present.

❖ We lived in very crowded houses that the workers made themselves of dried mud and they were closed with doors made of
boxes. I helped my father make our house. Now the company
gives the workers good houses.
  There was little pleasure. We only worked; we always suffered.
We were badly fed. I was the eldest of four brothers and three sisters. We ate chuño [dehydrated potatoes], guinua [highland grain],
llama meat, papaliza [a small tuber], bread, sugar, coffee, and tea.
The mine had a pulpería [company store] and vegetables were
brought in from Tacna.
  When I was young, we didn't know school, In the mine there
were chilenos. They didn't even know my name. We were totally
isolated.

Efraim concentrated his criticism on the priests who dominated the
isolated mining town.

✧ The *cura* [priest] lived like a king. The police came with a *chicote* [whip] to take us to the church. The cura enjoyed everything. They were nationals. They wore black clothing. We were pure Indians. The only king was the cura. The curas dominated us as they wished. They lived in a regular house with everything arranged. The Indians carried baskets full of things for them, and entered on their knees. Now it is a little better. The only gods are the saints.

My *mamita* worshiped Santiago. She had an image of him in a little box with twelve saints. Tuesday and Friday they chewed coca and did the *ch'alla*. The most important saint was the Father of Spain, the same Santiago, he who brings storms and lightning. She said when there was a lightning flash, "The Father is riding around heaven on his horse." We believed because we were stupid.

We adored the Pachamama since the time of the pre-conquest kings. We worshiped her with the *sullu* [foetus] of llama, *pastillas* [cakes], and we threw alcohol in the house and the patio. We chewed coca and smoked cigarettes, kneeling like this. We had faith only in Santiago, not in Jesus. The cura worked with the saint, taking our money. Jews, evangelists, communists—all those came later. The cura dominated with a chicote. His helper came to the houses with a chicote and beat people until we gave him food. In the *pueblo* [town] near the mine, there was a church full of saints. We had to go to the pueblo to enter into the church. Four Indians carried the cura like a king. As he came in a procession, the Indians made a road with their *awayus* [shawls], all of them knelt. They brought chickens, cheeses, and barbecued goat to receive the cura. The Indian is totally ignorant.

Mallcu, Pachamama—these beliefs never helped us. I was never baptized because one has to pay for the ceremony. When I was born, the Chilean administrator of the mine gave me my name when my father went to him.

The cura used to say, "Respect the *patrones* [owners]!" How they did deceive one! If a wedding or a mass for health was needed, they received money. For less than a quarter of an hour, they received six hundred pesos. When a girl was going to be married, they told her to come to the rectory for three days before the wedding for instruction. Then the padre took advantage of her and in addition she had to work for him. The padres said, "*Amayuyu, amakeya, amasua*" [don't lie, don't be lazy, don't steal], but they were the worst of all.

We ate dirty food, but I was never sick. When I was small I learned Spanish with the Chileans. We worked twelve, fourteen, fifteen hours a day. When it was dawn we entered, and when it was sunset we came out. When we died they threw us out. They buried us in the field without a mass. We had a wake, we chewed coca and drank hot alcohol. The chief mourners gave food. Everyone went to the funeral drunk. After nine days, they gave a mass. The company didn't give anything for the death, even when we died in the mine.

When I was eighteen years old in 1910 I left home with one of my brothers. Our mama was a drunkard. We went in the *ferrocaballo* [iron horse or train]. We went to a Chilean company in Coro Coro. There young girls worked. Women in boots carried the mineral in *picas*. Some of the girls were no more than twelve years old. In Carnival, ugh! they ruined the girls.

I worked with silver and copper since I was eighteen years old. I believe that it does not have as much effect on the lungs as tin. Before, in Llallagua, they drilled with dry drills. There was a lot of dust and the men didn't last a year. Now they give waterproof clothing and boots. Before we used *p'olkos* [handmade hide boots]. Formerly they didn't have arched tunnels. The men crawled into their work places on their hands and knees. The miners advanced only where there were veins. There were no technicians. We didn't have helmets. We made caps from sheep hide. We put hide patches on our elbows and knees. Formerly we worked with kerosene lamps. It makes a lot of smoke. In Llallagua, in 1910, we used candles. First they had a Chilean company, and afterward Patiño came. They didn't even have houses. When I arrived we didn't have any place to live in. I had a woman. We made a little house and we lived like pigs. She didn't work. In 1914, during the first war, there was more production in the mine. I was in Huanuni where they used mule teams. Patiño was the owner. The work was the same as always. In that time, Llallagua was the best company. We earned three and a half pesos a day. Milk cost five centavos, cheese ten centavos; it cost five centavos for a big bread, twenty centavos for meat a kilo, eighty centavos for pants, eighty centavos for a whole sheep, potatoes were fifty centavos an arroba.

[Did you save anything?" I asked.]

Nothing! We were drinkers. We lost ourselves in the *chicherías*. Now I have nothing. When I was a child, I could buy things for five centavos: garlic, salt, etc. We had all kinds of American merchandise. They made everything with machines in America.

We lived in bad conditions in the encampment. We were packed in like sardines in three square meters. It was very backward. We got our water in a tin. In the mining camp there were two classes: the worker and the patron. They didn't want the workers to live like human beings; they didn't want civilized people. They couldn't stand that! In 1925 it was a little better during the time of Bautista. If someone had sickness of the mines, they gave him a pension. There was a social security agency. While the worker died before without anything, now they gave to him according to hours of service.

I was in Oruro when the Chaco war came forty-five years ago. They came and got me, taught me to shoot a rifle. The military are brutes. Bolivia was not prepared for war. I was in it a year. There was no water, no food. We sucked green plants. The war was a disaster. The heat burned us in the Chaco.

["What changes have there been in the life of the miners since then?" I asked.]

When Villarroel was president, we got a bonus. Then in the new year, the *rosca* [oligarchy of the owners] hung him because they didn't want us to have anything. After the overthrow of Villarroel's government, Urriolagoitia, *el chivo*—he had a beard like a goat—didn't want to work with a union. Anyone who was in the union, they took out his card and sent him out. After Paz Estenssoro, the union ruled. Why should the people work? It was very vicious after Paz; everything was in scarce supply. The miner could get things cheaper than anyone. I earned three to five hundred pesos in 1952, and I worked in the *cancha* [concentration pits] until 1959.

In 1957 the owners wanted to close the mine. It was a political decision. They said the mine was exhausted, but it wasn't. The veins will never leave. It is because they didn't make any preparations. It was to punish the workers that they closed it. San José will last for millions of years. It is because of imperialism that they want to control the worker by closing the mines they organized. When Barrientos came in, he threw everyone out for communism. Those who were fired for union activity are returning. The unions are reforming, but I don't have any interest. When the unions ruled, the people didn't want to work. Now many people get work.

Efraim has a more developed consciousness of the world he lives in than does Alejandro, who was more concerned with finding a patron than in identifying himself with the rest of the workers. Efraim cast the life conditions he described into a framework of class opposition. His disillusionment with the union movement of the fifties caused him to reject this form of class action to secure the rights of workers. He was still obsessed with hatred of the priest, who, with his pious claims to obey the patron and work hard, preserved the status quo and his own privileges in it.

Early Years of
Union Organization, 1910–1930

At the turn of the century, worker organizations were almost totally dependent on financing by liberals, whose political ideology was directed toward reform, not a change in power relations (Alexander 1972:376). The link between political and economic goals influenced the working class movement until the present. Only those unions which succeeded in organizing a national base were able to gain some autonomy. The railroad workers were the first national organization of workers. In their first congress in 1918, they were joined by miners, commercial, and printing workers (Barrios 1966). By the second decade of the twentieth century, two major trends in working class organization emerged. The first represented the policy of government-sponsored official unions organized under the Federation of La Paz, in which the state played the role of mediator, arbitrator, and harmonizer of labor conflict. The second was directed against the government, and was linked with the international revolutionary movements. This latter trend began in 1912 with the formation of the federation of international workers (Federación Obrera Internacional) and was followed by the International Federation of Labor (Federación Internacional de Trabajo), an organization with international links reinforced by the success of the Russian revolution (Lora 1969:170). Anarchists, syndicalists, and Marxists vied for control within the federation (Troncoso and Burnett 1960). The international movements in Bolivia linked their demands for full social legislation with the seizure of power by the workers (Lora 1969:235).

Despite the radical attack on imperialism and international capital, these international organizations were paper tigers that did not provoke the retaliation of foreign or domestic firms. This situation changed with the entry of the working class into immediate struggles in the enterprises in which they worked. From the beginning, workers' demands were met with the massive opposition of the army, which received its commands from the company managers via the government.

Miners, who were organized late in the second decade of the twentieth century, became leaders in direct action of the rank and file. When the Patiño Mine Company refused to pay a bonus to workers in Siglo XX in 1918, the miners, in a spontaneous uprising, assaulted the shops and the cashier of the company. The employees and the superintendent, armed with pistols and carbines, counterattacked. The workers used the tools of their trade, dynamite and explosives, to defend themselves. President José Gutiérrez ordered the infantry sent to the mine center, and in the resulting encounter several workers were killed. The corpses were burned in the calcination ovens where the minerals were concentrated (Lora 1969; Rivera 1967). A strike in the Huanchaca Company resulted in the discharge of seventeen employees who were replaced with chilenos. There was another setback in September 1919 when the Catavi contract workers objected to decreases in their pay and their delegation to the administrators was received with army gunfire, causing several deaths (Barrios 1966:50). Again their bodies were disposed of in calcination ovens, and the company strengthened the armed forces quartered in the barracks adjacent to every major mine (Lora 1969:37).

Despite these initial defeats, the mine workers of San José, Oruro, decided to go on strike in 1920. The date chosen for declaring the strike was July 30, the eve of the celebration of Supay. It is probably more than coincidental, since the ritual reinforces the solidarity of the rank-and-file workers and has in other events tipped off rebellion (Nash 1972). Following the lead of the Huanuni miners, the workers agreed on their demands for an eight-hour day, a 20 percent increase in salaries, and lower prices in the company store. In the course of this strike, which ended on August 19, the miners of Catavi began a spontaneous strike against the Llallagua Tin Company on August 12, attacking the company store. The Ballivián regiment ended this with gunfire, killing three and wounding four (Lora 1969:294).

Jorge, the son of a carpenter in the mines, experienced these strikes at second hand as a child. His memories of the mine begin in 1920 when the men went on strike.

❖ In 1920 the men had a strike to gain the eight-hour day. My mother was afraid to let us children go out of the house because they were shooting. The Partido Republicano supported the strike. It was one hundred percent effective from the point of view of rank-and-file support since all the miners stayed out. But it lasted only three days. The leaders tried to get a settlement, but they failed when the troops were sent in.

Notwithstanding the use of violence against strikers, Uncía workers organized a union in 1923. Their attempts to gain union recognition resulted in a major massacre despite the moderate demands made by the leaders and the discipline with which they presented them. An account written by one of the labor leaders, Gumercindo Rivera, stresses the lack of anarchism, revolution, or violent change implied by their acts (1967:81, 127).

The massacre at Uncía was a response by the tin owners to the organizational activities that began with the anarcho-socialist unions in the early decades of the twentieth century and climaxed in the formation of the Uncía Workers Central Federation of May 1, 1923. On that day, five thousand workers entered the football field, where the program of speeches by union leaders was received with "enthusiasm for the idea that very soon they would leave behind what they had been until that moment," as Rivera (1967) prophetically stated. They were to break the paternalistic relations, the crippling, competitive individualism promoted in contract work as they tried to promote for the first time collective action. It was a break too with the anarchistic actions, as the union leadership tried in the following weeks to provide legal channels for grievance proceedings and worker representation. When the audience with President Salamanca failed to produce a positive recognition of worker demands, a strike was called. Union leaders were imprisoned on June 4 and government troops sent in. When a mass of workers met in the Plaza Alonso de Ibáñez to protest government action, the army opened fire and killed four and wounded several men and women.

I interviewed a retired miner, Melquiades Maldonado, who had been an organizer of the federation and active in the commission that organized the May 1 meeting and subsequent interview with the president.

❖ In that time there were many conflicts in the mines. They used to dismiss the workers if they had any suspicion that they were engaged in organizing. They sent them on the train with their beds and their belongings on the railroad. Some would go to Huanuni and others to Chuwalla and other mining companies. They would discuss where the best conditions were, what they were paying in the other mines. Many left on their own with their families and their bundles, walking on foot because they didn't have money for the railroad, or they had to sell their things for next to nothing to go look for work in other places. The workers moved from one place to another like that. It was a pity the way they lived. And when they got to the mine, there was no place to live, even in Cancañiri. They lived in caves in the hills. There were these natural caves where they put up walls and a metal door and these were the living quarters for the workers. We began to demand that they give encampments for the workers, but the company didn't want to do that. They didn't have any water; they had to go get water from streams that were often polluted. And so we wanted something to benefit the workers. This was the beginning of the organization—to demand something for the welfare of the workers.

Maldonado did not want to describe his own actions in the strike because he said it was all down in the book which he presented to me, *La masacre de Uncía* by Gumercindo Rivera (1967). I asked him whether the strike at Uncía had changed anything and what the effect of the massacre was.

◈ Well, the massacre, according to them, had the effect they wanted. However, I would venture that we gained a great deal. Soon after that, the mining companies thought about building camps for the worker and gave a little convenience to him. They began to get schools whereas before they had just a few teacher trainees with very poor quarters.

After the strike, Maldonado and the other organizers fled to Argentina to avoid being imprisoned. There were no paying jobs in Bolivia other than in the mines, and since they were blacklisted Maldonado and other union leaders who followed him felt that he had no recourse but to seek another country in which to earn a living.

The strike and massacre at Uncía proved two things to the workers: the possibility of collective action and the force of reaction to it. Although forced to leave the country, they felt that the risk was justified since they won the right to demand more humane conditions and the right to make other claims on the company.

The government use of violence against workers continued throughout the decade. Jorge, who experienced the strike when he was a child through his father's involvement then (see p. 42), was forced to enter the army because of general unemployment. There he was forced to become a strike breaker, but his early experience made him conscious of the dilemma workers faced as recruits in the army.

◆ When my mother died in 1925, I went into the army. They sent me to Sucre and to Potosí, where there were strikes. We recruits were slaves for the government. We had the task of shooting at the workers. The workers came to us and said that when we got out of the army we would be in the same position as they, and we shouldn't shoot. They would come up to us while we were on guard duty. There was no shooting. The issue during this strike was higher wages, and all the problems we workers have. Then they sent us to Potosí, where the situation was much the same. The company paid us all. They gave us cigarettes, coca, and alcohol, and when the strike was over, they gave us fifty to one hundred pesos as a tip.

I came directly to Oruro when I got out of the army in 1925. I rested six days and went into the mines. I entered at seven in the morning and came out at five o'clock in the evening. In 1926 I was a master carpenter earning two pesos fifty centavos in silver.

Tomás, who was five years younger than Jorge, was also the son of a miner. However, he was more unfortunate in that his father died when he was still young and he was forced to work inside the mines.

◆ When I began work in the mines at the age of thirteen, I earned eighty centavos a day as a *chasquiri* taking out bags of ore. We smaller boys would go into the new shafts that were sunk below the existing levels. We climbed up these shafts about twenty meters with twenty-kilo sacks on our backs. We could stand up in the tunnels. We worked with paraffin candles, and following this, with *carbón* or with wax candles. It was dangerous because the light would blow out and we would fall in some of the open shafts. We didn't get electric lights until ten years ago.

In 1926 there was a strike. My father was *mayordomo*, and as a work gang leader, had thirty men. He earned very little, just two or three pesos a day, and it was not enough. The men asked for an increase in the salary. The men destroyed the pulpería. I was still little and did not know what was happening. I asked my mother, "Mama, what's happening?" and she said that the workers were taking food and clothing from the pulperías. A little while after, they increased the salary to three pesos and up to five pesos and work went back to normal. The directors of that mine came to Oruro. In those days the supervisors entered very rarely in the mine. They did not bother themselves about the workers. They were well set with money.

In those days, money was worth more. You could buy bread for five centavos, a sheep for sixty centavos. With five pesos a day you could buy food and even clothing. Now it is more. Children nowadays live differently. Children are much more wide awake. They go to the movies and enjoy themselves more. Formerly there was more control over children. Parents didn't know how to read or write. I went to school and the teacher beat me. My mother said it wasn't worth the trouble for me. The professors marked me absent and sent a note to my father. He said to me, "Why didn't you go to school the last three days?" and I said, "My mother said I didn't have to go because the teacher beat me." He sent me back. But I didn't stay long. I repent of this, because I can only work in the mine. I have a brother thirty years old who is a chief of the pulpería in the mine and earns twelve hundred pesos. He went through the fourth grade of secondary school. My father always said, "You don't want to be a miner like me."

The Chaco War and Its Aftermath, 1930–1951

"The MNR," one miner advised me, "was born in the War of the Chaco." He had never learned this in the primary school he attended, where the war is still whitewashed with patriotic slogans, nor had he read the histories that trace the roots of the revolution of 1952 back to the disillusionment and alienation engendered by that war. He deducted that conclusion from his father's account of his experience in the war, of the betrayal of enlisted men by their officers and of workers by the government. The movement, in his view, was a product of discontent with the old order, less in agreement on what they wanted than on what they were against.

At social gatherings in the mining community, when some of the older workers try to strike heroic poses as veterans of the Chaco, the younger workers burlesque them, and most of the veterans mock their own role in the war. "They say we were fighting a war for oil in the Chaco," one worker said at a ch'alla. "We weren't fighting for oil; we were fighting for water. Over each puddle we waged a war with the Paraguayans because we were dying of heat in that blazing sun."

Older miners defend the position of the common soldier and criticize the officers for the war. At a celebration of the ch'alla in Mina Itos the conversation turned, as it always did when the chicha flowed and deep feelings were expressed, to the Chaco War. Mario talked of his experience as a 19-year-old draftee in the Chaco:

❖ The people of Paraguay are very backward. We helped them advance. The majority of us soldiers were well prepared. We served as schoolmasters to the Paraguayans, teaching them to read and write. It was a backward country, a poor people that had never reached the level of Bolivia. We contributed another view of the world to them. We taught them about medicines, the Work Code. The War of the Chaco advanced Paraguay. Thanks to us they know how to read and write. We even taught them to work. In comparison, Bolivia lost a great deal. We had bad leaders, and Standard Oil was pushing its interest in the oil.[3]

Eduardo had a good word only for the priest in his company in the Chaco. He claimed he never saw any other officer when he was on the front lines.

❖ We were one or two hundred meters from Concepción when there were seven hundred wounded. During the last assault on the Chaco, I fell prisoner along with the padre, Captain Tapía. There we were bleeding to death trying to save ourselves from our enemies because we couldn't walk. Father Tapía was like a father to us.

The Chichas Regiment was inundated in mud. They told us, "You have to clean this well so that there will be water." There were snakes in the water and in the mud. *P'ucha, hermano,* the snakes were as thick as this finger and more than a meter long. Each of us who entered cut them in two or three pieces. The soldiers were fighting for the snakes from hunger. Each of us soldiers ended up with rations of snake, a third for each.

Jorge, whose experiences in the army as a strikebreaker are recorded above, was again recruited into the army during the Chaco War.

❖ In 1932 I was in an accident. I was in a lift when it fell three hundred and eighty meters. One of the men died. I was in water at the bottom of the shaft for twenty-four hours. When I came out, I

---

[3] This view is contested by Klein (1969:196), who points to the myth making involved in claiming the war was fought for oil.

stayed home because I did not want to go to the hospital although my back was hurt. My two companions were not found for three months. Shortly after that I was called back into the service because of the Chaco War. I went to the recruiting station with my liberation papers, bent over from my accident, and they said to me, "A cripple like you can't do anything else but enter the service."

In the Chaco War, I was wounded two times and just got well on the line. Sometimes for three or four days we had nothing to eat. We were walking around like drunks, with nothing but tea in the morning. Then I was taken prisoner. I went to Paraguay. I was taken with about forty men when we were surrounded. In the prison in Paraguay I worked in a carpentry shop only for my food for a year. They beat us with a metal rod there. I was released when peace was declared.

I went to the army barracks in Bolivia and was released. Then I came back to Oruro. The supervisor, a Dutchman, said, "Jorge, you are going to enter the mine." He gave me the choice of working there in a carpentry shop or one league away. I never wanted to go into the mine after the accident.

Basilia, who was three years younger than Jorge, was also affected by the Chaco War despite the fact that she was not recruited into the army. She left her work at the surface of the mines to enter into the pits as a replacement for the men who were fighting. An excerpt from her autobiography (Nash and Rocca 1976) is included below.

❖ I entered the company to work when I was sixteen years old. My family told me I had to help support them with the work. I have worked since I was a child.

First I worked in Colquiri. There were three shifts there; one was at night, another in the day, and another at two in the afternoon. We didn't rest a minute. We ate quickly and returned to work. There was a lot to earn at this time with Patiño and Aramayo. Now there is nothing to be earned. A few work in the mine of Colquiri now. Before, a lot of men used to go in, and there were four or five shifts of women, and now there isn't one. In the time of the Chaco I worked in Llallagua. I worked in the placers, pressing the metal from the water. When the press broke, the stones went *patajjj*, like flying arrows. There were accidents there. One of my comrades, a woman called Olimpia, was by my side. Suddenly, "Aaaaayy . . ." she yelled. They took her to the hospital. What a miracle that I didn't have an accident too, being at her side! Then during the Chaco War, we women went inside the mine to work when the men left. We used to dance and laugh on top of the haul as we went down into the shafts to work.

Tomás is like many of the veterans in blaming the military hierarchy for the disastrous defeat in the Chaco.

❖ In 1933 I went into the service in the Chaco War. We soldiers didn't lose the war; it was the officers who lost it. They lived behind the lines and never came out where there was fighting.

Another veteran, called "Gazelle" by his mining comrades because of his ability to run (proven in the Chaco), said that the generals sold out the country. He castigated their failure to prepare the infantry adequately.

❖ I couldn't fight in the low country. I would like a war with Chile in the altiplano. I don't like the forest. When the *choque* [clash] came with Paraguay we went to war without shoes, barefoot with straw hats. It was lost because of the officers, not by the troops, not by the soldiers. As an ex-soldier, I know how the War of the Chaco changed the outlook of those of us who have studied it and analyzed why we fought in it. We have many natural resources, but there is a great deal of envy among the nations of South America. In the course of time, outsiders have robbed our country and we have lost a great deal. There is no organization to advance the country. After the Chaco we lost a piece of land. There are European countries that have less than we, but they do not lose what they have. We lack initiative.

The analysis of the "Gazelle" reveals some commonly held ideas: Bolivia's national riches were lost because of the stupidity and blundering of the leaders. The lack of organization at the top caused the inefficiency and disorganization at the bottom. This miner, like most of the veterans in the "Chaco generation," does not attribute the war to foreign imperialism. That accusation, made by the MNR leaders, was filtered through the union leaders who had read Marof (1934) and other theorists who repudiated liberal government rule under Salamanca.

The net effect of the Chaco war was to descredit military and political leadership. The following decade was marked by the conflict between populist forces under the MNR and the old leadership manipulated by the *rosca* of tin magnates. The mysterious death by suicide of the popular young military leader Busch, who had led the rebellion of junior officers against the top hierarchy, left the presidency vacant in 1941.

Labor unions and workers were universally opposed to the Chaco War of 1931–35, but resistance was lessened by recruiting protesters into the army. Following the war, President David Toro established a Ministry of Labor with the leader of the typographical union as minister. German Busch, who followed him into the presidency, established the first labor law with collective bargaining. The apparent increase in pro-labor sentiment was not tested until World War II when, in 1942, the workers of Siglo XX and Catavi drew up a petition demanding a 100 percent increase in wages. When the company refused to negotiate, the union called a strike. The response was to arrest all union officials. When the workers protested their arrest, seven miners were killed. In response, 7,000 workers went out on strike on December 15 and remained out until December 20. On December 21, a group of workers moved in procession to the office of the management. In the following demonstration, the army fired from 9 A.M. until 3 P.M.

The official death count was 19 dead and 40 wounded, but workers reported up to 400 deaths, a figure which M. Kyne, a CIO organizer from the United States sent to investigate the event, was inclined to believe. Summarizing the meaning of the massacre, Kyne (1943) reported that "collective bargaining does not exist in Bolivia at all . . . no genuine written collective contract has ever been adopted." He attributed this to the reserved and suspicious attitude adopted by the authorities, the economic control exercised by companies over employees, and the hostility of employers to union organization. After the incident he reported that Hochschild, Aramayo, and Patiño, the three major mine owners, met to plan a joint strategy, and with the support of President Peñaranda mounted "a political front for the mine interests" (Kyne 1943).

Juan recounts the event on the occasion of his birthday when he had invited all his old working comrades to help him celebrate his retirement from the mines:

> ❖ I am going to speak a little about the massacre of Catavi, that occurred in the year 1942 in the field of Maria Barzola. This was the year in which the miners of Siglo XX and Catavi asked for an

increase in the pulpería. It was not a general increase in wages but only an increase in the pulpería, especially in the bread rations that we received daily. In this time the Siglo XX and Catavi company gave us three loaves of bread a day and this was not enough for the whole day. It was very little for the family. We asked that they increase it to ten loaves. Finally the Patiño Mines company restricted us completely and denied us our petition. Despite this, all the miners of Siglo XX that had been honest workers, disciplined workers, workers who were looking to the future of our country, met in a general assembly. It was the greatest meeting that they had had in all the life of the company of Siglo XX. The workers decided to march to the administrative offices of Catavi and Siglo XX. The armed forces of the Colorado regiment positioned themselves on the hill. They began to open fire on the first of the miners who appeared. Hearing the firing of the machine guns, the miners turned around and ran back.

There was a woman named Maria Barzola who said, "We are women. No one can shut our mouths. As daughters of the country, as mothers of the country, as mothers of our children, no one can shut our mouths. We shall seize the flag as women and put ourselves in the forefront."

The army was positioned on the hills. The women started to pass by with the flag. With them were the children of the miners, children of the women of the miners. Despite that, the massacring army did not respect either the children or the wives. They fired the machine gun on the field and killed the woman Maria Barzola. The workers did not threaten the administrators, nor the employees, nor the other persons of the company. Many women and children died. The army did not respect anyone.

There was a woman who said, "May the countryland live! May the miners live! The miners are those who give dividends to our country!"

There was a Second Lieutenant Rodriguez—I remember his name well—who drew his pistol and planted a shot. Then the woman fell to the ground. She had her son with her and they say the child also fell to the ground with her, not from the bullet but from fright. Mother and son died. The army of the government did not respect fathers nor mothers nor children.

Basilia was living in Siglo XX and working inside the mines when the massacre took place. She describes her experiences that day:

❖ I was living in Llallagua when they had the massacre in 1942. The bullets rained on us like grains of rice. One could not escape anywhere. Some of us went inside the mine. We were in there a week, starving. When we couldn't bear the hunger and thirst in that hot air, I made a hole in the pipes that carry water for the machines and I gave it to the babies to drink. We tried to blow open the door with dynamite, but there was an earth cave-in. I climbed out the chimney and looked for help. Then they opened the door with a tractor. Then all of us came out. They invited us to eat. The soldiers seized some people and threw them in the lake, where they drowned. I barely escaped by the hill with my children. Then some of us came to work in Oruro, panning metal in the hill of San José. . . .

Ceferino was a decade younger than these workers. He is highly politically conscious, just reaching maturity at the time of the MNR revolution of April 9, 1952. He started working in the mines as a helper in 1933 in Patiño Mines.

❖ In 1941 I spent one year and seven months in the army. We were sent to supress the Huanuni strike. There wasn't any massacre then—they used workers to break the strike. We were stationed outside the mine to guard it against sabotage by the workers.

When I got out of the army I worked as a pipe fitter for the air hoses and also outside on the compression machine. I earned nine pesos eighty centavos a day with a minimum wage of three hundred pesos a month. It was enough to live on.

In 1941, the Federación de Sindicatos de Trabadjadors Mineros de Bolivia was organized in Siglo XX. I was happy, young and not interested in workers' rights and demands. My work comrades talked me into joining. Some of the leaders were Cerafin Dorado, dead, and Cerafin Rodriguez, also dead. Then came the strike of 1942. We had fifteen to twenty days of strikes. The company announced, "The miners who do not want to work will be killed." They paid every man who went to work a bonus of two hundred pesos. With this tip, almost all of the workers came in. Then the massacre came on December 21, 1942. Five hundred to eight hundred of the seven thousand workers were thrown out of work or killed for failure to conform.

On the morning of the massacre the workers of Cancañiri, Socavón, and Miraflores united at ten o'clock. There were six thousand of us. We were going down to the administration, calmly, without any weapons. We were a mixed lot, women, children, men. Maria Barzola was a delegate for the pallires. When she approached the soldiers, they shot her. We were about four hundred meters from the office, and they were firing on all of us. We couldn't advance, and so we escaped. We were surprised by the attack on us.

There are many versions of the story, as many, possibly, as there were women who fell that day. Some say that Maria Barzola was an elderly woman who was dedicated to drinking chicha and chewing coca and picked up money for her vices working on the slag pile.

Another version, preferred by Nestor Taboada (1960) was that Maria Barzola was a prostitute who ran out in a drunken stupor, leaving behind her lover who was an administrator in the company, and seized the flag without knowing what she was doing. The one miners give—and this is supported by some nonminers who have lived in Llallagua, the town that has grown up near Siglo XX—is that she was a regularly employed pallire who was the representative for the women in the union and acted in full consciousness in her heroic act.

In another version of the event, other words have been attributed to her as she took the flag. One miner told me that she said, "We women know better than the men the suffering of our children from hunger. It is better to die than to live in this misery."

All versions, except for Taboada's account, point to the sense miners express of the women sharing the misery and the struggle to change conditions along with their men. The massacre marked not only a tragic memory, but a milestone in changing the status of workers in national political life.

The Populist Movement and the Revolution, 1944–1952

With the old guard discredited, the MNR supported Villarroel, who became president the year of the massacre. During his period of office, a ministry of labor was created and Juan Lechín became the first representative.

In 1944 the Federation of Mine Workers Union of Bolivia (Federación de Sindicatos Trabajadores Mineros de Bolivia, FSTMB) was formed in Huanuni and elected Lechín as their leader. The principal element, but not the controlling force, was the National Revolutionary Movement (Movimiento Nacionalista Revolucionario, MNR). FSTMB presented a reform platform calling for collective contracts, institutionalized social legislation, minimal legal wages, and a Day of Miners, celebrated on December 21 in memory of the dead of Catavi. Their demands were supported by Gualberto Villarroel, who succeeded Peñaranda in 1943. The alliance of labor, junior army officers who had opposed the Chaco War, and the lower middle class was abruptly ended when President Villarroel was killed in 1946. The coup, brought about by a paradoxical alliance of the pro-Stalinist Revolutionary Party of the Left (Partido Izquierdo Revolucionario, PIR) with the conservative Falangist forces (Falange Socialista Boliviana) backed by mining interests, brought into power the pro-rosca government of President Hertzog.

Juan speaks of this period:

❖ I was in the army at the Chilean frontier in July 1946. Our discharge papers did not arrive because of the bad luck that a revolution broke out in La Paz. They overthrew our president, Villarroel. The university students and the traffic police rose up and they were to blame for the fall. Enriquez Hertzog entered the presidency, but because of old age he was replaced by Dr. Mamerto Urriolagoitia. This was the most *carnicero* [butchering] government because it made the most massacres. In this time, Patiño gave meal and clothing and barracks to the soldiers although they were under the order of the government. More than five hundred soldiers were in the mines of Siglo XX and Catavi. The soldiers that didn't want to carry out their orders were killed. In the year 1949 there were various killings and some small political agitation. In 1951 they wanted to put the PIR in power. There was a rebellion of the unemployed in that year. In the presidential elections in May the MNR triumphed, but they did not give power to the party. The leaders barely escaped being killed and left the power to the *bota militar*, and this was under General Hugo Balivan, I think. This lasted until the eighth of April, 1952.

The MNR and the Revolutionary Party of Workers (Partido Obrero Revolucionario, POR) gained the support of the workers as the PIR lost its credibility. In the 1946 Congress of Miners in Pulacayo, the POR led the delegates in formulating the doctrine that was to influence labor policy for the following two decades in the Thesis of Pulacayo. Asserting that Bolivia is a "backward capitalist country," and a "link in world Capitalism," the document points out that "the national bourgeoisie is incapable of carrying out the democratic tasks of eliminating the latifundia and other pre-capitalist forms of the economy," of uniting the nation and "liberating it from the imperialist yoke." As a consequence, the proletariat "is obliged to combine the fight for bourgeois democratic gains with those for achieving socialism." The "feudal-bourgeois state justifies itself as an organism of violence to maintain the privileges of the dominant classes." The proletariat of Bolivia, because of its youth and vigor, because of its near "virginity in the political aspect," because it does not have "the classical parliamentary and collaborationist traditions," and because "the class struggle had reached extreme belligerency, we say for all this, the Bolivian proletariat has been able to convert itself into one of the most radical" (Lora 1970a 361–390).

With some prescience, the framers of the document pointed out that the objective conditions for a socialist revolution did not exist, but that the revolution would be "bourgeois democratic in its objectives and only an episode," needing the alliance of the rural workers and the petty bourgeoisie. Rejecting reformist solutions, they called for "Death to capitalism! Death to reformist collaboration!" The themes developed in the Thesis of Pulacayo were to influence subsequent proclamations made in Colquiri in 1963, in La Paz in 1965, and at Siglo XX in 1970. Although the feudal character of the state stressed in the thesis was in decline throughout this period, the link between bourgeois capitalism of the nation with imperialist financial and military interests was stronger.

Labor gains in the thirties and forties were eroded in the government of Enriquez Hertzog, who was backed both by the rosca and the PIR. Labor expressed its discontent with a series of strikes and protest beginning in September 1946 and lasting throughout 1947. The miners were in open rebellion against the Patiño mines, which responded with a plan to fire all the workers and rehire only those who were not designated "labor insurgents." A sit-down strike was called by the FSTMB in February 1947 that paralyzed the mines for eight hours, but still no settlement was reached. The unions were convinced that management wished to destroy the labor movement, and management opposed what it called "the obstruction campaign against the reorganization plans of the company." They blamed the conflict on outside agitators and appealed to the patriotic sentiments of the workers not to paralyze the national economy. They did not accept strike action as legitimate. In an attempt to break the impasse, the workers called a general strike in forty-nine mines in August 1947. The strike continued with no progress in negotiation until it was forced to an end on September 5. Union leaders, including Juan Lechín, were imprisoned and union funds were frozen, all with President Hertzog's approval. On September 7 the FSTMB scored the president's unconstitutional behavior. Hertzog responded to attacks on the basis that he was defending the workers from "a small group of aliens" who had established dictatorship over workers, "who sow chaos," and he asserted that he froze the funds of the union leadership so that Lechín could not use them for personal needs. On September 18 the company fired 7,000 men; Patiño's strategy was to rehire only non-union workers in order to break the national federation. Claiming that the strike was not supported by the majority of the workers and that it was therefore not legal, the company refused to negotiate (Patiño Mines and Co. 1948:87–93).

The union struggles in 1946 and 1947 reveal an increasing polarization of the workers and management, and simultaneously an intensified class consciousness. As the conflict escalated, there was the beginning of an alliance between Bolivian technicians and the workers based on a nationalistic definition of common goals. The fact that Juan Lechín and the union leaders in general were aware of it can be seen in the petition cited earlier in which the workers attacked "foreign technicians" and claimed that Bolivians could run the mines themselves. The conflict never reached settlement since management, recognizing the subversive threat to the old order, resorted to armed repression.

The government of Mamerto Urriolagoitia began its move to crush the labor movement in May of 1949 when a strike broke out in Catavi. None of the issues raised in the two years of strife preceding the outbreak had been handled, and the administrators of the mines ruled autocratically, backed by a president who carried out their orders. Also, when the government exiled Lechín, Torres, and other leaders of the FSTMB, the workers began a revolt in August of the same year which threatened to lead to a civil war. The president sent in additional troops to Siglo XX–Catavi. Ceferino recalls his part in this strike:

❖ There was another movement to increase salaries in Siglo XX: We presented twenty demands, all well stated. We were getting nine pesos forty centavos, and as a result of the strike we got a fifteen

percent increase. On the twenty-eighth of May we declared a
strike. We got up at seven o'clock as the army entered our houses
forcibly. Some were sent to La Paz as agitators. I was at my work
when they came to get me. The *sindicatos amarillos* sold us out and
gave the administrators our names.

Those of us who had been in the army were given twenty-four
hours to get out or else get killed. I left and came to San José. Here
we worked by the day and made nine billetes [pesos] a day as
makipuras. We would work for a few days and then get laid off.

The wife of an employee in the Catavi administration described
the massacre in Siglo XX when the army marched in:

❖ The massacre began at five in the afternoon. I recall very well that
a plane flew over the region of Siglo XX and flung out a sign which
said, "Viva Juan Lechín." The miners gathered, and at this moment a terrible revolt broke out. It appeared that it was a signal for
them to rise up, since this man was the leader of the workers not
only of Siglo XX but of all the country in all the mining centers and
even in factories. They began to make a small demonstration. Then
at five in the afternoon I saw the army station themselves where
the drugstore is and behind the turn of the hills. This time the
Colorado regiment was mobilized, and I saw how they killed people without pity. If they saw a child, the child died. Any man
walking they shot, even though there was no indication that he
was going to do anything. And afterward they began a rainfall of
shots. I saw how the poor women fell down below the Racing
Club. They fell as if they were tops, their *polleras* [skirts] spinning
around, these poor women.

The following day the soldiers used mortars. Since it was the
first massacre I had seen, I went with a friend to see what would
happen. There was firing on all sides because the miners defended
themselves with dynamite as well as they could against the mortars, the bullets, and all the superior weaponry of the army. We
saw some macabre scenes. The union building was a small house,
and when we entered to see after the firing, the roof was all caved
in. On the walls we saw pieces of heads, blood on all sides. There
the radio transmitter of the "Voice of the Miner" had functioned.
Now they have a great building for the union below that place
they call "Chaquivayu."

After that we counted how many coffins passed to the cemetery.
We reached fifteen at noon and we returned to re-count in the afternoon. We have no idea how many people died this time, because they put the dead in common graves and these bodies were
not buried as were those we saw carried in coffins. They were

bodies of those who were completely destroyed, they just threw them in. This always happens in the mining massacres when they use mortars, although in the year 1967 in the massacre of San Juan they did not use mortars; they used bazookas, which were worse.

In any case, Catavi has been a mining center that is the vanguard of unionism, and so they have always destroyed it.

Celso, whose brother was in the army at the time of the massacre, recalls what he had seen and what his brother told him of the attack:

❖ My brother, who was in the army, knew the whole problem of the civil war from close up. The soldiers did not want to participate in the Civil War, as many in the army resisted. But they obliged the cadets to go and they lost many of them. One of the soldiers told me that if they did not shoot, others shot them. I believe that many were killed that way resisting the attack, because soldiers that resisted, soldiers that did not shoot, were soldiers that died by the shots from officers. For example, there was a soldier in the civil war of 1949 who was serving in the Camacho regiment here in Oruro. The Second and Third Battery who went to Catavi had many soldiers who were children of miners. The papa of one of them was a union leader. He was one of the soldiers who resisted, and his immediate superior threatened to kill him, and then he shot to kill. When the shooting was over and they took the union building and the soldiers were masters of the situation, then the soldier found his papa was dead exactly where they shot. The soldier almost went insane, and in order to go to the wake the same night, he had to put on civilian clothing or they would have massacred him if he had gone as a soldier.

This always happens with the Bolivian soldier. The Bolivian soldier is very brave, but the officers are cowards. This they proved in the War of the Chaco, where they were completely compromised. They put our campesinos forward as cannon meat. They were not prepared, they had only a month in the service and then put them at the front. One can't deny that the military in the city are brave, massacring students, massacring workers, while our frontiers are completely left unprotected.

Like all miners, this worker distinguished the military from the enlisted man who is forced into the service. Miners blame the massacres on the officers who give the order, not on the soldier who is forced to shoot by the threat to kill him if he fails. Others have told me that scores of soldiers were killed both in the 1942 massacre and in the 1949 massacre.

The revolution of 1952 was an outgrowth of the repression of the forties. Most of the miners who had reached maturity in 1952 took an active role in the revolution of April 9. Their ranks were well organized and they had a leader everyone felt confidence in, Juan Lechín Oquendo. In order to understand the role miners played and the effect of those events on their lives, I asked several miners what they did on April 8 and 9. Eduardo, who was 18 years old at that time, answered:

❖ Well, in the year 1952, I worked in the interior of the mine in level three hundred and forty. One morning they came and told us to come out and join the demonstration that was taking place in the plaza. But we didn't even get down to the city because the firing was strong down near the barracks. It looked as though the alert forces of the population had come to the barracks to take it, and because of that there was firing. A few of us workers of the interior had got down about a seventh of the way when we could no longer cross over. We had to jump into the river and stay there until eight at night in the aqueduct. There were only two of us, and so it was logical that we could not cross to the other side because of the armed civilians circulating. It looked as though we had been cut off with barbed wire. Afterward the army barracks shot the mortar toward our section. Soon a group of civilians came and obliged us to collect the wounded. There were people with their bodies destroyed. We had to take them to the hospital. We did this all night.

From there we went to San José and stayed in the tunnel to Itos until six in the morning. At six we went down and found that the civilians had taken the barracks and the armed forces had yielded. So then we made a demonstration. Everything was over on the ninth of April here in Oruro. After that they took over the whole country.

[I asked if it was true that the general in command of the armed forces in Oruro had promised to yield and then fought, as I had been told.]

Yes, it was General Salinas, if I am not wrong. He said that he was going to surrender the troops without bloodshed, but once they had arrived in the barracks he gave the signal and they fired the machine guns. That is why over a hundred people died or were wounded. We had another encounter with the Regimento Ingavi quartered in Chaplapata. When this regiment entered Oruro, the civilians positioned themselves at the curves and were shooting at them, but they were firing from all sides. They killed many people, and as many soldiers died as civilians.

Because men, from the age of nineteen, always enter the army and acquire some experience of battle, when there is an opportunity we know how to make our battle. I had not yet had a chance to enter the army since I was not draft age. But that is why I say that the man tries to improve himself in every way, seeing the economic circumstances in which the country lives. In our case, here in Bolivia, one becomes aware of the despotism of the high bosses, of the big capitalists. And these are the circumstances that make the worker have this desire to overcome, to try to be something more in life, not only a sad proletarian. Well, I say this with experience because I suffered in my own flesh, because I have worked at everything. I have seen this inequality, this lack of opportunity, although logically a worker can be better than any professional in any respect.

Analyzing all this, I would say that humanity is one, only there are economic differences. The worker can be superior to another not only intellectually, he can also be more cultivated in general. This is the curious fact about men; if we are going to be inert, only dedicated to work, we are going to see that a man is looked down upon by others. From that point of view, I believe it is just that a man tries to improve himself, although it might not be a great accomplishment, in order that he should not die without knowing what life can be and what his place is in the social milieu in which he lives.

Eduardo had raised himself to a mechanic and had the opportunity to travel to all the mines. He was ambitious and intelligent, and had cultivated interests in music and travel. In his soliloquy on the revolution he moved directly from his own frustrated ambitions to an acceptance of revolution as the only solution given the inequality and despotism that he had experienced "in his own flesh." Workers assimilated their army experience with, as he put it, the expectation that they would find an opportunity to use it "in their own fight."

The revolution of 1952 was a total uprising of the people. Celso, who was 14 years old at the time the fighting broke out, recalled his role in it:

❖ I was working at the time in San José, where I had started work that year at the age of fourteen. I would have continued with my studies, but my mama didn't have enough for our food much less for our education. I began to work, then, in my early youth, and for this I am leaving all my youthfulness here in the mine and I have nothing to show for it.

In that year there was a great deal of killing, after which the worker won his independence and the proletarian class won. President Victor Paz Estenssoro, who now lives in Peru, had been very humane with the workers and we improved our conditions somewhat.

San José started this revolution. My brother-in-law had fallen wounded—my wife's eldest brother—and so I seized his gun. Then I was in the fight, but fortunately nothing happened to me. We fought the Regiment Ingavi in Papel Pampa. San José was waiting the fall of Camacho in order to take the barracks. I had learned to use a rifle in the barracks where I had gone since my eleventh year as a volunteer. I still have my gun underneath my bed.

I asked his wife what she had seen on the day of April 8.

❖ That day they were fighting in the street when the soldiers came to the mine. I saw them when I was in the pulpería. My brother went in a truck that left with other workers on the third shift. Afterward he fell wounded. His foot was broken. The women were looking for their relatives, because most of the men had gone out to fight.

The revolution began in La Paz and afterward the biggest blow came here in Oruro and afterward in all the mines. The miners rose up and took the army in their undershorts because they were attacked by surprise. They wanted to call in another regiment, but it was late because they were surrounded by the civilians and they had mined the roads. When they arrived, they made the mines explode. And so they had to surrender. The officers made them come here to the city, barefoot and without their pants, and surrendered them.

Many died, both soldiers and those of the working class. It was a great catastrophe, a massacre. They told me that it was the betrayal of the general of the Camacho regiment, who had promised that he was going to surrender the barracks without a fight. And so many people fell there dead because the commander of the regiment Camacho had said, "There isn't going to be any fighting. Let's arrange everything satisfactorily."

Her husband went on to say,

❖ After having run through the plaza in a demonstration, a group went to the barracks. At the door of the barracks they said that nothing was going to happen, but they were positioned on the roofs of the barracks. When the group was rounding the corner to the Avenue Dalance where the railroad goes up to San José, advancing with the Bolivian flag, the firing began in cold blood.

Many people died there. I can't say how many. We were watching from here in San José. There were many dead hereabouts. There weren't as many houses as now, and on the field many many men and women died.

Some came to the dunes on the south side and others went behind to await the Regiment Andino from Achocalla. Those that were from the side of Machacamarca were the Regiment Ingavi, fourth cavalry and another section.

They say that at five in the morning the soldiers escaped from the barracks along with the horses by a false door. Then they took the barracks. A few fell there, but the revolution was won.

There couldn't be another battle like that because the army is much more fully armed and with more modern armaments. Now, frankly, we are under military command. We can't do anything without much more bloodshed.

I recorded some of these interviews in the first weeks of my field trip in July 1969. The mining police that Barrientos sent into the mines were still stationed in San José and the other major mines, and in addition, sindicatos amarillos served as spies to advise the management of any agitation. Considering the repression, it is extraordinary that my informants were as open in their declarations as they were with me, a stranger from a country identified with the military regime that seized power in 1964. I think it reveals how strongly motivated they were to find a wider audience for their struggles and saw an opportunity in me that they were willing to take despite the risks. When I reflect back on these early days of my field work and recall the eagerness with which my informants poured out their suffering, their frustrations, their resistance to what they identified as the agents of imperialism, I am impressed with the human need to record its own history, and through that to find a future course of action.

In the biographical approach, more important than the events recorded are the impressions made on the person who experiences them. From these we can gain an understanding of the impact of historic events on the individual consciousness and ultimately on the collective consciousness drawn from this. Efraim's awareness of exploitation came indirectly from uncovering the hypocrisy of the priests who helped maintain the subjugation of the Indian workers. This diverted him from the main elements in the class struggle, since he gave priority to the attack on the priesthood, no longer a primary opponent of the working class, rather than to attacking the managerial or capitalist elite. He was made acutely aware of the dehumanization of the working class in the early years of industrialization by his mother's debauchery, and his own when he worked in the mining camps. The success, in his eyes, of the workers' struggles to obtain a human level of subsistence blunted his awareness of the persistence of the class struggle.

Alejandro's close contact with the foreign technicians gave him a false sense of the security to be gained through paternalistic ties. This search for a patron is at odds with the development of collective identity with a class. In the early years of industrialization there were more opportunities for the favoritism he benefited from than later, especially after nationalization, when new forms of structural opportunity (see chapter 8) arose. Alejandro rued the passing of the old order; Efraim celebrated it and regretted only that it was replaced with new forms of imperialist exploitation.

Basilia had a worker's consciousness that was not linked to class. The surrogate roles she played vis-à-vis her male comrades, those of mother, sister, and possible sexual partner, limited the worker solidarity that all the men profess. However, when she worked inside the mine she became aware of the suffering of the men in their work. She said,

> ❖ Once when I was drilling the machine kicked me. I thought about how the men-children work. The men-children have a right to complain. I know about their work.

But her rivalry with men destroyed the comradeship she felt in the work:

> ❖ Work is very scarce for women. But in the small mines the ores branch out. One day I was hammering metal in the slag pile, and I piled up three pounds. But the men-children do not know how to do that. All the men-children fail to get out anything where the women work. You always have to go look where they have thrown it out and take out the good metal. The men-children do not know like the women how to select metal.

The very marginal position of the women, who acquired the skills for selecting metal out of the lower-grade ores, stirred up a rivalry toward men, who had a competitive advantage over them. Since

WOMEN IN SIGLO XX LOST THEIR JOBS IN THE CONCENTRATION
PLANT BUT PETITIONED FOR WORK ON THE SLAG PILE, PICKING UP
ORES THAT CONTAIN MINERALS THROWN OUT IN PAST YEARS,
WHEN ONLY THE RICHER ORES WERE PROCESSED.

women of her generation did not enter into the male-dominated
hierarchies of unions and politics, they did not always discriminate
between populist and oligarchic presidencies. All governments
were a succession of exploiters to Basilia, who said,

> ❖ I bore all this with so many governments, with so many presi-
> dents. And what do I have for it? Nothing. I have wasted my
> lungs. My lungs are spent. They have thrown me out in the street.
> In the street they strike me.

Basilia expressed her willingness "to go into the service to defend
the country against Paraguay," but instead she entered the mines to
replace the men who had gone into the service.

Basilia is unable even to enjoy the devotion of her children in
her old age. The accumulated resentment of harsh though devoted
upbringing—Basilia tended her babies in a basket set near her in
the mines because she feared that the attendants in the nursery
provided by the mine could not answer their needs—the short
temper from working a double shift, twelve hours a day, so that she
could feed them and clothe them, resulted in an accumulated resentment. When her eldest daughter was 24, she hit her mother

over the head with her hand drill and ran off with her B $5,000 in retirement pay.

In contrast with the contradictions and lack of social and personal reward in Basilia's life, Jorge was able to save enough not only to buy property and thus security, but also to educate three of his children so that they became professionals. Although he was conscious of the exploitation in the mine and of how the soldiers were nothing but "slaves of the government," he nonetheless found a niche within that structure. His motivation became the desire to buy the lives of his children out of the mines. This is, ultimately, the trap of a politics predicated on class consciousness: No working man or woman desires, for himself or herself, to continue in that status, and the more successful they are as workers, the more likely they will be to rise out of the class or to buy their children out of it.

Tomás, although of the same political generation as Jorge, was less critically aware of the deception played on the workers in the Chaco War and postwar strike-breaking period, perhaps, as I suspected, because he was not Jorge's intellectual match. Jorge spoke ironically of the military recruiters' statement, "A cripple like you hasn't got anything better to do than go into the army." Although Tomás showed class resentment of the officers leaving the fighting up to the recruits, he later became one of the vigilantes in the post-Barrientos phase of military control in the mine. The Chaco War generation to which these men belonged was a generation of defeat.

Eduardo, Celso, and Juan had just reached manhood when the Civil War of 1949 drew them into the events of history. Their generation of *movimentistas* was a generation of victory, but a victory which turned to ashes as they were betrayed by politicians and some of the union leaders.

In the euphoria of the early post-1952 revolution, the class struggle was relegated to the past. The disenchantment with the populist government which began in 1956 with the Stabilization Act came to a climax in 1965 with the military occupation of the mines. During the Barrientos period, the gains the workers had made in the early years of the revolution were erased. Two decades of a frustrated revolution have shaped the consciousness of the miners. This will be explored in detail in the following chapters.

CHAPTER 3

◈◈◈

Belief and Behavior in Family Life

◇FAMILY BEHAVIOR contains the paradigms that orient social behavior. Ideology is not explicit except during rites of passage, when elders take the opportunity to make role models known to those who are about to enter them. It is the daily acting out of implicit assumptions that has a lasting impact on the child and determines behavior in a way that ideologies adopted in later life cannot control.

In the Bolivian mining family there are three basic paradigms for relating to others: dependency, competition, and cooperation. These provide complementary ways of adjusting to a harsh environment of limited opportunity. Paradigms of dependency arise in the interaction of parent and child or surrogate parent and child, and wife and husband. Age and sex priorities are established early in the consciousness of the child as it sees the prerogatives of elder over younger and male over female enacted in the domestic scene. Siblings provide the dramatis personae for the paradigms of competition and cooperation. Economic limitations in the mining family intensify the interplay along these axes of dependency and competition, but the hard reality of poverty gives priority to cooperation. Strategies for survival learned in the family serve to orient people throughout their adult life. It is not, however, a single, coherent body of rules and meanings. What appears to be totally contradictory behavior is often found in an individual. The triggering off of a particular action is not predictable only in terms of the individual, as "basic" or "modal" personality theory suggested, but rather the historic context in which it occurs.[1]

---

[1] The concept of "basic" or "modal" personality (DuBois 1944, Kardiner 1939) was developed when anthropologists worked with a model of isolated homogeneous

Latin American social scientists, especially Matos Mar, Cotler, and others of the Instituto de Estudios Peruanos have begun to apply the model of dependency in international relations to intranational social relations (Matos Mar 1968, 1969). Matos Mar (1968:22 et seq.) had analyzed how a relatively small group who control decisionmaking in Lima and in a radial network throughout Peru depend on external sources of power, and Salazar Bondy (1968:59) shows how this power of decisionmaking by one group or person over another makes for alienation, or living according to "modes and forms of existence inferior or far from their full realization." Deference and obsequiousness, slavish fulfillment of the required task countermanded by strategies of subterfuge and deceit, are the basis for success in authoritarian structures. These strategies are learned within an authoritarian family and are perpetuated in adult life as men and women enter as workers in enterprises over which they have no control, and by women in the domestic scene itself.

Authoritarian characteristics are not lacking in the mining family, but along with the strategies cultivated within such a structure there is respect for the father because of his personal sacrifice as a breadwinner that goes beyond a response to arbitrary authority, as well as a sharing of tasks and recognition of the contribution of each member that breaks down the more corrosive aspects of the dependence found in middle class family life. Necessity sharpens the acuteness of dependency while at the same time contradictory tactics of cooperation are given the opportunity to arise.

The organization of the mining family has changed almost more radically in the past half century than any other institution in Bolivian society. The change has been in a conservative direction, tending to minimize the political radicalization of miners, as the nuclear family emerged out of the shambles of the communal *ayllu*. We have little literature on which to base a reconstruction of the family life of the early decades of the twentieth century, only the memories of older workers who recall the dislocation of workers and the disruption of the family caused by movement to the mines. There was no provision for housing accommodations that would lead to stable marriages. Men burrowed into caves in the hillside to

people. Wallace (1964) broke the mold by showing the compatibility of mutually contradictory ideas and behaviors not only within small-scale societies, but even within individuals.

accommodate themselves until they could move the encampment as housing became available. There they were often quartered in barracks style, with four or five sleeping in a windowless hovel. Married couples had to share such quarters with each other and with the bachelors. The conditions Marx (1906:542) described for British miners in the eighteenth and early nineteenth centuries prevailed in Bolivia up until the forties, when some minimal rights were won. Wages were not high enough for a man to support a family, and so women and children worked even when the husband or father was working. Whatever stability was maintained in family life against the odds of severe emotional stress built up in these inhuman conditions could be lost at any moment because of accident or sickness.

The transition for the family was not directly from an extended to a conjugal family, as Goode (1963:2) predicts, but rather took the form of the consanguineal family analyzed by Gonzalez (1969) as typical of migratory or marginal work groups in the New World and other areas. It was marked by a loss not only of the extended family ties but of the nuclear core itself. Men were the immediate victims of the industrial system. Their bodies were blown up or crushed by falling rocks, or they spit up their lungs once they contracted silicosis. Women and children died less dramatically of malnutrition and a less malignant form of silicosis they contracted on the slag pile or in the concentration pits.

Greater family stability came with the winning of a modicum of social security benefits, hospitalization, and pension rights in the forties and fifties. The beneficial effects of a stable family life in creating a more dependable work force were recognized by the administration of the mines after nationalization. Industrial relations managers extolled the virtues of family life and social service workers were sent into the homes to teach women improved homemaking practices. Family life was seen as a competitive alternative to political and union activity by both men and women, and the administration undoubtedly appreciated its deradicalizing effects.

Household Composition and Family Relations

Table 3.1 shows the number and frequency of household composition for workers in the sample interviewed with the help of two

Table 3.1. Household Composition

◈◇◈

	Interview Sample		10% of Personnel Statistics					
	Workers		Workers		Employees		Engineers	
	No.	%	No.	%	No.	%	No.	%
Nuclear Family:								
parents and their children	52	65.2	76	61.8	15	55.8	4	100
Nuclear Family Plus								
Grandmother			14	11.3	5	18.5		
Grandfather			4	3.2	1	3.7		
Both grandparents			6	4.8	2	7.4		
Grandparents and sibs			3	2.4				
Grandmother and sibs			9	7.3				
Grandfather and sibs			2	1.6				
Grandparents, Grandchildren			1	0.8				
Grandmother, Grandchildren	3	3.6						
Single Parent and Children								
Mother	4	4.8						
Father	2	2.4						
Mother and grandmother	11	15.1						
Father and grandmother	1	1.2						
Joint Family: siblings of spouse and nuclear family								
Wife's sibs with children	1	1.2						
Widow, her sib, children	1	1.2						
Wife's sibs, no children	3	3.6			2	7.4		
Husband's sibs, children	1	1.2						
Bachelor	1	1.2	1	.8	2	7.4		
Unknown	—	——	7	5.6	—	——	—	——
Total	80	100.7	123	99.6	27	100.2	4	100

students in the mining barrio along with statistics from employee records in the personnel office.

The interview sample reflects the actual household situation in the mining barrio most accurately because it includes the surviving families of dead miners, while the personnel statistics only refer to households of employed workers. Also, the personnel statistics included all dependents whether or not they were actually living with the nuclear family of the miner. Both sets of statistics reflect the preponderance of the nuclear family, and the data from the interviews in the barrio reveal the familial resources for patching up fractured nuclear families.

Although children are no longer as great an economic advantage now as they were in the early decades of the twentieth century and still are in the rural economy, most mining families welcome them and do little to prevent conception. I knew only one woman who used birth control pills, and her husband was the butt of jokes for his failure to produce an offspring in seven years. Most women had heard of the rhythm method but did not have much faith in it because they knew of so many failures. Many women tried to limit intercourse with their husbands. This was facilitated by a preferred sleeping pattern in which men slept alone or with a male child and women slept in a separate bed often with the youngest child. Both men and women adhere to the Catholic ideology that children come from God, but women are more concerned with trying to limit their arrival on earth. One woman, who had worked all her life in the mines and at the surface, said when I asked her if she had wanted to have the children she bore:

❖ Children are in the world because God sends them. It isn't the women. If it were up to the woman, there wouldn't be any more. A woman alone cannot have children. But the men are pigs and they get the girls in trouble when they walk in the street.

One of my comadres had heard of condoms from her sister-in-law, whose husband had failed using one. She insisted that she learned the following about rhythm from the doctor:

❖ The doctor in San José hospital advised us that a little before the days of menstruation and afterward are the most dangerous. My husband sleeps in another room from me. Once when I was washing the baby I said, "Francisco, take your child," but he didn't want to. "It appears to me you ought not to have children," I said. Then I told him, "Don't open my door—go to your own room tonight."

My sister has five children. I don't see how she can stand it. I get nervous with just these three.

Abstention, rather than prevention, is generally taken to be the only sure preventive. Despite the interest women express in finding out about birth control, there is a great deal of misinformation available, and it is difficult for them to sort the truth from speculation. Birth control pills are available in pharmacies in the city, but they cost the equivalent of two days' work, and this makes them inaccessible.

Workers who want to improve their children's lot in life try to discourage them, particularly daughters, from early marriage and even marriage in general. Jorge, a very ambitious man who worked in the carpentry shop, had two daughters who were spinsters. He remarked: "I advised my daughters not to get married. Men nowadays are worthless. They get drunk and do not support wives. One of my daughters is a teacher and the other is a pharmacist. The others are not yet old enough to get married."

Inadvertently the mine management supports a policy of uncontrolled family expansion by a wage policy which subsidizes each child throughout its student period and gives an outright sum of B $200 plus a child subsidy of B $12 per month per child in addition to B $14 for the wife. Maternity care is provided for miners' wives. Uncontrolled reproduction is further encouraged by giving prizes to families with the most children. When Ovando's wife visited the mines of San José in 1970 she gave sewing machines to the five families with the most children. One disgruntled worker who had ten children said she should have given them to families with the most living children, because some of those families who received the machines had fewer alive than he. While such subsidies and prizes do not directly affect reproduction, they underwrite an ideology that encourages unlimited conceptions.

The privilege of uncontrolled reproduction accorded to male workers, who are acclaimed and congratulated by fellow workers and management alike as their family grows in size, was not extended to women workers when there were large numbers supporting themselves and their children in concentration work. Administrators with whom I spoke commented sarcastically on how the company did nothing but foster the spawning of children by employing women in the concentration.

The institutional support of unlimited birth delays the feedback to the workers on the dangers of overreproduction that operates more efficiently in the rural areas. The campesinos feel more immediately the drain of a new infant on limited resources. Abortifacients are used by women for themselves and for the livestock. The effectiveness of these herbal remedies can be seen in every Bolivian market, where heaps of llama fetuses are sold for ritual purposes with no apparent decline in the adult female llama population. In extreme cases of deprivation, infanticide is also practiced in rural areas. One of the missionary priests said that he had been called in more than once to baptize and give last rites to a child who appeared only to be suffering from extreme hunger. In contrast, the miners do not feel the pressure of additional children until the declining years in their own productivity. Juan reveals the accumulated burden that workers face with each successive birth:

◈ When I had only one child, life was very good, like any life that one could live normally. We had everything, and times were good then, not like now. Afterward when I had another child, things were still good. I didn't have to worry about anything. After that, Anibal was born in January of 1958. Then there were two students in the house, but things were not too bad. There was another daughter born in 1961 and then there were three students. After that, in 1966 I had another daughter, and three years later, in 1969, I had my last. I do not know if he will be the last or if I am going to have more children. Everything depends on God, everything comes from the heights.
["Did you ever try to prevent conception?" I asked.]
No, in no way. I just waited the will of God. Everything is the will of God; it is not up to us.
My eldest son is now grown up and is working in my place in the mine. In one year Margarita will graduate and go to nursing school. But I can't even think of educating the rest. My health is finished. I have one hundred percent silicosis. I have no lungs; they are empty. I cannot work any more because my life is ended.

I was inhibited in getting data on the use of birth control and, except from very close informants, on any sentiments about family planning, because of a strong attack by left-wing parties against campaigns to limit population, especially those promoted by "North American imperialists."[2] I limited my census survey to questions concerning live births only. The data from personnel records and my census are included in table 3.2. Data for the surface workers (who are generally clerks in the offices), hospital workers, and others with at least an elementary school education seem to indicate a greater limitation of reproduction than among the subsoil workers.

[2] *Yahwar Malku* (Blood of the Condor) was shown while I was in Bolivia. The film presents a scathing picture of Peace Corps volunteers sterilizing Indians in the interest of imperialist domination.

Table 3.2. Children per Family According to Age of Woman

A. Birth Records, Personnel File

Number of Children

Age of Wife	0	1	2	3	4	5	6	7	8	9	10	11	12	?	Total
Subsoil workers:															
Under 20 years		1													1
21–30	2	1	5	1	1	3									13
31–40	1	7	6	7	6	5	13	16	3	3	2				69
41+		8	5	7	6	9	7	9	3	5	3				62
Unknown														6	6
Total	3	17	16	15	13	17	20	25	6	8	5			6	151
Surface workers:															
21–30			1			1									2
31–40		1	3		1		4	4	1						14
41+	1	2	4	1	2	4	—	1	1						16
Total	1	3	8	1	3	5	4	5	2						32
Engineers:															
31–40		1	1	3	2										7
41+		—	—	1	1										2
Total		1	1	4	3										9
B. My Sample from Interviews															
21–30	1	3	5	4	6	1	1								21
31–40		1	1	4	2	9	5	5	1	1				1	30
41+	—	5	2	3	7	5	4	5	2	1				2	36
Total	1	9	8	11	15	15	10	10	3	2				3	87

Women are the central force maintaining continuity in a family life broken by the sudden deaths or desertion by the father. Both men and women agree that the mother-child relationship is the most important tie in their life, and often times the only enduring one. The self-sacrifice by the mothers, many of whom worked two shifts of six hours to keep their children fed and clothed, even eking out money to educate them, gave children a rare understanding of the human potential for love and devotion. Long after their mothers had died, adults, especially men, could hardly speak of their passing without crying. "My mother left me an orphan," said one miner whose mother died when he was 45 years old.

The reality of daily work and devotion to their children reinforces a belief that most of one's blood comes from the mother, although mixed with a small contribution from the father. Devotion to the Pachamama, a concept which has devolved from a more abstract time and space continuum to a mother-earth image, reinforces on the spiritual level the mundane commitment to the mother.

Motherhood is sentimentalized and enshrined in the Spanish-Creole culture handed down to the cholos. However distorted this may become, there is a real sense of pride in motherhood. Mother's Day is celebrated on May 27 in memory of the women of Cochabamba, who fought the Spaniards on that day after their men had been killed, a kind of recognition that underwrites a male value premise in assigning importance to women. A youth says this of Mother's Day:

❖ The day we devote to mothers commemorates the action the mothers of Cochabamba had taken in the War of Independence when they took over the guns of the men after they had been killed by the Spanish army. In honor of this, to remember this act of sacrifice, we give them this day of celebration. I always give my mother a small gift. When I was small, I gave a little card. Two or three weeks before Mother's Day I pleaded with my father to give me some money to make something. Then I hid it until the day arrived. Sometimes I would dedicate a poem that I would read to her and I would give her an embrace with confetti. What my mother liked most was the program we held at school, after which we went to the union hall, where we had lunch and we danced.

A man's tie to his family is through his paycheck, or more precisely, his credit in the company store. Men feel no need to disguise the fact that their ability to earn money and hand it over to their wife forms the basis for their maintaining a position in the family. For most miners, the family provides the object and motivation for living and working. One worker told me during the ch'alla in the Colorado mine, a ritual in which most of the workers wax more and more philosophical as the drinks flow:

❖ The miner knows how to work for his children, knows how to support his children. But *la vida esta comprado* [life is bought, meaning at a high price]. Eight people died in Colorado. Why? To support their children. Three of the men stayed up here and escaped. They couldn't get the others out. We expose our life and our soul to buy the daily bread for our children. Sometimes life plays with its deck of cards bringing death or loss of the workers' strength. A miner works with his love, not with bad intentions, to look for his daily living. Do you know why these deaths happen? Because for earning his way, united with death, with destiny, we don't know what road we are going to reach. Now I am speaking the truth. That's the only thing I am going to say.

Men feel obliged to earn for their family even when they have to steal. A miner told me, after he recounted how he had stolen a drill from the company when he was fired because of union activities: "When there are necessities in the home, a man is responsible for doing what is necessary. The only man who is not respected is one who does not work, a parasite who asks for money to live."

The miners' devotion to family, expressed in turning over their earnings to their wife, is underwritten by the priests, especially those of the missionary sects, who identify with the workers. In his sermon at the mass held in level zero of the Itos mine during Carnival, the Oblato priest said,

✧ There is no difference between the sacrifice that you workers make and what the priest makes. You workers who bring food home to feed your children are in your sacrifice acting as a minister of the Lord. The minister is in you, in your house, raising children, liberating silver, lead, and tin for the use of man.

A generation ago, boys growing up in the twenties and thirties often had to start work when they were eight or nine years old if their father died. This happened so frequently it was almost a general expectation because of the short life span of the miners. Mothers favored their children almost in direct relation to their earning power, giving those who worked the choicest selection of meat (if there was any) and the bulk of the protein. Boys in particular competed for the attention of their mother by trying to increase their earning power. One man related how he tried to attract his mother to the mine where he was working in the *rancho* when he was twelve, but he could not compete with his older step-brother, who was earning more as a policeman in the city. He resigned himself to her visits, which lasted only long enough to take supplies out of the pulpería on his account.

In case of the death of a parent, children may be absorbed along with the surviving parent into a larger kin group, the child may be sent to live with a grandparent, or a nuclear family may be reconstituted with the surviving parent getting married. Steparents are called *mamay* or *tatay* if the children are young when the relationship is established, or they may be called *tío* or *tía* or their Quechua equivalents *tiyoy* and *tiyay*. Relationships between step-parents and step-children are usually strained, but the exceptions prove the adaptive potential of family life.

There is a strong sense of the material obligations between parents and children. Basilia, who had worked all her life in the mine and in the concentration plant, expressed the sense the older generation had of what was due to them from their children: "Why do you have children? It is because the children are going to return the *aini* [reciprocal aid]. The child is going to give back all the aini. But they aren't doing that any more."

Children expect to inherit something, even the smallest token, to validate the relationship after the death of their parent. The same woman commented after her mother's death: "Since she was my mother, she should have left me something when she died instead of casting me out to suffer like a dog."

Sibling rivalry often becomes a vicious competition, stirred up frequently by parents who mete out love, food, and the opportunity for advancement through education according to preferences that follow the values of the dominant group. Boys are generally preferred over girls, especially by the mother, and whiter and brighter children are given priority by both parents. Sometimes one or more of the siblings will succeed in rising from the chola subclass to being a *gente de vestido* and enter into the professional class. This usually causes a rupture with the family in which they were born. One miner's wife, recalling her hardships as a child when she went to work as a housemaid and later as a palliri, said of her older sister:

❖ I have an older sister living in Santa Cruz and married to a clerk in a commissary who is a *señorita*. I went to visit her after I was married and she said, "I am not your sister. I don't have a sister of your class."

I was devastated. I said, "Yes, Marta, thanks," I said, "Thanks! If you are not my sister, it isn't necessary that you should be."

My informant had worn de vestido garments when she was a child and up until her teens, when she went to live with her grandmother in the mining community and started to work as a palliri, she had adopted chola dress, the pollera. She went on to say,

❖ I looked just like my papa. It is for that reason they say I was the favorite of my papa. I was the most beloved child. But he died without leaving anything for us—he would have, but my grandmother took everything. She became the inheritor of everything. We got nothing. And so we were thrown into the street. Then my mother got married again and so she didn't claim anything. But her other children became señoritas: one was a typist and the other became a hairdresser. They were children of my stepfather and so they received their studies while we got nothing.

The separate favoritism by father and mother stirred up the competitive rivalry of the siblings. This is frequently aggravated when children by a previous marriage may be sloughed off when the mother remarries. In the Indian family, favoritism was accorded by age order rather than the competitive norms of chola culture. The youngest child, *sulk'a sulkitan,* was expected to receive and usually did get the most affection and material inheritance from his or her parents, since he or she usually received the house along with some agricultural land. This objective favoritism, built into a culturally accepted norm, probably minimized some of the hostility acted out in the chola family.

Hostility engendered during the developmental years in the family often continues throughout adulthood. Older people speak of siblings having used witchcraft against them. Basilia railed against her brother, who because of envy of her greater earning capacity used witchcraft against her. She claims he put a spell on her by grabbing a toad and burying it with a photograph of her along with her nail parings and some of her hair. She would have died, she said, unless a neighbor discovered the place where the toad was buried and dug it up.

Sibling rivalry over the inheritance of goods from parents can continue for years after their death. The custom of equal inheritance of goods is complicated by the degree of responsibility taken in the care and maintenance of parents in their old age and the burial expenses incurred by one or more of the children.

Despite this avowed hostility and competitiveness, the brother-sister relationship can be the basis of the warmest and most cooper-

ative relationships. This is characterized more in the extensi
the sibling relationship to co-workers in the mine, who often
each other brothers—ñaña—than it is between biological brother.
However, the very extension of the metaphor for brotherhood to
those relationships which subsume the deepest and most intimate
cooperative relationships demonstrates the ability of the family to
generate the ideal if not the actual behavioral concomitants of this
bond.

Marital Relationships

Couples in the mining community enter into a communally
recognized marital union with the traditional *makemanaku* (request
for the hand). The betrothal differs from the campesino customs in
that the couple initiate the procedure rather than their parents. The
man goes with his parents or other older relative to the house of the
girl's parents. If all parties are agreed, the couple then enters a kind
of trial marriage, which a few still refer to as the *tantakuso tukuyinchis* (they are before everyone). If the father of the groom is dead,
his brother, uncle, or another older male of his family plays the pa-
ternal role, calling upon the youth to respect his *padrinos* of baptism
and confirmation and his future parents-in-law. From the moment
that the man lives with his future wife, her mother has a right to
make a claim on him for goods from the pulpería. When the man
has assumed sexual rights without confirmation or advice from the
parents, this is demanded somewhat vindictively.

The frequency of different types of connubial relationships is
shown in Table 3.3 from data in personnel records. The miners have
a reputation for being *muy picaro* (very adventurous) in their relationships with women. This was probably more justified in the
years when contract workers were earning much more than men now
employed in mining. Table 3.3 indicates that only one-fifth deviate
from a monogamous norm.

Padrinos of the tantakuso tukuyinchis ceremony are charged
with checking up on the behavior of the couple, particularly the
man, toward each other. They advise the couple at that time:

◈ At any moment we may enter your house and see what you are
doing. If you [the future wife] are wasting potatoes or vegetables

JUAN AND HIS FAMILY BAKE POTATOES IN AN EARTH OVEN IN THE
PAMPAS NEAR HIS HOME.

or other things, we are going to call it to your attention. And this
is not so that we will be a bother; you have to take advantage of
the man's work with a level head and with a great deal of care,
because if the woman does not save, then the man's work does not
serve to form a home. If the woman saves very much, she can form
a home quickly. We beg you both to bear with your padrinos,
your padres, and all the family.

The *novios,* first the man and then the woman, pardon themselves, kneeling in front of each of the guests, saying to them,
"From now on we shall take part among you in good grace," and
the padrinos say when they have finished, "You are pardoned."

In the intervening period before a formal marriage, the couple
refer any of their problems to the padrino. I asked one man, who
had several *ahijados* (godchildren) of marriage what advice he gave,
and he replied:

◈ I tell them, when a man is angry, the woman ought to listen
quietly, because when the woman gets angry, there is never going
to be an understanding. All their life they are going to fight. If one
of you is angry, then if one remains calm you will overcome the
misunderstanding quickly. You aren't always going to remain two.
You are going to follow the same road as we old ones. You are
going to have children and once you have children you have to

Table 3.3.   Marital Relations of Miners

Marriage Form	Workers		Employees		Engineers	
	No.	%	No.	%	No.	%
Same woman, married	73	59.3	28	62.2	2	50
Second wife	3	2.4	2	4.4	2	50
Concubine*	22	17.7	7	15.5		
Divorced	2	1.6	7	15.5		
Unmarried	6	4.4	1	2.2		
Common law	5	4.0				
Unknown	12	9.7	—	—	—	—
Total	123	99.1	45	99.8	4	100

*One man with three wives.

show discipline. You have to think of feeding your children, of clothing your children, and particularly of their studies. And if you proceed in this manner the children will respect you as they should.

When the couple have saved enough money to have a formal wedding, they put on a celebration that extends to the outer limit of their resources, often requiring that they burden themselves with aini for years to come, since the loan has to be repaid in double. The major expenses are drinks (beer, cocktails of fruit juice spiked with alcohol, and chicha), flowers, candles, an orchestra, the rings, and dinner. The liquor and food are usually given in aini; the other items are often given by someone named as padrino of the rings, the orchestra, etc. They are accorded honor at the celebration strictly in respect to the size of the contribution. The wedding may last as long as three days and the expenses mount up to two or three months' salary.

Weddings in the mining communities differ from those in the country in the influence of parents, the range of guests invited, the kind of gifts given by guests, and the responsibility of the groom to his guests. Both parents and offspring agree that if a man is earning his own living, he has a right to select his own mate. The request his parents or surrogates make to the girl's parents is a formality, and the couple usually have an alternative strategy worked out if they should refuse. In the mining community, friends of the couple and of their parents compose about half of the guests in proportion to relatives, while in the country, at least in Cochabamba, the entire community unites at marriage. Guests typically bring items such as glasses, dinnerware, and silverware in the mining community whereas farmers pin money on the groom. In the mining community the groom is expected to enjoy himself drinking with his comrades of work rather than spend his time caring for his parents and future parents-in-law, serving them drinks and attending to their needs and those of their generation as he is in the rural areas.

These contrasts in behavior reflect a different relationship with the elder generation and kinship groups. Miners do not have to defer to the parental generation since they expect no inheritance in land from them. More importantly, they reinforce the relationship between working peers. In contrast to the men, women who marry miners do not have the reinforcement of the kinship group that the campesinas benefit from and do not gain any solidarity with a work group. They are expected, as the padrino I interviewed above expressed it, to listen quietly and remain calm if a disagreement occurs in order to maintain the marriage.

The ideological issues in the fit between family form and industry raised by Goode (1963:20) express the masculine viewpoint in the mining community. They include (1) the right of an individual to choose his own spouse and place to live, and which kin to associate with; (2) the right of an individual to assert his worth in contrast to the inheritance group; (3) the encouragement of love; (4) the right to change marriage partners; and (5) egalitarianism among the sexes.

With reference to the first set of rights, male priorities determine all but the choice of kin to associate with. The choice of spouse is male initiated. Women are resistant to marriage, especially those who have been brought up in a mining community and know its hardships. Most of the women I have spoken to professed uninterest in marriage and speak of their courtship and marriage as a deception. Petrona, one of my comadres, related the following story of her courtship:

❖ My husband told me, "I want to ask for your hand. I want to marry you." I replied, "What will be will be. I am going to ask my mother what I should do."
I went and asked her and she did not even get angry. She said,

"You can think about it and you can take the road that goes forward or back. I can't tell you anything," she said, because she is very understanding. She wasn't anybody's fool.

I did not know my husband hardly. He told me that if I didn't marry him he would throw himself into a shaft. I was a fool and I believed him.

My mother-in-law came from Cochabamba directly to speak to my papa. She told him, "I want your daughter to marry my son because she is very well brought up and bright."

My father treated me badly. He said, "It looks as though you must be having relations with her son."

"I don't even know him. Don't talk to me like that, Papa!"

Then my mother-in-law came directly to me and said, "I had a talk with your father and your father told me, "You can speak to her directly."

"I don't know. I am not at the age to marry yet," I said.

Then my mother-in-law came and took me and I lived with Juan.

Resistance to forming an alliance with a man is not just a pose on the part of women but an awareness of the endless succession of childbirths in a community where birth control is little known and not accepted and where the abusive treatment of wives is an institutionalized norm. Another miner asserted that when he proposed marriage to the assembled family of the prospective bride, she said,

❖ "I cannot marry."

"Then what do you want?" her family asked. I thought we had been in agreement before we went to see them.

"I want to live six months with Manuel," she told them. She was earning money as a palliri and had her responsibilities helping one sister who was in school and her parents.

I said, "No, that isn't what I had thought. I want to get married." My mother had by then succumbed to her vices and was unable to prepare a meal to send to me in the mine. Flora would have had to stop working.

Although there is not complete correspondence between male and female ideologies with respect to marriage, there is complementarity. Both believe that parents' wishes should not prevail and agree that it is the man who chooses, the woman who yields, in the choice of the partners. However, with respect to legal marriage, men prefer to believe that they enter into the contract freely, but women recognize the pressure their family puts on the man once they have been joined in common-law alliance and have children. Legal marriage does provide security for a woman, particularly after she has children, although the mining company pays subsidies to the concubine of a miner once she has established common-law status. In the case of the first couple whose courtship is described above, Petrona spoke of the three years between the time of her joining her husband Juan until their marriage as a period for saving money for the ceremony. He maintained that he had never agreed to a specific time for marriage, and in fact he resisted her father's attempt to force him into a legal union after their first child was born and a dispute between him and his wife over how much pulpería he should give his mother broke out. He asserted:

❖ Although they obliged me to get married, I announced that I am master of my will and no one can force my will. "My position is firm," I told them, "No one can force me to change my mind."
I got angry and so there was no more pressure to make me marry because I had my child and my wife didn't want to give me up. She has always been at my side.

Petrona says the marriage, which occurred a year later, was precipitated by her father:

❖ When we were in Cochabamba, my father came to Juan and said, "Until when are you thinking of being joined with my daughter? It is now three years, going on four. I don't want you to continue in common-law union. I want you to marry my daughter."
He spoke to my uncle, who was very rich, and so he got us married right away.

Her husband persists, however, in his view that he made the decision:

❖ We went to live in Cochabamba and lived with a brother of her father for three months. Then I decided to get married.

These self-images, dramatized in the narration of their life histories, reveal how the individual maintains intact a view of self that conforms with his or her world view.[3]

The right to divorce is preferred by women only when they are not burdened with children because of limited opportunities for self-employment. Choice is exercised by men from the time a ro-

[3] This excerpt is taken from the life history of Juan Rojas (Rojas and Nash 1976).

mance is initiated until another is contemplated. Women for the most part have neither the money, the power, nor the opportunity to initiate romantic adventures before or after marriage. I am not referring now to commercialized sexual relations involving widows and other unattached women, which are said to be frequent and usually stem from contacts made in the chicherías. Freer marital relations benefit the male when opportunities for gainful employment for women are limited.

A generation ago, when there were many women employed as palliris, they were considered to be much freer in their sexual adventures. In Huanuni, where the palliris were attached to a particular *cuadrilla* (work group) whose load they handled, I am told that the men did not seek sexual relations with the women in their work group but preferred those assigned to another cuadrilla. While I am sure exceptions were made in the Carnival festivities after the *k'araku* (see chapter 5), I think the comradeship developed in the work mitigated exploitative sexual advance.

The tie between a man and his home during his working hours is the lunch bucket. If there has been any trouble between a couple, the man can assess how seriously his wife has taken by the quality of his lunch. They expect three servings: soup, *segundos* or seconds consisting of meat and potatoes or noodles, with a cooling herb tea in a bottle tied to the three-tiered metal tins. If any course is lacking, or even worse, if the lunch does not arrive, they know they are in trouble. There is a great deal of joking and comment during lunch hour, when the men usually congregate near the main shaft where there is more ventilation, about their comrades' familial relations as evidenced in the lunch. Once I began to appreciate the importance of the lunch break for social and nutritional purposes, I could sense the lunch bucket as a kind of lifeline extending from the home to the mine. Women bring the bucket to a specified depot where a company truck comes by at eleven o'clock to pick them up and take them to the mine, where they are lowered in the haul. The men wait expectantly below and each comes to the shaft to claim his. If a man has had a bad fight with his wife, he won't even come to the shaft to avoid the embarrassment of being the neglected one.

Marital problems are referred first to the older, respected members of the family, oftentimes to the padrinos of marriage, and

THE MEALS ARE A LINK BETWEEN THE HOME AND THE JOB, THE
WOMAN AND THE MAN. IF THE COUPLE HAVE A FIGHT, THE MEAL
IS NOT DELIVERED TO THE TRUCK SENT BY THE COMPANY TO
PICKUP STATIONS IN THE ENCAMPMENT, AND THE MAN KNOWS HE
IS IN TROUBLE. HERE WOMEN BRING THE LUNCHES THEY HAVE
PREPARED TO THE STATION.

later, if the trouble continues, to the judges. Legal agreements are
drawn up at a charge of B $10, almost a day's wage, for the writ and
as much more for the court fees. The couple feel a kind of investment in the marriage after this expenditure and seem to show a
greater commitment to maintain it. They are often assigned to the
guardianship of older relatives, who visit them and check on their
well-being.

The major reason given as the source of friction is money mat-
ters, although this may be only the overt expression of deeper with-
drawals. People express their emotions by giving or withholding
money, food, or obligatory demands. In the fury of a fight, a man
will often flaunt his superior economic power, threatening to throw
his wife out of their house, or he will beat her physically. One
woman, who wanted desperately to find work on the slag pile, told
me she never had to put up with as much abuse when she was
working, but with seven children, her husband did not take her
seriously when she threatened to leave him. Commentators on the
outrages to the working class in the development of indus-

trialization have rarely considered the special abuse that working class wives take. A ragged, undernourished wife and children symbolize the man's frustrated ambitions and he takes the brunt of his anger out on them. They are probably the only major working segment of the population outside of a slave system which is daily subjected to beatings and threats regardless of work performance. Conflict within the family is endemic in an impoverished society. Poverty is a social relation, not an absolute condition; the miner is poor in comparison with the campesino who lives in an economy of scarcity. Although the campesino has fewer material goods than he, he feels the impoverishment more bitterly as self-defeat. His poverty is portrayed to him in the anguish his family must endure. One miner said to me:

❖ In my work I am happy. I joke with my comrades, I work in peace. And then I come home and I see my wife and children undernourished, poorly clothed. It is then I have a sense of the problems in my life and I get filled with rage.

Wife beating is common enough to be considered a major threat by women. When I asked my comadre Petrona what were the biggest problems in living in a mining community, she replied, wife-beating, and went on to relate the troubles her comadre had with her husband:

❖ One of my compadres fought a lot with his wife. Sometimes he hit her when she was pregnant. I had to stand there in the middle like a devil defending her so that he wouldn't wound her. He would come in at three in the morning from wherever he was drinking. We lived beside him. A wall separated us. One could hear everything.

My poor comadre cried out, "Comadre! Comadre! What is he doing to me?" I would be sleeping on this side, when I heard her from afar, in my dreams I would hear her shout. Then she would come in with her great stomach, and afterward he would come in beating her pitiably. He was a bad one!

I was very strong although I am thin. I pushed my compadre on the bed. "Why are you beating this poor woman?"

He would say, "I want to throw her out like shit! This woman is a spendthrift. She doesn't know how to save money. She doesn't know how to do anything, comadre. You have to pardon me because of what I am doing. She isn't like you, cleaning house, sewing for the children. You can see how dirty, how ragged the children are. She doesn't mend anything. She just walks in the street at her pleasure. She passes her time with her sisters, and my poor children are in the house without anything to eat or to dress themselves. You can see how it is, comadre.

Marital conflict is epitomized by a story that I thought was fictional when I first heard it. A woman in Siglo XX killed her husband and then made *chicharrón* of his body, leaving only his head, hands, and feet. The husband was reputedly a drunk and beat her often. The story is related in a joking way—I heard it from several different sources—and I did not take it seriously until a man reputed to know something about anatomy claimed that he was called in to reconstruct bones found in the woman's house to verify whether they were human. What is considered the most bizarre part of the story is that she *sold* the sausage in the mining encampment. The story not only reveals the intensity of hostility that can be worked up in the marital union, but also epitomizes the chola reaction to exploitation in commercializing the remains. Women particularly seem to relish the part of the story, "Y se ha vendido su marido!" ("And then she sold her husband!")

The Wider Kinship System

The kinship system offers a set of relations which are potential but not always actualized networks. Geographic mobility, class mobility, and a short life span limit the horizontal spread and vertical depth of kinship ties. If the movement is limited to the highland mining communities, there is likely to be continuous interaction since the mines are linked into an effective communication network and there remains a common interest. However, movement to another department, especially Santa Cruz, or to Argentina, the flight areas the most often mentioned, usually means an end to interaction even by mail.

Kinship relations are extended bilaterally rather than lineally since the life span is short and geographic mobility breaks up the continuity. Even those miners who speak Quechua in the home use relationship terms that are derived from Spanish. Spanish terms with Quechua suffixes are commonly used: *tiyo* and *tiyay* are widely extended to bilateral and affinal kin as are *sobrinoy* and *so-*

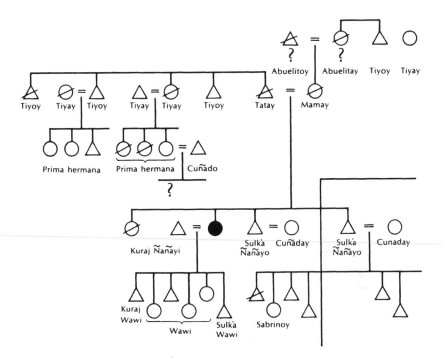

FIGURE 3.1 KINSHIP TERMINOLOGY (FEMALE EGO)

brinay. Collective terms for relatives are more often Quechua than Spanish, as *ñañasni* (my siblings) and *aylluani* (members of my *ayllu*), which is used alternatively with *sobrinotusni*. These extended consanguineal groups rarely have an opportunity to get together unless the older generation holds onto land and remains in the countryside.

Age is of greater importance than sex in ego's generation. Older siblings are referred to as *kuraj ñañay* and younger as *sulka ñañay*, but names rather than kin terms are commonly used in speaking to the person. The reference system is, if one presses hard enough, Quechua, while the vocative system falls into the Spanish idiom.

The kinship terms of the family of orientation are often extended to in-laws if they are amicable relations. This is especially true of parents-in-law, called *mamay* and *tatay*. Siblings-in-law are included in the collective term *ñañasni*.

Compadrazgo

Compadrazgo relations illustrate the adaptive potential of the fractured geneological system in its capacity to expand and acquire new social resources to compensate for those lost by death or geographic mobility of the mining family. The egalitarian ritual kinship terminology obscures the distinct differences in the quality of the relationship that is related to the occasion which generates the tie and to the nature of the status relationship existing between the compadres prior to the ceremonial tie.

The most important compadres are those of baptism. Members of the nuclear family of orientation are often named as compadres, thus reinforcing grandparental or avuncular ties with the compadrazgo tie. Old friends from the father's army days or from the town of origin of either parent are often preferred, especially for the first child, but neighbors and working companions are also included in those cases where an egalitarian relationship is reinforced with a respect relationship. Sometimes the parents try to gain some security in the job by choosing superintendents of the mine, *mayordomos* of a level in the mine, or clerical employees in the administration. When opportunistic motives are the basis for making vertical ties with superordinates in the social hierarchy, most show a preference for gente de vestido. When I asked Basilia, "Who are your godparents?" she replied,

> ❖ I have a padrino and he is called Francisco Lazcano. My madrina is Carmine Lazcano. She is de vestido. She is well read, like you, señorita. My family doesn't have cholos as padrinos. All are de vestido, puro de vestido. My mother's padrinos are the same. When they married, my mamita lived above Palca. Her madrina and her padrino are rich.
> None of my children are chola. They just wear suits and dresses, because people have more respect for the vestido. But for the cholas there is no respect. Whenever they want us, they yell at us. They do not have the cross in their mouth; they do not have the escutcheon that this brings. The padrinos take charge of their godchildren in good form. There is respect for their godchildren. For that reason my daughter is de vestido, señora. They have patience, a decent word for them, but if one is a chola and doesn't know how to read, *niñita*, they don't have any good words. "The cholas don't know anything," they say, "just speak ten words or so of Spanish." For that reason I didn't want a madrina or a padrino to be like that.

This woman, like many of her generation born before the twenties, accepts the alienated chola view of what the chola culture is like. She aspires to gain admission into the class of gente decent by choosing de vestido people as compadres for her children. This viewpoint, embracing self-hatred along with strong mobility drives, is significantly linked to the compadrazgo relationship which provides an alliance with the dominant culture at the same time that it gives a refuge from one's indigenous culture.

After having studied the institution of compadrazgo in an Indian community where age structured social relations both within and outside of genealogical ties,[4] it was significant to me that age had little to do in defining respect or superordinate relationships. People could, and did, choose as padrinos persons younger than they. I asked Juan, who was padrino of marriage to a working comrade senior to him, what the special conditions of the relationship were in this case. He responded:

❖ Although he is of greater age, the godchild has to follow in the steps of the padrinos, with mutual comprehension. There are some who are older who do not conform. Rufino was very bad. He drank chicha and he used to beat his wife when he was drunk. When his wife came to me and complained, I had to beat him with a lash. He had to receive his punishment. If I had left him in peace, he would have been ruined. He calls me papa and I call him ahijado, or son.

This ability to ignore age and seniority as linked with prestige may be related to the job situation, where seniority is less significant than ability and skill. Many men in superior positions are younger than men in their work gang or partnership team. With the aging process there is a loss of the higher paying, more dangerous and strenuous positions occupied by men in their thirties. Juan's ahijado worked as a *peón por la casa* (free-floating worker) while Juan was working on contract with good wages.

The padrino relationship is initiated when those desiring the alliance make a formal visit to the padrinos. They usually go with other relatives, since they feel that there will be less chance that they will be refused. Padrinos of baptism are chosen during the first year of life. If the child is sickly there is a special emphasis on

4 Nash (1970) develops this comparison more fully.

baptizing as soon as possible so that the child should not die without a name.

The ceremony of baptism is performed at a fee of B $10,000 in one of the churches in the center of the city, preferably the cathedral of the Virgin of the Mineshaft, which has the most prestige. The madrina holds a girl child and the padrino holds a boy child as the priest anoints the child's temples with oil, gives it its name, and utters the benediction. The padrinos provide the baptismal garments, with which they themselves dress the infant before the ceremony. They pay for the baptismal registration. More traditional Indian couples bring a *t'anta wawa* (bread baby) to be blessed along with the infant, and this is given to the child's parents as a kind of surrogate for the child they were given spiritually. After the church ceremony, the parents of the child treat the compadres to a banquet of *piquante* of chicken or other fowl. They are regaled with chicha, beer, and alcohol cocktails in quick succession. Following the eating and drinking, each of the members of the kinship group of the child's parents who are present formally embraces the padrinos and showers them with confetti.

The obligations of the padrinos do not end with the ceremony. Their formally prescribed duties are to give instructions in church rituals and teach their godchild to be religious, to respect Christ and to know Jehovah, and to teach their co-godparent how a father should behave to his children. Informally they are expected to respond to the needs of their compadres as they are requested. Juan went so far as to invite his godchild, the son of an Indian campesino, to live in his house so that he could send him to the mine school and have him get the same education his children got. On New Year's Eve compadres often invite their co-godparent to a chicken piquante. This is especially the custom when compadres are of the same social status and when they are neighbors.

If the child should die, padrinos are expected to buy the coffin. When a child is still an infant, the godparent carries the coffin. They should be present at the wake and the funeral. After the mass in the church, the godparents stand with the parents shaking hands and thanking the people who came to the ceremony.

One of the characteristics which I found on the occasions when I accepted the compadrazgo alliance was the encouragement of advice-giving. It struck me perhaps because of the general negation of this practice in our society, and as ethnologists we are expected to maintain a culturally relativist position. However, compadres expect the persons of their choice to give them advice on their own conduct and that of their child and seem cheated when they don't get it. They appeal to their compadres for their opinions on behavior problems and help in making decisions almost as the parents of our society seek out a therapist. This constant search for advice and for lessons in self-improvement is premised not so much on a sense of inadequacy, which I have seen played out in other relationships besides that of compadrazgo, but on an optimism about the possibility of progress and change.

Compadrazgo relations, like marital relations, can be formally dissolved by a return of all the gifts exchanged at the time the relationship was made. In one case when a fight between a woman and her comadre's daughter occurred over an accusation of theft, the woman returned a cooked chicken and two barrels of chicha consumed during the baptism ceremony. She added that it was not necessary to return the potatoes or noodles, always an accompaniment of a meal, because she herself had provided them. She expected her former comadre to return a pollera and an *awayu* (shawl) she had given as gifts at New Year, in addition to the B $20,000 she owed them, and a t'anta wawa which was given at the time of the baptism. The very fact that the relationship can be undone proves not its fragility but its strength. Like marriage, it is a relationship that must be publicly rejected in order for people who have become enemies to be able to relate to each other without the contradictions becoming overpowering.

The rites of passage of baptism, confirmation, and marriage require the formal alliance of compadrazgo. We can include with these rites the compadrazgo relationship formed at a health mass, since it shares the same quality of concern for the health and welfare of the child between surrogate parents and consanguineal parents. Another more exploitative compadrazgo relationship has developed when people seek help in sharing the financial burdens to which they have overcommitted themselves. When people have undertaken the *carga* of a fiesta, they may ask someone to become a padrino or madrina of a specific item such as the orchestra, or they may ask a person to bring the cake for a wedding or birthday. A soccer team may seek a padrino, who is then expected to contribute the shirts or some other item of the uniform or equipment. The item contributed is publicly announced and much acclaim is given to the padrino. Children in a neighborhood will even try to exploit the relationship in getting a ball for their team. It is a polite way of getting the wealthier to share the wealth without getting into the burdensome aini or pauper relationship.

In the compadrazgo relationship, mining families express all the competitive norms in their culture. When several compadres or padrinos are involved in the same ceremony at the same time, it is a contest to see who is given priority. The politics of who should be served first, to whom the best portions of a fowl should be given, who should be seated inside the house and who should be relegated to the patio require a lifetime involvement in the culture to finesse. I recorded the following conversation while I was gossiping with my comadre Rosa, which gives some insight into the complexities:

❖ The comadre of Francisco by his illegitimate son, an Indian cotmaker, came asking for an orchestra for the child's sixth birthday. She wanted five players for from two to eleven at night. I took offense and got very angry. I went to the band members and advised them that there should be only three players, one accordionist, a drum and a saxophone, and I told them that I would get them at three in the afternoon. She had wanted them at two.

I went at three and the madrinas of the baptism were there inside and the madrinas of the orchestra were outside in the patio. And so much wind! And when the madrinas of baptism were served beautiful meals, they gave a tower of *chuño* with a sauce and for meat a little wing of the chicken. That day I said, "When my son is a year old I am going to screw them for the aini!"

Only a week later he was a year old and I went, with a huge invitation, this size, and I said, "An orchestra, please, comadre. It is Tito's birthday."

"How many hours do you want, then?"

"Whatever you wish."

"How many musicians do you want?"

"Whatever you wish."

And in the afternoon they came with four musicians. And so it was that I won. And they told me that the musicians didn't drink any chicha, only beer, and that they wanted a *fardo*. I served it in little glasses.

My mama came for Tito's birthday and I told her what the Indian cotmaker said, and my mama told me, "We are going to serve her the same." And I said, "No, mama, we have to do better."

I made a *fandango* and served a mountain. I gave her the chicha in a pineapple shell with peach juice so she would get drunk right away.

But your compadre is very good. He said, "Good, go ahead, send the orchestra at two." But I didn't. He would take the shirt off his back and give it to anyone who asked for it. These padrinos are killing us. Those who want a fandango and everything ought to pay for it, or if they want padrinos they ought to pay in the aini as I made my comadre the cotmaker do.

Usually, when the compadrazgo relationships stems from an exploitative base, there is an aini or the relationship is ended. Contract workers are the most subject to being named for such semi-exploitative relationships, but they preserve their own honor by permitting their wives to fight the encroachment on ground rules worked out in the rural allyu.

The compadrazgo relationship provides an arena which both displays as well as channels hostilities that arise in the tightly packed encampment. The relationship, predicated as it is on respect, reinforces order and peace in the encampment, especially among the neighborhood group. When contract differentials used to be higher because of payment according to ore content rather than cubic meters of output, compadrazgo obligations heaped on the young contract workers in their prime minimized the envy that could have destroyed the sense of community based on an egalitarian ideology.

Ideological Disparity between Familial and Collective Goals

The nuclear family is underwritten and supported by the major institutions that affect miners: the administration of the mines and the church. The former recognizes the rights of dependents in both the nuclear family of orientation and of procreation, and provides allotments to them even when the worker has broken from his wife or family. The church provides an ideology for cultivating family bonds and an institutional base for the rituals that validate the social relationships on which they are predicated. In addition, it gives a framework for expanding relationships in compadrazgo ties established in those rituals.

The nuclear family has been analyzed as a complement to industrialization. This should be qualified to indicate its complementarity to an industrialization based on private capital where the nuclear family, because of its mobility, can conform to the vagaries of changing jobs. In addition, because it is a small, self-sufficient unit dedicated to aggrandizing its own consumption ends, the nuclear family creates a dependency of a woman and her offspring on the male breadwinner and thus ties a man to his job. If industrialization were based on a cooperative egalitarian system, the boundaries of the nuclear family would probably be merged in a community in which collective action for wider social interests would be encouraged.

The dialectic between cooperation and competition enacted in the family roles has changed dramatically in the past half century. Those workers who have survived from the early decades of the twentieth century reveal that, in the transition between agricultural and industrial adaptation, hatred was turned inward against oneself and one's family. The nuclear family was in many cases destroyed by the constant disruption, the poverty and the lack of minimal housing facilities to maintain privacy and nutritional needs. The inability to sustain the family led to self-doubt aggravated by the anxiety and uncertainty in the new situation. It required the development of class consciousness to overcome the internalized tensions engendered by the industrializtion process, and this has not yet been completely effected.

The liberation of men from control by the extended family over their choice of mates, of residence, and of the disposition of income was won at the expense of increasing the dependency of women. Cut off from the opportunity to do productive work as the mines became increasingly capital intensive, women had no basis for working out an egalitarian basis implied in the ideology of the modern nuclear family based on romantic love. This dependency of women and children on a single wage-worker in the family increased working class dependency on the job and reduced their ability to cope effectively in the political arena.

Chapter 4
◆◇◆
Community Integration
and Worker Solidarity

◆THE SOLIDARITY of miners as a work force is an often noted but sel-dom explained phenomenon.[1] I shall try to show here how the class solidarity that emerges in production is linked to class consciousness that exists in the community and home as well as the work site.

In most modern industrial societies, the home life of the workers is physically separated from the job. The motivations and activities of the domestic unit are antagonistic to those of the work group. The shared consumption drives of the family cultivate conformity to a given job structure, while the shared work conditions promote a sense of alienation and hostility to the company.

In the mining community, the contradiction between home life and work life is less evident. Houses are often an extension of the mine buildings and it is hard to see where administrative buildings end and the workers' housing begins. Workers' families share the same basic conditions as the miners: their water supply, electricity, and other facilities accorded them are an extension of the mine facilities and are contingent on the wage-workers' relation to their jobs. Most of the basic foodstuffs, oil for their stoves, and clothing come from the pulpería, or commissary operated by the company. Any breakdown in this administrative organization is felt immediately in the home and community as it is in the mines. When workers are fired, killed in accidents, or sick, their rights and hence their

[1] Kerr and Siegel (1954) note the cohesiveness of miners as a work force in their comparative analysis of strikes, and Lipset (1963) refers to miners as the work force with a high degree of solidarity.

families' claims on these job benefits are lost or at least threatened. Moreover, in periods of industrial crisis the community and family are immediate social conduits of the effects; when there is a "white massacre,' or mass lay-off, children suffer hunger and anxiety equally with the adults. When, as often happens in the labor strife of the mines, there is a "red massacre" or bloodbath provoked by a strike or worker protest, children are killed along with women and men. The shared sense of *communitas*, of belonging to the same social group and sharing equally in its destiny, reinforces the solidarity of class gained in the work group.

The Oruro Mining Center

The active mines are Oruro and Itos, on the southern periphery of the city, and Colorado and San José on the northern side. The oldest mine center is no longer active, and the Church of the Virgin of the Mineshaft has been erected at the entrance. Company housing flanks the hills near each mine entrance, and the new national cooperative housing are grouped in a grid pattern on the lower slopes.

When I first approached the mining center of San José on the northern border of Oruro, I had the sense of an integrated physical organism. The mine whistle controls the rhythm of the workers' lives: a loud blast awakens the workers at five o'clock in the morning and another marks the time for their entry into the mines at seven. In the hour between six and seven putty-colored figures in a constant stream move quickly up the hill to the mine entrance, the muffled sound of rubber boots on the gravel road increasing in tempo as they approach the mouth of the mine. At three the first shift emerges into the blinding sun as another stream of workers approaches to take a turn. And finally, at eleven at night the graveyard shift workers are the last to enter the mine, almost welcoming the warmth of the sulfurous interior as they escape the cold winds that have lacerated them in their climb up the hill. There is no movement that is not directly related to the mines. Even nature seems dead; there are no birds, no green grass or trees in the winter months of June, July, and August when I first stayed in this center 13,800 feet above sea level. Miners have a sense that their life de-

ENTRANCE TO ITOS MINE WITH ADMINISTRATIVE BUILDINGS
SKIRTING THE MOUTH OF THE MINE AND WITH RAILS LEADING UP
TO THE 60-METER CONE.

pends directly on that of the mine. Once their lungs are infected
with silicosis, there is little chance that they can adapt to another
climatic zone where colonization lands are available, nor would the
skills they learn serve them in any other capacity.

Some of the impact of the productive setting is minimized in
the mines of Oruro, where the urban center that has grown up to
service the mines—the banks, the university, the legal offices, and
the stores and market—diffuses the focus of social, political, and
economic control. But Oruro would not have developed if it were
not for the mines and the wealth that permitted these secondary
operations. The mines that were opened by the Inca in pre-
conquest times in Paria and Sica Sica drew the Spaniards, who discovered the nearby San José silver mines in 1595. The purpose of

establishing the town (called Villa de San Felipe de Austria) in 1606 was "to draw together some of the Indians who live in the surrounding valleys and *sitios*" and "to bring to them the doctrine" (Archivo de la Municipalidad 1606). The importance of regularizing the labor force made it imperative that "churches should be established first, and the rest necessary for a well-ordered republic." The first Spaniards to exploit the mines, Diego y Francisco de Medrana and his brother Juan, were forced to rely on wage-workers rather than forced labor because of the scarcity of local productions. They attracted workers from Salinas, Berenguela, Pacajes, Sicasica, and even Potosí by raising wages from four to five reales. Mining reached a peak of operation in the colonial period in the years 1678 and 1679, with 32 large mines and 258 small mines operating. After Independence, in the year 1877, all the mines of the area passed into the control of a central mining concern, the Companía Minera de Oruro. As the hub of a transportation network that included both rail and highway transport in addition to telegraph and telephone lines in later years, Oruro maintained its central position in the mining network even when the mineral content of its own ores was declining. Oruro's position as a center for other mines of the department of Oruro was assured when Simon Patiño opened the pre-concentration plant in Machacamarca at a few kilometers' distance. Rail lines brought in the tin from Catavi–Siglo XX, Uncía, and Hochschild's mine in Huanuni.

The Oruro mines were able to weather the transition from silver to tin at the turn of the twentieth century because of good deposits left behind in the earlier extraction. In 1910 Blanco (1910) reported a production rate of 250,000 metric tons of silver and U.S. $115,000 for tin in San José with employment of five hundred workers. The mines continued in operation until 1946, absorbing the shift from silver to tin. In that year the mineral content dropped to 1.69 percent, and it was no longer commercially feasible for the Companía Minera de Oruro to continue exploitation. In order to avoid unemployment, the government took over the mine and operated it under the Banco Minero de Bolivia, until in 1952 it was nationalized under COMIBOL (Aguirre Zeballos 1959). The mineral extracted today is a complex of tin, silver, copper, lead, and gold.

The oldest of Oruro's mines in the hill called Pié de Gallo (Foot of the Cock), rising on the western flank of the town, is now closed. A church and paved plaza, constructed at the entrance of the old mine, are the setting for the cult of the Virgin of the Mineshaft, to whom the Carnival is dedicated. Each mine entrance is surrounded by its own encampment of workers, but recently many workers have chosen to move into town to be near the stores, market, and entertainment offered by the city. The most isolated of the encampments, Itos, is partially abandoned since the entry of the army in 1965 (see chapter 8).

Social Services in the Mines

The Company Store

Mining encampments are, by virtue of their geographical location and their social organization, paternalistic settings. Because of their isolation from settlements based on farming or pastoralism, they are dependent on supply lines that extend far away, often into foreign supply centers. Building supplies, furniture, all of the amenities of life have to be brought into the community from outside. This is true even of Oruro, which is a large urban area with a developed commercial section. Since the fifties, a persistent drought has limited harvests even more narrowly than the short growing season permitted in the past, and only a few villages subsisting on quinua and herds of llamas, goats, and sheep provide agricultural products for the city. In some of the more remote mines, the pulpería is the unique supply center for basic necessities, and the few vendors that come to the encampments are not regular suppliers. Even in Oruro, where the urban center provides competitive supply sources, the miners depend on the company store for the four basic necessities: flour, rice, meat, and sugar.

The pulpería is a social center and meeting place for the women of the encampment. When the fresh meat supplies come in, women get up as early as three or four in the morning to come stand in line in order to purchase the limited supplies sold at the reduced rate. There is strict recognition of order of arrival: the first to arrive may return home before the store opens to do errands, but her companion will hold her place in line. Some of the mines have a ration card to control the purchase of the price-controlled basic necessities according to family size, but this was not the case in Oruro. It is on these waiting lines that the women get together to discuss their problems. The protest that led to a major strike in Siglo XX began with the women in the pulpería, an event dramatized in Sanjines' film, "Courage of the People." The walls of the pulpería are lettered with the initials of parties and federations, slogans and battle cries.

The pulpería is the very center of the crunch between diminishing wages and rising prices. It is the source of the vulnerability for both management and labor. On the one hand, the administration can never provide the necessary quality and amount of supplies, and in operating the company store it opens itself to a constant attack by the workers, who sense the double exploitation as consumers and as producers. On the other hand, by accepting dependency on the pulpería because of its lower price policy on the basic necessities, workers lay themselves open to being overcharged on all other items.[2] Furthermore, when the workers call a strike, the company can break it within a week by stationing the army in the pulpería and cutting off all supplies, as they have done on numerous occasions. Without the pulpería, the small private dealers and the cooperative action of the women, who on occasions have risen to the need during strikes and expanded their own marketing activities, would come into action. The union not only failed to mobilize these energies when there was an opportunity during the Paz Estenssoro period, but also defeated the women's cooperative in Siglo XX after the crisis of the strike was over.

Housing

Since most of the workers are uprooted populations, they require housing supplied by the administration. Miners have a strong preference for being near the work site because of the long hours and difficulty in transportation. The administration provides housing for 753 workers, 566 units of which are within the mining encampment. Housing ranged from the old row houses, called *casas blancas*, 52 of which were being repaired and 179 in the process of being replaced, to new units with four and five small rooms instead of the old one-room row unit. The new housing was allocated to

---

[2] Valdivieso, Sanjines, and Brown (1965) point to the distortion caused by the pulpería in Colquiri.

ROW HOUSES CONSTRUCTED IN THE TIME OF THE TIN BARONS
PROVIDE CRAMPED, SINGLE ROOMS IN WHICH TWO OR MORE
MINERS' FAMILIES OFTEN LIVED. THESE LIVING QUARTERS IN THE
ENCAMPMENT OF SAN JOSÉ HAVE BEEN INCREASED TO TWO ROOMS
FOR A FAMILY AS THE WORK FORCE WAS CUT DOWN.

former inhabitants of the old units who were good workers and had
large families. Separate encampments in Colorado and Itos mines
included 25 and 161 of the old units respectively, with 75 unoccupied since the military invasion of the mines in 1965. Both new
and old units lack any plumbing or sanitary facilities or even a po-
table water supply. Dust and garbage mingle on the bare ground
surrounding the mine buildings, rising up in swirls as the harsh
winds of autumn and winter increase in the late afternoon.[3]

The tightly packed settlement requires rigid rules to control individual usage of communal facilities. Water is limited and controlled, with a ticket permitting eight 16-liter cans of water to each

[3] For years, mining inspectors for the national Ministry of Mines repeated the
same criticisms of housing in the San José mines: complete lack of hygienic facilities,
lack of light, ventilation, patio in which to raise animals with the result that these
enter into the house, air pollution in kitchens that lack chimneys and flues, lack of
pure water, etc. Most of these same criticisms can be made even of the new construc-
tions, which lack plumbing, water, and adequate yard space. Depopulation of the
mines has meant that the problem of crowding is not as acute, and there are no
longer cases of multiple family units living in the same room.

family a day. Electric light is controlled by hours: 5:00 A.M. to 7:00 P.M. on weekdays, and noon to 1:30 P.M. on Sundays.

The only restrictions on commercial activities are those put on the sale of liquor and on prostitution, but both exist with the payment of strategic dispensation of these services and goods as gifts when the threat of expulsion occurs. Women, usually widows of miners with no other source of income, ferment the popular chicha beer and sell it, often laced with liquor. Since there is little pressure on housing now with the reduction of the work force, widows are allowed to stay in the encampment after the death of the worker. This avoids one of the cruel spectacles of the old private mines, when the family of a recently dead worker, often an accident victim, was forced to find alternative living accomodations shortly after the death. Neighbors often justify the continued residence of relatives of former workers, saying, "She has a right to be here: her husband left his lungs in the mine." The sense of the direct relationship between the job and the right to live in the encampment was best expressed by a miner's wife who said to me, referring to their house: "My husband lends his lungs to the company and they lend us this house."

In the old row houses, the immediate contact of neighbors leads to a forced cooperation and a sharing of misery as well as the joys of family life. Before the introduction of vaccines, contagious diseases spread through the rows of housing in almost a chain reaction. This supported the belief in Lari Lari, a malignant spirit believed to bring illness to children who was said to lurk on the rooftops. There are few secrets that can be contained within families; neighbors can hear almost all conversations carried on in a normal voice, and the disputes between husband and wife are immediately communicated. When a worker is fired, neighbors share their own food because, as one woman told me when her neighbors were left in this condition, "We could not bear the sound of the children crying with hunger at night." Family celebrations are an open house for the neighbors; the mass for a dead member of the family, the offering of food given to whoever passed by to enter and pray for the past members of the household on the occasion of Todos los Santos, the chicken piquante eaten on Christmas Eve or New Year's shared with neighbors who had been named compadres—all these oc-

casions serve to knit together in a set of constantly renewed reciprocal relations those who work and live together. This web of neighborhood exchanges is made formally explicit at the time of the
pasamanku, when the family that has borne the expenses of a fiesta
for a saint venerated in the neighborhood hands over the fiesta to
one who has accepted the charge for the incoming year. All the
neighbors gather to share the food and drink and dance to the live
music contracted for the occasion. On the last day of the fiesta, the
entire party bids goodbye to the saint in the house of the *pasante*
and dances in a line to the house of the receiving pasante, and there
everyone is locked in from midnight to the following day. This celebration epitomizes the sense of necessary cooperation and integration enjoining members of the community.

SOME WORKERS BUY
HOUSES IN THE BARRIOS
OF THE CITY OF ORURO
TO PROVIDE MORE
SECURITY FOR THEIR
FAMILIES.

Surrounding the company housing are the *barrios mineros* composed of houses bought by miners through the Cooperación Nacional de Viviendas, or housing cooperative. The barrios are outside the control of the mining administration. The first cooperative for housing in San José was promoted by the secretary of the union shortly after the revolution of 1952. The first of these units had a lot valued at B $3,000 and houses valued at B $2,200. The new occupants built their own walls, which were an increasingly important mark of the individualism cultivated in these neighborhoods in comparison with the encampment. The monthly cost of purchase was set at B $30, and when rented, they usually commanded a price of B $50.

Each of the barrios is named for one of the nearby mines in the department where blocks of housing were sold to workers from the same mine, mainly for retirement. This reinforces the neighborhood solidarity developed over years in the encampment where the workers lived in their productive years.

The mine management now prefers that the workers find housing on their own, partly because of the pressure for improved conditions and partly because of the increased administrative burden the management of company housing imposes. For this reason, they have provided a bus line that operates free of charge to take workers from the town center to the work site. In addition, they give a flat B $50 for housing for those who do not live in the encampment. Workers seem to be more aware of the crippling dependency of relying on company housing than they are in the case of the pulpería, and they have been alert to finding their own housing. This would, of course, lessen the community integration that is the basis for solidarity.

The dialectical relationship between dependency on the company and the sense of community that arises among those who consider themselves victims of a shared experience cannot be resolved by any simple solution. At this time, it is quite evident that the company gains by divesting itself of the "social benefits" of a paternalistically organized company policy with regard to housing and stores. These become a target for criticism uniting the workers in their opposition to the company. Even when they are well organized, these services are a constant reminder of paternalistic attitudes and relationships. Combined with the high unemployment rates and the lack of alternative jobs, the management has no need to use these attractions to gain workers.

Education, Health, and Social Welfare

Education

The social benefits won through the labor struggles of the twenties to the revolution of 1952 tie workers to the mines more effectively than the wage alone could do. Mine schools are considered by worker and townspeople to be superior to most public schools, especially those in rural districts. San José mine has eighteen grades, from pre-primary to fifth grade, with over 800 children. In 1970 there were 437 boys and 366 girls under the supervision of twenty-five teachers, fourteen of whom were women and eleven men. In addition to these regular teachers, over half of whom have a normal-school education or are working for a degree, there is a specialist in manual work for boys and for girls, a music teacher, and two physical education teachers who have twelve years of education. Their base pay of B $600 is almost twice the base salary for miners, although some contract workers are able to earn as much. A director and a secretary take charge of the administrative duties of the school.

The schools give milk and bread four times a week to the children. Teachers claim that the children, especially those of underground workers, are sent to school unfed and ill-kempt. Although the teachers all insisted that they noted a definite difference in the alertness, competence, and appearance of the children of mine workers and those of the office workers, I was not able to note this in my observation of classroom behavior. The teachers are possibly transferring their attitude toward parents to the children. The Parent-Teachers Association, they claim, is marked by the absence of parents who work inside the mine. Workers have told me of their own personal sacrifices to send their children to school, and of the contributions made by work groups to the school equipment, especially in the surge of enthusiasm after the revolution.

Teacher-student relationships are authoritarian and tend to inhibit original or expressive behavior. This conclusion is based on six hours of observation in the mine school and the John F. Kennedy school, an adjunct to the main educational facilities in the mine barrio (see Appendix).

The discrimination against the children of interior workers becomes acute in the distribution of scholarships for higher education. Miners feel strongly about the scholarships because, as they put it, the only inheritance they can offer their children is a higher education. San José mine gives only eight scholarships, and of these, only one to the child of an interior worker. Raul spoke bitterly of these scholarships:

◈ COMIBOL gives these scholarships with the money that the workers produce, but they do not conform to the national reform that called for help for the workers. Some of those who have received scholarships turn against the workers and try to throw us out of the courses in advanced studies. This ought not to happen; on the contrary, they ought to come and teach the workers. This happened to Doctor——, who received his lawyer's title with our money. . . . When the students are in the university, they share their ideas with the workers and sign pacts with them. I guess that they are just trying to gain a political position within the union movement and the moment that they go out, they lose all this. They come out with prestige and they can go into the political parties or direct a union. Once they get out of school, they forget the worker. They only take advantage of the weakness of the workers.

Up until World War II, even a primary school education assured a person of a job other than that of a miner. The very fact that workers won the right to free primary education minimized the opportunities that were available. In 1970 workers' children who had twelve years of education and in some cases one or more years in the university had no other opportunity than to follow their parents in the mine. The fact that their father or their mother had "given their lungs to the company" gave them a claim on a job, and the overweighting of surface-level workers meant that increasingly the only work available was in the interior.

Health Care

Another of the benefits provided the workers is hospitalization and medical services not only for the worker but for the family members. For the most part, mine hospitals and the doctors associated with the mine are considered superior to those available in most towns, and there is not even a comparative base for the campesinos, who have no more than herbal practitioners to care for their illnesses. Raul, who commented on the schools above, complained of the medical practitioners by whom they were treated:

✧ COMIBOL contracts with doctors who do not specialize in the body of mine workers. A miner will go, for example, and say, "Doctor, some part of my body aches," indicating where, and the doctor says, "What could it be? First I have to look in my book." So he isn't a good doctor. This often happens with the doctors and it is a calamity what happens. COMIBOL does a favor to the professionals, handing over the workers to them like meat, like lard, for them to go study at their pleasure. When one deals with a sickness like silicosis, there is no cure for that. Thanks to COMIBOL and other companies, silicosis is an inheritance that one has to bear for all time, for all one's life. In the university the students do not specialize but just study general medicine. A doctor who comes out of the university is a kind of encyclopedia who is trained to cure any sickness, and then only in his place of work does he learn of the special sicknesses. I want to tell you what happened in Siglo XX and Catavi. They couldn't cure the working masses because they were opposed to those sectors. They even poisoned them with their drugs and injections. Overnight the workers would die. The ventilators they have in levels four-eighty-one, five-sixteen, and five-eighty-six aren't sufficient to handle the dust. In the Number Seven Block it is permanently black. You can't even see light up to ten meters because the air is so heavy. . . . It is very possible that the doctors are compromised with COMIBOL to avoid giving the workers a series of social benefits, because in the social security office they grant compensation in accord with the degree of the silicosis.

Distrust of the doctors is widespread, particularly among the pensioned workers. There is the suspicion that they receive inferior drugs, and even worse, lethal doses of oxygen with the injections so that they will be removed from the sick rolls permanently. They look on the bronchial-pneumonia hospital as a morgue and try to avoid being sent there.

Social Security

Bolivian workers point out that their social security law is one of the most advanced of South America, but the actual benefits are often not forthcoming. The first retirement compensation was the Sistema de Compilación de Maldonado, passed in 1905. In 1938 Busch increased coverage to other sectors of municipal workers. The code was revised after World War II, first with changes advised by United States adviser MacGruder and then by Dr. Emil Schombaum of the United Nations in 1948. Social security was mandatory for most sectors in 1949, and following the 1952 revolution it was extended to the entire republic.

The miners were the first to gain accident security in 1924 during the presidency of Bautista Saavedra, but there were no accident pensions until 1956. Since then there have just been fill-ins in the law to make it easier to interpret. For example, if a worker was unhappy with the settlement of his case, he could go on to the supreme court to make a settlement. The loopholes for managers enabling them to avoid compensating workers were eliminated. Formerly, the worker did not receive compensation for an accident, if it were proven that he was drunk or that the accident was the result of an event such as a flood or landslide which could not be blamed on the owner. Formerly the code listed occupational diseases for which the worker could receive compensation, but this was changed to a listing of the agents, such as gas or landslide, which caused the illness or death. The current law covers all workers for sickeness, maternity, professional risk, invalidism, old age pensions, and death.

Despite the liberal social security law, most workers are dissatisfied because of delays in receiving their benefits. In Oruro, the *rentistas*, or pensioned workers, of whom there are over 4,000, frequently are forced into demonstrations such as a hunger strike or invasion of a public office in order to gain the compensation due to them. At one of the regional centers for dispensing pensions, workers come from all over the department to receive their payment, and when it is not forthcoming they must sleep in the cold parks or scrounge for food. As a result of frequent past failures to get their payments on time, pensioned workers are organized in a union with a representative who is a full-time paid agent for his clients.

On one occasion when the pensioners were delayed for three days, I saw over 200 restless men and women lined up in the partially constructed hospital which was to have been a haven for sick workers and turned out to be temporary quarters for the social security disbursement. I spoke with a few of the workers.

Florentino came from Catavi for his retirement pay. He was a hand driller and got the professional disease after working in the mine for twenty-eight years. He had been receiving the pension for ten years and commented that formerly, during the time of the private mines, it was easier to get compensation for disease. "Now it is like asking for charity," he said. "There is no pulpería for the retired. Everything about the way they handle payments is abnormal." I asked him how he would solve things, and he said that there was no solution. I asked if the union leader was helpful, and he reported, "He only robs from us in the discount of one peso each month."

The widow of a miner said, "We who have nothing but the miserable pensions that our husbands left when they died, never received any help from charities. The *ricachos* don't let us get to the goods. Las Caritas [the Catholic charity] only serves the padres."

A man joined the conversation, saying, "I'd like to see the United States give tools, machines, so that we could farm. We are losing our morale with this treatment of us like animals." I asked him if there were any mines where the conditions were better for the pensioned workers, and he replied, "They throw out the people in all of them without giving any compensation. People used to complain to the government, but they have given up." Another man took up the same theme, saying, "We would like to have land and work it, but we can't do anything here without irrigation." This man had worked twenty years in the mine and left voluntarily. He received B $150 a month on which he supported three children.

A widow nearby said that she received B $72 and that after paying a rent of B $30 she had to work washing clothes to pay for the food.

The secretary general of the sindicato came on the scene and climbed up on a pile of gravel to tell the waiting rentistas that he had consulted the commissioner of pensions and that he was going to put money in the *caja* [social security office] immediately. He said that it was not just a question of Oruro, but that the office was not able to pay anywhere. He kept insisting that it was not a question of negligence on his part or that of the union, but was due to the change of officials in La Paz. The new commissioner was not yet fully introduced into office, and the central bank was waiting for the key to open the deposit. As he left he said, "I am going to my office. I don't want to make any enemies and I don't want to prejudice anyone." When he saw some of the pensioners making threatening gestures, he invited them to go with him.

The delays caused by bureaucratic inefficiency as well as the inability to make payments because of the raids the military and the government make on the social security funds have tragic consequences for workers who have no margin of security. I was in close contact with Juan after he had been diagnosed as 100 percent incapacitated in 1968 and had not received his compensation in 1970. He was working seven days a week as a night watchman in order to make a bare living for his family of eight. He described his visit to the caja in 1968:

> ❖ The director told me to wait a month and I would get my disability. I told the director, "I have paid my quota monthly. I left my youth in the mine working for my country. My life is playing with death." The director simply responded, "We do not have any authority to send you your pension. You have to continue working." Each month I take the trip to La Paz to learn that nothing has arrived. I am caught in the bureaucracy of the caja. If I don't get the pension, I won't be able to keep my son in college.

When Juan started his suit for his pension, he was told that he would get three months of salary without work, but this was stopped and the pension was not forthcoming. He had to go back to the company begging for work. Two of his friends who left work at the same time had not received their social security, nor had they been able to get work because that would ruin their chances of getting the pension. One of these men, Emilio, was without a salary since he left work in 1968 in order to get a lump-sum payment to send his son to college. He had not received any money since then. His wife was working in the neighboring department of Cochabamba selling food, and he helped her. He had 100 percent disability. The other, Maximo, left work in 1968 with 100 percent disability. He was making and selling chicha, and worked occasionally in a small mine. Juan said that up until the time of the military leader Barrientos the workers used to receive their checks within three months of their retirement.

I visited the caja and sat with workers waiting to be served in the reception hall. One woman broke into tears about her poverty when she was turned away again at the director's office. The secretary treated an older couple with the utmost contempt, calling them "hijos" and not even trying to conceal the irritation in her tone. Repeated medical examinations to confirm what has already been diagnosed, trips that expend the energies and the meager financial resources of the workers seeking compensation, loss of documents out of inefficiency or deliberate attempts to delay the case are the lot of the workers seeking their legal claims. A miner with 100 percent silicosis told of his fifth medical examination:

❖ I traveled up to La Paz on Monday. The director of social security sent us to the clinic. They took blood from our veins. They made us run after they took the blood and then breathe into a tube from the mouth with the nose stopped up. I almost fainted and saw stars. Then they made us go without food until two in the afternoon. Afterwards, in the office of COMIBOL, I said, "I only want to know what degree it is." They said, "We cannot say. The caja has to say." In the caja they told me, "This afternoon we will go over all the data." But they never told me. They don't want to advise us, nor does COMIBOL. COMIBOL pays the doctors to say we have less. But it costs too much to go to a private doctor. Here the caja waits until you die to pay.

The rentista, or pensioned worker, is a specter to the miner of what he will be in the short span of productive time accorded to underground workers. Their problems are given attention during national meetings. One of the main demands made during the national congress of the Federation of Mine Workers' Unions (FSTMB) in April 1970 was for an independent social security board to avoid the raids made on miners' social security funds by other workers and employees. A commentary by one of the delegates to the congress expresses the sentiments of the miners toward the caja:

COMIBOL, is, let us say, the fountain of enrichment for other organizations and other institutions, particularly political ones, and COMIBOL manages the caja with political ends. Therefore, what has happened to COMIBOL also influences the caja, which serves as a bank for the government and its propagandists, who go there for their own motives. They have created a series of measures cutting off payments to our comrade pensioners. One of these is to set the pension on the basis of twelve months of income rather than the average of the past three months of work, and this is always a lower rate. We ought to call for the autonomy of the caja for the mining industry. The miner carries the greater burden of the caja because he pays his quota on the basis of his whole income while the teachers and other public employees pay on the basis of only a part.

Another delegate picked up the argument for an autonomous caja, adding that the presidents are named by the minister of work based on political favoritism and are consequently not responsive to the needs of workers.

Each of these presidents has his own favored *camarilla,* [cohort] and this camarilla comes to work for the caja. When the government changes, another comes in with his camarilla and so it goes on, accumulating a mountain of bureaucratic people in the caja. With the creation of an autonomous caja minera they ought to bring in miners. When I called for this in 1965, the FSTMB rejected the idea, but now people see that I was right.

The complaints of the miners against the caja were summarized in the social commission at the 14th congress of the FSTMB:

Fourteen years have passed since the promulgation of the Social Security Code and the organization of the caja. In the passage of this time, the mine workers have been able to observe a complete distortion of the fundamental provisions of this institution, which ought to protect the workers and their families. This is so because since its creation the Caja Nacional de Seguridad Social has been managed with a political bias. Far from signifying a hierarchy for the social stability of the family of the insured, it has been transformed into a gigantic farce, bureaucratic and unmanageable for lack of a technical plan in its organization and a scarcity of scientific focus in the operation of this entity. Today, the living experience of the children of the pensioned comrades who walk in the streets in search of their daily sustenance because the allowance isn't enough to feed them or for minimal necessities shows us the incompetence and lack of feeling for those whom they should serve. To what has already been noted we ought to summarize other reasons which underwrite the clarification of our proposal:

1. The miners are charged on the basis of total earnings to support the national social security, while other working class sectors such as the factory workers are charged on the basis of basic earnings, benefiting over the extra percentage we bring in.

2. Because of the agreement between the caja and COMIBOL and

the FSTMB, the miners should support only 5 percent, but since 1968 they have supported it with 7.5 percent. . . .

3. Constant influx into the caja of workers who are not charged even though they receive its benefits.

4. The excessive bureaucratic plant and the monuments raised prejudicing the building of complementary cajas for different sectors of the affiliated workers.

The demands that flowed from these complaints were for an independent caja for workers, concerned with the illnesses of workers and with control exercised in administration by miners.

In the course of nationalization and revolutionary reforms, social services for the mining communities were increasingly taken over by national agencies created as a response to demands formulated by workers in the years of labor struggles prior to the revolution of April 1952. The growth of the middle class bureaucracy that served in professional capacities the roles miners used to perform for themselves, and the decline in the services offered, became the source of a new alienation from the administration of the mines and the government. The revolution caused the workers to see these benefits in health, education, and social security as rights, not gifts of the *patrón*, but their increasing dissatisfaction with the quality of services offered and the disillusionment with the opportunities for them within the system negated the gains made on paper. Summarizing the gains and losses of the nationalization process in the 14th congress of the FSTMB, they reveal their own awareness that the mining administration improved the position of the middle class who came in professional capacities to serve the mining community and became a parasitical burden on the productive workers.

Games, Sports, and Diversions

Children's games reflect, more than the leisure-time activities of the adults, the patterns of small groups within the encampment. The favored games are soccer, basketball, marbles, hopscotch, and jumprope. The children fashion their own toys out of the refuse thrown on the margins of the slag pile: vehicles made of sardine cans that roll on used batteries, box carts, and beanbags. Mutilated dolls pass on from hand to hand until they are thrown out with the refuse, only to be rescued by other children who will adopt them.

Young people tell me that in their childhood they played more team games than presently. One song-dance described to me that used to be popular in the thirties and forties and that is now disappearing may be a holdover from competitive rivalry between segmented districts of the encampment. A line of boys approaches an opposite line of girls singing: "Buenos días, mi señorita, mandundirum," and the other line responds: "What do you want, mi señorito, mandundiru dirundan?" To which the first replies, "I want one of your daughters, mandundirundan" and the girls reply, "which of them do you want mandundirundan?"

The reply comes in choruses explicating the virtues of the chosen daughter, for beauty, grace, etc. One young man said that the children didn't play this game because of embarrassment or self-consciousness that prevented group play.

Another kind of game that was frequently played during the forties was based on cowboy and World War II pictures exported by the United States. The winner of a game of chance based on colored dried beans determined who would be on the winning cowboy side since, as was predetermined in the film script, the cowboys always had to win. World War II games were favored by the children in the fifties, as one young man explained:

❖ Then there were the pictures on the second world war, this was what we liked to play best. We always wanted to be on the side of the *chinos* [inclusive term for all Asians]. In the battles the Americans always won, and so we always played it that way. [I asked him why, since the Americans always won, the children always wanted to identify with the chinos and he replied as follows:] I believe that it could be related to politics, no? But what politics can children have? A few liked to be Americans because their uniforms were attractive and the armaments were good, while the chinos had large rifles with bayonets and their helmets were not well adjusted to their heads. Their boots were not even the same as those of the Americans. Nevertheless everyone wanted to be chino, although nobody knew even what class of chinos they were, whether Japanese or what. They didn't know who American soldiers were nor from whence they came. They only played for the fun of it.

With remarkable dexterity and an authenticity of detail, these Third World children fashioned weapons used in the wars of First World nations portrayed on screen, keeping pace with technological advances from arrows to rifles to machine guns. The sound effects they produced in their play were equally authentic, from the *fiuuu, fiuuu* of arrows to the *ban, ban* of pistols and the *tataratata-a-a-a-a* of the machine gun.

Soccer teams are an expression of the segmentation of social groups in the mining community as well as an exhibition of the overall solidarity of the work force. Each major level of the mines forms a team which plays competitive matches in the encampment of San José and Itos. The best of these players make up the first-string team that plays against other mines and in national competitions. The nationalized mine company, recognizing the importance of the game not only for much needed distractions in the isolated mining communities but also to reinforce the image of COMIBOL as a national enterprise, hires good ball players who have a nominal job in the mine but who are released for games and practice. Some of the underground workers are considered to be as good players as these stars, and in San José the five best players are said to be carters. The entire population of the encampment attends the big matches with outside mines. During the play, workers have an opportunity to vent their hostility not only against the visiting team but also against certain of the less liked administrative staff, who might get hit in the cross-fire of refuse thrown, supposedly, at the field to express disgust with the visitors.

The players gain industry-wide recognition for their feats on the soccer field, and this can contribute toward a political and union leadership position. Juan Lechín Oquenda was at one time a soccer goalie and became well known before his rise to eminence as the leading figure in the union movement.

It is perhaps obvious, but nonetheless important, to point out that the sports activities reinforce the solidarity of male groups in the mining communities while women participate as spectators only, except possibly as madrinas of the team, a status gained by contributing some of the equipment to the players on request. It is another way in which male leadership is sponsored and consolidated in the male-dominated mining communities. Women participate enthusiastically in volleyball, but team play is otherwise absent in their school or postschool life, and none of their team play allows them to travel to other mining camps and become figures in the wider political and social setting.

Golf, billiards, and sometimes bowling are available in some of the social centers of mining camps, but the charges were prohibitive to underground workers and these sports were patronized almost exclusively by employees and technicians. Films and radio are the almost exclusive diversions available for ordinary workers, since in the larger mines isolated from the city anyone can enter with a monthly fee subtracted from the worker's paycheck. Most of the films shown when I lived in Bolivia were from the United States. In the case of export films, as in the case of currency, bad films drive out the good, and those from dominant nations drive out those of local provenance. Bolivian film-makers have made a few films in the postwar period, but neither these nor the films made in other Latin American countries could compete with U.S. films because of the distribution system. Radio, however, broke the monopoly of foreign cultural expression when the workers themselves operated radio stations in the major mining centers from the early days of the revolution of 1952 until the fall of the mines to the military in 1965. In addition to broadcasting news of the mines, sports events, and national news, there were many amateur programs that gave an opportunity for musicians, singers, and reciters of poetry to find expression for their talents. Manuel, who worked in Itos throughout the time of the MNR, spoke as follows about the programs:

❖ Well, the program had to be something in relation to the miners, no? Since it came into the ether from the heart of tin—that's what it was called, "From the Heart of the Tin," a theatrical program.
[And what was the theme of the plays? I asked]
Precisely about the workers, how they ought to know the suffering and the sacrifice, and especially about the integration with the politics of Victor Paz Estenssoro, because everyone was for him then—not everyone, but they had to be.
[Did they have any stories that continued?]
Yes, they also had them, but I don't remember very much of that. They had many programs, especially the Day of the Miner, December twenty-first, in memory of the massacre of Siglo XX in 1942. They prepared many programs that day, and once they narrated "The Price of Tin," but they never finished it because there

were all these troubles.[4] They often had to post militia in the radio [station] to protect it.

[Was the line they took too strong?]

No, it wasn't for that. There were parties that attacked it, they used to come right up to the transmitters, and to avoid that, they used to station guards. If people came who were not workers, the guards interrogated them.

The first building to be seized in the military invasion of the mine in 1965 contained the radio transmitter, since this was the center of communication to mobilize the workers. For five years, the radios were silenced until Ovando's period as president was nearly terminated. The new transmitters were not as strong as the old, and the broadcasts, at least from San José, lacked the originality that characterized the old programs. The old stations, especially the "Voz de Minero" broadcast from Siglo XX–Catavi, had welded a single community of all the workers in nationalized mines and even those from the smaller mines within hearing distance.

The political significance of the radio was recognized not only by the political parties but also by the priests. The missionary priests arrived in Siglo XX about 1955. The first director of the mission, Father Line Grenier, recognized the significance of the "Voz de Minero," and thought that the best way to fight communism was to have a radio station. Radio "Emisoras Pio XII" was set up in competition with Radio "Voz de Minero" and broadcast in both Spanish and Quechua. A counterattack began on radio waves. Some workers threatened to attack Radio "Pio XII," and a guard was set up. "We tried to get the people to think for themselves," the young priest who was informing me about the radio station told me.

The young priest's feeling that the workers needed help to think for themselves is contradicted by Domitila Chungara, who was head of the housewives' association of the encampment.[5] When I asked her if Radio "Pio XII" was good, she replied:

[4] *The Price of Tin* is a novel by Nestor Taboada based on the massacre of December 21, 1942 (Taboada 1960).

[5] Domitila Chungara was invited to the Tribunal of the International Year of Women held by the United Nations in Mexico City in 1975 as a result of efforts made by myself and Elena Ladd, who featured her in her film, "The Double Day." There she met Moema Viezzer, who transcribed her taped autobiography, now published (Viezzer 1977).

❖ Yes, it is good, but I believe that all the organs of the press depend
on the people who operate them, since everyone thinks in accord
with how he lives. I think that sometimes it is in the service of
other than workers' interests, and sometimes it is in the service of
the pueblo. During the strike of 1964, Radio "Pio XII" even attacked the housewives' association, saying that it was bad. The
women had organized the association to protest to the managers
because they didn't pay the salaries here, and that is when they
turned against the workers.

According to this same woman, a mother of six, the children used
to enter with confidence into the station of "Voz de Minero" and
sing and play their instruments without inhibition, because they
were not made to feel inferior as they were in the radios of the town
centers or even in Radio "Pio XII." This is an important aspect of
socialization, and only when community control of the radio is effective will there be an opportunity for such self-expression.

In the resurgence of the mining movement after May 1970, the
executive committee of the FSTMB laid out a cultural plan for the
mines. The plan projected secondary schools for those mines that
lacked them, expansion of the radio network, courses in leadership
for union work, theater, chorus, plastic arts, film clubs, music and
social assistance (*Presencia,* January 26, 1971). Even before the formal plan was worked out, leadership courses were launched on
June 24, 1970 (the anniversary of the massacre of 1967) in Siglo XX,
and university professors gave lectures in other mine centers. Those
that I attended in the months of October and November in San José
were given at a high theoretical level, since the professors had
learned from experience to respect the intellectual capacity of the
workers. These plans, like the other expressions of community regeneration in the brief time in office of J. J. Torres, were left unful-
filled with the military coup of Colonel Hugo Banzer in August
1971.

Community Reciprocity and Exchange

The mining community depends on traditions inherited from
the rural ayllus, or kin-defined local groups that were the basis of
the pre-hispanic Quechua culture, for accumulating capital or mobilizing assistance. These include the aini, or reciprocal exchange,

and the pasanaku, a kind of lottery in which participants draw lots and distribute agreed-upon objects of sale.

The aini implies a sense of interest payment, since the person who lends money, goods, or services receives them twofold when they are returned. The time for reciprocation depends on the occasion of the gift and the relationship obtaining between the people entering into the exchange, and extends in time from a month to half a lifetime. Commonly, exchanges occur when a ceremony requires extra expenditures that cannot be met out of regular income, as on the occasion of weddings, accepting the fiesta of a saint, graduation, and funerals. For weddings, aini may be requested from a number of people for specific items such as the band or the liquor and may not be returned until the lender is engaged in a similar obligation, at which time the borrower is expected to give back double the amount. Usually this exchange occurs among close relatives, since the relationship is assumed to be life-long. When someone takes on the obligation of the fiesta for the saint, they take advantage of all the aini they have accumulated in the past to farm out various expenses for the bands, the chicha, the alcohol, items of food, and the cost of the banner which announces their patronage of the fiesta, usually drawing on neighborhood and compadrazgo ties as well as kin. If they farm out too many of these obligations, it detracts from the respect they gain for having contracted the obligation in the first place. One way of avoiding the onerous interest rates of the aini is to name certain padrinos of special features of the ceremony: there may be the padrino or madrina of the band, of the flowers, of the wedding rings, or of the cake. The payoff comes at the fiesta itself, when the padrinos are treated with special respect and attention. The problem comes about in judging the various weightings of the gifts against the givers, and giving the respectful attention expected to all the padrinos present.

The pasanaku operates as a kind of saving pool in which participants draw numbers to determine the order in which they will receive the money, furniture, basic supplies of flour, sugar, or rice, etc., for which they have contributed shares. The advantage comes in getting wholesale prices for items which are distributed in units of one. For example, a group of women might pool their money to buy cots: one of them who is accustomed to bargaining in the marketplace goes to a distributor and gets ten cots at a discount. Then each receives his or her bed at a saving of from 10 to 20 percent. Sometimes the woman in charge of the distribution on such large items gets a part of the profit, which is considered her due for her time in making her trip, paying in advance for her bus fare, and the charge for the items, as well as for her skill in bargaining with the vendors. In such cases, the pool serves to capitalize incipient entrepreneurship.

When money is the object of the lottery, the pasanaku operates as forced savings and the participants gain only in terms of the time of payment. Thus the person with the lowest number in the lottery gets the first disbursement of cash, and so on in order of the drawing number. Although only persons known to be responsible in their credit obligations are permitted to enter, there are no personal ties within the group and accounts are kept in order. A housewife spoke of her involvement as follows:

> ❖ I began to play with money the first time this year. I wanted to go to Copacabana on my husband's vacation for the fiesta of the Virgin. I had to give one hundred pesos each month in order to get the sum of a thousand pesos. In this, no one can fail, because if you fail, we are all ruined. One time in the concentration plant they played for fifteen hundred pesos, giving one hundred and fifty a month. Where do they get so much money? Here up above (in the *campamento*) they play with oil, rice, sugar, meat, and bread and even flour. We have to give our twenty kilos to enter the play. I don't remember the name of the nurse who handles this—it is on the tip of my tongue. We also play with sheets, mattresses, cots from Argentina—that is beautiful. But with that kind of merchandise the *pasanakera* earns a lot because she charges more than it is worth. She gets the overhead that a shop gains, since the sellers give her a better price for buying in lots. Also we do it with vegetables. We put in a peso, two pesos, three pesitos and then the pasanakera buys tomatoes, onions, squash, or whatever. For instance, let us say that there are ten of us, then one ought to divide it in ten heaps, including the person making the division. But they make eleven piles and the distributor takes two heaps, one for her and the other for her gains. Even the shop owners have their pasanakus in the name of the co-op. Sometimes we do it with shoes and make an agreement with the owner of the shop that ten pairs will be sold at his shop. Then when our number comes up,

we go to the shop and he sells them at the agreed-on price. Then
the person who has the lottery ticket goes to the shop and picks
out his shoes, as happily as though he had not paid for it because
it seems like a gift.

In both the case of the pasanaku and the aini, primary group controls operate as a selective mechanism determining entry and as a
kind of diffuse social control, but once the contract is made the behavior is characterized by segmenting it from other features of the
interpersonal relationship. In the case of the pasanaku, it is sufficient that one is a known member of the community with a reputation for being responsible in order to enter the pool, whereas in
the case of the aini the exchange is kinship, fictional kinship, or
neighborhood bonds. The sanctioning system relies on primary
group interrelationships: If any member fails, the sanction is exclusion from participation not only in future aini or pasanaku but also
extends to daily social intercourse, and ultimately the person is
forced by shame to leave the community, in the case of the pasanaku, or to break the initial social relationship, in the case of the
aini. The mining community thus shares a characteristic technique
of cooperation with other non-Western rural communities, i.e., explicit, socially sanctioned obligations embedded in primary group
affiliations.

The Housewives' Association

The special nature of the mining community cultivates a total
participation of all those who live and work in it, in part because of
the isolation and in part because everyone is directly or indirectly
dependent on the same enterprise. The rate of pay directly affects
men, women, and children. When there is a massacre, all are killed
without discrimination. As a result of the solidarity that grows in
such communities, women have formed a housewives' association
that has been active in demanding better food supplies and in defending the civil rights of men imprisoned for political activities.
Men and women have joined together to demand improvement of
their lot in economic and political action.

Because of its greater political mobilization, Siglo XX has a
greater history of women's involvement in protest than does Oruro.

CHOLA MARKET WOMEN ARE THE LINKS BETWEEN REGIONAL
MARKETS BRINGING THE FRUITS OF THE YUNGAS AND VEGETABLES
OF THE COCHABAMBA VALLEY ALONG WITH POTATOES OF THE
ALTIPLANO TO SELL IN THE CENTRAL MARKET OF ORURO.

In 1962 the wives of labor union leaders and other women of the encampment Cancañiri in Siglo XX mine entered into a hunger strike
called to protest the lockout of workers in a plan to "rationalize" the
working force. Domitila spoke to me of the movement in which she
took part:

❖ The housewives organized themselves because they did not pay
the salaries on time. The army came and imprisoned the union
leaders. Then all the workers declared a strike. Those women
whose husbands were in jail, the wives of Escobar and Pimentel,
went to get their husbands' liberty, but failed. They decided to
unite and make a solid front to ask for their liberty. The committee
went to La Paz and declared a hunger strike. Radio "Pio XII" cen-
sured the act because it was immoral—they said a person could
not declare a hunger strike because it was against God's law.

But the hunger strike was successful because they brought in the
food and pay and also their husbands. At first there were only
seventeen women in the strike, but it grew.

When the miners took European technicians as hostages in order
to back their demands, we women organized a twenty-four-hour
watch to protect them because the men had threatened to kill them
if the company did not respond to our petition. We thought that
that would give an excuse to the government to send in the army
for a massacre, and we wanted to prevent that.

The organization of housewives that grew out of the strike of 1962 faltered after the crisis was over. Domitila explained it to me as follows:

❖ The women hadn't yet arrived at a level of understanding among themselves and the organization declined in 1963 or 1964. They imprisoned or deported the husbands, and sometimes these men turned against the women. They told the women not to get mixed up in things. We organized the committee again in 1965 and it included both the women of the parish as well as of the encampment. The priest had tried to split the women of the parish from those of us in the encampment, but we overcame this. We used to have our meetings at the door of the pulpería. There were three or four hundred women that made demands, and we would elect a representative.

After the worst massacre in history took place in Siglo XX in 1967, taking the lives of over eighty-seven men, women and children, the housewives revived their organization. When the leader of this group, Domitila, spoke out against the massacre, ordered by Barrientos, she was imprisoned and her husband was fired from the mine and put on the blacklist. She spoke to me of these times:

❖ I have a deep rancor in my heart for all the outrages we have suffered. . . . Repression is very strong and the family suffers a great deal. It is precisely for this that I believe that I ought not to be quiet since we have suffered so much. I lost a child when they imprisoned me—I was pregnant at the time—from the abuses I received in jail. So for all these reasons there is a deep hatred in my heart. I cannot keep quiet. I do not want my children to live the same life I have lived. We feel for our children when they cry because of their decayed teeth, when we can't give them proper food. They must have a better life! Look at this room: in this room we have to prepare two beds right on the floor. There are from twelve to fifteen people sleeping here, children kicking off the blankets so we are never properly covered. We eat on short rations. I believe that the fundamental thing is to speak out for everyone. I don't like to be selfish. I do not want only the happiness for my children. I have seen the rest of the children suffering and I want all to be happy.

Although Domitila is unusual in her forthrightness about what she experienced, she expressed the sentiments of the majority of the women in the encampment. She was delegated by the housewives' association to speak at the inauguration of the 1970 Congress of the

FSTMB. As she spoke in the crowded union hall, where she was of
the very few members of her sex, the murmur of voices rose as the
men showed their lack of concern with woman's talk until she
spoke out as follows:

> ⋄ I echo all the widows in the massacres, those of September and of
> San Juan, when hundreds of children were orphaned. I asked that
> all the goods of General Barrientos be confiscated in order that the
> proceeds be used for the feeding of these children and the educa-
> tion of these children.
>
> All the delegates who have preceded me have referred to the
> problems of the working class; we also echo these because we are
> participants in the exploitation of our workers, of our husbands.
> We want this Congress to take certain means, always working in
> unity with all of the working class, to take the responsibility of the
> vanguard. And all of us are disposed to support the means which
> are developed in the Congress. Also, I want to echo the inhuman
> exploitation of the wives, mothers, and the children of workers of
> the slag pile, and I want to invite all of the delegates to visit such
> places of work and see with their own eyes the inhuman exploita-
> tion of these women.

The sense of exploitation expressed by Domitila and the plea for
unity in the struggles of the working class is not recognized by the
men. The union leaders not only failed to support the cooperative
organization the women formed to bring supplies into the community, an organization that might have helped break the workers'
dependency on the company store, but they were the first to order
their wives back to the kitchen. When the women were fired en
masse from the concentration pits in 1967, only one leader tried to
help them. It was through their own effort that the women of Siglo
XX won the right to work on the slag pile, but they were not contract workers and had none of the benefits of regular wage earners.

The housewives association in San José mine has not taken
nearly so militant a role as that in Cancañiri. While I was in Oruro,
they were being mobilized by the missionary priest with the assistance of the nuns in cooperative activities described below.

Community Development and the Church

The Catholic Church, whose genius for conforming and adjusting to social change at the margins, while maintaining the structure

and hierarchy of the establishment intact, is especially marked in the case of the mining communities. The colonial priests for the most part acted as an arm of Spanish imperialism in extending colonization and breaking down the resistance of the indigenous population to external control. The criolla administration in the Independence period tolerated the presence of exploitative priests in mining communities as long as it found the church useful in maintaining its own domination. The excesses of these priests, who had almost unchallenged control of remote communities, is summarized by Efraim, who began working in the mine when he was eight years old at the turn of the century (see chapter 2). "The priest said, 'Respect the owners!' " he told me and went on to exclaim, "How those priests deceived us! If one had to get married, needed a mass for the soul, they always got money. For that reason I was not baptized when I was born."

Following the revolution of 1952, few priests found any opportunity to extract their portion of the surplus value generated in the mines, and the parishes were left almost abandoned. In the middle fifties, missionary priests and nuns were sent from Canada, France, and the United States. These young, zealous missionaries rejected the trappings of the church and tried to deal directly with the souls and consciousness of the people. Often children of proletarian families, these priests identified with the miners and wanted to share their way of life.

I spoke on several occasions with a priest born of a poor Irish family in Massachusetts. His theory of community development was to work directly within established communities, finding useful roles for himself and the nuns that were acceptable to the people. He contrasted the new thinking with the past, when priests created an artificial community by drawing people into the church. He, like many of the young priests of his generation, was inspired by the papal encyclical of 1967, which pointed to the new direction that missionary work took throughout the world. This often meant taking a stand against political powers, all the way from local *prefecturas,* or governors, to the president. President Ovando found the clerical opposition to the increasing reactionary trend of his government so intolerable that he had several priests expelled in 1970.

The priest in San José attempted to divest his role of supernatural affect and relate directly with men both in his sermons and in his behavior. On the day of the Patrón de Compadres he held a mass in level zero of Itos mine, and in his sermon he said that the working man who sacrifices himself in his work to bring home his pay to his family is as much a servant of God as he. Except in the mass, he wore ordinary clothing and rode a bicycle on most of his parish visits. Like other priests and nuns in the Oblato order, he learned Quechua and translated hymns into the native language for the mass.

The new image of the priest emerged with striking effect during the Congress of the Federation of Mine Workers Unions in April 1970 in Siglo XX–Catavi mines. The priests held a mass for the martyred union hero, Federico Escobar, the man who was feared by the nationalized mine administration in the early part of the sixties. The earlier fight between Oblatos, who had come to Siglo XX to oppose the "communistic" tendencies of the mine in 1957, was forgotten as the priests offered the mass in an impressive open-air ceremony. Following the mass, the priest divested themselves of their priestly garments, acting out the principle that they were the same as other men when they completed the mass, and walked with the workers in the procession to the graveyard.

Miners accept the alliance with the priests in their everyday labor struggles, and they appreciate the new attempts to identify with the workers, but as one union leader said at a meeting: "We will work along with them as long as they oppose the enemies of the working class. But when we all die, they will go to sit on the right-hand side of God, and we will go to Hell where we belong." It is, so far, a temporal alliance, and one that does not commit the workers, as they see it, to an acceptance of church ideology and church-controlled behavior.

In addition to carrying out religious services, the priests and nuns of the mission have organized a clinic for the sick of the poor barrios and a credit union. They have helped the people organize a housewives' group and a youth group in an attempt to overcome some of the problems of a growing number of unemployed youths with few outlets for diversion.

Internal and External Definition
of the Community

The mining industry defines the size, the location, the extent, and time schedules of the workers. There seems to be little room for self-definition by members of the community. However, by drawing on pre-conquest cultural roots, tempered by the massive cultural offensive of the Spanish colonial period and elaborated by the scraps of technology and organization acquired from modern introductions, the workers have fashioned a way of life that enables them to defend themselves in the wider society and provide meaning and interest to both young and old members of the community. The workers are alienated from the social relations defining them as subordinates in the hierarchy of the mining administration, but they are not culturally or socially alienated in the community they have created. This is important in providing them with the strength to resist cooptation and personal dehumanization from those who exploit their labor and try to rule their lives.

Following the 1952 revolution, there was a brief period of cultural and social development in the mining communities. The radio, the expanded sports program, the enlarged educational opportunities all provided new avenues for self-expression. Until 1964 the union was the main channel for the energies that were released. However, the creeping bureaucracy of the national mining enterprise gradually took over worker control of these outlets. The gains of the revolution in health, education, and welfare were real gains in the objective conditions of life, but since they often served to squelch the initiative of workers and to put them down and convince them of their inferiority at the very site where the service was offered, the workers turned against them. The combined efforts of the Office of Industrial Relations, with its corps of social workers trained to teach the workers how to live "in a civilized manner," the teachers who instilled a sense of inferiority in the children of underground workers, and even the missionary priests, who tried to reach out to where the people were and raise their sensibilities, but always in a vision of a better world defined by the church, served to sap their self-esteem, their ability to define their self-interests for themselves and their talents in projecting themselves beyond their immediate circumstances. For those who resisted conforming to the mold of the dominant class, there were the military police whom Barrientos sent into the mines to spy, to share in the earning of the jucos, and to carry off union leaders who continued to struggle underground. These police spies and undercover agents were under the orders of the Departamento de Investigaciones Criminales, whose senior officers were trained in some cases in United States universities and received advice from CIA agents in the arts of counterinsurgency and cooptation of leaders.[6]

The attempt made by workers in the 14th Congress of the Federation of Mine Unions in 1970 to reorganize the trade union movement and regenerate the community agencies in a program administered by themselves was dashed when Colonel Hugo Banzer seized the presidency from General Juan José Torres, who had permitted a wider degree of freedom than his military predecessors, Ovando and Barrientos. Again the mining communities were forced into a stalemate, their militant trade union leaders exiled, their wage increases wiped out by the inflation that followed Banzer's devaluation of Bolivian currency in relation to the United States dollar.

[6] During my first month of research in Oruro, an agent of the DIC came to investigate what I was doing. Although his manner was somewhat brusque in his first visit when, in my absence, he demanded that he see copies of our field notes which a student carried to La Paz before his return, later over coffee he revealed that he had been given a United States scholarship to the University of Wisconsin, where he said he studied "counterinsurgency." He commented that the United States CIA agents who were in Oruro during the guerrilla movement of Che Guevara were not effective because of a lack of cross-cultural perspective.

Chapter 5

◆◇◆

The Natural and
the Supernatural Order

◇MINERS RELATE to a superhuman world of saints, devils, deities, and enchanted beings with which they live in the mine, the encampment, and the region. Although they may deny belief in these spirits and deities at some levels of their discourse, they continue to relate to them in their everyday behavior and in their subconscious fantasies. In the rituals and celebrations to these forces projected in pre-conquest concepts and mythic animals, post-conquest Catholic saints and deities, they arrive at an understanding of their being and destiny that enables them to transcend the definition of themselves as meaningless cogs in an industrial enterprise.

In the competition for the souls of subject people, missionaries, spiritual leaders of the traditional order, viceroys, governors, and populist leaders have tried for over four hundred years to create a sense of dissonance between the views they propose and other contending world views. This has been a means of promoting and maintaining their leadership and holding exclusive authority. The people of the mining communities have resisted these attempts to wipe out their own beliefs. They tend to encapsulate the widely disparate, apparently contradictory ideologies to which they have been exposed in a unitary world view not by syncretizing indigenous and colonial beliefs with modern ideologies, but by separating out and assigning a separate place, time, and context in which each is appropriate. Tuesdays, Fridays, the week of Carnival, and the month of August are the appropriate times for giving special recognition to the Pachamama, the ancient space/time concept immanent in the earth, and for the enchanted demons and spirits. Supay, the lord of the hills, sometimes referred to as Huari and as the Tío, was transmogrified by the Christians as the Devil, and Pachamama is sometimes identified with the Virgin. However, this technique of syncretizing elements as developed by the Spaniards in the early years of conquest seems alien to the Bolivian way of thinking. It relates to a mode of thinking that accepts only a single, hierarchically defined system of ideas. Indigenous thought is capable of entertaining coexistant and apparently contradictory world views. The identifications made between figures and concepts in the two systems are only superficial categories, and as one becomes familiar with the culture, people deny the fit. In the following discussion, I hope to clarify this point of the segmentation in time and space of the two systems, since it defies the model of acculturation as a homogeneous blend.

The Belief System

The ritual cycle in Oruro is structured on two axes, one dealing with agriculture, the earth, and the Pachamama, the other with mining, the underground, and Supay. The overlay is Spanish colonial and post-Independence Catholicism, but the deeper structuring is pre-conquest agricultural rites, concerned with preserving the fertility of the land and maintaining harmony with the supernatural. The miners fit their industry into the old structure, maintaining equilibrium by sacrificial offerings to Supay for the mineral they extract.

Ritual time relates to the preindustrial agricultural cycles. The warming of the earth ceremonies in June with the onset of the cold dry season, the preparation of the soil in August for the planting in September, and even Carnival, the season for harvests and joy, relate to an agricultural culture. It is not as clear, however, that space is structured in terms of any significant social groupings in the four quarters of the compass. The ceremonial shrines related to the monsters of the myth recounted in chapter 2 stand like sentinels at these compass points. But movement and activities in other ceremonial occasions relate to the location of work and residence.

Although miners defer to Supay in their productive base

within the mines, the cycle of Pachamama is still the most pervasive. The ch'alla, or offering to the Pachamama, is performed in
all the life-crisis ceremonials. It can be as simple as an offering of
liquor or a "table" made up of a llama fetus, sugar cookies, q'oa
(wool), and confetti, or as complex as a full meal served to neighbors and kin. At these ceremonies, no drink is imbibed until some
is poured into the ground for the Pachamama, and this etiquette
prevails in casual social gatherings as well as the ch'alla within the
mine.

Alliance to the Pachamama relates the individual to life, while a
contract with Supay brings luck and the chance windfall that might
change one's circumstances but inevitably causes death in a short
time. The Awicha tempers the anger of the Tío; when a thundering
blast of dynamite shakes the underground and threatens a cave-in,
miners call on the Awicha, who figures as a companion of Supay
and who is their intermediary with him.

This complementarity of the two forces is found along other
dimensions of contrast. The Pachamama is a female force of continuity in subsistence production. Offering to her ensures continuity
in the returns from crops and flocks. The offering of chicha, or in
some more elaborate ceremonies the fetus of a llama, guarantees
equilibrium in the productive and reproductive forces. Supay is
clearly a masculine force; offerings to him are in the form of propitiation to gain his good will, not for maintenance of a status quo,
but for enrichment from the hidden treasures of the hills. A live,
white llama is sacrificed and its heart interred in the mines to gain
his good will twice yearly. It is both an offering to satisfy his vora-
cious appetite so that he will not eat the men who work the mine,
and a request that he yield to the workers some of the riches of the
mine. Ceremonials to him are characterized by abandon and release
of passion in dancing, drinking, and chewing coca. Considering the
peasants' awareness of the need to limit their flocks in order to
maintain the life of the herd, it is perhaps justifiable to see in the
offering of the aborted fetus to the Pachamama a recognition of
human intervention to assure an equilibrium between the food resources and the animals that graze on her pastures. In contrast, the
offering of a mature animal is a direct substitute for the human lives
that Supay might otherwise claim.

The time-space concept implied in the Pachamama retains its vitality after over four centuries of alien domination in mining communities. Erroneously translated as Earth Mother by the Spaniards, who held a more personified conception of the supernatural, the Pachamama is often equated with the Virgin of Christian belief. I learned how miners felt about this identification one day when a Baha'i missionary joined me and a carpenter in the mines, Manuel, in a discussion of supernatural forces. Manuel rejected the identification of the two forces:

❖ The Pachamama cannot be considered the same as the Virgin Guadalupe or the Virgin of the Rosary. No, it is not the same. Others call it the "Virgin Land," and this is more like it. We speak of Pachamama as the opportunity to live in the mother earth, but it is more than that. We receive all we need from the mother earth in the time-space continuum. She produces all the foods that serve us, including the clothing we wear. And so in this the Pachamama differs from the Virgins of this world, no? It is another force far superior, far stronger, if you wish, far more positive. And so in this sense we cannot speak of the Virgin of Guadalupe, or of Carmen, or of the Virgin of Copacabana as the Pachamama. Undoubtedly our belief in another respect is similar to all that, but it is never equal to the Pachamama. It is a concept much greater.

The missionary present asked Manuel if it might not be the same difference as that between God and a saint, and he replied:

❖ Exactly, God is everything as creator of the land. And just so we think of the Pachamama, as creator of the land, creator of mankind.

He went on to discuss the cosmic equilibrium:

❖ We think of the moon as the force that generates cold. If only the moon existed, we would all die, frozen by the cold. Well, if the sun only existed, and not the moon, who knows but what we would all die, burned to a crisp. And so there is this belief that these two worlds give us an equal temperature. Furthermore, the rotation of the world includes the change of seasons. In the winter when the sun is far away we are closer to the moon, although this is only a theory for me since I have never arrived on the moon. This belief is expressed by the campesinos who say, "Killapacha karancha," the moon is far away, "Rupayta k'askaman. Chay új killaspiri Juyapaj rupaynapaj ya k'askamun chaymanta chirita k'onipataj pasanchaj."

Undoubtedly from the point of view of scientists there is a profound variation, although the variation of the rotation of the earth
does not differ. The campesinos, without knowing astrology,
without knowing the movement of the earth, have taken into account what you see, Juanita. Intelligent as they are, they imagined
that in time the earth is rotating in a way so that they are farther
from the sun and get closer to the moon, and know that when the
world approaches the moon it is cold, and when it is near the sun
it is hot. Many people have distorted all this form of thinking.
They tried forcing new things on us, and they killed us. But now
the moon has been violated! [Our conversation occurred just after
the first moon landing. The verb *pisar*, to step, is also metaphori-
cally used for rape, and Manuel alluded jokingly to this.]

The conflict between these two cosmic forces comes to a climax
at the time of the winter solstice, which occurs on June 21 but is celebrated on the eve of San Juan, June 24. As happens so often, the
Christian calendar provides a framework within which indigenous
people accommodate their own ceremonies. Some miners have heard
the story of how San Juan entered into a competition with Jesus
Christ to split a rock by blowing a wind so cold it could cause frost.
Campesinos celebrate the day by burning the stubble grass over
their fields, and in this way they help the Pachamama maintain the
balance of heat and cold. Miners to this day celebrate the eve of San
Juan by lighting fires around which they gather to drink and dance.
For the campesinos, lighting the fires signifies the maintenance of
fertility for the land and their flocks, and each faggot that they burn
stands for the life of one animal for the year. The miners have generalized the theme of maintaining an equilibrium such that life can
continue on earth. In Siglo XX the celebration has a particular significance, since it was on the eve of San Juan in 1967 that General
Barrientos sent in the troops to massacre the inhabitants (see
chapter 8).

Carnival

The character of these supernatural forces and the roles they
play in society are revealed in the communal celebrations. These are
occasions for expressing community solidarity and continuity with
the past. They are also the time when conflicts are dramatized and

transformations made explicit. Rituals from the pre-conquest can reinforce identity of a people in such a way as to strengthen their resistance to external domination. The same ritual acted out in a changed historical context can have a new meaning. The essence of these celebrations is to maintain in equilibrium opposed forces in the environment through ritual offerings in the ch'alla. This sense of the need for human intervention in the cosmic equilibrium is so great that neither priests, mining administrators, nor governing agents could wipe out the rituals or the beliefs on which they rested.

In the week of Carnival, the schedule of events defines the structural dimensions in time and space that underlie the pre-conquest and hispanic tradition (table 5.1). The weaving together of the two separate strands retains the distinctive features of each. Tuesday and Friday are the days for the featured events of the pre-conquest traditions. Saturday is the day for weaving together these themes in the pageantry of the grand procession and dance. Sunday is the day for honoring the Virgin of the Mineshaft. The dancers, who have masqueraded as devils, condors, temptresses, blacks, Indians, llama herders, and cowgirls, remove their masks and reveal themselves.

Carnival is both a climax to and a beginning of the year's ceremonial cycle. Just before the advent of carnival, Manuel talked to me about its meaning to miners:

> ❖ Carnival is a pause, a rest, a spiritual release, a moral flushing out, an escape, a liberation, a form of expressing one's sorrow and at the same time one's joy. You must understand that the miners work the year round in the mine, and sometimes when they want to have freedom to make a fiesta, to dance in a team, to make a ch'alla, they cannot do it. And so they wait until the fiesta of Carnival, when they give vent to all these pent-up desires.

Carnival is a highly organized series of events occurring immediately before Lent and involving all the workers' unions and fraternal groups of the city (see Table 5.1). The coordination of these events depends on the municipal organizing committee, but the impulse comes from a base made up of dance groups from an urban zone or occupational group. These groups meet throughout the year in the house of the *pasante,* who has charge of the image of the

Table 5.1. Carnival Week Events

Day	Event	Performers	Place
Friday	Ch'alla to serpent	A few dozen, since his true day is May 3	Shrine near stone image in south side
Tuesday	Ch'alla to house	All houseowners, particularly those who have just moved into new houses, and shop-keepers	House, yard, and market
Wednesday	Ch'alla to toad	Most of townspeople	Shrine near stone image in north side
Friday	Ch'alla to condor	Most of townspeople	Shrine near stone image in west side
	K'araku in the mine	All of active miners	Below level zero in mine
	Mass	Priest, about 75 miners and family members	Level zero in mine
Saturday	Entrance of dancers	Dance groups, entire town, and tourists	Streets, plaza in front of Church of Mineshaft
Sunday	Mass for Virgin	All dancers, with masks off	Church and plaza

Virgin of the Mineshaft owned by each society. Those favored by the miners are the Incas, who call themselves Children of the Sun, Tobas (Indians of Iquique) Indians of the jungle, *diabladas* (devils), and *llameras* (llama herders).

Each of the acts of Carnival is associated with historical precedents relating to the pre-conquest or early post-conquest days. The traditions of the indigenous and Spanish populations are woven together but as distinctive strands, not as homogenized elements, and appear in the dances and dramas that interpret past and present. There are two main dramas: The first is the triumph over the monsters sent by Huari, which took place sometime before the conquest but which, over the centuries, incorporated post-conquest spirits and powers. The second is the conquest of the Indians by the Spaniards and their subjugation in the labor force of the mines and the vineyards. The first drama is played out in the Devil dance and is recognized in the propitiation of all the vestiges of the monsters in the area. The second is enacted by the Children of the Sun on the plaza on Sunday of Carnival as well as in the dances, especially that of the *Diablada* and the *Morenada*.

The Dances

The dances in Carnival are both a propitiation of the supernatural forces as well as a temporary taking on of the powers they represent. The magic of the identification is contained in the mask; as long as the dancers wear the mask, they are the figure impersonated. On Sunday the dancers remove their masks and dance under the arches laden with silver as they enter the church to pray. Although the magical element is not always assumed by many of the dancers today, there is a sense of transformation in the dance as they perform what seem to be impossible feats, leaping and cavorting as devils, or weaving to and fro, bearing the heavy suit of the Morenada, or pole-vaulting as Tobas in the long procession from the north of the town several miles up to the plaza of the Church of the Mineshaft where the Virgin is ensconced. The dancers prepare themselves for this arduous exercise in practice sessions that begin on the first Saturday of November and continue each Saturday until Carnival in February or March, when it falls due. Even in the practice sessions the dancers wear uniforms: matching caps, sweatshirts, and pants or skirts of the same color. What sustains them in the final display is the strength of their faith and the devotion to their promise to the Virgin.

I shall concentrate here on two dances, the Diablada and the Morenada, for their significance for the consciousness of workers in relation to their work. Both dances show an evolution over time in which the dancers move from a representation of themselves as miners or slaves along with a single devil in each group to a predominance of figures representing the prohibited but desired incarnation of evil. In the case of the Diablada, miners became the devils, and in the case of the Morenada, slaves became the casks that contain the wine they made. The change of costumes reveals the shift. People said that in the old days the miners wore their work clothes as they moved out of the mineshafts on Friday afternoon, carrying a single image of the devil. In the case of the Morenada, the dancers formerly were stripped to their waists and wore simple cotton trousers of the slave, while today they wear the elaborate jeweled and tiered cask-like form. We can only speculate as to how this transformation came about. The attractiveness of the costuming of the few who represented devils sprinkled among the mass of miners may have drawn the fancy of more and more participants, as might the ornate cask instead of the semi-nude body of black slaves; or it may have been the desire to assume the mask worn by these figures representing temptation, to enjoy for a fleeting moment the world of self-indulgence denied them in their ordinary lives. According to one of the students of Rodolfo Kusch, who conducted an Institute of Indigenous Philosophy in Oruro investigating Carnival, in the process of the dance the slaves transform their hatred of the *caporal,* the black slavemaster who is the immediate agent of their enslavement, into joy. They become transformed into a container for what they make, and the wine as the agency of liberation makes this possible (Alessandri 1968).

The costuming of the dancers, particularly those in the Diablada and Morenada groups, sustains a year-round industry of a group of artisans who make the plaster of paris masks of the devils and black faces, sew the capes with jewels and mirrors, and make the pointed red-tipped shoes of the devil. The devil's mask has three serpents springing from its forehead between two arching horns, representing the monsters that threatened to devour the Uru Urus who inhabited the town before the arrival of the Spaniards. That of the Morenada shows the caricatured negroid features with spreading nostrils, protruding lips, and bulging eyes. The *cabecilla* is the most elaborately dressed of the Morenadas. He carries a pipe and cracks a whip as he leads the other dancers. The cost of the costume, which amounts to from B $200 (US $18) for rental to B $2,400 (US $200) for purchase is an important symbol of their devotion to the Virgin and the sacrifice they make to her. Each elaboration in the costume becomes a manifestation of their faith and devotion. When Orureños talk about progress, they often refer to this increasing elaboration in the Carnival masks and costumes.

The devil dance captures the essence of Carnival in Oruro. According to legend, the dance began when a miner fell asleep after the ch'alla to the devil in the mine. As he woke up, he saw the devil himself dancing and he followed him, dancing out of the mine. After that, the miners continued to dance in the streets following

FOLLOWING THE DANCING IN THE STREETS DURING CARNIVAL,
DEVIL DANCERS ENTER THE CHURCH OF THE MINESHAFT TO PRAY
TO THE VIRGIN.

the ch'alla on the Friday of Carnival. Miners can voice the evolution
over time from the beginning when the miners predominated with
one or two devils dispersed among the dance groups to a dance in
which the devils predominate. Initially the miners were dancing in
homage to the devil, according to Celso, who still has the mask he
wore as a dancer ten years ago. The dance of the miners was a kind
of flowing out of their hopes, ambitions, fears, and joys. In the process of dancing, drawn to the devil, or Supay, who danced among
them, they transformed themselves into the attractive, luring figure
to whom they gave homage. Celso spoke to me of this evolution:

> ❖ At first it was the miners who danced the Dance of the Miners.
> Then it was a flushing out of all of their cares as well as their joys,
> not like now when they have masks and costumes. From this, luck
> has gone, evolving, changing, and transforming the dance until
> they have arrived at the luxury of dissipation which the Diablada
> is today.

I asked him what the meaning of the dance of the miners used to
be, and he replied:

> ❖ It was a dance to the god Momo, to the devil, to the Tío himself.
> But it was a paradoxical situation, because at the same time that
> they bowed to the Virgin of the Mineshaft, they went with this

devotion of faith to complain of their troubles and to cry about
their problems; and afterward they thought that the Virgin of the
Mineshaft gave them her blessing, which they took as a consent
and reason for what followed. Then they began to dance with all
brakes off, releasing them to their liberty. Carnival contains both
these factors: first an accounting of their problems and their suffering and finally release to one's joy.

The Morenadas are a mythical rendition of the African slaves
seen through the eyes of the Indians among whom they came to live
and work. The slave labor brought to work in the mines of the altiplano made a deep impression on the Indians. Many of the older
miners speak of stories they heard from their parents, who saw the
brutality of the caporals exercised to an even greater degree against
the slaves than against the Indians. Alejandro, the seventy-year-old
miner said that Indians of his parents' generation would bury the
dead bodies of slaves thrown out of the mines when they died. According to legend, their inability to endure the climate of the highlands was the reason for their being sold into slavery in the Yungas
tropical plantation area, where they worked in the vineyards. Their
relocation may also have been due to the decline of mining in the
nineteenth century as the silver deposits were exhausted and capital
was invested in agriculture. The dance represents the motions of
the slaves stamping on the grapes to express the liquid. They accompany themselves with the noise of the *matrakas,* which replicate
the sounds of the cranks turning the wine presses.

The Morenades in the Zona Central have a quite different costuming from that of the other Morenada groups. They have chosen
dark suits, vicuña ponchos with white scarves, and black felt hats.
Their matraka is made of the body of an armadillo, which is considered the typical animal of Oruro. They carry a silver flask containing chicha, which they drink as they dance. The costuming is more
conservative than that of the other groups, and almost makes explicit the professional base from which these dancers are drawn:
doctors, engineers, auditors, lawyers, and dentists.

In one of the dramas worked out in the choreography of the
Morenadas, the legend of a rebellion against a caporal in the vine-
yard called Maria Antoinette is enacted. A young black woman who
was the delight of the old despot attracted the attention of the

slaves. Burning with desire for her, they caused the caporal to become drunk and then overcame him in a rebellion. Then they forced the caporal to stamp on the grapes and move the winch, while they ridiculed him in satiric verses. It is an incomplete rebellion, one in which the agent of oppression, not the forces of repression, is attacked and forced to take their position in the productive process (Alessandri 1968:10).

The organization of the dance groups provides an institutional basis for forming important friendships and contacts. In Oruro there are four major groups among the eighteen dance societies. Diablada Artistica Urus, formed in March 1960, Conjunto Huacathocoris Urus, formed in 1968, and Congregación de la Virgen de Socabon de la Diablada, formed in 1960. Since Carnival depends ultimately on the faith and support of the individual dancers, we must explore how the individuals are inspired to enter into this collective manifestation of their faith and what its meaning is to them. Mario, whom I met in level 540 of the mine where he works as a carter, began dancing when he was three years old. His father had worked in the mines in Chile and liked to dance, so when he returned to Bolivia he formed a dance group with most of the miners from Chile. The dance was that of the Indians of Iquique, called Tobas. The dancers wore a skirt and a turban of feathers. Some of the miners who fought in the Chaco War had seen Indians of the southeastern tropical region and were impressed by their customs, which they translated into the dance. The musical accompaniment was of cane flutes. The dancers carried lances with which they performed their great leaps. The original "Chunchos" group changed to "Gambas" wearing slim costumes and carrying a machete, finally evolving to the present Tobas. The headdress of feathers remained the distinguishing feature, but now the dancers wear white shirts and green vests with gathered pantaloons over long underdrawers, a concession to the cold of the highlands, that diverge from the tropical model.

During the weeks of the buildup for Carnival the dancers meet alternately at the house of each member. They wear their practice uniform. The house is adorned with paper decorations and confetti, and the host invites the others to cocktails. The ch'alla for the Pachamama is offered before each drink.

I asked Mario how he felt about the dance. He said he danced with faith, believing that he would have no problems. I asked if it had helped him, and he said that he fell 15 meters in the mine and did not break a single bone, which he attributed to the intervention of the Virgin. Manuel was active in the union before the fall of San José to the military in 1965. He hid three days in the mine, and every night he lived in fear that the authorities would come after him. Now he doesn't want anything to do with the unions. He has put all his energy and dedication into the dance group he helped organize and maintains.

I spoke with another leader of a dance group who worked as a clerk in town. His group, which has 375 members, is very proud of its Virgin, which they say is identical to that in the Church of the Mineshaft. "It is she for whom we sacrifice ourselves," said the leader, sweeping aside the wine damask curtain over her image with a flourish. "The artist who made her spent six months in the production." The evening I attended the meeting there were 25 or so members. Before the altar were five tables of graduated sizes, each with a doily and artificial flowers in plastic vases. As I looked at it, an image of all the front reception rooms in all of the houses I had entered in Oruro, each with a table with vases and plastic flower set in the center of the room, came to my mind and I saw it now as a culture pattern, impregnated with a sense of reverence. In front of these tables was a footstool where each of the members knelt as they arrived and prayed to the Virgin.

"The Virgin goes out only on the Friday of Carnival," the leader of the society told me. "At Wednesday night socials when a smaller group of us get together, a smaller image of the Virgin goes to the house of the society member holding the meeting. Friday evening is the night of veneration; on Wednesday there is a business and social meeting when people draw up plans for action and install officials while they drink chicha or chocolate."

In addition to the president and the vice president, there are committee members in charge of public relations, hacienda, statistical control, press and publicity, culture and sports. There is a Secretary of Piety who prepares people for confession at the time of their first dance. She has the special task of praying every Saturday to the Virgin.

The expenses of the organization are taken care of by the *quota pro fiesta* of B$100 for men and B$50 for women. This is spent on the band, the dinner, drink, the costs of B$10,000 expended during the Carnival celebration itself. There is competition among the dance groups, which makes for pressure toward maintaining high standards of costuming. The competition is, however, contained within a strong sense of regional pride and a deep awareness of the cultural tradition which all the dance groups are keeping alive.

Ch'alla

Two separate acts, during Carnival, divided by time and place but linked by the common elements involved, are the ch'alla to the Pachamama and to Supay. The first is performed in the house and yard at midday on Tuesday of Carnival week and the second is per-

DRINKING *chicha*, A FERMENTED CORN BEER, AND DANCING TO THE MUSIC OF A GUITAR AND CHARANGO, MINERS CELEBRATE THE CH'ALLA INAUGURATING A NEW HOUSE.

formed in the mines on Friday evening beginning about sundown and lasting until midnight. The first brings together the members of a household and assures their health and welfare and the productivity of whatever subsistence crops they grow in their gardens. The second reinforces the solidarity of the work group and ensures the safety of the men against accidents as well as the yield of the minerals. In both cases offerings are made to gain the good will of the spirits of the earth and the hills. Both are performed by all the people involved in each setting.

The ch'alla to the house is performed every Tuesday of Carnival Week and the first week of August every year, but an especially elaborate one is performed the first year the family occupies a house, whether it is new or old. Relatives, neighbors, and fellow-workers are invited to participate in the ch'alla and share a meal. At one of the first year of residence ceremonies I attended, at the house of Aníbal, a plumber who worked on contract for the mine, and Christina, his wife, the guests included her parents and siblings along with five men who worked with Aníbal. His parents lived too far away to come. It was a new experience for him, since his kin believed in Sebaya and performed different rituals.

The family bought a sheep, which they slaughtered for the meal, reserving the blood, and prepared six barrels of chicha which they served with liquor and beer. They bought a prepared *mesa,* or table offering, for the Pachamama, which consisted of the fetus of a llama, q'oa, and sugar wafers sprinkled with confetti. They decorated the house with crepe paper ribbons and balloons, both for the benefit of the house and to welcome the guests. As the guest arrived, they were wreathed in streamers and sprinkled with confetti. Sometimes confetti would be stuffed in the mouth of the guests as they were urged to "eat the fiesta." Aníbal poured the spiked chicha over the bricks in the center of the main room of the house and in the four corners, calling for the health and wealth of the household members and that there be no fighting. Because he and his wife had lost two children from contagious diseases, they were especially eager to make a good fiesta and ensure the health of their two-year-old son in their new home, which was borrowed from the mine enterprise. He sprinkled chicha in the center of the plot and in the four major compass directions. Each of the guests was served

MARKET WOMEN AND MEN MAKE THE OFFERING OF THE CH'ALLA
TO THE PACHAMAMA IN THEIR STALLS ON TUESDAY OF CARNIVAL
TO ENSURE MORE SALES DURING THE YEAR.

liquor, some of which they poured in the ground before sipping.
Following this the mutton was served with corn kernels and *chuña*.
They passed the rest of the afternoon dancing to the music of the
radio and a *chiranga* (a small stringed instrument made from the
shell of an armadillo) that a neighboring youth brought with him,
and drinking.

All shopkeepers hold a ch'alla on the Tuesday of Carnival to ensure good luck in their business. The market area was decorated
throughout with streamers and confetti when we arrived after leaving Anibal's house at three in the afternoon. Teenage youths were
engaged in dousing people with water, especially those of the opposite sex. It reminded me of the Burmese water festival in March,
and the Holi festival of India, and it is similarly related to fertility.

In contrast to the open sharing of the ch'alla to the Pachamama
in the sunlight and open air, the ch'alla to the Tío is withdrawn into
the inner recesses of the mine, where just the work group of a section share their drink and coca with the Tío. The year I was in
Oruro, the ch'alla to the Tío had been resumed after five years when
it was banned by Barrientos. The men took the reinstatement of the
ch'alla as a sign of greater freedom in the Ovando regime.

In the old days, when the palliris worked in the concentration

"LONG LIVE THE CH'ALLA!" SHOUT THE MINERS AS THEY INVITE
ONE TO THE FEAST FOR THE TÍO CELEBRATED ON THE EVE OF
AUGUST 1, WHEN THE MONTH OF THE DEVIL BEGINS.

pits at the entrance of the mines, the men used to take the large
images of the Tío out of the mines after they had made their offering and joined the women, where they danced and drank together.
According to one palliri, some of the women tried to gain more on
their contract by flirting with the Tío, wearing their best satin polleras and dancing provocatively before him. Nowadays, women are
not part of this celebration unless, as happened in one of the mines
the year I was there, the women prepare the food in their houses
and carry it down to the mines.

In the morning of the ch'alla the men bring the streamers and
confetti with which to decorate the image of the Tío in their *paraje*
(work site) into the mines. Each of them brings a flask of liquor,
often prepared with fruit juice, a bag of coca, and cigarettes, and
those who play bring a chiranga or guitar. First they decorate the
image with the streamers of colored paper wound around the neck
of the Tío and set a cigarette in his mouth. They sprinkle alcohol,
being careful not to drop any in the eyes of the Tío because this
would make them burn and they might lose the vein of ore. The
men then light the cigarette for the Tío and offer coca leaves. They
sit and chew coca and smoke cigarettes and drink. Someone begins
to play the chiranga and the men dance "like Indians."

The Awillachu or K'araku

On Friday of Carnival, the smaller mines sacrifice a llama or sheep in the open, at the entrance to the mine. They bring the palpitating heart with the "table" inside the mine as an offering to the Tío. The ceremony is the same as that of the k'araku performed in the larger mines, but because it is performed in the open, at midday instead of midnight, it is more closely related to agricultural offerings to ensure greater productivity of the crops. In Oruro the miners pour the blood of the sacrificed animal on all the machinery of the sink-and-float plant. One miner explained to me that the machinery would produce more and would not cause accidents when this offering was made. It is possible that the ceremony is effective in overcoming the workers' alienation from machine production. They welcomed mechanization and were proud of the increased productivity it meant, especially in the early years of the nationalization of the mines.

The year I was in Oruro the sacrifice of the llama in the mine was not carried out at Carnival as in former years because of lack of money. When the "tin barons"—Patiño, Hochschild, and Aramayo—owned the mines, the sacrificial animal was purchased by the owner, who often attended. After nationalization of the mines in 1952, the rituals continued. In fact, some of the miners complained that they were done in excess of the Tío's needs. Juan told me that going into the mine shortly after the revolution was like walking into a saloon. There was a tapering off of such secular abuses of the ritual in the latter part of the decade, and following military control in 1965 the rituals were entirely cut off. This intensified the hatred the miners felt for the regime of Barrientos. Although the rituals were again permitted under General Ovando, the administration did not subsidize the cost of the llama, and the ritual I observed on Carnival was limited to serving hot beef stew brought into the mines by the wives of the workers. It was not until the accidents that occurred in July that a complete k'araku took place (see below).

Ch'alla of the Serpent, Toad, and Condor

The Friday before Carnival is devoted to a ch'alla of the serpent at the southern end of town. In the following week, people attend to the toad on the north side of town on Wednesday and on Friday they congregate at the image of the condor. The last two ceremonies are the chief recognition these enchanted images have during the year, and the congregation is great. The special day for the serpent is on the Day of the Cross, and the Carnival offering is limited and attended by only a few people.

When I arrived at the figure of the toad about three in the afternoon, there were about one thousand people scattered over the hills near the statue. Both the original crumbled remains and the new cast-iron image were given offerings and decorated with streamers and confetti.

In 1935 during the discontent against the Chaco War, rebellious groups used to congregate at the site. In an attempt to disrupt the subversion, the general stationed at Oruro barracks ordered that the image be blown up. Within a month he was paralyzed and he died within a year. The people reconstructed an image and set it on a pedestal at the same site.

Each group that arrived, usually composed of a nuclear family, made the offering of a "table" containing q'oa, the fetus of a llama, sugar wafers, and confetti, burning it at the base of the image and shaking up beer which they poured foaming over the image. Each family group went from the toad to the field at the foot of San Pedro hill and built a small house of rocks. These they decorated with yellow flowers and wound with streamers, and poured liquor or beer over it. Then they sat down and ate the picnic lunch they brought with them, some visiting with friends they encountered.

Almost the same ritual is performed at the image of the condor. People arrive in family groups, burn their offering, wind confetti and streamers over the condor, and pour beer or liquor over him. They then retire to build their dream house of stones on the nearby slopes. One act that I did not observe in the first occasion at the toad was "mining" gold; people go with a hand drill and hammer to the steep rock that looms on the hill overhanging the condor and mine the yellow rock. They take the nuggets to the house which they have constructed and "ch'alla" it with liquor. The belief is that the "fool's gold" will attract real gold, or currency, to their home. The trick to having one's dreams fulfilled is to go with complete faith in the venerated image, and the reward for the devotion expressed in the offerings will be forthcoming as reciprocated aini. While most of the people were cholos, judging from the women's dress, there were a few dozen mestizos sprinkled among the hundreds of people in both areas. The condor attracted even more people than did the toad.

These are active cults that reveal the intensity of the desire the people have for material improvement in their lives. They provide the kind of inspiration needed for maintaining a notion of the desired object. Most people I questioned said that they were successful in gaining desired objects in the past and attributed their success to the power of the venerated image.

The Mass in the Mines

A direct counterpoint to the other events that take place on Friday of Carnival is the mass for the Saint of the Compadres performed by the North American missionary priest at level zero of the Itos mine. The niche for the saint is in the main entrance, where the vaulted ceilings of the vast open space give the appearance of a cathedral. The remains of confetti and streamers on the winch from the celebration on the eve before could still be seen.

In his sermon the priest identified Jesus Christ with Viracocha (the Inca ruler) as a herald of the Lord come to earth to put in practice the will of God. He said that the miners who bring their wages home to feed their children are in their self-sacrifice acting as an agent of the Lord just as much as a priest. "You too are a priest," he told the miners. Then the priest blessed the new niche, commenting, "The image is just a remembrance of somebody. It is not here so that we will have more luck. We want to consecrate our mine to the Saint of Compadres so that we will be honoring the Lord. This niche is in memory of our comrades who have died so that some can arrive at the State of Christ. We want to put this here as a remembrance of the son of the Lord." There were about seventy-five to a hundred miners, women, and children in the congregation.

The priest's sermon is a direct confrontation with the sentiments miners hold about their relationship to the saints. The Señor de los Compadres is a particular favorite of the miners, since it is felt that he brings luck to those who undertake his fiesta. Their expenditure on candles, liquor, food, and incense is considered to be the beginning of aini, a reciprocal exchange which the saint must respond to by protecting them from accidents and enabling them to earn well. The missionary priests tried to overcome years of opportunistic exploitation of mining and agricultural communities by alienated priests of the older orders who encouraged belief in the magical powers of the saints to increase their hold over the Indians.

The Entrada

Saturday of Carnival is the first day of dancing in the streets. I went to watch the preparations in the house of Tito, the son of one of the office workers in the mines, who danced the temptress with one of the Morenada groups. Both his sisters danced with the Llameradas. Tito's shoes were not yet back from the cobbler, and there was a note of desperation as the family waited for him to return. The father, who worked in the pulpería, was stitching one of his daughter's many petticoats on the sewing machine; men often take on domestic tasks, cooking or cleaning when their wives are otherwise occupied. Some neighbors dropped by to drink chicha and admire the costumes. They asked the younger daughter, a girl of four, to dance a few steps to show off all the petticoats. Each of the costumes cost from B $900 to B $1,500 (about US $75 to US $125), over a month's pay. When Tito returned with the shoes, made of straw with patent leather and stiletto heels, he donned the gold-cloth dress he had made for himself and his mask of a leering, voluptuous chola. Only men can dance the role of the *chinas*, or seductresses who are the consorts of the devil, since the obscene gestures required would make the role too much for a woman to overcome after Carnival, I was told. The role often attracts men with homosexual tendencies, like Tito, who can find in the Carnival an acceptable outlet.

The procession in the streets began at two and continued until six in the evening. Each group danced to their band on the five-mile stretch until they arrived in the plaza, where they performed the special dance steps they had practiced for months. All the streets were lined with people who enthusiastically applauded each of the groups. Many of the dance groups had bears, big and small, who pulled female spectators from the crowd and danced a few steps with them. Special features such as an astronaut with a U.S. flag on his space suit and a machine gun in his hand gave a modern touch to the traditional groups. A Volkswagen made up as a float with porcupine quills drew strong applause. Flora, the widow of a miner, who stood beside me as the dance groups entered the plaza, told me that one of the special features she remembered from the thirties was a child dressed in cotton batting who represented the balls of gas that attack workers in the mine and knocked against the other dancers, who pretended to faint before him.

What characterizes Oruro Carnival processions, in contrast with celebrations in other places, is the order, the precision of the dance steps, and the lavishness of the costumes. It is not a wild excess of sexual and drinking indulgence, but a precise channeling of some very deep passions and sentiments. It is both an expression of discontent and a solace for them. As I watched the succession of dance groups, I could appreciate the tremendous excitement I had seen in the preparations for it.

Veneration and Mass for the Virgin

Sunday of Carnival is devoted to the worship and veneration of the Virgin. The dancers arrived at the Church of the Mineshaft at five in the morning and climbed up to the grotto set high above the plaza, where an image of the Virgin is ensconced behind bars. The niche set in the hill is almost like a balcony seat in an opera house, and I realized more than at any other point in the celebrations that she was the chief spectator. The setting of the church is designed for just this celebration. When I looked out from the height of the grotto, I could see the devils dancing on the round plaza in front of the church. At the circular platform at a higher level, bands stopped on their way up to play. At the smaller clearing in front of the grotto, the dancers came to kneel and pray. As I stood among them, I could feel the thump of drums and brass, and the sound was overwhelming. As the dawn rose, each dance group came in with their band and the dancers knelt before the Virgin and prayed. They wore their practice dress, a way of announcing to the Virgin the months of preparation that went into their performance in her honor. Some of the distinguishing marks of their costume identified the dance group to which they belonged: the devil shoes (red-tipped sneakers of the devil dancers), scarves, or the matrakas of the Morenadas. The four bands playing simultaneously were nonetheless able to maintain the theme of their special dance groups. It illustrated the segmentary character sustained by the dance groups throughout the celebration. The pressure of each dance group threading its way into the packed arena near the Virgin set up almost magnetic currents as the dancers moved up and down or in and out of the plaza, occasionally colliding. Following their devotions to the Virgin, each dance group entered the church and prayed before the altar.

At 6:30 A.M. the mass was said. The priest asked the dancers to leave so that he could proceed with the mass. In his sermon he hardly mentioned the Carnival proceedings.

The Hijos del Sol (Children of the Sun) present their drama of the conquest in the main street at 10 A.M. The protagonists include Pizarro; Diego Almagro, his cohort; the cleric Vicario Hernando Luque; the king of Spain; the king of the Incas, Atahualpa: Hualla Huisa, chief diviner; and fifteen Ñustas, or Inca maidens. The Spaniards were costumed in leather boots, velvet capes, silver helmets, and satin pants. The priest wore a black cassock and basin-shaped hat, and carried a large book with which he menaced the Indians. His mask was a contrast to the actor's brown face, which one could see through the semitransparent pink gauze with brightly rouged cheeks and widely staring blue eyes. The actor often broke into a smile from behind his mask as he angrily threatened the Indians in his role as the domineering priest. King Ferdinand also wore a bright pink mask topped by an elaborately curled wig on his head. The Inca were dressed in short, multicolored robes, aprons of coins, plumed headdresses, and golden sandals. Atahualpa, who was played by a handsome young Indian, wore a crown with mirrors. His scepter represented a star over a crest of moon, a symbol I have also seen on the image of the Virgin of Copacabana. His prime minister, followed by a young boy who announced his presence with a tambour, danced in and around the Spaniards, burlesquing their words with beats on the tambour.

It was very much "theater of the street" with many outbursts of laughter from the audience, who stood in an oval at the same level as the actors and barely giving them space to move, when they saw the mocking of the Spaniards. They cheered and clapped as the Inca made inroads in their clash with the Spaniards. When the Inca women got into the fray, they were even more enthusiastic. The priest's role seemed to highlight the Indian view of Spanish deception and treachery. His gesture of beating people with the Bible is an ironic statement of how supernatural powers were abused by the conquerors. An even more striking act revealing the use of spiritual powers to deceive and destroy occured when the priest baptized Atahualpa and then the Spanish army moved in and immediately shot him. A nice touch at this dramatic climax was the appearance of a small child who ran into the arena where the performance was held and spread out a plastic tablecloth for the Inca king to fall on so that his costume would not be soiled as he fell. The king lay dead, occasionally craning his neck to see how the rest of the play was going on without him, which caused some hilarity in the crowd. The Inca maidens gathered around him to sing the mourning dirge in Quechua to a Spanish hymn. The final scene showed Pizarro banished by the Spanish king for his cruel and treacherous acts, which was roundly cheered by the spectators.

The final irony in the presentation of the drama that I witnessed was when the theatrical group entered the Church of the Virgin of the Mineshaft to pray to the Virgin and ask for her benediction. The Italian priest who officiated at the mass railed against them for their banner proclaiming them as Hijos del Sol, saying, "You are not Children of the Sun, you are Children of the Lord.' "

In the enactment of the death of Atahualpa, the players reenacted their own conquest and subjugation. The drama reveals their rejection of the unjust act and the spirit of rebellion that they keep alive through such recapitulations of Pizarro's betrayal of his promise to release Atahualpa. The dialogue in Quechua is an assertion of their own cultural survival in the face of Spanish domination. The effect of the drama is to sharpen the sense of resistance and the moral triumph over unjust domination.

The Cargamiento, *or Bearing of the Arches*

Every fiesta in honor of a saint requires that arches bearing ancient silver objects such as plates, vases, spoons, and bowls be raised before the entrance to the church. The number of the arches and the weight of the silver are an index to the devotion of the pasantes, or persons charged with the carrying out of the fiesta. Although aided by friends, relatives, and compadres, the pasante must reciprocate each of the arches when those who have made the contribution take charge of a fiesta. This form of reciprocal aid in the aini is an indigenous element entering into the Spanish ceremonial context.

The silver arches are prepared on Monday following the entrada. According to Estanislao Aquino (1968:9), the armament of the silver burden replicates the construction of the Inca empire in four parts: in the center of a hand-woven mantel is placed a large soup bowl, and two chalices representing Cuzco are set on the forehead of the mule who carries the burden and another at the rear, on which rests a cushion with goblets, pitchers, three spoons, and a pillow with jewelry representing the four provinces of the empire: Antisuyo, Contisuyo, Collasuyo, and Chinchasuyo. In present-day ceremonies, the silver is rented for the occasion, but is nonetheless a show of wealth and a sign of devotion to the saint.

The year I witnessed Carnival, there were 65 arches; this represented a decline over the previous year, when there were 190, and two years ago, when there were 217. People attributed it to hard times and inflation. Many of the arches were donated by the vendors who sold food, candy, ritual objects, and lottery tickets. It was a kind of insurance for good luck in the following year by recognizing and paying respect to the Virgin.

Each of the dance groups, dressed in their costume but with the mask removed, danced through the arches and entered the church with their band. There the priest blessed them with holy water, they sang their farewell song to the Virgin, and left. Many had tears in their eyes as they sang. The dancers were accompanied by the pasante, who had borne the burden of expenses. They came with their boxed Virgin and banners announcing the name and founding date of the group.

Carnival is a time for cultivating one's luck and overcoming the destiny that one seems committed to. It is a time for the pursuit of the ordinarily unattainable, contained within a specified time and place. Luck is available even to the lowliest, and the only investment is faith and a modicum of ritual expenditures to secure the aini due to the devout. It is a time to store up aini with the powerful allies available in the immediate environs of the city in the hope that, with enough faith, the payoff will surpass the amount invested in the offering. It is a time to reassess the past and to stock up credits for the future.

I was often told, and I have seen it written in most tracts about Carnival, that it is a drama reenacting the triumph of good over evil. My own reaction, after eight days of ceremonial offerings, processions, displays of faith in the Pachamama, the Virgin, the devil, and the enchanted images, was that good and evil become blended. Fortune, power, riches, sex, strength, were available by appealing to the devil. But access to these values required the intermediacy of the Virgin, who had acquired her own court of devils as well as guardian angels. She too combined good and evil. Her very existence in the Church of the Mineshaft was due to a thief who by his veneration was able to transubstantiate her.

Why has Carnival not only survived but grown more elaborate over the years? Whenever people spoke with me about their problems, about the political repression and revolution, they concluded by asking me, "But have you ever been here during Carnival?" and proceed to describe past processions and their role in them. I grew to expect this as I sensed that it wasn't a shift in the dialogue but an extension of it. Carnival is an expression of a people's view of their history and an account of how they have transmuted their defeat into a triumphant statement of the value of survival and self-determination. Josermo Murillo Vacareza (1969:9) says:

> [The Diablada] is more splendid when the disenchantment that invades the spirit of the pueblo that contains the frustration of those forces that direct it, falsifies itself in its very vitals. The daring and impetuous dance is the hidden impulse, equal to that of their ancestors to demolish, fight and subvert against which they oppose themselves, either to subjugation or to inferiority; the epochal music is a stimulus to a movement of insurgency, as a trumpet of

permanency; its rich and beautiful clothing derives from a system of impoverishment, as if to say in the hyperbole of fired imagination, that we dare to believe that there is an end to it.

It would be simplistic to say that Carnival is a substitute for revolution; it is more accurate to say that it is a reminder to the people of the necessity for revolt when the historical conditions are appropriate, just as it is a denial of the misery and drabness of their everyday lives and expression of what they aspire to.

The Life-Death Cycle

In the rituals relating to death and rebirth, the basic notions of equilibrium between extinction and regeneration are worked out in the annual cycle. After death the soul goes on to live in an afterworld that is very much like this world, but where everything is in abundance. The souls are invited to return to earth on Todos los Santos, the day of all souls, when feasts are prepared in the homes of surviving relatives. Fertility and regeneration are most strongly linked with the celebration of Chiripujo, the shrine of the stone reptile, which takes place on the Day of the Cross.

Todos los Santos

There is a precise scheduling for the arrival and departure of the souls during the three days' celebration of Todos los Santos. The souls of children arrive on October 31 at noon, and adults on the following day at the same time. They prepare to leave heaven at 5 P.M., Juan told me, so that they can be reviewed by God to see that they are clean at seven. God has a list and checks them off, and those who are late cannot go on their visits. If the day is sunny the souls are joyful, and if it is rainy they are sad and it is a bad sign for the crops. Juan remembered a cloudy November 1 when the potato crop failed. November 2 is always rainy because of the sadness of the souls in leaving. If anyone is late in getting back after their twenty-four-hour leave, they are locked out.

In preparation for the arrival the family bakes bread, which is the major offering for the souls and guests who drop in to pray. Juan, whose mother had died during the year, was making a large tomb to receive her soul. Petrona bought the following items.

flour, 2 cwt at B $.95	B $190.	carrots	B $3.
yeast	3.	paper and ribbons	3.
alcohol	30.	basket of sweets	4.
lard, 7 kilos at B $5.6	39.	sugarcane, 2 stalks	5.
chicha	10.	pineapple	5.
rental of ovens and hired		drapery cloth,	6.
help of baker	30.	cookies, 2 doz	6.
eggs, 100 at B $0.50	50.	horse-shaped sweets	2.50
4 ducks	12.	birdlime	2.
potatoes, 2 25-bl sacks	26.	bananas, 25	2.50
chuño	35.	oranges, 25	3.
sweets	2.	squash	2.
tomatoes	2.	onions	3.

I helped Juan and Petrona shape loaves of bread from the 200 pounds of flour. We worked all one afternoon shaping the dough into bread babies (t'anta wawas), crescents, ladders (so the souls could climb back to heaven with them), butterflies, toads, serpents, pigeons, moons, and whatever imagination dictated. The bread babies, which our gingerbread boys resemble, are made with dough blackened by oven grease to mark the features. The family also made whipped egg-white cookies, which represent the breath of souls, and shortcake.

The family laid out a huge table in their main room to represent a tomb. They decorated the poles supporting a purple canopy with stalks of sugarcane and with pineapple and other fruit. They cooked the chicken, duck, and other favorite dishes of the departed, which they arranged on the table around a picture of Juan's mother.

Acculturated families tend to lay a simple table with the cakes and wine and spongecake. The tomb for children is laid out with a white cloth and decorated with white flowers.

Guests who were invited for the midday meal began to arrive at 11:30. They sat on the chairs arranged around the wall of the room, very much like the arrangement when the body is laid out for the wake. Juan came into the room at 12:00, carrying a tray of burning embers and copal. He stood with his family in front of the tomb and said, "Our Father, pray for us. My mother perhaps had many sins, but forgive them and receive her in heaven." At 12:10 Petrona brought in a bowl of soup which Juan placed in front of the chicken on the table. The guests were then served bread with wine, then soup followed by chicken piquante. There were about ten guests in addition to the family.

We visited the houses of miners who died that year. José was killed in the fighting in Oruro during the attempted coup by Rogelio Miranda when Juan José Torres came to be president. José's widow, two daughters, and their husbands had laden the table in the main room of the new house the mine administration had allotted them that year with bread representing ladders, doves, t'anta wawas, and a huge figure of José himself. José's son-in-law told me, "It is a sacrifice that we must make on the first year. We have to give the best we can." The picture I had given them of José at a union meeting was displayed in the center of the tomb.

Domingo, who had died of a heart attack in the mines, was served by his widow, who is de vestido, in a much simpler manner. There was only a table, without the canopy we had seen in the other houses, laid with wine and bread. While we were there some children came in and caroled. Then a group of about five women entered, asked for the name of the deceased, and sang a chorus.

None of the members of the family are expected to pray for the departed, since their prayers are not expected to carry as much weight with God. The idea is for friends, neighbors, and even strangers to pray on the basis of the rewards that the family will provide in the sweet wine, cakes, and bread. Juan told me of the rivalry in the mining encampment of Siglo XX when he was a boy, where the children went to as many houses as possible, singing prayers for their rewards. He described one great fight when the boys from another section of the encampment invaded what he and his group considered to be their territory. There is a price for each prayer: one bread baby, twenty-four Padre Nuestros, and twenty-four Ave Maria Gloriadas. Some families prepared a list of the names of the departed so the guests could fill them into their verses. We saw children with large bags running from house to house, much like the trick-or-treaters in the United States.

The very next day, on November 2, the tryouts for the Carnival dance begin. I think this is more than coincidence. Death is constantly juxtaposed with the assertion of life in the mining communities. I learned to overcome my own repulsion at the idea of eating at the wakes in view of the body laid out in the bier. The bread babies themselves seemed to me to be the assertion of new life in the face of death. When I watched Juan, with his arms whitened up to the elbows, passing out the vibrant dough to his children for them to make figures, it communicated a sense of the worth-whileness of life. Dough, which has a life of its own, became the medium for transforming the message of rebirth. Although no one was able to connect the bread babies directly with a meaning of this sort, the metaphor was there throughout Todos los Santos.

Todos los Santos offers another opportunity, like Carnival, to invent songs and perform, since the prayers are often given in the form of sung verses. Some that were related to me follow:

> In the sky there is a pillar
> Carved with pilgrims
> That San José carved
> For the Virgin Mary.

Each song has a chorus, such as that which follows the above verse:

> Praised be the Lord
> Sacrament of the altar
> And the Virgin conceived
> Without original sin.

Another common song is:

> White pigeon, white pigeon,
> White pigeon, where are you going?
> Carry me close to the Virgin Mary
> And the Lord Saint Joseph.

But as with everything in the mines, these songs are politicized:

> There comes Paz Estenssoro
> Raising a cloud of dust
> To put a bullet
> In Walter Guevara
> In his skull
> For having formed the PRA.

and the chorus is picked up:

> Praised be Juan Lechin,
> Leader of the Miners
> And without original sin.

These sidelights serve to remind people of life at the time of mourning. The comrades of men and women who died in the year, in accidents or of the occupational disease of silicosis, come to their houses and partake of the food and drink offered to them. It is a time to enjoy their visiting, but on the following day they must leave. At noon on November 1, people say there is a gust of wind as all the souls leave to reenter heaven before the gates are closed. The family takes all the remaining food to the cemetery to leave at the grave of the departed.

Chiripujyo and the Three Miraculous Jesuses

The stone images of the giant lizard at Cala Cala and Chiripujyo and the sand dunes that are a reminder of the hordes of ants that threatened to devour the people of Uru Uru are now the sites of churches which are dedicated to miraculous images. The first two are those of Jesus, said to be related as elder brother in Cala Cala to younger brother in Chiripujyo. The third is devoted to Santiago, who some say intervened with his sword to stop the swarms of ants from descending on the town. The three cults are favored by the miners, who often become pasante or past officer of the fiestas in their honor.

The Señor of Chiripujyo is celebrated on May 3. Up until about fifty years ago, it was the time for a kind of communal betrothal custom in which couples arrived in pairs flanked by the unmarried girls and boys. They walked up to the mouth of the serpent which is just beyond the church yard and there they prayed for marriage and a home. The married couples talked to the single people about the experience of domesticity and about the problems and responsibilities of the marriage state. Along with this they talked about the reproduction and raising of cattle. Each couple made an offering of incense and q'oa before the mouth of the serpent, both holding the smoking burner. They prayed for their own home and for many offspring and animals. Some say that to ensure the fertility and richness of their home and flock they offered their first-born child as a sacrifice at the mouth of the serpent. Chicha and coca dealers, who are said to still carry on these practices, are particularly fond of the place because it offers a good market for their products.

Chicheros had until some time ago a factory set up just below the mouth of the serpent.

The sense that the Señor de Chiripujyo is still related to fertility and abundance attracts many people to his shrine on the three days of his fiesta in May. When I visited the Church of Chiripujyo on May 1, I saw freshly painted white llamas on the interior walls of the church as well as on the door outside. I was told that the pasante had painted them. The outlined figures looked very much like the sculpted and incised figures of llamas that were in the local museum, but I was unable to find out whether they had any reference to the old pre-conquest cult. There were about fifty persons inside the church, as many de vestido as chola, and a few Indians. There was a constant turnover since their individual rites took only a short time. People entered the church, some, especially women of the chola class, with incense burners piled with copal which they blew toward the crucified Jesus figure, incongruously draped in a blue and silver loincloth. Only one man, an Indian, performed this act in the church. They then lit a candle, sometimes two or more if they were carrying out the ritual for a friend, and then retired. The cholos usually proceeded to the serpent's mouth to offer chicha or beer and a "table," offerings of cookies, candies, and the fetus of a llama.

The theme of sacrifice in the interest of perpetuating life was also part of past celebrations at Cala Cala. Until recent years when it was prohibited, the Indians of different villages nearby performed a T'inku. This is an encounter between men armed with chicotes, metal-toed boots and varnish-hardened rope boxing gloves, who used to fight until someone died. Celso had seen one a few years before, but the government prohibition was effective enough either in preventing it or forcing it into hiding, so that I did not witness one. I saw the armed warriors carrying out a circle dance with women waving the white banners. Celso's informant at the event he witnessed told him that the Indians felt that they had to offer a man bleeding to death to the Señor de Cala Cala. There is still some feeling that a celebration is improved by the drawing of blood. Petrona's father was congratulated when he blew off a hand and part of his ear at a celebration in the mines when he tried to set off a dynamite charge, and animal blood is still considered to be a poor substitute.

Cala Cala has recently modernized the facade of the old church in the community of the same name about ten miles east of Oruro. I arrived at 12:30 just as mass was being said. The image of Christ was impressive: a grayish tint to the body with bright spots of blood, wild black hair, mahogany-colored lips, and a silver crown, nailed to a silver cross draped with a fish. After the mass, people crowded to the altar to get the priest to bless the toy cars and houses they had purchased outside in the market, as a token of the promised reward for their devotion to the Señor. There were about two hundred and fifty people in the mass, Indians, cholos, and ladinos. Outside groups of Indian musicians came with pan pipes and drums, which they played outside the church in reverence for the Señor. Pasantes of the mestizo social class carried out their devotions in the four corners of the churchyard with the help of the priest, and similar groups of cholos with their pasantes performed the same rituals. It was a completely segmented performance, with each group pursuing with deep devotion their own opportunistic ends for self-improvement and wealth. Most of the participants went to the huge figure of the lizard. The lake was dry at this time, which was just the beginning of the rainy season, but people say that when there is water one can see the tinge of the blood he shed when slain by the intervention of the Ñusta.

The priest emerged with assistants to pray at the four stations marked with crosses in the churchyard. As the priests moved with each group of pasantes, the brass band and the native flute and drum players played simultaneously as a group of lechuayus danced. Most of the participants proceeded in the afternoon to the huge figure of the lizard. There they made an offering of liquor and a "table" at the hump of the lizard's back and withdrew to a small chapel, where they meditated and inscribed a message to the miraculous Señor asking for his favor: "Señor, I ask for a good husband," one modestly requested. Another stated. "Your children await a profession in order to be great men for our country and devotees of our Lord of the Lakes, [Signed] your sons, J.P. and C.E." "Pardon me, Sr. [abbreviated to fit the limited wall space], give me your benediction with a house and a truck. I shall return, [signed] your son and servant, Dionicio." Another simply asked for work. As I left at 5:00 the market was doing a thriving business in toy carts, houses, popcorn, and amulets.

Mario, one of the organizers of the Tobas quoted above on Carnival, also dances for the Señor de La Laguna of Cala Cala. He attributes the acquisition of his house to the Señor, since, during one of the fiestas he attended, he and his wife made a house of stones near his shrine and two years later he acquired one. Mario's account of his career dancing for the saints revealed some important features of the interrelation between miners and the saints they worship. The basic notion is the reciprocity due them as devotees of the cult, in return for which they get security and the objects they request: a house, an auto, or whatever. The real benefits they receive are the sense of security which enables them to work in a dangerous place and the motivation to work. Their faith that the saints will respond to their prayers inspires them to make concrete their nameless desires, which they then translate into the small replicas of the desired object, available at all the celebrations. When I purchased a house at Cala Cala, the vendor offered me a deed without my requesting it. I was then told to get a witness to the sale, just as though it was a real house, and the vendor cosigned her name releasing any claim to the property. The transaction not only confirmed my sense of the attainability of the dream but instructed me in some of the techniques of getting it (the bill of transfer, the cosignees, etc.). It was a step farther than the way North American advertisers take the workers down the garden path of consumer dreams, but possibly the greater literacy rate and familiarity with contracts of the American workers obviates the need for this final step.

The cult of the saints and the pasantes that serve them promote consumption desires and the knowledge of how to gain them. Plaster-of-paris replicas maintain the image firmly in view, and since the house or car is equipped with a coin slot, it serves as a bank to hold whatever of the portion of the wage that can be saved from immediate consumption needs. Ultimately consumption desires are the hold that this system of production has over the workers.

Warming the Earth Ceremony

When the June solstice arrives and the earth grows cold, the campesinos believe that the people must care for the Pachamama so that there will be renewal of life. Since the fiesta of San Juan coincides with this date, June 24, it has become the time for warming the earth with bonfires. Each stick of wood one throws in the fire represents a llama that the Pachamama will give to the person who remembers her. In the mining community as well as in the center of the city, people light bonfires and dance and drink until dawn. Although their concern is not that their flocks will die, they maintain this ritual as a life renewal ceremony.

For the miners the night of San Juan has had a special meaning ever since the massacre of 1967, during the Barrientos regime, when many miners had been fired and there was cut in wages. Despite the repression of union activities, the Federation of Mine Workers Unions called a meeting for June 24 to plan a strategy for regaining their wages. Delegates from other unions gathered in Siglo XX on the eve of San Juan and joined the miners of the encampments of Siglo XX and Catavi in the festivities. While the community celebrated, the army entered the encampment and killed over 87 people (see chapter 8).

When I visited Siglo XX on the second anniversary of the massacre I walked through the fire-lit streets, talking to the men and women who offered me chicha. "It is our history," one miner answered my question as to why they celebrate San Juan. "We must remember that night and carry on the earth warming, since it is an agricultural custom: The campesinos warm the earth to get more animals and crops for a greater life. We do it now more than before the massacre because we feel the need to assure more life, and assert our right to live."

The Month of Supay

The month of August is the time for the preparation of the land for planting in September. It is a time to propitiate the power of the hills, which is identified with both Supay and Huari, sometimes called Supay's father. Among the miners, the two beings are treated as one. It is simultaneously a time to recognize the Pachamama, since one must avoid the destructive potential of Huari at the same time that one wins the benefits of the earth's fertility. Therefore there is a special ch'alla for the Pachamama on Tuesdays in the houses and garden plots, as well as special attention to the ch'allas on Friday for Supay in the mine and for the enchanted stone images throughout the area. It is a time to ask for both fertility of the fields and mineral wealth from the mines.

K'araku in the Mines

The k'araku, or sacrifice for Supay, was in abeyance in nationalized mines throughout the military occupation, and there had not been the money or spirit to reinstitute it until the year I came. In the first week of July, three young workers were killed in the mines. The workers asserted that the deaths were due to the failure in keeping up the ritual offering of the sacrificed llama to Supay. A delegation of workers urged the superintendent of the San José mine to permit them to carry out the ritual on the customary night of July 31, which was that very month. The superintendent agreed to this and offered to pay for the llamas when he saw that the men were reluctant to return to work. I arrived at 10:00 P.M. on the appointed evening. Many workers were gathered in level zero at the elevator shaft. One man offered me a drink from a plastic fish he wore suspended from a string around his neck. "The k'araku is held in order that there be some development in the mine, or so that we might discover a vein that would benefit the company," he told me. "If they [the managers] had come, we workers would want to work with greater enthusiasm and will. Here we are waiting for some improvement to take place so that all can benefit. But what benefit would it have? Only so that the administrators could take trips out of the country."

At 12:20 the men charged with the llamas brought them into the main elevator, the male on the right and the female on the left. "It is the same in marriage," one man said, as the pure white llamas, decorated with streamers around their neck and sprinkled with confetti, the female with the colored wool "earrings" in her ears, were lifted on to the dollies on which they were conveyed to level 340. Twenty minutes later two *yatiris* (curers who deal with natural and supernatural physical disorders) arrived and were escorted below.

At level 340 the men gathered around the llamas as the yatiri cast liquor in all directions, asking the awichas, the malcus, the tíos to protect each level in the mine, beginning with level 340, pleading with the Tío not to eat any more workers and that he yield them much mineral. In this part of the ritual the yatiri used one bottle of *pisco*, two of alcohol, and one of wine, which he sprinkled on the floor. After doing this, he called, *"Hallalla, hallalla"* (life, life) and the miners removed their helmets. They sat down and began to *pijchar* coca (chew in a meditative fashion). One miner noticed that the female appeared to be crying, and he kissed her, trying to comfort her. The yatiri instructed the miners that they had to approach the llamas kneeling with their arms behind their back. They were then to kiss the llamas as they begged pardon for having to sacrifice them. The reason for their keeping their arms stretched out behind them was so that the llamas would not know who killed them and revenge themselves after their death. As the miners followed these instructions, the yatiri called on the malcus, the Awichas, the Pachamama, and the tiyulas of the mine.

The first llama to be sacrificed was the female. The senior yatiri grabbed the female by the head and the assistant yatiri held the body. The first cut the throat with a knife and the blood flowed into the white enamel basin which the miner in charge of the ceremony held. Then the senior yatiri took a smaller knife and made an incision at the heart. He took hold of the still beating heart and pulled it out of the llama and put it in another white basin. The miner in charge of the ceremony laid on top of it a cigarette with q'oa, alcohol, and coca. With the men following, he proceeded to the main gallery of the level where the large image of the Tío was ensconced. They buried the offering of the heart covered with coca leaves before the image and sprinkled the dirt with some blood. The men asked for safety and that there be no accidents in the mine. They spoke in Quechua, in a low, intimate tone. They spoke of the accident and pleaded that no others come to pass and that they have good metal. At this point in the ceremony no drinks were allowed.

The men returned to where the other llama had been left still alive. The yatiris cut the throat of this llama in the same way and received the blood and the beating heart in the two basins. The yatiris prayed over the blood, asking for safety and life of the awichas, machulas, and tiyulas. They called out all the danger points in the mine, the elevator, the winch, the machines, asking for safety and that there be no accidents in any of the work sites, each named in turn. Then five men brought the heart to a remote gallery which was rarely frequented. Each man entered near the spot where the second heart was buried, calling for his own safe-keeping and that of his companions. Returning to the place of the sacrifice, the men proceeded with an *acculli* or chewing coca in a social mood, as the yatiri sprinkled the blood that the llama still gave forth in the gallery. Throughout this part of the ceremony, none of the men drank any alcohol. This was destined for the Tío, the Pachamama, and the awichas.

Following this, four men carried the body of each llama to the elevator shaft, a fifth carrying the head, in a form of procession. The carcasses were carried out to be cooked the following day.

The next morning the same men charged with bearing the carcasses of the llama out of the mine brought them to a bakery, where they were cooked in the large ovens. Then they delivered them to the mine entrance, where the miners and their families were gathered for the meal. The female had had a fetus in her, and one of the men carried this draped around his neck, its forepaws hanging over his shoulders. He commented:

> ❖ This is the luck of the working class. It is our thing because of our faith in the Tío Lucas. He is the owner of the mine. We walk with him. He takes care of us and we arrive with him. He is still owner of the mine. Before, we worked with greater strength and without accidents. It is the fault of the security engineers that we had this accident. They are in collusion with the administration. We make claims without any effect.

The men rubbed the body of the fetus with alcohol, saying, "Ch'alla, ch'alla, viejas [old women], awichas."

There were some complaints about the proceeding of the ceremony. One of the miners said that the two plates of blood should have been left at the place of sacrifice so that the awichas could sit down and eat with the Tio. Another said that the fetus should have been buried along with the heart inside the mine. Someone rescued it from the burning pile of bones heaped up as people passed them on from their plates after eating the meat, and was prepared to bring it inside the mine, but another objected that any reentry at this point would disturb the Tío while he ate and so it was cast back on the pile. No one, however, dissented with the idea of the sacrifice. Young and old alike were in accord that this was the appropriate action to take in view of the increase in accidents.

Ritual and Ideology

What is the meaning of these rituals and how do they relate to the new ideologies that express the class consciousness of the miners? These questions have to be answered on at least three different levels: (1) What happens with the people relating to each other in the scene? (2) How does the ritual relate these participants to other significant reference groups? (3) How has the significance of the ritual changed over time?

A simple Malinowskian functionalism helps us to answer the first. The ch'alla integrates men within the work site and thus promotes the solidarity of the primary group. This is best expressed in Manuel's words, when he told me:

> ❖ This tradition inside the mine must be continued because there is no communication more intimate, more sincere, or more beautiful than the moment of the ch'alla, the moment when the workers chew coca together and it is offered to the Tío. There we give voice to our problems, we talk about our work problems, and there is born a generation so revolutionary that the workers begin thinking of making structural change. This is our university. The experience we have in the ch'alla is the best experience we have.

Manuel, who was one of the top leaders in the union in the pre-Barrientos period, was perhaps unusual in equating primary group solidarity with the basis for revolutionary action. Although it is a basic Marxist proposition about the beginning of class consciousness, many union leaders seem to negate it and are often critical of traditional rituals. This may stem from the fear of deep-rooted levels of consciousness and self-determination that are not controlled through the bureaucracy of union management.

The second issue of how the ritual relates workers to other significant reference groups requires a historical perspective. In the days of the tin baron before the nationalization of the mines in

1952, the owners, especially Patiño, would come to the celebration of the k'araku and dance with the palliris and the men as they celebrated the feast. His administrators gave each miner a personal gift of a skirt or jacket, in return for which they gave him a lump of the richest metal they had uncovered in their work. This exchange of the t'inka (the management's gift to the worker) and the achura (the workers' gift of ore to the owners) symbolized the basic reciprocity in the labor relationship. It reinforced a set of paternalistic ties that gave the workers greater spirit to work and sacrifice themselves. In those days, the workers within each work group were paid according to a contract figured on the basis of the mineral content of the ores they produced. There was a great deal of competition between each work group to secure the richest vein, and the hostility engendered was worked out in witchcraft. Alejandro, the old miner who had worked in most of the mines of Bolivia and a copper mine in Chile, described these customs:

> ❖ The men in the mines who got high returns on their contracts were most often the targets of witchcraft. The miners used to go seek the shamans from among the campesinos who know more about this. These shamans have animal spirits. Here, and especially in Colquecharka, many miners use witchcraft to make their more fortunate companions lose the vein. They went into the mine with the shaman and they threw water with salt on the vein where their enemy was working and this made it disappear. Sometimes the miners knew they were being bewitched and they called on the Pachamama.

Other miners reported pouring the milk of a black burro mixed with garlic on the veins of their enemies to make them disappear. The miners also had to protect the veins against the "evil eye" (bankañowi) of any workers entering their sector. When they struck a good vein, they sometimes slept in the mine to protect it. The miners never brought garlic into the mine, because this could make their own vein disappear since the Tío did not like it.

In short, hostile competition was intense, and the solidarity built up in the ch'alla was limited to the immediate group of men working on the same contract. Following the nationalization of the mines, the base pay was raised and equalized for all the mines, and the bargaining for the contract was carried out by the union agents in open bargaining procedures. Workers felt that one of the most important gains they made was to have the contracts figured openly with the superintendent of the mine, the mayordomo of the level, and the head of the work group witnessing the contract statement. After the revolution the contract was paid to work teams of two men rather than to a work gang, and it was based on total output measured in cubic feet regardless of mineral content. Thus the solidarity of the work group was weakened at the primary group level, but a larger unity was maintained in the work force as a whole as the union welded together not only the work units within a mine, but through the Federation of Mine Workers Unions of Bolivia (FSTMB) created a massive political force of all miners and, through the Workers Central of Bolivia (COB), linked miners to other industrialized workers.

During the period of nationalist solidarity within the populist revolutionary government, the ch'alla in the mines served as a recreation more than a point for mobilizing rebellion and focusing on dissatisfactions. This brief period of amicable labor-management relations came to an end with the Triangular Plan reorganization of the mines after 1960 and deteriorated still further after the military occupation of the mines by Barrientos in 1965. The miners say that Barrientos suppressed the ch'alla because he was afraid of the solidarity promoted in these drinking sessions. The suppression of the ch'alla added to the resentment of the workers against both management and the government.

Along with the suppression of the ch'alla came a sharp drop in the production of high quality ores. This was coincident with a falling off in exploration. Furthermore, the nationalized mining administration has never succeeded in developing work incentives. The wages of the workers were frozen at the level to which Barrientos had reduced them in 1965. This fact, coupled with rising salaries of administrators and army officers, has resulted in both alienation of the workers and stagnation in production. A brief respite came with the Torres regime in 1970 when wages were reinstated to the pre-1965 levels, but his presidency came to an end after ten months with the military coup of Colonel Hugo Banzer. The alienation of the worker expressed to me during the ch'alla reveals the complete transformation of the ritual from one in which worker-management solidarity was reinforced to one in which the ritual becomes the basis for communication of rebelliousness.

We have answered our third question, how the ritual has evolved over time, in the course of analyzing the changing structure of relations. This has not been a one-way street from paternalism to revolution. When the conditions were ripe for revolt in the past, especially in the early labor struggles of 1918 and during the Chaco War, the ch'alla became a point for mobilizing discontent. It did not surprise me in the least to learn that in 1918, when the management of the private mine of San José rejected the workers' position for higher wages and union recognition, the workers chose the night of July 31 to declare the first strike recorded for the mine. Again when there was extreme discontent over the Chaco War, the shrine of the Sapo (the toad) was chosen as an assembly point. Recognizing this, the general ordered it to be dynamited, with the disastrous result that he became paralyzed and died within the year. The cycle of which I observed the latter stages was one in which there was a shift from sponsorship of the rituals by the former owners and their foreign administrators, reinforcing an exploitative labor system, to a rejection of the belief and repression of the rituals of the ch'alla by the indigenous bureaucrats and technicians who entered after nationalization. These men probably rejected the rituals because of their fear of being identified with the Indian and chola classes from which they came. When the ritual was outlawed, the Tío was transformed into an ally of the workers. As one worker said, on the occasion of the k'araku, "The Tío is the real owner here. The administrators just sit in their offices and don't help us in our work." When Ovando permitted a limited ch'alla to take place in the 1970 Carnival, the men expressed some hope that their lot would improve, but the failure of the administration to make the traditional exchange and the impoverished nature of the celebration, because of lack of funds, minimized the impact of the celebration. "The Tío is still hungry," the miners said, "and so are we."

Assumptions about traditional and modern systems of belief often fail to capture the complexity of selective changes in symbol systems. The Tío is more important now in reference to accidents than as a generator of riches. This is tied to a contract system in which, after nationalization, the payoff depends on the total tonnage output rather than the mineral content of the ore. Its significance is directly related to this changing reality.

One evening Manuel visited us accompanied by his cousin Jorge (a pirkiñero who panned the outflow of the mines), who had converted to Protestantism. When Jorge rejected the traditional customs, Manuel objected, saying:

❖ Jorge says that this country, as a consequence of the old religion, drinks too much and does not take advantage most effectively of their earnings. Those values do not pertain so much to religious principles; if we analyze them, they are more a cultural process. From the purely orthodox religious point of view, these customs should be eliminated. But man has his defects. The miner must believe in the Pachamama and the Tío because of accidents that occur. Man is spiritually weak from the point of view of accidents or propensity to accidents. Without this belief he does not work in confidence. He is always uneasy. He thinks that even if not today, tomorrow he may have an accident and does not work, looking around to see if he is going to fall or if it is going to happen. But he does not work.

Therefore, the miner, particularly in the month of August, buys his wool, grease, coca, and other things that he offers, saying, "Pachamama is not going to punish me." With this, he internally believes he has fulfilled a proposal of giving something to the Pachamama and from that moment he can arrive at a point of forgetting an accident. Then he can continue working with tranquillity. It is a custom that the priests have not forced on us. We ought to think that our own race formed it, and that it was not formed by the priest. In the time of the Inca, they had forms of serving God, the Sun, and the Mother Earth. It was always in his [the miner's] feelings. He serves God in his offerings now as before in the time of the Sun.

The majority of workers do not question the presence of the Tío or the Pachamama. When they are startled, they yell, "What are you doing, Tío?" or "Don't get angry, Mama!" When an accident nearly happens, they offer more liquor and coca to the Tío with thanks for saving them. Some miners say that the fears men constantly face in the mines cause some to lose their virility. When this happens, the miners turn to the Tío and ask him to make them as potent as he. When three men died within a short period of time in San José in 1969, the men were convinced that the Tío was thirsty for blood. A delegation requested the administration to give them free time for a ch'alla, a collection was taken, and three llamas were purchased. A yatiri was hired to conduct the ceremony. All the miners offered blood to the Tío, saying, "Take this! Don't eat my blood!"

The Tío is an explanation for the inexplicable, a rationale for the irrational destiny which is forced on the miner. Their faith in him enriches a barren existence of unremitting toil. In the colonial period, when he appeared before the workers, he had the face and figure of the enemy of their enemy, the devil, red-faced, horned, and dressed in the royal robes of a medieval underworld denizen. In the period of imperialist exploitation, he appeared as a gringo, wearing a cowboy hat, boots, red-faced and larger than life. When one makes a contract with him, one is assured of riches even at the price of one's life, but he pays off with a greater certitude than government bureaucrats or officials. Supay transcends the medieval conception of the devil imported by the Spaniards; he is the source of wealth and desired power as well as the agent of evil. As Josermo Murillo Vacareza (1969:7–9), a folklorist steeped in the traditions of Oruro, says,

> The ancient figure of "Supay," by a process of acculturation-transculturation, acquired the characteristics of the Western Devil; but the natives, instead of hating him as a malignant being, maintained by instinct their ancestral conception of the "Supay" in the depths of the mines, where the *mitayo* is condemned to die in a fatal and exhausting labor. There as with religious images, he received tributes, adorations and invocations.

As the central figure in Carnival, Supay is both an expression of the frustrations and anxieties of the lives of these people as well as a projection of their desire to overcome them.

Huari and the Pachamama

One myth which gives us some sense of the link between the two powers, Huari and the Pachamama, was related to me by Eduardo Ibañez, a painter whose work is inspired by the folklore of his homeland. The condor, who epitomizes the romantic life that is the basis for human reproduction, is the son of Huari, and his adventures are as follows:

> ◈ Legend tells us that Huari, the god of evil, had a son completely different from him. He was a good and pious son, who always

came to the town of Uru Uru transformed into a condor. When he touched his feet on the earth, he turned into a handsome man. He fell in love with a beautiful maiden who appeared to be an Indian princess. The people of Uru Uru had a great deal of faith in the maiden, believing that she was sent by the gods for their salvation. Sensing that the son of Huari was in love with the maiden, they threatened him that, if he tried to steal her, he would be turned to stone. The *curacas* [town officials] met and they reached an understanding that he was going to steal her. They prepared to change him into stone. Late in the afternoon of a day in the month of the preparation of the earth, [August] they saw a white condor flying high, a young and handsome condor. Hardly had he put his feet in preparation for the flight at the foot of the Luridanchu hill, then he was converted into stone. And there he remains petrified.

Since a petrified soul has a great deal of hunger, the people had to give him food each Friday. On the other side of the hill there is a great round stone that the people call the Round Stone. And there the couples who are in love go to leave food for the condor who was in love. In our days, many of the couples still go there on Tuesdays and Fridays and ask that it be possible for them to make a home and that they should not be left disillusioned and petrified as the condor. After making a ch'alla, they construct a small house at the foot of the condor, arranging rooms for the children they think of having. They go down rapidly and without looking back. And in many cases, because of their faith or some real act on the part of the son of Huari, the lovers begin to form a household and have the children that they ask for.

In the celebration of the ch'alla to the condor on the first Friday of August, I saw couples, both married and unwed, go with their offerings to the site of the stone image and there build their dream houses. The time of arrival should be an odd hour, 11, 1, 3, etc., or midnight. The group, called "chain," of persons should also have an odd number of adults. Children represent the spirit and mature women represent the body. White offerings are preferred: popcorn, rice, and sugar, which represent the spirit. The coca they bring is the encarnation of the Pachamama and the fire that they light to burn their offering is the human desire for unity and a representation of the sun. The liquor offered represents the good and bad thoughts people have.

The first act is to sprinkle liquor, beer, or chicha on the condor and drink some, then sprinkle confetti and wind *serpentinas* (streamers) around the head of the condor. The first act is terminated with a prayer asking the condor to give what they need.

The second act is to build a house of rocks in the vicinity of the condor. I watched Elsa, a schoolteacher, build a house in which she laid out a patio and stuck little twigs representing fruit trees. When I commented on how well she had constructed the house, she agreed, saying that she had many nieces and nephews and wanted to provide a good house for them in the future. When the house is finished, one must sprinkle it with liquor and stretch streamers over the structure and sprinkle confetti on it. Some stock the house with items needed—cloth so that there would be no lack of clothing, sugar, corn, rice, so that food would not be lacking, etc.

The final act is one of meditation, while the group smokes a cigarette and chews coca leaves. Finally some go to the "bank" to take out the yellowish stones which will be taken home. The last act is to burn the items stored in the house and the "table" for the condor.

The Day of Spring

September 21 is the day for crowning queens in schools and colleges all over highland Bolivia, and to celebrate youth. It is a time when the first crops begin to appear in the earth after the spring rains have come. The secular nature of contemporary festivals is a transformation of what might have been a fertility ritual honoring the Pachamama, at least if we can judge from a legend which Eduardo Ibañez related to me:

> ❖ This happened at the foot of the Andes in a very high place called the Land of the Chosen. The people had a great conception of women. Some women of the town lost this respect, thinking that woman was the same as man. But a lord [Viracocha] of the town showed them that woman has a great gift, a secret that only the gods know. In order to demonstrate this greatness that only women possess, that only women bear in their organs the offspring that they want so much, he prepared himself on the twenty-first of December to return to the Pachamama. He made a great opening in the earth to bury a jar. He began to heat everything around the earth and he invited those who did not believe in the greatness of women. He put himself inside the mouth of the jar and everyone was astonished as he prepared to close himself in

with bits of earth. He called upon them to kill him, saying "I am going to show that, by entering into the Pachamama with my blood, she will hold me in her breast and give birth to a new being."

No one believed him, but he urged them to kill him. They poured all his blood into the vessel, without losing a drop outside. They kept it completely shut for nine months. All those who had participated in the sacrifice dedicated themselves to caring for it all the time, because no one opened it or he would die.

After a while, when there were only three days lacking until the date that he would fulfill the term, they all heard some revelations as he said to them. "So it is as women bring from the earth their children without knowing what is in their womb, without giving account of this great mystery, of this respect of their childbearing. Many times they give birth to the gods. Don't forget to unearth me in three days at midnight, because if you do not open me at this hour I have to die."

The twenty-first of September arrived and the people came to the place where the lord was buried. They took off the top and a white *malku* flew out and moved its head, looking at all who were present. It seems that the people cried because they had awaited this sacrifice believing in the value of women. After this, the malku rose up and flew into the Andes. From then on, the white condor is the protector of women.

Like all pre-Hispanic days of celebration of the solstice and equinox, both the twenty-first days of December and September are charged with a special affect which enters into the political sensibilities of the contemporary inhabitants. In 1942, the miners of Siglo XX-Catavi marched up to the administration offices to demand a raise in wage. The ensuing massacre (chapter 2) resulted in this day being comemorated as the day of miners.[1] In 1970 the Day of Spring became the chosen day for students and workers to enter into the streets in a major protest demonstrating against the government of General Ovando for his treatment of the *guerrilleros* of Teoponte. In the month of July, leaders of the National Army of Liberation (ELN) of Che Guevara had gone to Teoponte in a desperate attempt to offset the turn to the right that Ovando's government had taken

[1] In 1977, December 21 was chosen as the day that wives of miners jailed for their participation in a strike in 1976 should go on a hunger strike calling for political amnesty. The strike grew as the army menaced them with jailing and death. By January, international pressure resulted in capitulation to their demands, release of the prisoners, and return of the exiles.

in the preceding weeks. Failing to capture the ambassador of the United States, whom they had planned to hold hostage in order to gain some position for the Left in the government, their members were captured by the armed forces when they were sleeping, and while in captivity, a dozen of their leaders were completely destroyed by hand grenades and bazookas. Fearing to reveal the cowardice with which the army overcame the rebels, Ovando had resisted the pleas of the parents and the priests who demanded that he turn over the bodies, until the pressure had built up to a fever pitch in the early weeks of September. Finally he yielded, and the destroyed bodies were given over to the student group in the Universidad Mayor de San Andrés. The horror of the Bolivian populace grew, and the procession, uniting students and workers, made a public demonstration on September 21. Shortly after, the government was ousted by a right-wing junta led by General Rogelio Miranda, who proved so unpopular even with the armed forces that the way was paved for the entry of Juan José Torres into the presidency.

Rituals in Contemporary Belief and Behavior

Pre-conquest beliefs provide deep roots for the people's sense of their identity and a baseline for their resistance to oppression by alien forces. Although this may lie at a nearly subconscious level, it nonetheless has a pervasive influence in determining the choice of timing for political acts of protest and consequently the reaction of the ruling group. The first strike in Oruro in modern times took place on July 31, 1920. Although there are no records to indicate how it started, I can imagine scenes such as I have witnessed on the occasion of the ch'allas in the mines, when the workers were determined to take their destiny into their own hands after offering the ch'alla to the Tío. Perhaps it was an obdurate administrator who refused to let the men close the mines for three days after making their offering so that the Tío could eat in peace, and the workers decided to act in response to the dictates of their own custom and strike. The massacre of December 21, 1942, occurred on the day the malku interred himself in his own blood, when the miners of Siglo

XX and Catavi marched, ten thousand unarmed men and women, to the administrative offices of Patiño Mines Company to demand higher wages and a share in the war-inflated prices for tin. The massacre of San Juan took place when a congress was called to reinstate the wages Barrientos took from the workers when he ended their revolution. Finally, the students and workers called a demonstration against the government on the Day of Spring, September 21, when the white condor was born and spirits were high.

Whatever the deep-lying connections are, it is during these rituals that the spirit of rebellion comes to the surface. Resistance takes many forms, but it is always strengthened by the self-determination of a people who have not yet lost their self-identity. The rituals and belief combine to reinforce the myths which encompass their history, and the celebrations of Carnival, the ch'alla, and the earth-warming ceremonies prepare the people for a time when they can shape their own destiny. Sectarian political leaders usually reject ritual protest as deviance. However, if one thinks of it as a rehearsal that keeps alive the sentiment of rebellion until a historically appropriate moment, it may reinforce political movements.

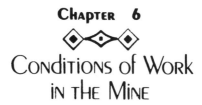

Chapter 6

Conditions of Work in the Mine

◇MINERS TALK of the mine as though it were a living organism. This is not a survival of animism, but a poetic metaphor that strikes anyone approaching the entrance. The pulsating thump of the *chancador*, or compressor, that breaks up the rock is like a heartbeat, and the hum of the pumps that draw out water from the lower levels and feed water into the lines for the drills is like the respiratory system of a giant mammal. As one nears the mouth of the mine, the odors of hydrogen sulfide are expelled like the gases from an overtaxed digestive system. The reddish-brown *copajira*, or cuprous liquid, drains from the interior like pus-filled blood from suppurating wounds. The miners often refer to the interior of the mine as "the bowels of the earth," and they jokingly say that one of the reasons Bolivia does not have earthquakes is because all the explosive gases that build up inside the earth are released through its mineshafts.

Three shifts of eight hours maintain a 24-hour servitude to the mines. As each shift changes, the workers, wearing their helmets and boots, their rain gear rolled under their arms, move toward the mouth of the mine. Throughout the day, men move in and out on rail cars like Lilliputians serving the needs of Guilliver. There is a cannibalistic quality in the relationship between the workers and the mine. "We eat the mines," one man told me at a ch'alla, "and the mines eat us." Their feelings about the mines are expressed in the names they give the work sites: Moropoto, Black Anus; Veta Dolores, Vein of Sadness; Sapo, Toad; El Tambo Mata Gente, People-Killer Inn, a work site where seven men were killed in a cave-in; Carnavalito, Carnival, or the last time to eat meat before Lent. In the smaller mines, the dried blood from the sacrifices of llamas splashed on the mouth of the mine gives an even more carnivorous look to the hills.

Conditions of work within most mines can without exaggeration be described as inhuman. There are no conveniences for workers in most mines. The lack of latrines, the absence of any drinking water except for the lines that feed the machines, are inconveniences that make men aware that their physical needs are considered irrelevant by the administration to the operation of the mines.[1] Once, when the men in Itos prepared themselves a lunchroom so that they could sit down and eat at a table instead of sitting on a pile of ore in a shaft as many do, the management arbitrarily closed it. Extreme changes in temperature within a few yards mean that the danger of respiratory infection, especially grave with men whose lungs are vulnerable because of the silicosis everyone suffers from, is great. Temperatures range from 10 to 41 degrees Celsius (50 to 105 degrees Fahrenheit). Those who work in the high temperatures often have to take breaks every five or ten minutes, hosing themselves down with water to replace the body fluids they lose. Men who go into these hot areas lose several kilos a month and are unable to sustain the work for more than a short period.

In order to appreciate fully what the conditions of the mine were like and how they affected one's physical, emotional, and mental outlook, I was determined to enter the mines for an eight-hour shift. The engineer in charge of safety tried to talk me out of it, first on the basis of danger, and when he saw that made no impression on me, on the basis that the workers objected to the presence of women in the mine because, he said, of "suspicion that it would bring bad luck to the operation." However all the miners with whom I consulted wanted very much for me to enter so that I could understand with my own senses what the conditions were like. Whether they suspended belief in the adage about a woman's presence in the mines, or whether they reclassified me as a nonwoman because of the more prevailing role of a foreign investigator, I do

[1] In cooperative mines, where workers make decisions on many of the expenditures for safety, there was less attention paid to security than in nationalized mines (Widerkehr 1975).

not know, but none objected. When I obtained permission from the central headquarters in La Paz, I entered the following day. I include notes taken that day to convey a more immediate impression of underground work.

The Tempo of Work

The mine company sends out the bus that takes the men to the mine. I got on at 6:20 A.M. the morning I was scheduled to enter the mine. It was cold in the early morning before dawn. At the security office I was given a helmet to protect my head from falling rocks and from bumps where the corridors are low, and a belt to hold the battery that lit my headlight.

MINERS DESCEND INTO THE "BOWELS OF THE EARTH" TO START THE DAY'S WORK.

I entered with the carpenter, Manuel, who promised to let me observe his work day. We descended to level 180 (180 meters below ground level), where Manuel and his partner changed into the patched *bayeta* or homespun shirt some wear when working. I recalled the words of one miner who told me that Urriolagoitia, the president in the time of the tin barons, swore that he would have all of the workers wearing bayeta, a material that evoked the humiliation of the peasantry from which miners were escaping. The drillers helped each other tie closed the sleeves of their rain gear so that the wet clay that sprays them as they drill does not run down their arms.

After dressing, the men sat on rocks at the edges of the rail lines, chewing coca leaves in a meditative mood. This was in preparation for the work day ahead.

We walked about 200 meters and climbed seven ladders to Manuel's work site, where he was preparing a chute. He climbed up a chimney to do some hand drilling for a niche for the wooden beams in the rock wall. Although it is more difficult to prepare a hard-rock shaft for exploitation of the minerals, the men prefer it to soft walls because there is less chance of a cave-in later. He put on his inhalator as he prepared to work. Manuel is unusual in the care he takes to use his inhalator, a protective device to filter out the silicates that suffuse the air in the shafts. It was about 10 degrees Celsius in the shaft where he worked, but he sweated profusely because of the extreme exertion in rigging the heavy eucalyptus beams that support the tunnel. The carpenters are the most strategic personnel in determining the security of the mines, since they prepare the scaffolding for the work crews. He used a hand drill since the power and air lines were not as yet installed in the new shaft. Hitting the drill with the 3.5-kilo (8-pound) mallet was hard work. Manuel worked twenty seconds pounding, he stopped to measure the distance on the other side to see that it would line up evenly, then pounded the mallet one minute, rested fifteen seconds, breathing through the inhalator, worked another three seconds, paused, hammered another three seconds, stopped as another worker sidled by in the narrow passage. The driller was scheduled to work in this corridor and came in to discuss the job. The work has to be in accord with the advance he is supposed to make. He wanted it to bend in one direction, but Manuel argued that it had to be in a firm place. Manuel won the argument on the basis of safety.

The air was filled with a fine dust from a drilling operation that was going on nearby. Manuel proceded to work again, striking one minute, taking a five-minute break, striking thirty seconds with a thirty-second break, working twenty seconds with a fifteen-minute break to adjust the strap of his inhalator. A workman from another gallery came to get a part of the plumbing to rig up the drills. Manuel greeted the man briefly and took a break to measure the hole again, holding a meter stick at the level where the rocks joined. Using a stone attached to a line as a plumbline, he marked where the cross-bar should enter for a support. He hammered for ten seconds, then laid the beam on the niche he had formed, testing it for fit. He worked one minute, hammering hard, stopped ten seconds and adjusted his inhalator, than worked ten seconds, stopped five seconds to check firmness of rock. Despite the hard surface of the rock, sudden fissures can mean that the whole operation has to be redone in another place. He resumed hammering for forty seconds, stopped to look at the hole, breathing very hard, resting twenty-five seconds, then worked ten seconds and rested fifteen. Another workman came to go down the ladder to the next level below. Manuel took the opportunity to break for ten seconds, then hammered another five seconds, breaking to breathe heavily.

Manuel was balanced on cross-beams astride a shaft that dropped ten meters below. The shaft was a little wider than a meter and about two meters above the supporting beams. He commented to me while pausing in his work that, while the drillers had machines to work, the carpenters had only their own power. He worked another thirty-five seconds, tested the rock, hammered another ten seconds, working and pausing to regain his breath, which was labored because of the inhalator muffling the intake of air. If he were to slip on the clay-covered beams that supported him, he could have another of the bad falls he had suffered in the past. The young, inexperienced workers have many accidents before they learn the caution that Manuel, in his twenty-five years inside the mines, has learned to master as second nature.

Another driller came by looking for a drill. Manuel stepped

back to allow him to pass and took the time to measure the second niche he had begun to form for the beam. A rock dislodged and fell below, a reminder of the danger he himself was in in his precarious position. He worked thirty-five seconds, tested the rock for ten seconds, worked fifteen seconds, stopped two seconds, hammered seventeen seconds with a four-second rest, another seventy seconds with a five-second rest, twenty-five seconds hammering and then a break to measure the ledge on which to set the beam. Meanwhile the sound of the drill from the nearby shaft sounded and the air became even more suffused with dust. A worker passing in the shaft below yelled if it was possible to pass, and Manuel stopped work so that nothing would fall as the man made his way across the passage below. Each man's life depends on his working comrades. If there is an accident, each worker has some feeling of guilt, even though it was not directly his fault, because the concern for everybody's safety is always in their minds.

Manuel's partner, Julio, arrived. Both men carried their tools in a cowhide bag with the fur side out and with a leather shoulder strap. Many of these old, hand-crafted items are still used in the mines since they resist the corrosive atmosphere of the interior. The two descended the shaft in which they worked to get a wooden beam, which they sawed to the size they had measured. They each brought up a heavy beam slung over one shoulder with a rope while they clung with the free hand to the slippery, clay-covered ladder. Manuel readjusted his inhalator, which he had taken off to make the 5-meter climb up the ladder. As he worked on the niche, his partner began hammering for eleven minutes and he taking over for ten. They tried fitting the beam in the rests, then took it down to chip away some more rock. A driller came by to take the nitrate bag I had been sitting on, to set the fuses in the adjoining shaft. All the charges are set off shortly before the noon break so that the workers can take the lunch time away from the narrow galleries where the dust rises with the charges and retreat to the open galleries near the elevator shaft. Together the men tried out the beam, setting it in different positions and testing it for durability. They took it down and chipped again at the niche. Domingo took over as Juan shook the pebbles, which had fallen from the ceiling of the shaft, out of his boots. When a big rock falls, the men call on the Pachamama not to be angry, but they accomodate to the small rocks constantly dislodged as they work.

Manuel took off his inhalator so that he could breathe more freely and helped Juan lift the beam in place. He took a block of wood, about 3 by 8 by 15 centimeters (1 by 3 by 6 inches), and held it as Julio pounded an adz 2.5 centimeters (1 inch) from the end, splitting it down. Then Manuel took over the adz and split the wood down to the end as Julio put his foot on it to hold it in place. The two worked in perfect coordination with few words spoken, accustomed to respond to the needs of the task without asking questions. When they were satisfied with the wedge they had fashioned, they hammered it into the niche where the beam rested in order to tighten the beam firmly in place. Manuel told Julio to prepare another piece, and when he finished hammering the wedge in place, he descended to hold his foot on the block from which Julio was cutting the second wedge just as Julio had done for him when he was preparing the first. Although the two men interchange roles, each doing the same acts, Manuel, as the master carpenter takes the initiative, sets the pace, and makes the judgments in each of the acts they undertake. It is a perfect blending of cooperative and managed operation, with the two men responsive to the total needs of the task. At the same time, the older master carpenter is accorded the authority to make judgments and issue commands which the younger man accepts, deferring to the authority without losing his own sense of initiative. Although the age relationship is the primary factor in their relationship since it corresponds with experience and skill, not all partnerships are decided in that way, since *peónes de la casa,* or general assistants to anyone, are often older than the person in charge. When they had hammered in the second wedge and tested their weight on the beam to make sure that it was secure, they prepared to leave and go down to another level. They seemed satisfied that the beam would hold up under the stress of the overhead weight it carried and was secure against the blasts of dynamite that were set off all around them.

Both men began to descend the seven ladders of 5 meters' length, each one staggered in the shaft so that if one slipped and fell it would not be a long drop. I followed them down. At the lower level, where they met the drillers who were to work in the shaft, Manuel told them that the engineer was coming and that they would have to wait for his decision before they proceeded with the preparation. The driller said that he knew better than the engineer what had to be done, but they waited for his appearance. When the engineer arrived shortly after, Manuel told him where the cross-beam would have to go, and the engineer pondered this a while and agreed with him. Julio took the measurements of the beams and the two sawed the wood below so it would be easier to take it up the shaft. As they worked, the drillers joked with them, laughing as they remarked that Manuel should be the engineer. The men do not have a great deal of respect for the engineers, many of whom have theoretical knowledge but lack the practical experience to be able to carry out the job. They noted that this engineer, a young man trained in the United States, had at least learned to accept their judgment of what had to be done in the two months he had worked in this mine, and they felt this was progress. After they carried up the new beams and stacked them where they were to fit in the upper levels, Manuel announced that it was time for lunch. It was then 11:30. They both washed their hands in the stream of *copajira*, the yellowish-red sulfurous water that winds in a sluggish stream in all the passages.

The lunchroom was a large niche carved out in one of the passages. Rough wooden planks lined the rock wall, on which the men sat. There were men there when we arrived. There was some joking and laughing as the men relaxed from the strenuous work. Soon the elevator arrived with the lunches packed in tiered metal containers and wrapped with cloths by the women so that the soup would stay hot. They were picked up at the mining encampment by a company truck which brought them into the mine.

On a second occasion, when I entered for a full day's shift, I recorded the operations of a driller, Celso. Drillers always work in pairs, a master driller with his helper. The drills, which weigh as much as or more than the man, can be used for up to eight years. With the newer drills, the men can get more production and earn more on their contract. It is almost impossible to determine the relative efficiency of the man and his machine, and while the administration blame the workers when production is low, the workers blame the poor performance of the machine, the low air pressure, the hardness of the rock matrix, or the failure of the engineer to assess practical problems.

I entered the gallery where Donato and Celso were working, a very damp, cool work site. Both wore the yellow slickers provided by the company, which were drenched with clay. The drill was constantly sticking into the clay surface on the ceiling of the shaft, and the two men spent more time trying to dislodge it in order to proceed with the next perforation then they did drilling. As they worked the drill into the face, they turned to hand work to pull out the shaft. I was reminded of a dentist working his way into the giant cavities of the mountain. They often had to use a mallet to release the drill. In one case it was stuck for eight minutes. The helper worked hard with the wrench for eleven minutes and the master took over for ten minutes. When they released it and began to drill, the helper stood at the barrel of the drill, watching the point of entry in the face. Any minute it could be side-swiped when striking a new kind of material, and he could be knocked over and even killed. The masters all admit that the job of the helper is even more dangerous than that of the master because of the erratic behavior of the drills.

When the drill stuck another time, the helper took the wrench and hammered it out. The foremen came by and watched for a while, commenting that it took a long time, sympathizing with them for the loss on their contract rather than criticizing. The helper adjusted the water hose, which sprays the perforation as the drill enters to keep down the dust and cool the machine, and the driller lets the air into the barrel. Neither the driller not his assistant wore the inhalator, since the suffusion of the silicates in the air was so dense that the filter would have been impregnated after a few minutes and they had neither the replacements nor the time to adjust this. Instead, they wore handkerchiefs and chewed coca leaves with the belief that this limited the inhalation of silicates that caused silicosis. They drilled for six minutes, stopped the machine, and took out the bore, replacing the 80-centimeter length with the 100-centimeter bore. (As the hole deepens, the drillers must adjust the length of the bore to the advance.) Celso turned the machine on, opening the piston slowly as the bore adjusted itself into the open-

CHEWING COCA, THE DRILLER BEARS THE SHOCK OF THE VIBRAT-
ING MACHINE AS HIS ASSISTANT HOLDS THE LINES OF WATER AND
AIR PRESSURE. ALTHOUGH MASKS ARE MADE AVAILABLE TO PRO-
TECT THE LUNGS, FILTERS ARE IN SHORT SUPPLY, AND IN THE
STIFLING AIR THE WORKERS FIND THAT THEY SMOTHER THEIR
RESPIRATION.

ing to avoid breaking the shaft. The master moved the drill in a ro-
tary motion, perhaps to keep it free so that it would not get clogged
in the clay. The helper stood to the side, constantly aware of the
danger. Water sprayed into their hands and sprayed their faces
with a wash of clay and mud. Pieces of rock fell as the shattering
blast echoed against the walls of the 70-centimeter-wide passage in
which they worked. They had no protection for their eyes. The
driller said that they had tried safety glasses, but too much smoke
and moisture obscured their vision and they could not stop to wipe
them constantly. Only the fluttering eyelid could respond with the
speed necessary to keep up with the machine. Three-minute spells
of drilling, one-minute breaks, water gushed out from the hole as
some vein of water was pierced. The caverns of the mine are like a
living organism, draining fluids from the wounds inflicted by the
workers. Cold, wet air whistled around in the narrow cavern in
which the men worked. Where I sat, only 2 meters from the drill

because of the cramped space, I was sprayed with the wet mud. The foreman came by again. He took his watch out of a shoe-polish tin in which he kept it to protect it from the dampness and checked the time. The driller worked the machine in three-minute intervals, stopping and checking the surface. He and his partner were drilling five holes in the ceiling of the gallery to insert the dynamite for the advance. They had to prop the machine on a log as the vibrations drove the barrel props into the floor of the passage. They did not stop working when the dynamite blasts went off below because they were behind in their work. The gallery filled with suffocating smoke from below as the driller set the machine in a new location, setting it up on a log to brace it. The helper struck a match to light a cigarette, and I could smell the acrid odor of the match in a split second, it was borne so quickly by the dense, humid air. As the helper changed the drill, he puffed on a cigarette, his check stuffed with the coca leaves. The helper, standing less than half a meter from the driller, could not make himself heard over the roar of the machine and used hand signals to communicate. I could hardly see either man although I was sitting two meters from the work site.

At 11:00 the men took a break for lunch. They "washed" their hands in the nitrate powder and rinsed them in the copajira. On this level they did not even have a bench to sit on, and the men chose hunks of ore to sit down on at the elevator shaft, where there was more open air space. Three of the men came up and offered me some of their soup when they saw that I only had a cold sandwich. I asked them to compliment their wives.

When we went back to the work site at 12:00, the driller let me hold the machine and try the advance. When I let the air into the piston, the jolt almost threw me, although I had been warned to expect it. It was like holding a tiger, something with a will of its own, and I realized fully the danger the men had spoken of in the operation of the drills. The vibrations of the machine numb the body completely. The men say that after several hours of drilling, they do not feel the pain of laceration from falling rock and are sometimes surprised to see blood flowing from a wound when they come out from work. A retired miner told me that after two years' relief from drilling, he can still hear the hissing of the pistons and the blast of

ADVANCING AT THE FACE OF THE ROCK, A DRILLER WITH A
HORIZONTAL DRILL FED BY AIR PRESSURE AND WATER LINES
WORKS WITH HIS ASSISTANT.

the drill hitting rock from his seventeen years behind the perfora-
tor, when he lies down to sleep.

I have spoken to other visitors in the mines who accept, without question, the managers' disparagement of the workers, their
laziness on the job, and their addiction to coca. I think that if they
were to stay for the entire work shift, they might gain some percep-
tion of the need for breaks from a routine which is the most demanding physically and psychologically that I have ever experienced.

Until the supervisor refused to give me further permission to
enter the mine, I spent five full-day shifts in the mine and made
about twenty entries. The questions raised by my observations
were: How do the workers relate to each other and to the technical
and supervisory personnel? What are the attitudes toward mechanization? How do they cope with the fear of sickness, accidents, and
death that are ever present? These issues are touched on in the following sections analyzing the organization of work.

Social Hierarchy in the Mine

Each mine has a hierarchical order comparable to that in figure 6.1, which corresponds to one section of a mine. The superintendant may be in charge of four or more such sections. The actual number of workers below the level of mayordomo differs according to the production plans, but the chain of command remains fixed. Drillers are deferred to by other workers both inside the mine and in the community because of the greater physical sacrifice required by their work and the authority they exercise over the other workers in the preparation of the work sites.

The Work Team

Formerly the work was organized in teams of six to a dozen or more workers called cuadrillas. The head of each work gang was a pirkiñero, an "empirical" engineer, a person of long experience skilled in gaining the cooperation of the men who worked with him. Each gang included at least one driller and assistant and the loaders and carters needed to handle the load. The men were paid according to the mineral content of the load they produced, and each team had a man skilled in detecting the quality of the ore in

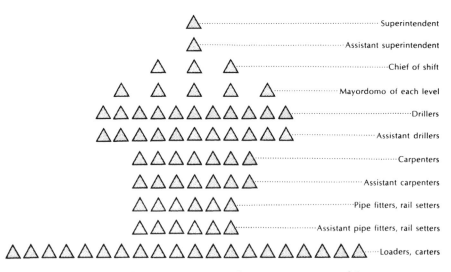

FIGURE 6.1 ORGANIZATIONAL STRUCTURE OF THE MINES

order to check the returns, which were distributed by the head of the gang according to set proportions. The solidarity of the team was great, as was the divisiveness between teams who competed to take over the best veins discovered by explorer crews. Pedro, *venerista*, told me about the old style of work:

> ❖Under the old system of work, the pirkiñero pursued the vein. They didn't cut galleries very tall because the miner was only pursuing the vein, and he went where the vein went. When it turned, he turned. Now the technicians maintain a width of eighty centimeters by two hundred and thirty in height. They orient the shafts in order to maximize the ease of removing the slag. But in the old days, the veneristas did not have any technical direction either in the universities here nor in Potosí. The work was very hard but at least it provided a base for making a living. They used to concentrate their own ores, and without any university training, they could produce up to sixty percent pure mineral, whereas now, in the new pre-concentration plants, they only get forty-five percent.

The organization of the work changed after nationalization as a result of the introduction of more machine-powered tools and the break-up of teams into partnerships of the master driller and his assistant, the carpenter and his assistants, while the carters and loaders worked for "the house." The contract paid to the two-man work team and the gains were measured in cubic meters rather than quantity of mineral contained in the load. The social consequence was the break-up of primary group solidarity and the broadening of ties with all the men on a level and even all those for each mine entrance.

Surface-level workers include the mechanics who repair the tools, the men in charge of the dynamite, the distributors of masks and clothing, and the light caretakers as well as the elevator operator on each of the three shifts. Lighter tasks above ground, including those of night watchmen and gatekeepers, are usually held by former underground workers who have contracted silicosis.

Despite the pyramidal form of organization, there is a good deal of camaraderie in the carrying out of tasks. Workers call each other brother (ñaña), including the mayordomo of the shift. Assistants to the drillers and carpenters are usually younger men who are learning the trade, and so there is an easy acceptance of authority based on experience rather than privilege.

Engineers and Supervisors

The real break in communication comes at the technical and supervisory levels. Workers complain constantly about what they consider to be an excess of supervisors. "Entirely too many *jefes*—here, there everywhere, but they do not cooperate with us," one man said on the occasion of a k'araku.

> ❖ Now we have more technicians than anything else. One will come and tell us to do something and we obey, but what they tell us to do often fails. They urge us to do something we feel is wrong and we say, "Yes, we will do it, sir, but under your responsibility." In short, I would say that the administration does not know what they are doing. Certainly they have learned the theory, but as far as practice goes, they know very little. And one who has worked knows from experience in the very base of the operations itself. For example in starting an exploration, in setting off a charge or in making a run, the worker knows how it is going to come out, while they, when they tell us something, it doesn't turn out as they predict. To make a perforation, there are different kinds of blastings: direct blast, *trazo fuego* pyramid blast, and side blast *saque de costado,* which you perform according to the kind of rock. In some sections the rock is soft and you can use anything, but in hard rock you have to know how to blast in order to draw it out. But these technicians don't take into account what the workers say as they did before. The pirkiñeros generally asked for the collaboration of the worker and the worker cooperated, but the pirkiñero himself knew how to work and there was comprehension. But now the technicians do not collaborate.

The workers resent the lack of respect on the part of technicians in supervisory positions who, they feel, do not know the work. Furthermore, the new system of work itself negates the skills developed in the old system. Formerly each cuadrilla planned and carried out a series of operations that demanded a high empirical knowledge of the mining operations, including concentration of the metals within the mine so that the contracts could be calculated according to content. With the new concentration plants handling the load in bulk with no separation of the product by work team, the only interest is getting the load down to the plant as fast as possible. The workers have not accepted the new system of work, and the failure of communication between technicians has meant that the antagonism has increased rather than diminished since the changes were introduced in the fifties. Thus, although the new system of work was introduced in the spirit of minimizing the self-exploitation of the workers that was the essence of the old pirkiñero system and equalizing the returns for labor for mines and work sites with different levels of productivity, the net result was to increase the hostility of workers toward the technicians and to alienate them from a job that was increasingly routine as the adventure of making a rich strike was taken out of the job, and the sense of controlling an operation was reduced.

In order to explore the question of the relations between technicians and workers, I invited a carpenter and a technician to discuss some of the conflict issues between these crucial segments of the work force. Despite the tension that always exist between people in these capacities, the conversation opened up dimensions of the roles that I could not have elicited from separate interviews. Manuel, the carpenter, initiated the conversation:

❖ I have the following criteria in judging a technician. A technician ought, when he is acting in his role, to accept sometimes the practical suggestions made by a worker. One example, Engineer. In level one-eighty they made a transport line to get the load which passes from one-fifty and Engineer Ortega agreed to it in his conversation with workers. The workers said, "Why don't we make a chimney with a ramp here, Engineer, and our load will fall right into the main shaft?" "Yes, good idea; let's propose it to the supervisor." But the idea was turned down, and instead they ordered another passage made with an enormous chute and an opening so small that we have a problem getting the load down. We couldn't use dynamite because it would blow up the track and even the corridor. We can hardly use it at all.

I think an engineering student ought to spend his vacations from study in the mine. Those who have are people who do not only theorize on a blackboard. One had to get down in the ground to observe and make his own study. Perhaps I am mistaken in this, but that is my judgment. And then perhaps when the student has finished his education he will have silicosis like a miner!

Manuel's sense of humor was wasted on the engineer, who took a very narrow managerial view of relations in the mine. When I asked him about the opportunities for advancement of workers into technical capacities, the engineer replied, "They have always trained both the technicians and workers and advanced them according to their ability."

Manuel interjected.

❖ It is just as the engineer says, if a man has capacity, they couldn't close the door in his face. Rojas, for example, formed a work team in the time of Patiño and his ability was recognized. There was, however, favoritism and some continued as workers despite their ability. One could see cases of injustice in all the ranges of work. There was one engineer *empirico* here who found the veins when a European geologist wasn't able to, and all the workers thought he would be named superintendent, but he remained a measurer of the work progress. He was demoralized by the experience. [In agreeing with the engineer, Manuel nonetheless subverted his assertion of equal opportunity.]

I asked the technician if he felt that the former foreign technicians were more easily able to maintain authority over the workers than the Bolivian nationals, an issue the miners had often raised with me, and he replied,

❖ My criterion is this: I believe that all workers respect a superior, the technician, when they see that he is right. I do not think it makes any difference whether he is a foreigner or not. But when the unions are given full guarantees, then discipline relaxes. This is a social and even political aspect of work, because sometimes the head of the union is a demagogue who wants to be owner of the mines, who thinks he shouldn't work. So then there is no respect given to the national technician.

I never knew if this technician realized that he was in the presence of one of these former leaders, who was said to be not only "owner" of San José but of Oruro during the height of the revolutionary wave, but Manuel, with great aplomb, said, on the conclusion of the engineer's speech. "I really have nothing to add to this opinion, Doña Juana. I am fully in agreement with him."

On another occasion, when I spoke with Manuel about technicians without an engineer present, he was considerably more frank in his opinions.

❖ The technicians are not capable of organizing the mines. They are using up the slag pile and not preparing for the future. They are trying to use these inflated production figures to justify their position, but it does not involve the costs of extracting the minerals

from the underground. In the mines you see the same problem as
a general with the army. A good general is always with his army.
He lives with his army; he fights with his army. But a general
apart from his army, at one hundred kilometers, is ineffectual.
And so it has been with the technician. He has to be with the
working class. He has to suffer the same misery, cold, hunger, and
desperation. We need discipline in the mine, to avoid absenteeism.

This was a recurrent complaint of the miners, that the technicians seemed to avoid being inside the mine. One driller commented that he had never seen the supervisor in his gallery, a remote and suffocating place where he said, he "worked alone like an
orphan." He contrasted this attitude of the post-nationalization Bolivian miners with that of the foreign technicians in the days of the
private mines, when they entered the mine and taught the men
how to do the work directly.

The supervisor was criticized by most of the workers for his
failure to go down into the mines to talk with the men. "He wants
to manage the workers like beasts," they said. On the night of the
k'araku held after the accident that killed three men, the superintendent and his staff were invited but didn't come. One of the men
commented to me:

❖ We invited him, and even without an invitation he should have
been here. Doesn't he know that we make the k'araku in order to
get growth of a vein to benefit the enterprise? He ought to be the
first to come here, and if he had come, we would work with
greater enthusiasm and will.

Most miners agreed that in the time of Hochschild, Aramayo,
and Patiño there was greater concern with productivity. Several
pointed out to me that, in the present bureaucratic structure with
generals who knew little about mining in the top supervisory posts
in La Paz, the managers of the mines at the local level were afraid of
investing in major exploration because they would show losses
which would be held against them. This lack of concern on the part
of the bureaucratized management in what the workers called "the
life of the mine" shook their faith in the technical staff.

The intelligence of the miners is discounted in the present organization of work in which the technicians seek to monopolize the

planning and organization in contrast with the former system, in which the intelligence and knowledge of the worker was exploited through the pirkiñero system. Engineers are unable to, or perhaps resist, communicating with the miners, who use both Quechua and Spanish names for the rocks and associated minerals that indicate to them the possibility of finding metallic ores. Pedro, who lost his job in the nationalized mines because of his union activities and who was working as a pirkiñero, explained some of the features they go by in discovering the metal:

❖ The only rock that carries mineral is one we call *allatullu*. In the cupriferous zones one often sees something green that makes the rock look as if it is going to cry and you can find silver or copper, but rarely tin. Sometimes we don't know what the rock is, but we know that we are going to encounter mineral in that zone. You might call it intuition; whether it comes from our own knowledge or the blessing of God, we don't know, but we know when we are going to come upon the mineral. It is the combination of many factors, and we live constantly with the hope of coming upon it. Sometimes one man will work up to twenty meters in a shaft and then abandon it, but another miner comes in for the first time and blasts the rock and encounters the metal.

I can tell you about one such case, a man named Bonifacio whom we called affectionately El Loco. The chief of his section wanted to take him out of the level where he worked because it was being inundated by water, but El Loco didn't want to go because he said he was going to find the metal soon. He stayed on, but he wasn't getting any metal. Finally the man didn't even go out to eat; he slept inside even. Finally he found the metal. He had a good eye.

His cousin who had brought him to visit broke in to say:

❖ There are some people who have what we call *bankañowi* [evil eye] that can make us lose the metal. We only let people we have confidence in come into our work site. We are always very careful about whom we let in. In addition we ought never to bring garlic into the mine because Supay would not like it. So the miners enter with certain patterns of caution so that the veins will not disappear.

Pedro continued with the theme of how the pirkiñeros worked:

❖ Well, a great many of the large mines of the state, the COMIBOL mines, are not practicing these customs because the work is measured according to cubic meters, and the only thing of importance is the number of tons. Before that, in the collective contracts, the pirkiñeros were submitted to work in which they gave all their heart, their tears, and their suffering. They had to work, and they were rewarded according to the amount of the mineral. Therefore they made these rituals in accord with their faith, and they didn't let any strangers come in except their own superintendent.

The miners are particularly sensitive to the favoritism toward technicians over the production worker. They note the differential treatment toward engineers who, if they make a mistake, are not chastised for it although they may waste months of work, while workers are publicly abused. When one engineer broke the code and criticized a colleague, he was transferred to another mine. The status prerogatives of the technicians underwrite a behavior of disrespect and even contempt toward the workers. Juan speaks in his autobiography (Rojas and Nash 1976) of a superintendent he worked with twenty years before whom the workers called Carajo (shit) because this was the man's typical explicative when he encountered workers in his inspection rounds. After enduring the insults of the supervisor, a Peruvian worker who had just arrived two months before attacked him physically and the supervisor was transferred. The supervisor, a gringo of undefined national origin, was perhaps reacting to the stereotyped image of the worker as a callous brute who required rough handling. My own observations of workers in the mine indicated an extreme consideration of other workers and supervisors such that this kind of practice was literally counterproductive, a condition that the former private managers were more sensitive to than the contemporary managers, who often ruled by repression and contempt. One young engineer, who at first antagonized the workers by his contemptuous attitude toward them, finally gained their respect by saying on one occasion to a carpenter who was explaining to him what should be done in the reinforcement of a difficult scaffolding, "Go ahead; you know better than I do."

Some of the antagonism between technicians and workers is overcome in the more remote mines, where there is greater interaction between them in the social clubs and at the movies and the soccer games. This may serve to stimulate the greater respect between supervisors and workers reported by miners who have worked in Colquecharca or Santa Fe rather than in San José. Manuel, who worked in Huanuni and Japo in addition to San José, drew this comparison:

> ❖ Here in Oruro, as soon as a worker gets out of the mines he is absorbed by the city. This doesn't occur in Santa Fe, Morococala, Japo, or Huanuni, where the relations between technicians and workers are closer. There are even cases when one can drink beer or a shot of whiskey with technicians because of this close social interaction. Here, after eight hours of work, the engineers go to the city and don't see the men until the next day, whereas there we only have the movies and we see the engineers there. We can exchange jokes, and we live closer.

There are many more cases of workers choosing supervisors and engineers as compadres in the remote mines, and this serves both as an index to greater respect and a reinforcement of existing respect patterns.

The Tío and the Gringo Supervisors

In the days of the former tin barons, the Tío used to appear before the miners as a gringo supervisor. This projection represented both the danger that these men represented as authorities and the collaboration they offered in extracting the riches of the mine. The following story that Juan told me about such an apparition in the Santa Fe mines conveys the fear and respect that these men felt toward them:

> ❖ One time in Santa Fe a carter—a short man, good worker, whose nickname was Cowboy—was pushing the mine cart on level forty-two toward the Fortune vein. In the middle of the road there is a turntable where he had to make a left turn to the Voyadora vein. There he said he saw a gringo, a tall thin man, approaching slowly with a huge lamp that lit up all the corners of the passage. With the light shining in his eyes, he almost went blind; the light was like a fire. Then suddenly the gringo began to climb up a chimney without any steps, even though it was very slippery. The carter was so frightened that he lost track of where he was going and went to the elevator. There the chief of the shift said, "What did you do with your cart? You were going for Rojas' load. Get going, Che; you are going to set us back. We have to get out a hundred

THE TÍO IS GIVEN HIS CIGA-
RETTE, LIQUOR, AND COCA DUR-
ING A COCA BREAK IN THE
MINES.

and twenty carts at a stretch, and if we don't they fine the cap-
tains." But the carter wouldn't go back. He went home with a
headache. When he arrived home, he went into a rage and broke
things that he had bought with a great deal of sacrifice. He said he
was going to kill his children. He walked around like a madman,
even threatening his neighbors. They say he went mad.

In the old days, when the workers tried to make a contract with
the Tío, they would bring a bright knife to the place where they
chewed coca and there talk with the little image of the Tío and
ask him to help them in their contract. They were usually desperate for money, since they knew that the contract would mean their
early death. An old miner told me this story of such an encounter:

❖ If you have faith in the mine, it always gives something. One man
was always drawn back to Potosí, where he worked. He entered
the mine with coca, alcohol, and cigarettes, which he offered to the
Tío, and he worked without losing the vein. One night a tall blond
man appeared dressed as a miner and said, "I am going to help
you. Bring me a jug of liquor." He gave the miner some dirt which
he was going to throw away but, thinking better of it, he put it in
his pocket, where it turned to gold. He thought of his debts, but

he went to get the alcohol. The shopowner didn't want to give him any until he saw gold. Then the miner turned and gave the alcohol to the apparition who said, "I will go ahead and you follow. Don't turn."

The miner threw back the ore without looking and took out mineral of the best quality. He bought a truck and a house with what he earned. It was the devil he worked with, and so his money was all gone in a month. So it always is with the miners. He came back to work in a month and the devil appeared.

"My children are sick," the miner lied to the Tío, "and I must come back to work."

"I will give you mineral for the last time," the devil said. "But don't look back."

The man, with the desire to know him, turned, and he saw the devil with his horns shining. The rock closed on him and he stayed inside buried.

Stories about encounters with the Tío reveal the anxieties about work and the rules developed to counter these fears. Conviviality and the companionships developed in work are so important for survival that those who work alone raise suspicions that they are working on a contract with the devil and that they are doomed to die shortly. Celso speaks of the danger of curiosity.

❖ I knew a worker at level one-fifty, and this worker never wanted to work with his helpers nor with anyone. Only he worked, especially at night. He entered his workplace with a mountain of coca and packages of cigarettes. On one occasion two youths of fourteen or fifteen years said, "Let's go see how our companion works." According to belief, he appeared a superman, and they wanted to discover how he did it. And so they hid in a place near his work site. The worker waited until all the others went to their homes and then entered his shaft. Shortly after a gringo appeared, a blond man with his lamp. He chewed coca [pikchaba], smoked his cigarette, and the other continued chewing while the blond man began to drill, or hammer at the rock. Each blow penetrated inches. When they saw this, the youths escaped and they almost went crazy. People asked them what happened, and they recounted this story. "We wanted to discover how this man worked and earned in one night what other people earn in two months. We saw this gringo come and he worked more than the other; the worker didn't work at all. Then we said that he was not a gringo, he was the devil." All of us workers listened and then went to make a k'araku to offer to the Tío.

So it is when they want to earn in their contract, they serve the Tío his coca and his alcohol and his cigarette.

The next day they went in to check on what the youth said. The worker who was in contact with the Tío was lost. So they looked in all the shafts—lost. Then, according to their belief, the workers said that the Tío had carried him off because he had fulfilled his contract.

There have been many such cases. For example in the year 1944, I met a Señor Vargas when he was already quite old and had the illness of the mine. His helper came to ask me for repairs for his machine. I sent them and, on his return, the assistant found the old man working with great interest. He said, "Maestro, what happened to you? Why are you working like that?" "Why not?" he replied, "Don't you see a gringo is sitting there?" The assistant didn't see anything there and replied, "Maestro, there isn't anyone there." "Yes, there he is sitting and smoking his cigarette. He must be the supervisor. Move it, man." The assistant didn't say anything. Finally the other said, "What has happened to you. There isn't any gringo there. There isn't anyone."

"But for me he exists," replied the master. And then he began to ponder. "That is the third time that this happened to me. I have only a month of life."

"Why do you say that?"

"The first time that this happened to me it was in Pulacayo. The second time in Colquiri. Therefore, I say that it is the Tío. I don't have a contract with the Tío, but here for the third time in this mine I see him. Therefore, I have only thirty days more of life to live. I am sure that I am going to die. Therefore I am going to teach you all my knowledge gained from experience, how to discharge the dynamite, how to manage the machine, everything."

Precisely after thirty days, we buried the maestro. We knew then that the gringo was the Tío, and he had called him. Señor Vargas had earned a great deal of money and enjoyed life.

The identification of the Tío with the gringo supervisor reveals a great deal about the worker/supervisor relationship in the pre-nationalization days. There was the sense that the alien technicians controlled the wealth of the hills and were both good and evil in their dispensation of its riches. There was also the sense of danger in the association that cut them off from their own social group and the power that resided in the primary group solidarity. All the stories I heard related about the Tío reveal that the contract was made by a single individual who worked alone. Some said they worked with the bull, which was the Tío's helper, who gored out the ore with his horns. I have never known anyone who has encountered the Tío in the form of a gringo in recent years, although belief in Supay persists. Perhaps it is because, as one miner said, "There is no longer any special payoff because of increased mineral production in the individual contract, and the fantasy was put to rest along with the promise of wealth in the old system of work."

Mechanization

The uneven mechanization of Bolivia's mines creates problems in the organization of work, the comparison of productivity, and the determination of wage rates. A driller is given a machine, but replacement parts are not always forthcoming or the pump is inadequate to supply all the machines in operation with air and water. A face mask is provided, but the replacement filters are in short supply or absent and so it is useless. Mechanical carts are installed, but not in the sections formerly worked by the pirkiñiris, where the irregular shafts and uneven terrain require the hardest labor of the manual workers. The deficiencies cause work stoppages and losses of contract pay that are a constant harassment to the workers. Although the workers recognize that the physical exertion is less with the introduction of machinery, they feel harassed by a system in which inadequate supplies constantly interrupt the flow of work.

Everyone agrees that the greatest physical sacrifice is demanded of the drillers, and they are accordingly paid somewhat more and treated with greater respect by other workers. Vertical drilling in shafts is more dangerous than horizontal drilling because of falling rocks and also requires a greater expenditure of effort than horizontal drilling. The drills weigh about 72 kilos (160 pounds), often more than the workers themselves. The drillers call the telescope *torito*, possibly an oblique reference to the Tío's helper, who is a bull.

I asked Juan how he felt after working seventeen years behind a drill, and he answered:

❖ After seventeen years of working, when I get near the mine I can still smell the sulfates and I feel suffocated by the gases. I remember how I used to feel nervous and jumpy, fearing the falling rocks. My body felt drugged. When I went outside, it was like bread for the spirit. It was as though my mind were uncorked. Although I haven't used the drill for two years, I can still hear the sound of the air hissing through the hoses when I lie down to go to sleep.

Celso described the physical effects of the drill on him:

❖ When one works constantly with the machine, one declines physically. I go out of work with my body numb as though drugged. And afterwards, the sound of the machine is such a strong blast, when I go to sleep I always hear it. When I first started to work, it was worse, but now I am used to it. I used to work in making the passages and that tired me out even more. It was in a very hard rock on level two-thirty. Water and clay came out of the rock and we had to hold the machine down by sheer force or it would kick back. The drill gets stuck in the clay and it takes more time pulling out drills than making the advance. While we are holding onto the machine with one hand and regulating the air with the other, the whole weight of the machine is in my arms. The mud runs down from the ceiling and soaks us. We used to get rubber gloves and this helped keep the water out of our sleeves, but now they don't issue any. Working with bare hands is very dangerous because rocks are constantly falling and cause many cuts.

After a day's work, the body is so numb that if one is cut by falling stones, the workers don't feel the pain until an hour or more after they leave work. Tension is built up because of the awareness of danger from falling rocks. If a drill breaks, it can knock you over and even kill you. It is even more dangerous for the assistant. I had a sixteen-year-old assistant—they used to go into the mine very young, and he wasn't experienced. I told him not to stand near the drill, but he was right next to me when the drill broke loose and fell down. He broke a rib, but he could have been killed. He left the mine and never came back.

The old hand-drilling was healthier, although slower in production. It caused less effusion of silicates and there was less danger of sudden rock falls. The carbon lamps the miners used to wear to light their work offered a safety feature, since the flame went out when oxygen was low, warning them that they were in the presence of dangerous gases. The newer drills are an improvement over the old models, called *chicharros,* which had no supports, so one had to rest every ten or fifteen minutes.

One driller spoke to me of the constant difficulties he has keeping his eight-year-old machine in operation:

❖ It is so hard to get repairs. The hammer pin is worn out as well as the drill shaft, and there aren't any bronze replacement parts here. They don't have any repair parts on hand. It would be better to have a shop right here in San José, but there isn't any, and we waste so many days waiting for it to come from La Paz. Yesterday, the water hose inlet was broken, but I continued working, and when this happens, the dust gets into our lungs even more. I thought that they were going to fix it by today, but they told me there isn't any replacement. Up until 1952 we didn't have as many problems getting parts, but after Paz Estenssoro entered, we began to lack tools. We have a lot of trouble with the lamps. We get down to the work site and start to work, and then the battery gives out and we have to go back and get another. The quality of the raingear we have is so bad it doesn't last the six months scheduled for it. And if we get wet, when we go out in the corridors where there are drafts, we get sick from the cold. Even if we have an accident and the boots get damaged, we can't get new ones. All the materials are under card control from the industrial security office. If anything is lost, the full value is taken out of our paycheck.

The mechanical shovel requires even greater pressure than the drills to work effectively. At some levels the pressure is so low that the men say it takes a half hour to do what could be done in ten minutes if it was working effectively. I was able to appreciate this problem when I worked with one of the mechanical shovels on the lowest level, 580 meters down. When a worker is on contract pay, it adds to the frustration and tension on the job.

The workers have not fought mechanization directly because the consequences in unemployment are not immediately felt. In the interior of the mine at least, the increased use of power-driven tools permits greater exploitation and in some cases greater productivity. A driller assessed the meaning of mechanization for him:

❖ In the case of San José mine, mechanization has more advantages for us. Undoubtedly from the point of view of society, the only way we support ourselves is by avoiding unemployment, but from the point of view of the economy, the mechanization is very good. As a worker, I can see that raising the load by shovel, which continues in some places, is nearly unbearable, especially in very hot places in the mine because of the dehydration of the worker and leads to rapid physical debilitation. Then in those cases, in my personal opinion, we ought to mechanize because we help the worker. If we analyze it a little more, mechanization brings advantages to some degree for the worker, especially for us, the drillers. Before, we used to have to mount the old drills on a brace and when we had to turn it, it was very heavy. We were always raising and lowering this mounting, and a man was overcome by the exertion. Now with the technical innovations this part of the drilling is no problem; the drill moves by the force of the air entering directly with less work. And so it is a form of caring for the human capital. So who is going to reject mechanization in a country like ours, or prefer to continue with the old techniques of the past?

Despite this worker's optimism about the process of mechanization, the capitalization of the mines after the Triangular Plan was introduced in 1960 resulted not only in the loss of some jobs previously done by hand, but lowered the wage of some of the workers. One of the carters told me that when he was given a mechanical shovel, they lowered the price that he received because it did not require as much physical effort. One man could do the same amount of work in a day that two men had done in three days since the work not only went quicker, but also there was no need to break up the large stones so that they could be picked up by hand. As a marginal mine, San José received many used machines from the mines that produced more, and so the contract was set at a level of efficiency that they could no longer maintain; thus the workers were the losers.

The greatest unemployment due to mechanization was in the female labor force. Over 250 women were fired from San José in 1967 when the concentration plant was installed, and their work force was replaced with 17 male operators. The women received an indemnity of only US $450 regardless of the number of years they worked. Only one of the union organizers supported their claims, and he was soon afterward imprisoned along with others who remained militant in the face of growing repression in the Barrientos period.

Theft of tools is frequent. Shortly after the military takeover in the mines in 1965, the mass firing of workers led to a near revolution as masses of umemployed attacked the mine guards. The number of mine police was increased, and the men, former soldiers, received higher pay than the production workers, B$600 base pay compared with B$350. Some of those who stole tools used them to enter the abandoned shafts and extract mineral while others sold the stolen goods. In 1968, in Itos, there was a battle between these clandestine workers, called jucos, and the mine police, with the latter using modern firearms and the jucos defending themselves with dynamite. The jucos seized two agents of the police and relieved them of their arms. They sought help from their working comrades in the encampment and, because of the sympathy most workers feel toward the jucos, they gained some support. The following day the administration fired over five workers without benefits, claiming they were assisting the jucos. Some of the people who had come out of their houses, just out of curiosity, were seized and held in jail. Following that, the security in the mines was even tighter. One man, whose telescope drill was stolen by armed bands of unemployed, was held responsible for the theft and nearly lost his job until one of the technicians intervened and said that he had seen the drill in the worker's paraje after he had left his job. But as the worker pointed out,

❖ Except for his word, we would have been fired; they humiliated us after all those years of work with the company. They do not have any confidence in the workers. How can a person go on working in conditions like that? If we are earning our daily bread with this machine, how can they think that we are going to steal it?

In Huanuni the management accepted a system of contract with the jucos, and they have fewer problems with theft than in Oruro.

Coca

The one solace the workers have on the job is coca, the gift of the Pachamama to her children to help them endure physical discomfort, fatigue and despair. Coca breaks in the morning and afternoon are as established a part of the routine of the mine as the coffee break is of the office. When workers enter the mine the first thing they do when they arrive in their work site and change their clothing is to sit down and pijchar, chew coca in a meditative and reflective mood, alone or, even in the presence of others, noncommunicating. Once when I arrived at the work site late with a miner because we were delayed by the security check I had to go through, the worker proceeded to chew his coca before working. The foreman of the level tried to hurry him up so he wouldn't hold up the other workers, but he refused his urgings. This was his moment to contemplate the day ahead, to prepare himself for the effort. He explained to me afterward why miners needed it: "It gives us courage, it serves us as energy, and it serves us as food. We can work sixteen hours below the ground with coca."

A young worker, who had to leave his studies at the university to work in the mine, said that he learned to chew coca despite his aversion to it. His working companions taught him that before the dynamite is discharged, one has to put a wad of coca in the mouth and chew it while waiting for the dust to settle after the blast. This is to avoid damage to the lungs, he was told. Many believe it prevents silicosis, and they prove this by pointing out that if you have coca in the mouth before the charge goes off, afterward you can taste the acrid smoke from the discharge in the coca, which takes the brunt of it.

The workers learn to divine their fate in the leaves during the coca breaks when they akulikar, or chew coca communally with their comrades in the special niches they cut out in the side of the corridor walls. A leaf with yellow spots indicates that they will find the vein of metal; a leaf doubled over indicates death, but if you wet it in the mouth and it opens, then one will live. All the workers are aware of the dangers of coca if you chew too much. The loss of appetite means that the worker will not maintain the necessary nourishment essential for his survival and he will shorten his life. The hallucinations sometimes drive one mad, and everyone knows stories of the *coca locas*, miners maddened by the narcotic. Most of those who have seen the Tío are reported to turn to coca addiction.

One of the miners told me about a custom similar to coca chewing that he had noted among the American engineers:

> ❖ I knew an American who had tobacco he used as we use coca; he put it in his mouth and commenced to chew it like chiclets [gum]. We saw him do it many times and so we wanted to see what effect it had. So we took a cigarette and tore off the paper and put it in our mouths and chewed it, but we felt very dizzy and it gave us a bad headache. Once Sr. Taylor had a little bag of tobacco and invited us to try it. He explained that you only swallow the juice. We tried it again that way, but we still got dizzy. They put in a great deal of tobacco and I don't know how they do it! They chew it almost all day without stopping.

Management is well aware of the importance of coca in that it makes inhuman conditions of the mine tolerable. As a result, they keep the pulpería well supplied with good coca from the Yungas. "If we ran out of coca," one administrative clerk told me, "we would really have a revolution on our hands!"

Sickness, Accidents, and Death

❖ When a worker is young, he works with a will, but little by little, as the years go by and his force is below that of the new young workers, then there is a fall in his production which the administrators view as laziness. But it is not laziness: it is the loss of force that has gone to benefit our own patrons. But this is no longer recognized, and there is no preference given to the older workers.

On the occasion of his forty-third birthday, when he retired from work, Juan summed up the life of a miner in those words. With 100 percent silicosis, he considered himself near the end of his life.

Silicosis

Silicosis is the "professional disease" of the miners. All miners get it, but the time of onset and the degree depend on how close they work to the face, whether they work with the drill or dynamite, and how well they defend themselves from it by adequate diets. As much as they are aware of its inevitability, they are surprised when it happens to them. They have all seen men—and women, who contract it in the concentration pit—die from silicosis; the suffocating gasps can be heard through the walls of the encampment housing by the neighbors. Juan sat watching a man dying of silicosis when he was six years old, and yet thirty-five years later he refused to believe he had 100 percent silicosis himself.

The search for a cure is desperate. Many miners fear the hospital, since they have heard that those with 100 percent silicosis die from the injections, which they say contain oxygen bubbles in the case of terminal patients. And so they try to cure themselves with yatiris, or herbal curers. Petrona's father went to one as soon as he was released from the hospital following the attack of grippe that resulted in his being diagnosed as 100 percent afflicted. His wife bought four lizards, two birds, the fetuses of llamas, incense, white dry corn, red wine, alcohol, q'oa and copal. She prepared a mixture of the wine and alcohol with which the yatiri rubbed his body. The yatiri then had the lizards and birds walk over his shoulders and back, in order to draw out the disease. He then threw them out in the dump after killing them. The diet for a silicosis victim is broiled black cat or dog and the blood of freshly killed vicuña. Others go live in Cochabamba, where they can get a fresh vegetable diet, but the problem is that in the low altitude their lungs might burst before they can get cured. The cure, as described by two miners discussing the problem, seems to be a metaphoric identity with pasturing animals.

❖ Generally, those who go to Cochabamba get up in the morning and eat fresh leaves of vegetables like the animals when they are growing, early in the morning—just go out and eat it fresh with nothing on it, no salt, and this will strengthen one. You have to avoid drinks, and hot sauce. It is better to eat the meat of animals that are docile, like the sheep. The meat of bulls does damage.

Flora, who watched two of her family die, described the symptoms:

❖ Mal de mina [literally the evil or sickness of the mine, which is the usual term for silicosis] causes a lack of oxygen, and because of this, the lungs do not work well. This starts a palpitation of the lungs and then there is a neurasthenic reaction. The first symptoms are that the patient can't sleep at night because of agitation. Because he can't sleep well, he is always fatigued. In this stage when he is not yet permanently incapacitated, there is a frothing in his lungs, and he has difficulty breathing at night. A yellowish spittle begins to develop. Later he begins to swell, sometimes to twice [normal] size and then the swelling goes down and he becomes paralyzed. He stops drinking, even men who love to drink. He cannot urinate.

My husband suffered a great deal. It was with desperation that I watched him. When his feet were swollen, he couldn't sleep nor rest, just breathe ahahaahaah. He couldn't rest because of the lack of oxygen. Many miners die this way.

Haperk'a

Fright, or haperk'a, is diagnosed and treated as a physical illness. Because doctors do not "understand" either the symptoms or the cure, people go to the yatiri directly for anything they suspect is etiologically traceable to fear. With children, fright is treated as soul loss, and the cure consists in calling the soul back to the body. With adults the tactic is to regain harmony with the powerful figures that control one's destiny: the Tío, a special saint, or one of the enchanted figures. Celso, who was nearly scared to death in the mine, recounts his cure:

❖ It was after lunch and I was hurrying, like everyone who works on contract—the worker has to accommodate himself to the work, not that the work is accommodated to the worker—in order to gain time. I went to see how the blast I had set came off. I saw that the discharge had been cleared out, but I did not notice a load hanging as I crossed the corridor. I took three steps back, and then the load fell, one and a half tons. My body didn't have breath to yell. I did not have the power to do anything. I couldn't cry, nothing— because nothing had happened! It was only the desperation I felt and my imagination seized me and I felt as though I had been smashed under the rock. And that was the great fear that seized me and I went into a deep depression.

Since I am a believer in the Tío, I took a little alcohol and a cigarette to smoke with the Tío and chewed a little coca and my head cleared up a little. It was sheer luck that I had turned back. The Tío protected me. Because I have this faith in him, nothing happened to me. When I spoke to my padrino about this, he told me that I would have to give devotion to Señor Santiago.

However, I still didn't feel well, and I didn't work with spirit. I went to a yatiri and we began to chew (pijchar, meditatively) coca, and he bagan to throw out the leaves and diagnose what was my trouble. He said that I had had a fright in the mine and that I was attacked. I said, "Evidently," because I couldn't deny it. He didn't even know that I worked in the mine, and so I began to believe in him since he told me the truth. Then he told me, "Go to the chapel, in the sanctuary of Señor Santiago, and support his fiesta." He told me that he was going to cure me, and that it would cost so much. He asked me for a white thread and a black thread and the "table" that they prepare with the fetus of llamas. We went together to the chapel and he prayed at noon to Santiago and said many things I did not understand. Now I am feeling better, but I have to go one more time.

Celso's wife told me that his great concern for his fear illness was that it made him impotent. This is possibily a fairly frequent affect of the fear, at least judging by a feature I noticed on one of the

Tíos in Siglo XX in the *lamero* section, the most dangerous in the mine, where the advance is with sheer dynamite and the danger is greatest. This Tío had an enormous erection, and the miners there told me that they appealed to the Tío in order to restore their own potency when they felt it diminishing.

In the old days, the cure required that the yatiri go with his patient to the exact spot where the fright had occurred and make the offering to the Tío. Some of the older yatiris used to wrestle with the Tío to retrieve the soul of the worker. In one case that I heard of, the yatiri lost and died soon after. No one expects that sort of professional dedication from the yatiris in these times.

Juan disclaimed belief in the power of yatiris to cure fear sickness. He described their treatment as a kind of theatrics which was occasionally successful in curing people even on the point of death:

❖ The belief is that the devil has seized their spirit, and for that
reason the sick person goes crazy. If he isn't cured right away,
they fear that the devil will carry him off. The yatiri claims to see
the spirit and he takes a little bell and a whip and the belt of the
scared person and he calls, "Come, come, we are going where you
are. Come, we are going," calling the patient by name. Then when
the spirit comes near, he takes the chicote and hits the spirit, saying, "Hurry up!" All the time he is swinging the bell or a bunch of
keys and at the same time swinging the belt and the whip. Then
he enters the house and the frightened one puts on his clothing.
This signifies that the soul has returned to his body. And many
times it coincides with his getting well, even where he is about to
die. But this has never happened to me. I have been frightened
many times, but I never got sick.

Juan's wife denied this to me privately. She says that Juan went on two occasions to the hospital with haperk'a, and the only thing that cured him were the rituals she carried out in the home with the yatiri without his knowledge. Many of the miners who profess not to believe in yatiris have faith in the curative powers of the *millu*, a white stone which, they say, has radium in it. Their wives rub it all over their bodies to relieve them of whatever symptom the fear sickness has caused, whether it is paralysis, pustules, or fever.

Fear is an ever-present condition for those who enter the mine. As they stand waiting for the elevator to take them into the lower depths, there is a great deal of joking and rough-housing to overcome the anxiety. No one ever denies his fear, for that would be considered foolish. By treating it openly they can hold in abeyance the anxiety that is the unattended accompaniment of fear. When the everyday techniques of overcoming fear are insufficient and the anxiety results in illness, the ritual cures are in many cases effective ways of vanquishing the hold.

Death

❖ Our husbands here in the mine die very young. One moment we will be playing, chatting, he enters to work, and in a little while he comes out dead. We remain widows with several children. For that reason, we asked for this work from the administration so that we could earn and feed our children.

It is difficult to get adequate figures on death and major accidents in the mine. The International Labour Office has reported seven thousand major accidents resulting in permanent maiming or death in 1947, but most visitors do not have access to the records. I was able to review the records for Oruro, all sections, for the year 1969. The statistics are presented in Table 6.1. In an information bulletin on the mines, the Secretariado Nacional de Estudios Sociales (1969) reported two to three accidents weekly in San José mines alone.

Table 6.1. **Accidents and Days Lost, San José, Oruro**

Month	Number of Accidents	Days Lost/ 1,000 Mitas*	Frequency/ 1,000 Workers
January	16	119	101
February	21	119	101
March	30	177	134
April	30	191	135
May	32	191	107
June	30	143	141
July	143	110	141
August	25	158	109
September	27	6,128	109
October	26	6,086	103
November	22	150	89
December	25		123

*One "natural" death in mine (equals 6,000 mitas).

In the accounting office a death is given the value of 6,000 mitas or days lost, or approximately twenty years of life. Sometimes there may be a contest between the family and the company. In cases such as heart failure or other circumstances where death can be attributed both to "natural" causes as well as working environment, and since the company has less financial responsibility to the survivors if a death can be proven to be nonaccidental, there is always a contest to prove the conditions of the death. In one death that occurred during my stay in the mining community, the company asserted that the dead man, who had fallen into a pit, had committed suicide. The widow asserted that he had no desire to die, although it was rumored that she was separated from him. Everyone will admit that it takes an active will to live just to go into the pits and emerge alive every day, because the moment one's guard is down, the faculties which ensure survival are relaxed. Suicide is common enough so that it is always considered, since men prefer to finish their lives in the mine or with a tool of the trade, preferably dynamite. The family of the dead man are defensively aware of the accusations leveled against them and assert, "He went off to work like any other day. Who would have thought . . ."

Five men died in accidents in the mine the year I worked in San José mines. The first funeral I went to, in March, of one of these victims was a contrast in the lavish display of the commercial funeral paid for by the company and the impoverishment of the worker and his family. Waldo was killed in an accident caused by dynamite falling out of its niche and blowing up in the paraje he was in. He had worked thirty years in the mine. His body was discovered at 10:30 in the evening, after rigor mortis had set in. I went to his wake in the social club of the union. The body was laid out in an elaborate casket with a window at his head. His mouth was open, his eyes closed, but the expression was of terror. He had a three-day stubble on his face. The casket was banked with a wreath of flowers sent by the union and another by the company. His mother was kneeling at the head of the casket, weeping. His elder wife and son were called in so I could take their pictures, since these are much cherished by the family. A younger wife took no part in the official funeral, although he was living with her at the time of his death.

A huge meal was served to the people who crowded into the social club to view the body. At 3:00 the funeral procession took off: a very luxurious limousine, followed by the COMIBOL truck laden with flowers, and behind this people walking. The first widow, the mother, and the sons walked behind the limousine. A grown daughter did not attend. Nubile women are not expected to endanger themselves or their future offspring "because they give us life," one man explained to me. As the procession took off, the mother beat the bumper and wailed. Thunder boomed and it began to rain. As the procession of about seventy-five people walked to the graveyard across town, the rain came down more heavily. The new union leader was in the front line of the procession. The eulogy at the grave site was given by an old miner and by the union leader.

When a man dies a natural death, his body is laid out in the home. I visited the home of Rigoberto, who had died in the hospital where he had gone with a pain in his back, caught pneumonia, and died. Compadres washed the body and laid it out. A meal was served to those who came to visit, one early in the morning following a night of the wake and another just before the body was taken out to the hearse—the assertion of life in the face of death. The following day all the dead person's old clothes were washed and burned. As the women laid out the freshly laundered clothes—tattered pants, rubber boots, a dance mask the dead man had worn in Carnival, shirts—the men prepared a roaring fire to consume them to an ash. This is done so that the soul will go to its final resting place and not stay with those things with which it had contact when alive. They discussed who would get his job; his children were too young; some said a brother-in-law would inherit it, but he was discharged dishonorably from the army and probably would not be accepted. His wife might get a job in the hospital washing clothes. Jobs are the only inheritance in a country where the wage covers a bare subsistence and there is high unemployment.

On the following day I went to the house to see the celebration after the mass. Women organized a game of chance with corn kernels, the winnings of which were to defray the cost of the mass. The host, brother-in-law of the dead man, put a blanket on the floor, then three kernels of white corn with one side marked in pencil, and covered them with coca leaves. As the women gathered to play, he served liquor and chicha. If the women didn't get three marked sides up in three throws, they lost money, which went for the mass. Outside, the men pitched coins into an iron circle with a slot. If they failed to get the money in a slot, they lost and the money went to the mass. B $600, almost two months' base wage, were spent on the food, and another B $60 for the mass. The widow did not know how much compensation she would get nor how she would survive with five children to feed on B $150 a month.

The biggest accident occurred in July, when three men were killed by a dynamite blast that fell through a chute from an upper level. One of the men working on the upper level described the circumstances:

> ❖ We were starting to load the cars when the accident happened. We heard the explosion, and we didn't know where it came from. We went into the work site to clean out the load, not knowing what had happened nor from whence the explosion came. Roberto [one of the dead men] was standing over there, and my comrade was on top of the cart. He was the first they took out dead. I was in the front car, and then the explosion went off. I didn't know what happened. I was completely stupid at that moment. I had lost understanding of my senses. Then I tried to escape to get help because there was no one there. I got two masons who went inside with me, and we found Roberto and put him on a cart and carried him out. Two beams had collapsed on Ponciano and we took them off and carried him out.

The word spread quickly in the encampment, and people came running to the union hall where the dead men were laid out. The men had carefully picked up all of the entrails and placed them on the box that contained what was recovered of Roberto's body. As the women entered the main hall and saw the bodies, they began to stamp their feet and started a ululating wail that was almost like a natural force, like the tide going out or thunder crashing.

The men of that section called for a triple burial: "We want the burial to be very symbolic, and we shall bury them together on this very afternoon." One man went to get the military band and the others arranged to go in a delegation to the administration to get the afternoon of the following day off so that all the workers could attend the funeral. There was some dispute over usurping plans for the funeral without the consent of the family of the dead men. The dispute over whether to bury them that day, since the company had already given all the workers the day free, or wait for a night's wake as usual, continued. Over the shouts of the men arguing how to best solemnize the occasion, the women's voices rose in a Quechua lament, "Imanasunchaj kunanka" (What are we going to do now?).

Hundreds, possibly even thousands, of people crowded into the funeral held that very afternoon. The union leader gave the main address.

❖ Again the mining classes are dressed in mourning for this infamous misfortune that inexorably accompanies the most exploited class of Bolivia. The necessity of bringing the crusts of bread to our homes obliges us to risk the dangers of work where there are no security systems necessary to care for our lives. The new misfortune that puts the hearts of miners in mourning serves to invoke the plea of the workers of the underground to the administrators of COMIBOL for better security conditions, more response to the requests for working materials and tools. If there is anything in our life, so full of petty economies, that we value, it is the tranquility and security of our children. They do not know what dangers we face when we enter work. The only thing they understand is the tenderness and joy of having you at their sides. Roberto, Ignacio, Ponciano, for you the hour to leave has come. Your comrades of work remain in solidarity with the struggles to secure better days in the welfare of society. We will remember always your heroic sacrifice working for a country that suffers from many injustices, in the hope of seeing a day of freedom from the yoke of neo-colonialism.

Each death becomes a grain in the scale of injustices totaled up by the union leader at the cemetery. Despite the recent massacres and the near-starvation levels to which the workers had been reduced, he still spoke as though someone was taking the ledger of injustices into account, but the people were skeptical.

Conditions of Work and Consciousness

The hardships and dangers that are a daily part of a miner's life weld the underground workers in a strong solidarity group. In the structural relations defined within the mine, they see themselves opposed to the technicians and administrators. Union leaders and the theoreticians within their ranks try to transform this conflict to one of class opposition and anti-imperialism, but it is not a spontaneous efflux from their experience.

The sense of being the most exploited segment of the working class is sometimes turned inward, as when the union director refers to the miners as a class in themselves, namely the mining class or the most exploited class. When the miners were the strategic element in the MNR polity and economy, this kind of thinking led to the plea for special privileges that cut the miners off from other sectors of the working population. When the identification is broadened to include the entire working class, this sense of being the most exploited becomes a motive for taking a vanguard role in the labor movement.

The most positive element in the miner's consciousness deriving from their immediate conditions of work is the sense that this sacrifice must be dedicated to a higher order of life. Sometimes the outer expression is limited to the family striving for the mobility of one's children. A few look beyond to the interests of the "mining class," and others to the working class.

In death the link between community life and work context is completed. The community rose as an extended family to mourn the death of the miners killed in the great blast of July. In the k'araku that followed (described in chapter 5), the full circle of communal, familial, and class participants took shape. The striving for significance in the death of the three young workers took the form of a sacrifice for the working class. No ritual or celebration is complete without the shedding of blood, and in the events that immediately followed the accident, the entire community became participants in a ritual that demanded that these senseless deaths be made meaningful. The meaning extracted from the event and made concrete by the union leader was the advancement of the struggles of the working class.

Chapter 7

◈·◈

Wages, Prices, and the Accumulation of Capital in Mining

◈THERE IS a delicate balance between wages, prices, and profits which, if tipped, sets off a wave of protest and political action or of repression. The distribution of the rewards from production is the crux of the issues relating to the political economy of the state. The failure to institutionalize the contest between claims for wages and profits in trade union negotiation makes conflict the basis for revolutionary action in Bolivia. Table 7.1 summarizes events in Bolivia from 1901 to 1972.

The struggle is sharpened in the context of a dependent economy in which the government responds to external pressures exerted by foreign capital interests and fails to act as impartial mediator or to respond to populist demands. It is further sharpened by the particular economic conditions of the mines. The surplus value, that is, the part of the total value of the price representing unpaid labor realized as profits (Marx 1969:215), is not reinvested in enterprises within the country to produce jobs or to raise the development potential of the country. On the contrary, it has been diverted to investment that threatens the very existence of the mine which is the worker's basis of subsistence. In the time of private capital exploitation, Hochschild built up Colquiri mine with the profits from San José and withdrew investment from the latter, which would have been closed if the Banco Minero had not kept it in operation. Patiño used the surplus value from Siglo XX and Catavi to build up the very competition in Malaya that is threatening the production of tin in Bolivia today. In the past twenty years

Table 7.1. Union Activities, Political Events, Tin Production and Value, Tin and Metal Exports, Wages, Consumer Price Index, GNP Population, and U.S. Aid, 1900–1971

Year	Union Activities[1]	Politico-Economic Developments	Tin Production Tons[2] (1)	Tin Production Value[3] (US$000) (2)	Price[3] (US$/lb) (3)	Exports[4] % Tin Total (4)	% Metal Total (5)	Balance Millions of US$ (6)	Consumer Price Index[5] (100=1937) (7)	GNP, Total Millions of US$ (8)	Per Capita US$[6] (9)	Population[7] (millions) (10)	US Aid[8] (US$000) (11)
1900			9,738										
1901			13,146										
1902			10,566										
1903			12,558										
1904			12,930			50[9]							
1905			16,614										
1906	Central Social de Obreros formed, called for regional federation.	Liberal party in power. Tariff and tax policy to encourage tin production.											
1907			16,608										
1908	Federación Obreros formed in La Paz.		17,964										
1909			21,342										
1910			23,130										
1911		Patiño invested capital in Williams Harvey concentration plant.	2,242										
1912	Federación Obrera Internacional.		12,166										
1913			16,754			73[9]							
1914			22,416										
1915			21,894			47[9]							
1916			21,224			42[9]							
1917			27,858										

Table 7.1. Union Activities, Political Events, Tin Production and Value, Tin and Metal Exports, Wages, Consumer Price Index, GNP Population, and U.S. Aid, 1900–1971 (Continued)

Year	Union Activities [1]	Politico-Economic Developments	Tin Production Tons [2] (1)	Value [3] (US$000) (2)	Price [3] (US$/lb) (3)	Exports [4] % Tin Total (4)	% Metal Total (5)	Balance Millions of US$ (6)	Consumer Price Index [5] (100=1937) (7)	GNP, Total Millions of US$ (8)	Per Capita US$ [6] (9)	Population [7] (millions) (10)	US Aid [8] (US$000) (11)
1918	Federación Obrera Internacional became Federación Obrera del Trabajo, backed by Pan American Federation of Labor, AFL and Confederación Regional Obrera Mexicana.		29,280			71⁹		191					
1919			29,100										
1920			26,230										
1921		President Bautista Saavedra increased taxes on tin from 5.5 to 13.3%. Minimal social legislation.	23,286										
1922			32,058										
1923	Organization of resolution on minimum wage, legal working day, protection against lockout; strike called to back demand at Uncia; army called in, resulted in massacre.		30,258										

Year	Events						
1924		32,064					
1925	President Hernando	32,598					
1926		32,184	29,521				
1927	Federación Obrera Local. Anarchists, sindicalists and Communists vied for control.	39,972	35,684				
1928		42,074	32,751				
1929	Concentration of rosquero control Patiño 38.84% Hochschild 10.04% Aramayo 5.10% Small holders 26.02%	47,087	32,491		69.6	88.7	
	Confederación Sindical Latino Americana, Communist controlled, IWW inspired; Asociación Continental Americana de Trabajadores de America Latina						
1930	Pres. Daniel Salamanca's government took greater interest in tin mining because of World Tin Accord; tin magnates took greater interest in government.	38,772	24,854	L172/MT[10]	76.2	93.3	
1931	Deflation, internal pressures for change; Chaco War with Paraguay over oil in which Great Britain had interest.	31,637	15,976	L122[10]	76.4	94.1	100
1932		20,198	12,701	L127[12]	72.3	92.2	126
1933		14,957	19,849	L161[10]	69.4	93.2	159
1934	Tejedo Sorzano, Vice President of Salamanca, succeeded in power.	23,224	34,778	L222[10]	79.5	96.6	200
1935		25,408	40,475		73.7	96.1	252

Table 7.1. Union Activities, Political Events, Tin Production and Value, Tin and Metal Exports, Wages, Consumer Price Index, GNP Population, and U.S. Aid, 1900–1971 (Continued)

Year	Union Activities [1]	Politico-Economic Developments	Tons [2] (1)	Tin Production Value [3] (US$000) (2)	Price [3] (US$/lb) (3)	Exports [4] % Tin Total (4)	% Metal Total [5] (5)	Balance Millions of US$ [6] (6)	Consumer Price Index [5] (100=1937) (7)	GNP, Total Millions of US$ [8] (8)	Per Capita US$ [6] (9)	Population [7] (millions) (10)	US Aid [8] (US$000) (11)
1936	Confederación Sindical de Trabajadores de Bolivia, first nation-wide labor organization with Trotskyists and Stalinists, Tristan.	Toro government established first Ministry of Labor. Labor had no immediate role: "Socialismo del Estado." End of Chaco War.	24,438	26,398		61.3		91.2		317			
1937		German Busch president in July coup (Nationalist-Social)	25,531	32,807		62.5	93.3		100	361			
1938	National labor code. PSOB took control of CSTB		25,893	25,011		63.3	91.3	8.5		462			
1939			27,648	31,601		66.3	93.4			627			
1940	Teachers Union formed, dominated by PIR.	Partido Obrero Rev. Partido de la Izquierda Revolucionaria formed.	38,531	47,847		71.3	96.0			799			
1941	Federación Trabajadores Mineros.	Falange Socialista Boliviana, right-wing party; Peñaranda, president, tool of tin barons; Movimiento Nacional Revolucionario formed.	42,741 (received)	58,015		70.6	95.7		1,011				From 1945 [12] to 1960 received $1,191,200,000 in mutual security & economic program aid, $500,000 in military aid.
1942	Strike, massacre of scores in Siglo XX-Catavi.		38,899	63,183		66.9	96.2		1,331				
1943	MNR gained force with miners.	Colonel Gualberto Villaroel MNR gained presidency, labor recognized gains.	40,959	77,882	.55	67.4	95.4		1,568				

Year	Events											
1944	POR vies with MNR in mine; Confederación Boliviana de Mineros formed with Lechín as President. Negotiation for collective contract begun.	39,341	72,646	.61	68.5	93.7		1,689				.4
1945		43,168	73,729	.61	74.9	91.7		1,829				
1946	PIR overthrew Villarroel with aid of rosca, July. Conservative regime. Miners split MNR–POR; Thesis of Pulacayo.	38,222	65,497	.64	70.6	98.9		2,045				.4
1947		33,777	75,559	.62	67.1	92.8		2,345				
1948	Formation Partido de la Unión Republicana Socialista coalition linked.	33,829	110,921		71.1	98.3	43.9		2,598			.4
1949	Massacre in Siglo XX–Catavi. Pres. Mamerto Urrilagoitia called "Butcher."	34,300	99,037	.73	70.8	96.2		2,794				.7
1950	Decree favoring large mining corporations.	31,320	90,911		67.4	96.6		3,426	537	178	3.0	16.5
1951	American CIO, AFL. Paz Estenssoro won.	25,506	145,873	.78	62.05	96.9		4,563				.5
1952	Central Obrera Boliviana formed. April 9 Revolution Paz is President co-government phase.	30,151	137,755		60.0	95.5		5,664				1.5
1953	COB dominated by MNR. Unions held 4 ministries: Ministry of Mines and Petroleum, Federación Minera; Transportes, Confederación Sindicos de Trabajadores Ferroviarios, Peasant Affairs-Peasants Union; Labor: industrial Union; enjoyed majority in Chamber of Deputies	25,340		.91	64.2	97.6		11,412				1.3
	Congress of COB	26,903	96,159	.89	55.2	96.7		25,613			3.2	18.2

Table 7.1. Union Activities, Political Events, Tin Production and Value, Tin and Metal Exports, Wages, Consumer Price Index, GNP Population, and U.S. Aid, 1900–1971 (Continued)

Year	Union Activities [1]	Politico-Economic Developments	Tin Production Tons [2] (1)	Tin Production Value [3] (US$000) (2)	Price [3] (US$/lb) (3)	Exports [4] % Tin Total (4)	% Metal Total (5)	Balance Millions of US$ (6)	Consumer Price Index [5] (100=1937) (7)	GNP, Total Millions of US$ (8)	Per Capita US$ [6] (9)	Population [7] (millions) (10)	US Aid [8] (US$000) (11)
1954	Communists and Trotskyists called for withdrawal from MNR; Juan Lechin and a few Poristas argued to stay.	Milton Eisenhower visited Bolivia; agreed to "fund revolution."						38.2					
1955			23,300	97,765	.92	56.0	95.5	18.2	46,102	562	166		33.5
1956		Hernan Siles, one of triumvirate of MNR, succeeded Paz; established stabilization policy.			.98	55.1	93.	23.3	128,518	536	158	3.5	28.0
1957	Oblatos entered Siglo XX; Radio "Pio XII" established.	General Strike against stabilization.	22,723	88,460	.94	58.8	90.6	5.4	276,483	518	146	3.5	26.8
1958			14,790	53,729	.91	56.0	83.0	-14.9	285,058	509	144	3.6	22.1
1959	General strike: reaction to stabilization.	W. Guevara Arce, 3rd of triumvirate, fought Paz; arms to miners.	18 of 20 mines losing money.		.98	68.1	89.0	12.7	341,000	502	133	3.7	24.6
1960	Christian trade movement gained in continent.	Paz elected; Lechin vice president and sent to Italy; PRA, split MNR.	14,409	59,623	.99	63.1	87.9	-5.2	381,444	533	144	3.8	13.8
1961		USSR dumped tin and tungsten on international market; repudiated Communists in mine.	15,017	68,704		66.1	90.2	-4.7	407,752	544	144	3.9	29.9

Year	Events											
1962	General strike; Hostages, Siglo XX against mine layoffs.	15,068	70,190		70.4	91.5	−22.0	431,483	575	149	4.0	
1963	Lechin split with Paz over Triangular Plan of West Germany, BID, US.	16,231	80,527	1.14		93.2	−22.2	428,433	610	154	4.1	38.3
1964	Paz overthrown; General Barrientos seized power. Student-worker strikes and protest.	17,951		1.55			10.7		637	158	4.2	78.9
1965	Barrientos lowered wages. Mines occupied by army.	16,902	124,403	1.77	70.6	95.3	−4.2	458,575	673	163	4.3	
1966	Officialista unions.	18,156	129,800	1.62	62.0	86.3	12.0		721	170	4.4	
1967	Congress of Miners called June 24 Massacre of Catavi.	18,315	166,300	1.50	54.7	78.9	15.4˙	519,080	742	171	4.6	
1968	Barrientos died; vice president Siles S. entered presidency.	18,098	173,600	1.42	53.3	60.0	17.8		786	177	4.7	
1969	Policia Minera "Yellow Unions" Ovando seized power in coup Sept. 26.	29,962	148,674	1.55			33.1		827	182	4.8	
1970	Reorganization of FSTMB, COB. Attempted coup of Gen. Rogelio Miranda resulted in J. J. Torres seizing power.	27,836	144,962	1.72			76.3					
1971	Return of wages cut by Barrientos. Union in Oruro confronts rebels, 8 dead. General Assembly of workers, students, peasants. Banzer coup Aug. 19.						46.2					10.1 credits promised 3.0 given

[1] 1900–1929 data from L. Peñaloza (1953); from 1930, data are from Alexander (1958) and Malloy (1970).

[2] Arce (n.d.).

[3] United Nations (1968). Figures vary for price of tin per libra fina; cf. Arce (1965:72): 1953, $0.96; 1954, $0.92; 1955, $0.95; 1956, $1.01; 1957, $0.96; 1958, $0.95; 1959, $1.02; 1960, $1.01; 1961, $1.13; 1962, $1.15; 1963, $1.17; 1964, $1.52

[4] United Nations (1970a).

[5] Wilkie (1969).

[6] United States Agency for International Development (1970).

[7] United Nations (1970b).

[8] Investigación del estaño en Bolivia (1935).

[9] Velasco (1964).

[10] Salamanca (1950).

under state management, capital from the mines has been diverted to the Department of Santa Cruz to develop oil and commercial agriculture, thus reducing the political potential of miners as the major producers of export goods. As a consequence, there has not been exploration for future development and mines have been decapitalized.

The declining productivity of ores combined with increasing costs for an inflated bureaucracy of the nationalized mining company caused COMIBOL to operate in the red until 1965. The squeeze has been put on the workers, whose wages have been reduced in a period of drastic inflation in consumer goods prices. This not only threatens the customary way of life of the community, but the possibility of survival.

Wages

From the early days of struggle to gain a living wage in the industrial mines of the twentieth century, workers' demands were met with the massive opposition of the army (chapter 8). Attempts to establish the right to bargain collectively for wages and hours culminated in strikes and terminated in massacres in 1918, 1923, and 1942 and the protracted struggle from 1946 to 1969. The mine companies were united in their opposition to labor union organizations and were able to resist any attempt to negotiate, except for brief interludes of support from populist presidents in the forties. Prior to nationalization, workers were earning on an average 85 centavos a day (Kyne 1943). Following nationalization, miners earned more than workers in other sectors of the economy. After 1965 they lost their preferential position.

Whenever workers gathered, wages were the focus of attention. During a ch'alla I walked up to the ledge above Mina Colorada with three miners to see the cross erected in memory of the seven men buried in a mine explosion eighteen years before. As they told me about the accident, they related it to their own experience:

❖ The mining administrators don't want to recognize the sacrifice of the worker. They aren't even interested in making us work—no, really, they want to kill us from hunger. Is it true or not, brother? [He questioned rhetorically the miners nearby.] But when a person attacks them, they say we are agitators. That's the way they treat us—like agitators. Even when it is a justified issue, even when we demand more wages in the interest of feeding our children. Our children walk barefoot, without proper clothing. Those seven men who died, they are happy now. [Others interrupted, saying, "Yes, it is true, brother. I swear to God . . ."] Let me finish, or are you going to talk? In the first place, what we call our "gross wages"— that is, what they don't hand over to us—I am not complaining about that. What I am demanding is that they should give us back our contract at the price we earned before Barrientos. I used to get eighty, seventy, or ninety pesos for what I am now paid forty. They cut our contract in half. And even as a contract earner I can't earn anything. To get ten pesos, you have to advance thirty meters. You have to work from seven in the morning to seven at night. But before we would get thirty pesos. It's nothing.

Change over Time

The variations that plague any attempt to assess the returns to miners' production over time are even more of a concern in trying to assess the return to miners in wages. Workers told me that they had greater possibility of gains from striking a rich vein during the days of private exploitation of the mines. When they left the mine, the indemnization they received often enabled them to capitalize a small business venture for themselves. Also when the workers figure how they did in the past, they immediately relate their earnings to the cost of food at the time. Thus one miner, now retired, who had entered in the mines in 1908, recalled that in 1914 he was earning the equivalent of B $3.50 a day in Llallagua, about a third of his current earnings, but he notes that 5 centavos bought a large loaf of bread, cheese was 10 centavos a pound, milk was 5 centavos a liter, 50 centavos bought an arroba (25 pounds) of potatoes and 20 centavos, a kilo of meat, while an entire sheep could be bought for 40 centavos. A similar grocery bag today would cost B $48.00 minus the sheep.

The big change in wages brought about by the revolution of 1952 was the setting of a basic wage regardless of productivity of the workers. Contract work was paid liberally, and miners gained more than industrial workers in most segments of the society, especially in relation to the subsidized pulpería prices on basic commodities. They began to lose this advantageous position in 1956 with the passage of the Stabilization Act. By 1965, when General Barrientos occupied the mines with government troops in May, miners earned less than workers in the rest of the industrial labor force. The basic wage was cut from B $11.50 to B $10.34 and contracts were reduced by a half or more. In an attempt to stimulate production in the face of these drastic measures, he provided an "incentive pay" of about half the basic wage for daily attendance at work if the worker reported at the job seven days a week throughout the month.

Barrientos promised an increase in wages of US $26,000 for all the nationalized mines, which he coupled with a demand for increased productivity in April 1965. In the following month, on May 23, the wages were cut from B $14.15–B $18.80 a day to B $9.79–B $11.40 per day. Although Barrientos promised this would be an austerity measure limited to six months, the rate remained throughout Ovando's period. On September 17, 1967, *Presencia* published a news story on miners' wages (table 7.2).

Mining wages became a major political issue in Ovando's year in office. When he entered the presidency after the coup in September 1969, he promised to return miners' wages to the pre-1965 reductions brought about by Barrientos. Workers were beginning to lose patience with Ovando's promises on coming into power by February, when they threatened to go out on strike if he reversed his position (*Presencia*, February 12, 1970). In March, at the first union meeting since Barrientos had seized power and suppressed labor organizations, one worker said prophetically, "Union liberty is a fiction. The continuation of the wage and salary freeze shows that the government does not have any interest in bettering the conditions of the workers so long as the decree of 1965 remains in effect." The issue dragged on until the congress of April, when the FSTMB outlined a strategy for gaining wage increases without contributing to inflation.

Table 7.2. Mining Wages, 1967

120 persons received	B $399.12	
120 persons received	733.77	Per month with night work ·
3,000 persons received	626.00	and profit sharing figured in
1,300 persons received	576.92	
200 persons received	2,029.08	

Both health and danger as bases for special bonuses were raised in the Congress of the FSTMB in April 1971 as central to the wage issue. There was a general preference for returning to the salaries prior to the cuts made during Barrientos' term, with the incentive system based on attendance at work and with cost of living increases. The delegates called for bonuses for unhealthy and dangerous work conditions despite the problems in this position, since most of the delegates were convinced that a demand for increases would start a cost of living increase. Their experience with the inflation following the 1952 revolution seemed to underwrite this argument. One feature of the wage demands made in the Congress which seemed to me to be defeating to long-range labor interests was the economic commission's demand for the right for all workers to work on Sunday and overtime if their needs were great, and that this should be established as a right irrespective of the needs of the company. This was a retreat from a position asserting the right to a living wage based on the basic pay. The final position taken by the economic commission with respect to a wage increase was a demand for a return to the pre-May 1965 wage structure except in those mines which had not been recategorized.

Some of the delegates tried to cast the wage issue into a more political vein:

> It is not we who regulate our wages, it is the North American imperialism of the developed countries that fixes our wages. Therefore we have to improve our institutional base along with other workers of Bolivia, of Latin America, and of the world to fight for liberation and national independence with all the underdeveloped countries against imperialism.

The key to the Federation's strategy was to combine wage increases with a reduction of the bureaucratic expenses. In an advertisement in *Prescencia* (September 19, 1970) the FSTMB presented a statement showing that the reestablishment of wages would amount to US $3,358,400 for all the mines each year, and could be met by reducing the expenses shown in table 7.3. The union directors, criticizing the administration for failing to apply modern methods of administration or for introducing advanced technology especially in the concentration of the ores, pointed out that the real drain of resources lay in administrative failures, not worker inefficiency. They called for an austerity budget for the bureaucrats,

Table 7.3. Proposed Reduction of Expenses for Mines

Currency exchange write-offs	US $370,000 annually
Accounting control	370,000 annually
Commission to the Banco Minero	931,000 annually
Mine police	300,000 annually
Import duties	755,000 annually
Reduction of bureaucracy	56,000 monthly
Travels of bureaucrats,	1,000,000 annually
daily living expenses,	
donations, insurance, materials	

maintaining that the annual increase of US $3 million for wages would be more than offset by reducing the above listed items. Using figures from Catavi, they showed the wage patterns given in table 7.4.

Wages in other industries had risen in the interim in response to cost of living increases. Salaries in construction rose from B $71 in 1966 to B $446 in 1969, and although they dropped in transportation from B $769 in 1966 to B $682 in 1967, they reached B $704 by 1969. The workers felt that the wage freeze in mining was a politically punitive act because of their role in resisting the stabilization act of 1956 and the Triangular Plan.

On September 7 Ovando finally admitted that the increase he promised on coming into power the year before could not be paid, a fact that he blamed on the fall in production. On September 30 the directors of COMIBOL said that the reinstatement of wages would mean the liquidation of the entire enterprise, leaving to their own fate some 19,000 miners (Patria, Sept 30, 1970). Extolling the "rationalization" of wages under Barrientos, they said they would leave the final settlement of the dispute with the president. General Ovando met with the directors of the FSTMB on October 1 and expressed his disagreement with COMIBOL's reestablishment of wages at the 1965 level. He tried to put off the wage increases until January 1 of the following year. Three days later, when Ovando went to Cochabamba, General Rogelio Miranda seized the "Burned Palace" and tried to establish a government. When he failed to gain support, even of the military branches, General Juan José Torres stepped into the power vacuum. A week later the miners resumed their demand for their wage reinstatement. General Torres set up a

Table 7.4 Distribution of Wages, Catavi

Monthly Wage	Number Receiving	Total Budgeted
B $ 363	166	B $60,258
370	136	50,320
429	69	29,601
451	278	125,378
484	36	17,424
528	95	50,160
550	18	9,900
561	10	5,610
572	10	5,720
594	77	45,738
627	11	6,897
649	16	10,384
660	7	4,620
682	2	1,364
700	21	14,700
726	1	726
748	15	11,220
770	3	2,310
792	1	792
804	3	2,412
836	12	10,032
847	1	847
915	3	2,745
975	2	1,950
1,050	1	1,050
1,100	13	14,300
1,150	1	1,150
1,200	13	15,600
1,300	3	3,900
1,400	2	2,800
1,500	2	3,000
1,600	1	1,600
1,800	5	9,000
2,000	3	6,000
2,200	2	4,400
2,300	5	11,500
2,500	7	17,500
3,000	6	18,000
Total	1,057	580,908

committee to study the problem, and on October 14 announced that salaries would return to the 1966 level in fifteen days. When the wages actually went into effect in January 1971, workers found out that, while some of the lowest income group gained, many of the contract workers lost money in their monthly paycheck.

The wage conflict was a restrained attempt to gain a minimum subsistence level for miners. In their public statements, the leaders of the federation rarely attacked the wage system itself (United Nations 1964:22–38). The issue at stake was life and the ability to survive, not the profits of the company. The increase in the cost of living (see column 7, table 7.1), not the increase in the price of tin, was the basis for the major thrust of the federation's argument. During the course of the negotiations, at least one of the leaders of the federation kept in view the ultimate goal of the workers' struggle: control of the means of production (*Presencia*, November 26, 1970). But the threat of military repression was too close and the workers' organizations too weak to press socialist demands. Both leaders and rank and file feared that this would threaten the moderate democratic processes sustained by the Torres government.

The Rationale for Wages

The worker's pay envelope reveals much of the value system that has evolved in labor-management relations. The establishment of a base pay, the family subsidy, the union dues checkoff, and the profit-sharing bonus reflect the history of wage negotiations.

The basic pay, measured in mitas, or a day's work of eight hours, is a victory of the revolution of 1952 and establishes earnings as a right regardless of the amount of ore produced. Before this, some workers could end up with negative earnings because of mechanical breakdowns or cave-ins.

The organizational efforts of the thirties and forties succeeded in establishing the family as the unit for a subsistence wage reinforced by welfare provisions. The family subsidy of B $14 for a wife and B $12 for each child per month is an advantage not only for the male breadwinner but also for management, since the security of the family ties a man to the job and reduces absenteeism. If a man leaves his wife, or concubine, management pays this share to her for support of their children. Special allotments for milk and a sum of B $120 for a layette on the birth of a child ease the crisis of each new arrival and probably minimize the use of abortifacients or infanticide practiced by peasants of the region. Each death appears to be compensated: B $120 is given on the death of a child, and when a worker dies, his wife receives 60 percent of two months' basic pay.

The rationale for the preferred position of the miners in the fifties was the decisive role they played in the revolution of April 1952. When George Jackson Eder (1968) came with his mission of "stabilizing" the Bolivian economy, he set the reduction of miners' wages as one of the principal targets in fighting inflation. With the simple logic of an Alfred Marshall economist, he stated that, if the miners demanded B $6,000 a day, then the exchange rate of the peso would have to be 6,000 to US $1 in order to keep wages to US $1 a day. He justified this position on the grounds that "there was no other way to escape this equation unless COMIBOL produced more tin or dismissed one half its miners" (1968:132). Mr. Eder even went to the extent of supplying President Siles Zuazo with the rhetoric for selling the stabilization program to the public; he emphasized that the president should state in his speech that the goal of no further sacrifices was linked to that of no further privileges (1968:171). Later Mr. Eder expressed satisfaction that the military regime of Barrientos "has not hesitated to arrest and deport the anarcho-syndicalist or Trotskyite labor leaders and to suppress violence in the mines with force" (1968:613).

When wages were cut in half after Barrientos sent in the army to occupy the mines, the incentive pay and profit-sharing plans were the new rationale by which management hoped to gain in productivity and keep the men on the job. The incentive pay provided an increment of approximately B $100 per month if the workers attended every day of the seven-day week. Even when the supervisor did not require attendance, men with large families often had to work overtime since they could not make ends meet without the extra pay. Workers complained about the profit-sharing bonus, since their share, based on 10 percent of their earnings, was a mere US $3–US $15 compared to hundreds and even thousands of dollars' increment to supervisors and managers (see table 7.5).

The company deduction of B $2 for the union is hardly a victory for organized labor, since the total for all workers is barely enough

Table 7.5. Corporación Minera de Bolivia, Average Monthly Wages
Before and After the Government Actions of May 1965

| | January–April | | July–December | |
	Number of Employees	Wage	Number of Employees	Wage
Mine laborers	8,529	B $867	8,076	B $527
Mine employees	623	1,221	554	1,086
Mill laborers	2,586	589	2,551	486
Mill employees	575	970	498	662
Surface laborers	4,531	514	4,711	452
Surface employees	4,587	862	4,074	690
Total	21,431		20,464	
Average		B $770		B $407

Source: Bolivia, Corporación Minera de Bolivia, "Estudio Sociológico de los Centros Mineros de COMIBOL: Salarios y Costo de Vida" (La Paz, June 1970), p. 13 (mimeo.). Taken from Burke (1974).
NOTE: Wages include base pay plus bonuses, overtime, and profit sharing (US $1 = B $12).

to cover a single trip of the directors to La Paz, and allows nothing for strike funds or other independent action by the union. Social security is another chimerical victory for the workers, since the bureaucratic blundering of this organization minimizes the pay-offs to the workers when they are in need of it, and they claim that both the military and the government use it as a public treasury. Entertainment, clubs, and movies, and other company-subsidized deductions are of greater significance in remote mines, since there is no other source of diversion than that provided by community facilities. Workers complained in Oruro that the B $5,000 given in 1970 was diverted to administrative facilities and the workers gained nothing from it.

One deduction I have never heard workers complain about is that for education; many workers came to the mine to educate their children and they take a great deal of interest in the schools. Workers tell me that during the strikes of 1957 through 1963 only the schools stayed open.

The paycheck of a contract driller shows the earnings of Celso for October, when he earned double due to working overtime (table 7.6). The months of September, October, and November are the basis for calculating the Christmas bonus, and all the con-

Table 7.6. Wages of a Contract Driller and His Partner

	Celso	Partner
Total mitas	B $371.25	B $326.25
Contract	1,481.52	467.96
Incentive	182.00	169.00
Family subsidy	63.56	75.42
Profit sharing	194.00	128.00
Total	2,292.33	1,166.63
Tax	20.61	
Social security	92.62	39.71
School	13.87	3.97
Pulpería	416.18	339.00
Debt	51.00	0.50
Union	10.00	1.00
Shops	11.00	7.00
Movies	7.00	7.50
Clubs	11.00	23.50
Cafeteria	10.00	111.51
Profit sharing*	18.13	197.56
Cooperative savings		4.42
Total deductions	661.41	735.67
Take-home	1,630.92	430.96

*In a decree of May 27, 1965, COMIBOL promised 50 percent of profits to be distributed among employees at 25 percent monthly by the mines and 25 percent trimonthly by the central office.

tract workers are eager to maximize their take-home pay. Celso and his partner worked ten to twelve hours a day and most Sundays for their pay. This is shown along with the stub of his partner's pay. As the only wage earner in a household with eight children, Celso was working desperately to keep his head above water. In the month following the bonus he fell sick, and his wife, who had been a palliri in her youth, went to work on the slag pile. When he returned to work, she continued to work, much to his dismay because of the shame he felt before his working companions. Despite the much-needed assistance, his pride, as the sole breadwinner, dominated over rational considerations.

A wage measured in hours, even when qualified in contracts by cubic meters taken out, fails to take into account the unhealthy conditions of some quarters in the mine and the danger of some jobs. The workers balance the sacrifice on the job against the returns and find them wanting. Celso tells of his experience working in an isolated paraje:

❖ The men can't continue sacrificing themselves so much for nothing, because some day there is going to be an accident and they do not receive anything for the danger in which they work. A worker who is in an unhealthy place ought to have his sacrifice recognized in extra pay. For the past two years, I have worked in a very narrow, suffocating passage which lacks oxygen. I was working down there alone, like an orphan, drilling, and cleaning up all the dust. I complained a lot to the section leader, saying that they ought to recognize this sacrifice. Finally I told him, "I can't work here like I've been working for the past eight months, because I am physically exhausted." So he put in a young man, but he didn't last more than three days. I don't know what happened, whether he didn't set his dynamite in well or what. They told me I had to go back in there, but at least they gave me a new drill, and so I was able to spare myself a little.

The superintendents don't recognize this. They come down to visit us for a few minutes with a good lamp, with a face mask that they don't take off even to speak to us. They look at us and make a few remarks, but we are there every day.

The difficulty with a system of wages geared to what appears to be a precise recognition of the level of physical sacrifice to the worker is that it validates the wage system by seeming to take into account all aspects of the sacrifice to the workers. Moreover, it divides the working class internally into favored and disfavored categories. In the wage negotiations of 1970 the FSTMB, while recognizing the hazards of some jobs over others, tried to avoid the traps of a wage system geared to such a definition.

Another respect in which the rank and file differed from the union representatives in challenging the rationale for wages and salary differentials was that the union concentrated on contrasts between workers and the supernumeraries in the COMIBOL bureaucracy, while workers focused on the contrasts between technicians and underground workers. The workers questioned the payment of technicians in U.S. dollars while they received bolivianos and hence were more subject to inflationary changes. The preferential scale was set in the early days of the revolution, when it was agreed that, in order to hold technicians in the country, their wage scale would have to compete with world payments for engineers. This discrepancy was exacerbated when bonuses, based on production were given and the percentage increase to workers would be in cents while that of the technicians would come to B $100 or more. The federation recognized the conflict between workers and technicians, and tried to overcome it and redirect hostility toward what they considered to be more parasitic sectors of the bureaucracy, but it was not easy to turn attention from the immediate targets of competitive hostility, the technicians who lived in the mining community while the administrators were out of sight in La Paz.

Unemployment

Guesses at the unemployment rate in Bolivia have been hazarded at anywhere from 5 percent nationally to 15 percent in urban areas, with an underemployment rate of 20 percent (United States Agency for International Development; 1969; ILO 1964:34) This is figured on the basis of 1.8 million in the labor force, most of whom are male breadwinners. It fails to take into account many of the women who have worked in the past, both in and outside of the mines. During the Chaco War, there were 4,000 women employed in the mines replacing the men who were recruited into the army. Some of them found work as palliris after the war. However, this source of employment for women was cut off when concentration techniques shifted to machine rather than mechanical separation of the ores after the Triangular Plan went into affect.

The Triangular Plan was deliberately aimed at cutting down the labor force in the mines. Towards this end, US $8 million was allocated toward paying indemnity to the men and women who were laid off. In the decade between 1960 and 1970 the labor force in COMIBOL was cut from 29,000 to 21,000 (Burke 1974:175). Paradoxically there were increases in the total labor costs during these ten years because of the change in the composition of the work force, with more higher-paid bureaucrats than underground workers. Due to inefficiencies in the administration of the social security program, many workers disabled by silicosis were put on surface work as guards or watchmen. While labor productivity increased in the sixties as capital was substituted for labor (Burke 1974:149), the resultant social disorder cost untold amounts (ILO 1964:39 fn 1). The government bore the costs for the army stationed in most of the mines to keep them running from 1965 until 1969, when there was a brief relaxation in military control. This separate accounting plus the rise in the price of tin in the latter part of the decade enabled COMI-BOL to show a profit and thus validate the Triangular Plan.

The desperation for work is revealed in the kind of marginal activity around every mine. *Veneristas,* or placer miners, pan the water flows and sell the mineral to the mine company or to the mine bank. Often the entire family is engaged in the work of concentrating the mineral they trap in the water flows. In addition to this work, women work on the slag pile picking up ores which were cast out years before when the interior veins were richer. There were more than two hundred of these women, most of whom were widows of miners killed in the mines or as a result of silicosis, in Siglo XX in 1970. They were paid by the bag, earning on the average 80 cents a day. They had no job security or social benefits, not even hospitalization. Around every major mine are hundreds of marginal workers sorting and re-sorting rock to scratch the last bit of mineral out of it.

The unemployed and marginally employed were represented at the 15th congress of the FSTMB. Proposals were made to form cooperatives of the veneristas, estimated at more than 1,800 in Catavi–Siglo XX center. The delegates called for concentration plants to provide work for the unemployed, and that they be recognized as regular workers enjoying the benefits of the school and hospital and other provisions for the miners. All of the workers recognized the importance of supporting the veneristas' demands, since they existed as a very visible reserve army of unemployed who could otherwise drive down the wage of all the employed. The solidarity the union showed with the phrase "the unity of the mining family" struck me as revealing an advanced consciousness of one of the basic problems in the economy.

Wage workers treated their jobs as an inheritance for their children, and this was respected in the community. When a worker was forced to retire because of silicosis or was killed by an accident, most people recognized the right of his surviving children to take over his work if they were of age. "He has a right to this job," fellow workers would say of a young man who won a job in the

company after his father died. "His father gave his lungs to COMI-
BOL."

Another group of unemployed, the rentistas, or pensioned
workers forced to retire because of health, were also represented in
union activities by a man to whom each one paid B $1 a month to
speak for them in La Paz. They received from B $150 to B $220 a
month, which could barely keep them fed on a diet of potatoes and
noodles, and frequently this was delayed in the bureaucracy in La
Paz. Shortly before the Congress of the FSTMB in April, they carried out a hunger strike in an attempt to get payments on time.
Since their labor power was no longer of value, their only means of
forcing action was to disgrace the government by this threat to destroy themselves. Despite their efforts, their situation did not improve. Three months later, a group of pensioners who had, as happens every month, come to the district center in Oruro and waited
two or three days past the time for their pension, staged a takeover
of one of Patiño's mansions in Oruro. I entered the building with
them. As I stood in the vast entry of the mansion towering above
the stunted, malnourished men and women, many of them wracked
by coughing, I sensed the failure of a nationalization program that
had failed to come to grips with the exploitative system inherited
from the tin barons.

The supply of labor does not, like the other products used in
the industrial process, respond to lowering in wages or other signs
of decreasing demand. In fact, there may be the reverse effect, as
parents hedge against an uncertain future by seeking security in
raising a breadwinner for their old age. While the campesinos of
the area practice abortion and even infanticide when necessity
forces them to recognize the limitations of the environment, miners
live in a somewhat false climate of security built into the family
subsidy in their wage. Thus their sense of anxiety at the birth of a
child is lulled, and they may not feel the burden until their own
strength begins to fail, often before their children are grown.

Facile solutions for the overpopulation in the altiplano often ignore the cultural obstacles to such a violent shift as migration to the
Yungas agricultural area in the latter part of the fifties. Just the
climatic change itself discouraged migrants accustomed to the cool
climate around the mines, and the lack of housing, medicines, and

agricultural tools made it impossible even for the hardy to stay. Those workers who had silicosis were often unable to survive the higher atmospheric pressure at lower altitudes. When the migration program failed, the U.S.-sponsored birth control clinics adminis- tered by the Peace Corps. It was rumored that these served as centers of involuntary sterilization, a theme developed in the film *Yahwar Malcu*. Whether or not the rumors were true, the sense of the castrating presence of the United States in Bolivia was symbo- lized in such institutions.

The Cost of Living

Barrientos' government succeeded in driving down the stan- dard of living of the most organized segment of Bolivian labor to a point that was below minimal standards for the survival of a family unit. Contract workers could, by working seven days a week, main- tain a family at a bare subsistence level, as Celso did, but there was no margin even here to allow for sickness of the chief breadwinner.

The symbolism of bread and its relation to the value of a worker's life is joined in a worker's sense of the meaning of work and the continuity of life. As the price of bread and the cost of living rose in the intervening years from the time that Barrientos broke the revolutionary trajectory of Bolivia's history, wages and the value of a worker's life went down. One morning a baby's body was found in the refuse heaps that surround the mining commu- nity, partially consumed by the dogs. The shocked horror of the women in the mining community almost seemed to confirm their growing fear that life no longer had a value placed on it. They tried to blame it on the *minifaldas,* miniskirted young women who re- sponded to cultural influences outside the community, but they sensed that the value of life was being negated.

In the first weeks of my stay, the administrators of the mine ad- vised me about the miners' inability to save, their lack of planning for the future, their drinking and fighting. These myths protect the sensibilities of the middle class, who would otherwise be over- whelmed with the inequalities which exist in a wage and salary structure that rewards the nonproducer and reduces the standard of the subsoil worker to a bare subsistence. The miners are well aware

of these myths. One miner told me, "They say that a miner is ignorant, is a brute; but I have worked twenty-three years as a miner
and I know that this is not so."

The high price of living in mining communities is a feature
since colonial times of the dependency on outside sources for acquiring the basic means of subsistence. Herédia (1966:93–94) notes
that in colonial times the richness of the mines contrasted with the
poverty of the people. Rents were ten times in Potosí what they
were elsewhere in the country. Iron tools, mules, wheat, and wine
were purchased at exorbitant prices. A city that produced an income of US $10.9 million a year in silver production lived in squalor
and misery. The uneven returns from activity in the mines sets a
kind of gamblers' tone to the life of a mining community.

The dependency on imports of basic foods has been growing in
the twentieth century. Stokes (1963:154) shows the following increases since 1925, when 22.3 percent of the food was imported, to a
small increase of 1.6 percent in 1940 followed by a major increase in
1952, when imports reached 37.84 percent of what was consumed.
Stokes blamed the jump on land reform, claiming that rice, sugar,
corn, bananas, vegetable oils, and tobacco could all be grown in
Bolivia on thousands of acres of undeveloped land. While his argument that there is an undeveloped agricultural potential in Bolivia is
based on fact, he ignores the distortion of the economy in which
productivity and capital resources have been channeled into export
production of minerals and oil in order to balance a continually increasing debt structure. Burke (1972) shows how the United States
policy of dumping surplus wheat at prices below the cost of production scuttled Bolivia's program for production of wheat in the
agrarian reform. The trend toward dependency for foodstuffs continued throughout the sixties, when US $158.6 million of imports
were foodstuffs. In 1967 only 22 percent of rice consumed was produced in the country, although in other cereals and potatoes Bolivia
produced nearly all of what was consumed (United Nations 1972,
Table 161, pp. 510–11). In 1968, 20 percent of the US $158.6 million
dollars of imports were foodstuffs (U.S. Agency for International
Development).

The stress on a working population whose wages were frozen
after the stabilization plan of 1957 and further reduced in 1964 can

be deduced from table 7.7. Monetary exchange manipulation has been a major cause of inflation when the country has depended on imported food supplies. Salamanca (1950:46) pointed to monetary manipulation of the exchange rate as one of the major reasons for inflation a quarter of a century ago. This became even more pressing after the revolution of 1952, as prices of meat and bread increased ten times the 1952 prices. A further major increase in prices after the devaluation of the peso in 1973, resulting in a median increase of 120 percent (Presencia, January 25, 1974), can give some perspective on the same process taking place two decades before. The exchange rate for bolivianos in reference to the U.S. dollar in the twenty-year period provides us with an index of inflationary potential. It rose from 110 bolivianos to the dollar in 1952 to 14,000 in 1955, and following stabilization rested at 12,500 from 1959 until October 1972, when President Banzer devalued it by 66 percent in relation to the U.S. dollar.

Although many of the businessmen of Oruro assured me that miners knew nothing about exchange rates, the miners' conversations with me convinced me of their understanding. I was discussing Zondag's (1966) book on the Bolivian economy with a driller, and he translated some of the issues into concrete terms for himself:

❖ We are earning about as much as we did in 1956 and 1957, but the cost of living has gone up. Since 1965 the daily pay has increased only ten centavos a day. But look at what has happened with prices. I have some data here that I can show you: before 1956 a peón, a regular worker in the mine, earned more or less the equivalent of three dollars and fifty cents for a mita. But today, a driller, who has the highest position in the mine, doesn't earn even a dollar. So you can deduce that the Bolivian money has been totally reduced. And along with that there has been a tremendous increase in the cost of living. They say that the mine has recuperated

Table 7.7. Cost of Living Index

	1962	1964	1965	1966	1967	1968	1969	1970
All items	101	110	113	121	135	142	145	151
Food	103	103	106	115	134	144	147	154

Source: United Nations Statistical Yearbook (1972), Table 178, p. 573).
Consumer price index from La Paz figures.

much of the losses, but it is not through the efficiency of the government but because of the misery of the miners, and of course the government doesn't want to understand that.

Another worker dates the awakening of understanding to the relationship he saw between wages and prices to the revolution:

❖ We didn't understand anything until the revolution about inflation and deflation. Now I know that in inflation, currency without value is put into circulation and in deflation money begins to disappear from circulation. Many miners who had saved in order to carry out different projects—buy a house or some tool for independent work—discovered after inflation that their money was worth nothing. Then came stabilization. In this period the workers, the poor people, became poorer and the rich richer. And in this process the financiers, far from doing good, did a great deal of harm to the pueblo.

The sense of exploitation is not an abstract quantity, measurable by some deviation from a generalized relationship to the GNP, but a very specific loss in terms of culturally embedded ideas of what is appropriate in the particular station in life in which workers place themselves. Marx (1969:226) points to a treatise by Mr. Thornton on overpopulation which shows that the average wages in different agricultural regions still conformed, a century later, to the more or less favorable circumstances under which the districts emerged from serfdom. I shall explore here some of those standards that provide benchmarks for resistance which Bolivian workers acquired in the three generations in which they have worked in industrial mines. Also, I shall show how their reaction to a rising cost of living that negated levels of living to which they had become accustomed related to these. These standards can be grouped in terms of (1) nutritional values, (2) the family as the consumption unit, and (3) expectations for the future.

Nutrition

People in the mining community have a good sense of the importance of nutrition in maintaining physical strength. All miners agree that a worker should not eat lard or grease because it disturbs the heart. They prefer vegetable oils in their cooking. Because of the greater physical exertion required of the drillers, some claim was made at a union meeting that they should get greater quotas than the other workers. Very few drink coffee in the mine; tea and lemon or lime drinks are preferred.

Most of the women are very aware of the relationship between good nutrition and health or disease. One woman, whose husband had died from silicosis the year before, told me:

> ❖ What the miner has to do is eat well. In the morning when they get up, they should eat beefsteak and afterward a cup of *cuaca* [tea] and bread with butter and cheese. At twelve they should come out to eat lunch, but there are many miners who can't come out. The administration makes them eat inside, along with the gas. That is the worst thing for a miner. It is for that reason that they come out yellow, depressed, dazed with the gases and pallid, because they lack light, air, and sun. When they get tuberculosis, they ought to eat better—milk, eggs, all of those things the miner needs—fruits, and this could stop the disease. But what we lack is money.

In 1970 basic nutritional standards were not being met; workers complained of living on "rations of hunger"—tea and coca—at the end of every month.

Familial Unit of Subsistence

The primary motivation for working, and for remaining tied to a job, is to sustain a family. It was on the occasion of the ch'alla in the Colorado mine that I sensed this basic drive as I listened to one of the miners commenting on the death of his comrades in the big explosion of 1956:

> ❖ The miner works for his children, to support them, but life is bought at a high price. Seven persons died in Colorado. Why? They had to support their children for their daily bread. They took out some of the bodies and couldn't find the others. We work for the daily bread of our children. Life sometimes plays with the miner like a stack of cards, with his death and with his strength. A miner works with his love, not with ill intention toward anyone, to seek his daily bread. Do you know why these things happen? Just to earn something he faces death, he becomes joined with his own destiny. We never know what fate has in store for us.

The men say that the frustrations they feel with regard to their lives hit them when they return home from work and see.their children hungry and dirty. It is then that the rage that they feel in sacrificing themselves so much for such low return wells up and they take it out on their wives and children.

The family as a unit of consumption with a single wage earner is extremely vulnerable to changes in the cost of living. The family subsidy of B$14 for a wife and B$12 for each child is unable to cover minimum daily requirements of even the cheapest foods such as potatoes, rice, and noodles. I have seen women deprive themselves of protein in the distribution of food in the meals they prepare. When the wage earner dies, widows receive a monthly check of B$150, which cannot even purchase the starchy foods available, and this is terminated in five years. In the early years of mining, the system was geared to the minimal needs of a single worker, and women found work in the concentration pits. The shift to the nuclear family with a single wage earner as the ideal occurred with some of the union gains made in the forties. There was a slow erosion of employment opportunities for women, a consequence both of improved technology requiring fewer hands as well as a deliberate policy of hiring men in the new, machine-operated concentration work. Following the Barrientos policy of wage reduction, the breakdown in a living wage adequate to provide for a miner and his family may have far-reaching consequences for the structure of the domestic unit and the reproductive levels of women. Some of the old supports of the familial unit of consumption are being lost. The private mines used to give certificates for purchase of subsidized articles with quotas based on family size for those articles sold below regular market prices. In San José mines this is no longer the case. Bachelors now sell the certificates for items in short supply.

Expectations for the Future

The major focus for workers' aspirations is the improvement of their children's lives. These hopes are concretized in a desire to gain education and professionalization, "to buy their life from the mine," as one father of six put it. This too is proving a mirage, since the jobs reserved for those with a secondary degree become less and less available as the general educational level of the population rises. Juan, who subjected himself and the rest of the family to many sacrifices to get his son into college, finally had to give up the dream when his own health failed due to 100 percent silicosis and his son took his place working in the interior of the mine. Many of the sons of workers who had entered college and were hoping to continue their education were forced to leave in order to work and supplement the family income when I was living in Oruro. This frustration of aspirations defeats the tendency toward embourgeoisement of the workers and reinforces a sense of class solidarity when they accept the fact that there is no escape even for the future generation. Aníbal, an "empirical" engineer who earned little more than the wage of a manual worker but who did the work of a technician, expressed the hopelessness of the situation to the workers today:

❖ The reality is this: we have in our household four boys who want to go to the university. But with the miserable wage that I earn, there is not enough to cover the costs for education. I would have to buy books, but look at how much they cost. My wage couldn't cover that. I asked the mining company for some help in a scholarship for my children, but how can I hope for that? When the government decides to give a scholarship they begin to ask what is the person like, because the person receiving a scholarship has to follow the official line. But the government is afraid that if they give scholarships to our children, many of them have the head to become a political leader of the workers. That has always been the fear of the government.

These interrelated problems of maintaining a culturally established level of living, of supporting a family, and of trying to improve conditions for the future are the basis for assessing the level of acceptance of a given wage system and ultimately the government that maintains it. Aníbal discussed these issues as a problem in the "political economy of the family":

❖ Formerly when I worked in Colquiri I had a wage of B$649 that was sufficient for me to live peacefully in my household. But now the B$300 that I earn has to go for food, clothing for the children, and more than anything else, for their studies for the future. That is an obligation that is absolutely necessary for a man to undertake because I never had an opportunity to be a technician, but now we miners can't do that for our children. So in balancing all these responsibilities, I would say that there exists a politics of the house. Politics is not only an international feature, but also something that one finds in the family. And in the family politics, the B$10 that I earn daily has to be stretched over the month. A Bolivian can't live like an American on ten bolivianos. For an American, the breakfast alone costs B$15, while for a national, it is only a little tea and a piece of bread. And so I say that our country is very poor. The 300 bolivianos that we earn a month has to provide food, study, maintenance of the house, and personal obligations that exist. If there are seven of us, the ten I earn is divided among us: one for each person and three remain for me to decide to whom to allocate it for a pair of shoes. And since a pair of shoes costs no less than 95 bolivianos, I have to take it out of our daily food allotment. And who is going to get that pair of shoes?

As always in our national life, the money itself has changed its value. I never suffered before as I am suffering now. We have suffered, but we always managed. Now that is no longer possible.

The bubble of rising expectations of the postrevolutionary period was broken in the sixties, but the workers are not prepared to go back to pre-1940 levels. Questioning of the lower-than-subsistence levels for a family is leading to questions of the legitimacy of a government and its state bureaucratic structure. The failure of the post-Congress efforts to reestablish that minimum standard has led to a sustained sense of rebellion contained only by military repression.

Family budgets were collected from four families for time periods varying from six months to a year. Although not all income was accounted for, the proportions are significant (table 7.8). In almost all the families, over 50 percent of the budget is spent on food, with from 15 to 31 percent on clothing; Case C is lower on food since the woman grows most of their vegetables and buys a great deal from relatives who live in Cochabamba. The youngest family, C, had a large outlay on furniture, B $959, since they were just setting up housekeeping. Two to three percent is spent on chicha, coca and liquor, far from the claims of personnel managers who try to blame the workers' poverty on their indulgences. Family A were buying their house and land through the cooperative and spent only B$438 for house and land. The other families were living rent free in company housing.

Consumer Dependency

The vulnerability of the worker as a consumer is based on the institution of the company store and the failure of community orga-

Table 7.8. Budgets for Four Families

A. *Carpenter in mine earning approximately B $15,000 annually: 2 adults, 3 children*

Food	B $5,335.98	50%	Social security	756.00	7%
Clothing	2,291.00	21	Rent	67.00	1
Bus	427.60	4	School	12.00	
Household expenses			Clubs	120.00	1
(kerosene, candles,			Cafeteria	36.00	
etc.)	335.30	3	Land Rent	150.00	1
Debt	377.00	4	Cooperative savings		
Union	12.00		and loan	240.00	2
Medical	84.00	1	School supplies	200.00	2
Miscellaneous	376.45	4			
Total				10,820.33	101

B. *Carter, earnings about B $700/month, Jan.–June: 4 children, wife*

Food	1,206.90	56%	Transportation	122.50	3%
Clothing	552.00	14	Coca	68.00	1.5
Household furnishings	999.00	24	Liquor	43.00	1
and expenses			Chicha	2.00	
Newspaper	14.50				
Total				4,007.90	99.5

C. *Pipelayer on contract, earning B $350/month, Jan.–June 4: 2 adults, 1 child*

Food	1,994.34	44%	Newspaper	18.50	
Clothing	1,437.00	31	Bus	74.40	2
Household furnishings,			Chicha, beer, coca	92.60	2
supplies	959.13	21			
Total				4,575.97	100

D. *Driller, earning about B $1,000/month: 5 children, 2 adults*

Food	3,459.90	49%	School supplies	87.65	1
Clothing	3,135.00	44	Coca	52.80	2
Household supplies	286.90	4	Liquor	51.50	
Bus	29.69		Cigarettes	18.00	
Total				7,121.44	100

nizations to develop secondary bases of supply. The first factor is tied to a dependency economy that fails to develop a broader productive infrastructure since the surplus value generated in industries is invested outside national boundaries or in specially favored regions of the country geared to the external market. The second is a failure by worker organizations to broaden their wage struggle to include housewives and their potential for organizing a cooperative base for distribution of goods. Both factors have deep roots in the culture of dependency that has grown up around the mines.

In the days of the tin barons, the company stores operated with imported foods and clothing, mostly from the United States, and sold them at cheaper prices in the pulpería since there were no tariffs. Manuel told me of this time:

❖ During the time of Hochschild, they had what was called a "dollar section." It was a store where the employee, or the worker who earned a lot, had the right to buy things that he couldn't get in the regular market with national money. They had, for example, English woolens, Camel and Chesterfield cigarettes. The worker who earned a lot had the right to buy a suit of English wool! Now, however, the only ones who can dress in English woolens are the high chiefs of the company. They have the right to dress, to smoke the Chesterfields or Camels; but before, the worker could too.

The "right" that this worker speaks of, to buy foreign goods, encouraged the sense of being a privileged sector of the working class and reinforced the paternalism of the old enterprises. At the same time, it tied the workers to a dependency on the company store as the sole supplier of goods while it discouraged the development of national supply centers. In mines where there was little or no competition from independent sellers, the miners were forced to accept low-quality food at high prices. Fresh meat, even in large mining centers like Siglo XX and Catavi, was often short and in smaller mines such as Santa Fe, workers lived on canned sardines, salmon, and milk for months without seeing fresh supplies.

Dependency on the pulpería is one of the major factors limiting the miner's ability to act freely in the labor market. As soon as the workers go on the job, they can draw supplies from the pulpería, but they are not paid for a month. At the end of the month, the pulpería account is deducted from the worker's paycheck, often taking up three-quarters of the total. His debts tie him to the job from then on. Encouraged to buy consumer items he can hardly afford because of apparently easy credit offered in the pulpería, the worker is never more than five days from starvation if he is cut off from this source of supply. Aníbal criticized the tendency of his companions to fall into consumer fetishism:

❖ The people go to Coro Coro mine to make a fortune and save money. There there are no distractions; their encampment is completely isolated from the city, from the whole society. But the miner, especially because he is wasteful, dissipates his money. He drinks, or he has this great weakness: he begins to buy consumer goods, for example furniture, radios, sewing machines. There in Coro Coro each miner has at least three sewing machines, three radios, a wardrobe closet. But what is lacking? Why doesn't he have a house? It seems a little absurd to me since they ought to think of buying a house in town first and afterward get the furniture.

However, the worker measures his satisfaction from the job in terms of concrete utilities. Many workers lost savings that they had put into the old mining companies when they were nationalized, or the money they had saved became almost useless as the inflation rose to indices of over 40,000 over 1937 base prices. When I asked one woman why she had three sewing machines, she said she had bought them as a dowry for her daughters. Suspicions about money and savings and not inherent wastefulness (as some of the personnel relations employees claim) are responsible for the failure to save money, combined with expenditures on concrete objects. Wage-workers bear the burden of inflation more than any other segment of the population, especially when their wages are frozen.

Even more important from the point of view of gaining control over their labor power, dependency on the pulpería limits the workers' effectiveness in a labor dispute. When the workers threaten to strike, the administration retaliates by closing the pulpería. As one worker told me: "If we enter into a strike, then they put the army in the pulpería, and then where are we? We are at the mercy of the company store, and we don't earn anything, so how can we buy in the market?"

This same tactic of coercion was used to increase "participatory democracy" during the MNR period; a woman at Siglo XX told me that the government used to cut the workers off from the pulpería if they did not vote in national elections.

One reservoir of potentially positive action in the political economy of the household is through the organization of housewives around the problem of consumer supplies. In the early days of the revolution of 1952, women were mobilized by the MNR and carried out some consumer protests. I spoke with Domitila, the president of the housewives' association in Siglo XX, and she told me about this movement.

❖ We protested the prices of milk, of sardines and other supplies. We went to La Paz to protest and we succeeded in getting better supplies. It wasn't a big deal, but at least we succeeded in getting more supplies of milk and cans of oil and lard. They also supplemented the amount of fresh meat available. Before we had to stand in line from three in the morning when the fresh meat came in if we expected to get anything. They used to give us one kilo a day and then they raised it to two. These were small things that we succeeded in doing, and we had to leave our homes and our families to travel to La Paz. We didn't know much and we didn't have any place to stay. But with the little preparation we had, we succeeded in making the people of the administration understand what we needed. We managed to get one cake of soap a week more, two jars of milk, a half liter, and two kilos of lard.

We women also tried to get quotas in accord with the size of the family. When we got into this problem we immediately realized the need to demand higher wages, because what value is the increased ration if you don't have money to pay for it?

The incipient politicization of women evident in this consumer protest fortified the workers in the strike of 1962. The housewives' organization provided the basis for the mobilization of women in getting provisions for the mining community when the company shut the pulpería. The women often started their protest as they waited in line at the doors of the pulpería itself (see chapter 4).

The fear working men have of women undertaking independent political action undermined this domestic base for reinforcing a wage struggle. Management is more aware than the union leaders of the potential force the mobilization of women might have in providing an independent supply base and in the public demonstrations which had an effective appeal to the wider population. Even the clergy were prompted to counter the women's hunger strike implying that woman's body, as a reproductive vessel, was not her own property to threaten by subjecting it to hunger strikes. This was never asserted in the case of the hunger strikes carried out by men.

Supplementary Income

Many families in mining communities use their skills and contacts maintained with agricultural communities to raise vegetables and chickens, make bread, and buy wholesale products. One miner who raised chickens, turkeys, and guinea pigs spent B$15 a month for the feed and had his own supply of eggs and meat. With chickens selling at B$8–B$12, he realized a saving of B$5–B$9 each on his flock of twenty chickens. Peasants make regular trips to the mining community to sell the feed, and they often develop compadrazgo relationships with the miners.

Women go to the country to buy potatoes and other vegetables during harvest time and make a saving for their family and sell the surplus. The pasanaku is one way of gaining capital to maximize purchases on these trips and spread the savings among the contributors. Others use the foods purchased from the pulpería at lower prices and exchange them for other products that the peasants raise. Sometimes they go in groups that regularly take these trips together. Their husbands take over in the home—most miners know how to cook and do not resent temporary chores of this sort, since they respect their wives' desire to enter into negotiations that will augment the family subsistence.

Families who have come recently from the country often make their own bread in one of the clay ovens on the outskirts of the encampment. The cost for making 600 small bread loaves is: B$1.00 for yeast, B$3.00 for lard, B$5.00 for an arroba of flour, B$0.50 for salt, and B$4.00 for wood to fire the ovens. At a total cost of B$23.50, they can make an amount of bread that could cost about B$120 if bought retail. They usually undertake this arduous job at the time of a fiesta so that they can make savings on their own costs and sell some in addition.

About 10 percent of the workers raise gardens on lands owned by the mine or by the cooperative housing. The variety of foods grown by one miner reveals the range of products they like in their diet. Juan showed me his garden, which filled his own yard in the cooperative housing barrio and extended onto other land owned by the cooperative. He grew parsley, peas, broad beans, sunflowers, wheat, radishes, and coriander, as well as a variety of potatoes: *papa t'ik'a*, *papa aili*, *mak'unku*, and *chuñu*. The latter is the small potato which is frozen and then pressed to preserve by dehydration. He grows enough potatoes for his family of eight for six months and enough quinua for a year. When I asked him how he learned to be a farmer he said, "Necessity taught me." Since he comes from Cochabamba, it is likely that he learned in that area choosing those crops which could survive in the higher altitude with a shorter growing season.

These attempts to overcome consumer dependency have not been underwritten by any community-wide organization nor by management. There are, however, reserves of human labor, especially youths, who could be activated to cultivate these soils which are fairly productive when watered. Delinquency among late teenagers unable to find work in the mines or the city was an increasing problem, and there were several cases of rape and robbery reported during my year's stay, a feature which was nearly absent in the past. The importance of such an activity has largely been overlooked by the union and other organized groups because of the unconscious acceptance of dependency on the company store from colonial times.

Cost of Production

The rising costs of production and the declining rate of profit in mining is a complex issue involving increasing bureaucratic expenses, interest charges on capital, declining exchange rates of the Bolivian currency, combined with a loss of productivity of the workers resulting from decapitalization of the mines, declining levels of mineral content, and lack of exploration for new ores. The difficulty of analysis is made more complicated by the accounting procedures of the nationalized mining administration, which is concerned more with concealing some of their operations than with revealing some of the basic problems. I shall try to sort out some of these issues in stating the case as presented by workers and by management, since it is the crux of the class struggle in primary producing countries whose economies are characterized by dependency on industrial centers in the world economy.

Bolivia represents an extreme case of dependence on the world market to which it sells tin and other minerals along with oil and on which it depends for basic consumer needs as well as manufactured goods. While colonial mining introduced European forms of capital goods, the items could be manufactured locally: hide boots and helmets, hand mauls fashioned in the form of animals by the workers, and drills of hand-wrought iron were all the tools needed in the early period. Industrial production at the turn of the twentieth century imposed the need to import all machine tools and most of the garments used by the workers. Dependency on foreign capital meant that investors wanted high returns with minimal risks, but the exaggerated fear of revolution nullified high-risk investment with the result that there was indiscriminate extraction and little planning for the future (Velasco 1964:17).

As the demand for tin rose in the world market, output quadrupled in the first three decades of the twentieth century (see table 7.1). A price drop following the depression in 1929 made possible a concentration of production in three major owners: Patiño, Hochschild, and Aramayo, who controlled 73.98 percent of all production. Their empires in Bolivia were consolidated with world tin magnates after the agreement of 1930 establishing the International Tin Council, which controlled prices in the interest of the tin consumers. Patiño's decision to invest profits in Williams Harvey Tin Smelters in England in 1911 and later in smelters in Dallas, Texas, instead of developing a processing industry in Bolivia, reinforced the dependency relation on the world market.

During the Chaco War with Paraguay (1931–35), production fell below that of the turn of the century and never rose to the pre-war high of 47,087 tons reached in 1929. Despite dips in productivity, tin was always over 60 percent of the balance of trade until 1953, when the mines were reorganized. Metals represented over 80 percent of the export goods except for a dip in 1960–61. Oil exports are lowering that proportion, but the development of the oil resources in Santa Cruz has in part drained capital from the mines of the altiplano (Zavaleta 1963).

Even in war periods when the demand for tin was high, Bolivia was unable to take advantage of the situation by raising prices. In 1941 the London Metal Exchange set a price freeze, and Bolivia's contribution to the allied effort was to maintain moderate prices on tin. Prices for tin did climb during the Korean war, possibly because access to Malaya's tin resources was threatened by the spread of communism in Asia and the consequent buildup of reserves beyond war-inflated demand. When the containment policy was set following peace, the United States dumped the tin reserves they had built up, bringing the price down to US $0.90 just at the crucial period when the mines were nationalized. Price, Waterhouse, Peat and Company estimated that COMIBOL lost US $124 million between 1952 and 1957 in price changes alone (Bedregal 1959), an effective way of controlling the revolutionary process taking place in Bolivia.

Nationalization and increased foreign aid from the United States following recognition of the National Revolutionary Movement in 1953 led to increased dependency. In the period from 1950 to 1964, exports dropped to a −30 index and imports rose by an index of 7 with 1953 taken as the base year (U.S. Agency for International Development 1965). After the passage of the Stabilization Act in 1957, U.S. advisers monitored every major economic decision made by the MNR government. All loans extended to Bolivia were tied to the demand that it buy an equivalent amount of goods from the United States. Bolivians claim that many purchases, particularly for capital goods in the mines, could have been made more cheaply in Japan and other industrialized centers. The Committee on Mines of the Alliance for Progress reported in 1962 (Ad Hoc Committee 1963) that "the stabilization measure adopted in December 1956 which were followed by a restrictive monetary policy and which has resulted in 1962 in interest rates of at least 20 per cent to 80 per cent per annum further discouraged domestic investors."

Bolivia was hard hit in this period by the increasingly unfavorable balance of trade due to the price exchange rate. CEPAL reported (1964:54) that "in the last six years, [1956–61] the growing contribution of independent foreign capital at long term loans for the financing of Latin American growth remained completely annulled by the unfavorable devaluation of the exchange relation. In this period, it is interesting to observe the losses as an effect of the deterioration of the relation of exchange (10,100 millions of dollars) represents almost six times the total net advances (1700 millions of dollars) according to the aid authorized by the official organisms of the United States and international institutes" (quoted in Canelas 1966:118; see table 7.1).

Dependency on the United States led to a negation of other sources of support. In 1959 the Soviet Union promised Bolivia a capital investment of US $10 million for a tin smelter. The United States counterpoised this offer with an agreement to lend the same amount for the recapitalization of the mines and for preconcentration plants. A later offer by the Czechs to set up an antimonium refinery with Swiss funds was turned down by the National Stabilization Council, thus ensuring American control over Bolivian antimony deposits (Canelas 1966:91).

The final capitulation to external control over the mines came with the Triangular Plan, a loan of US $37.75 million by the Bank for Interamerican Development, West Germany, and the United States, which tied the capital for modernization of technology and exploration to a demand for "rationalization" of the labor force. In the following three years, over a third of the workers were fired and another thirteen hundred were laid off after the military occupation of the mines in 1965. As noted above in the section on unemployment, these drastic policies did not result in real gains, since labor costs increased. The profits COMIBOL showed after 1965 were a result of rising prices of tin rather than success in disciplining the labor force (see figure 7.1).

The distortions in the industrial economy of Bolivia are reflected in the high costs of production and the declining returns of the mines. A cost breakdown from a report made in 1935 (*Investigación del Estaño en Bolivia* 1935:91) reveals the problems endemic to a primary producing, dependent economy (table 7.9). Fifty-three percent of the costs (expenses in Liverpool and depreciation) were incurred after the tin arrived in England, as the table shows. This kind of cost breakdown is impossible to get for current exports, but we can guess that, with the increase in the cost of the materials of production imported from abroad, the increased shipping charges and insurance costs as well as the rising rate of interest on capital and the devaluation of Bolivian currency, that the proportion of the costs attributed to out-of-country factors has increased over the years.

The fact that Bolivia did not have concentration plants within the country until 1970 has meant that it has had little control over the cost accounting once the mineral has left the country. Moreover, the smelting companies do not credit the sale for minerals other than tin that are contained in the shipment, and since most of Bolivia's mines produce a complex of minerals, the lead, silver, tungsten or other admixtures are counted as waste although the

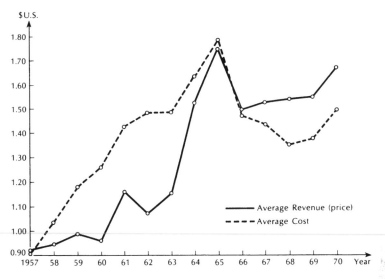

Note: Average revenue AR is the price received by COMIBOL; average cost AC includes
mine costs, regalias, and realization costs, or total cost placed market.
Sources: Bolivia, Corporación Minera de Bolivia, Departamento de Costoy Estadisticas
(unpublished material from the files of the department, La Paz, 1970) and Bolivia,
Corporación Minera de Bolivia, *Memorias anuales 1965-1970* (La Paz, from Burke, 1976).

FIGURE 7.1 CORPORACIÓN MINERA DE BOLIVIA:
AVERAGE REVENUE AND AVERAGE COST PER
FINE POUND OF TIN, 1957–1970

concentration plants make a profit on them. The additional shipping costs for sending out waste material adds to the cost factor so
that the producer nation is deprived of profits.

Bolivia's deteriorating position in the world market for tin was
reflected in the decapitalization of the nationalized mines. This was
a result of both mismanagement as well as a shift in interest to oil.
Arce (1965:15) blames much of the decline in the productivity of the
mines on failure on the part of management to invest in exploration. He attributes losses of US $106 million in the decade after na-
tionalization not only to a breakdown in administration but also to
the entry of workers in decisionmaking through workers' control.
The miners reacted against attacks of this sort, saying that the machines were breaking down frequently, there were often bad drills
which broke while in use causing accidents, and that weak batteries
for their lamps, poor work clothing which was inadequate in sup-

Table 7.9. Cost of Tin Imported into England, 1935

	Pounds	Shillings	Pence	Percent
Labor	30	15	11	18
Materials	24	15	7	14
Miscellaneous	16	14	11	9
Mineral adjustment		11	10	6
Expenses in Liverpool	55	15	6	33
Depreciation	34	18	3	20

ply, and other failures on the part of management to maintain equipment caused delays and accidents. The capital from the Triangular Plan that was to bolster the nationalized sector served to stimulate production in private mines (Burke 1976). The net effect was to leave Bolivia with a debt load that it is still struggling to pay.

The problem of operating a mine with worn-out equipment reached crisis proportions when I was in San José. As a marginal mine, San José received used capital goods from Siglo XX and Colquiri. Breakdowns in the compressor and water lines frequently caused stoppages in the work, and the inefficiency of the pump in draining galleries at the lower levels meant that whole areas were cut off from production. The frustration of the contract workers led to their holding a sitdown strike in May 1970. In an extraordinary reversal of labor and administrative roles, the men were demanding drills, a better compressor, and continuous operation of the water pumps. The supervisor of the mines claimed that it was their own fault that they didn't have enough of the 180-centimeter drills because they did not start with 120-centimeter drills and work up to the larger. When the men rejected this argument and called for a reliable compressor and pump, he turned to the issues of the pulpería and services in the encampment, saying, "Let's begin with the small problems and lead up to the larger ones," knowing that it would, as always lead to a stalemate. The men began to complain about quantity and amounts of basic necessities, the drillers wanted larger allotments of cooking oil because they made the greatest sacrifice, and so forth. The union leader, who was already compromised with the managers, fed the mine supervisor a line, "What about the hospitals?" knowing management was planning to build a new wing. This set the supervisor off on how management was doing more for miners than any other segment of the population and that they had just hired a gynecologist "who did nothing but put his hand up women's boxes all day." When the men laughed at his crude joke—which put him on a par with them in the sexist tradition—the conflict was over. Nothing was done to alleviate the situation, and it was clear that San José was doomed as an obsolete mine and the present supervisor was not going to do anything to change it.

I asked the supervisor of Colorado mine what he thought of the future of the mines. He was a *tecnico empirico*, a man who learned engineering from his long experience in the mines of Bolivia and who had come from Chile during the Chaco War. He told me,

❖ Four times the owners of this mine have tried to close it. First it was closed when the silver was exhausted; then tin was found to have value, and it was reopened, but in 1946 when Hochschild was the owner, he wanted to close it after he had capitalized Colquiri with the profits from San José, but the Banco Minero took it over to keep workers employed. In 1957 the nationalized mines wanted to close it, but then they got better machinery to concentrate the ores and it was kept open. Now they are talking about closing it again because it is a marginal mine. But in time they are going to find other methods of concentrating the minerals and the mines are going to live. No technician can say that the mine is marginal. Oruro ought to live for a hundred years."

This was the only technician working at a supervisory level whom the miners respected. He said that the only reason they admired him was because, shortly after he arrived, a new vein was found that kept the mine going. I felt that it was because he shared their faith in the mine and had the same sense that their lives depended on the life of the mine. He respected their knowledge about ores, although they did not have the vocabulary to talk about it in a way that would convince the theoretical technicians. Other technicians, who in the process of acquiring their degrees became alienated from the culture they were born in, did not have his knowledge of the particular character of the veins in the Bolivian mines. The workers could smell and even taste when they were getting near to the key veins. Often when a miner who is doing an exploration returns to his gallery after a blast, he tastes the face of the rock to know if he is getting close. They know the concatenation of minerals associated with tin, and their empirical knowledge is often as accurate, or even more so, as that of the geologist. But they need support from the managers in order to act on their hunches. Patiño knew how to take advantage of this skill and knowledge and built it into the contracts that he made with the pirkiñiros, or workers who got paid according to the value of the ore they produced. This supervisor was one of the few who would have liked to see the marginal mines turned over to the pirkiñiros and enable the workers to maximize their skill and knowledge in some of the closed shafts in those mines. He told me of the 1914 law permitting any national to exploit an abandoned mine, but instead of recognizing the legality of such acts, the men who entered these shafts were treated as jucos and put in jail.

I investigated the threat to close the mines in 1957. First, I spoke with a retired inspector of the mine, Max Cladera, who was an organizer of the Bloque Minero in Oruro the year of the threat. He and other businessmen and engineers of the area who were concerned about the economic future of Oruro drew up a letter condemning the proposed action by the national mining administration. He showed me a clipping from *La Patria*, published in 1957 (exact date not given), with the headline "The Federation of Miners Urges Guarantees of the Prefect of Oruro":

> The director of San José, Augusto Saravia, said that the reserves of San José were finished. The leader of the mining syndicate said, "The union, in defense of the conquest of the nationalization of the mines, refuted such declarations, demonstrating before public opinion in a general meeting that there exist vast reserves, justified by statistical data found in the mine company office which are sent monthly to the central office in La Paz. We publicly denounce the administrators' attempt to abandon our enterprise. We declare that, knowing of this attitude, the workers are refusing to go to work in a justified protest." The Bloque Oruro approved in a confirming vote, congratulating the miners of San José for having refuted the declarations of Engineer Saravia and asking for the mobilization of the city of Oruro in defense of its riches, issuing a call to its institutions to oppose all political operation of the regime that pretends to inflict such grave damage to the citizenry, closing a mine whose conditions of production and reserves can be shown by technicians of known quality.

Julio Aguirre Zeballos (1959) published a study *El mito del agotamiento de la mina San José,* asserting that it was the richest silver mine left in Bolivia, and concluded that political rather than geological considerations dominated the decision of COMIBOL's administrators. He listed the following problems as the root of San José's low productivity: (1) although mechanized, over 80 percent of the work is done by hand, especially in the concentration process; (2) there is a continuous changing of technical personnel; (3) development and preparation of the veins that offer greater potential are not done; and there is an (4) excessively high percentage of workers in the exterior, a proportion of 35 to 65. He blamed the excessive costs on the following factors: (1) administrative expenses; (2) inappropriate acquisition of products and materials through intermediaries and purchase of unproved capital goods; and (3) lack of accounting control over wage payments.

Claiming reserves of 621,470 gross tons of silver with a content of 5.5 mineral, 760,904 gross tons of tin with a content of 1.77, and 30,209 tons of lead with a content of 8.09, he argued that the administration had falsified reports. He recommended reorganization of the administration, developing geological explorations, and a program of preparation and exploitation of new veins as well as abandoning some shafts because of flooding. Pointing to the experience in 1947 when the Banco Minero took over operation of the mines and grossed US $8,817,384.45 in a two-year period, he urged the rejuvenation of San José.

From the time that COMIBOL took over the administration of the San José mine in 1953, there were more than ten directors and eight superintendents of mines in a period of five years. Instructions from La Paz were sent by a number of different officials rather than through one, contributing to the lack of direction and planning. The authority of the director was weakened by COMIBOL annulling or reversing orders. The top-heavy bureaucracy apparent in San José was endemic in the entire structure of COMIBOL. Whatever savings were effected in ridding the lower ranks of the work force of supernumeraries in accord with the Triangular Plan were soon liquidated by increases in the hierarchy in La Paz and the mine police introduced by Barrientos. In 1945 there were 265 employees in the COMIBOL offices in the mine centers, and by 1970 this figure increased to 475. The La Paz office increased from 175 to 682, with administrative employees getting 100 times the wage of workers and

the president earning US $20,000. In 1970 union leaders called COMI-
BOL the "private purse for the military government." Instead of
serving as a "center for the entire transformation of the economic
and social conditions of the Bolivian Nation" (Bedregal 1959:14), the
mines were not able to maintain a minimal standard of living for
the workers themselves. They continued in operation at increasing
costs to the rest of the economy only to provide payments to offset
the soaring debts outside the country.

The case of San José illustrates the extremes to which the state-
managed operation was willing to go to crush the rising labor
movement, because it was the militancy of the leadership in this
mine and their concerted efforts to break the stabilization plan that
provoked management into threatening closure. The lack of concern
shown by the supervisor and his staff for economic conditions in
the mining center and even the national economy fostered opposition by middle class business and technical leaders, who joined the
union in opposing the shut-down of the mine. The attitude taken
by the mine management reveals the alienation of the national
within the state bureaucracy, and the loss of direction when the
profit motive that prompted a higher level of efficiency in the old
enterprises was not replaced with broader social concerns and
movement toward socialism. The failure of the nationalized management to plan for the future meant that the mines were in a
greater crisis in 1970 than when they were seized in 1952. While Patiño used to save a portion of each vein for the future, COMIBOL
exploited each vein to the maximum. As one Oruro university student said to me, "They worked without capitalist foresight."

The Relationship between Wages, Prices, and Profits

The wage structure in mining fails to respond to changes in the
cost of living and in the profits from production in accord with classical market theory in economics. In fact, the reverse situation has
taken place in Bolivia: wages are declining in response to increasing
costs in the subsistence products and the rising prices of tin. This
results from the dependent position of Bolivia's economy in the
world market, which has in the last decade been exacerbated by a
state bureaucracy backed by military regimes. Dependency in the

world market has always meant that Bolivia was vulnerable to measures carried out by the industrialized nations to control prices, such as dumping reserves to keep prices down or to threaten recalcitrant political regimes. Whatever profits resulted from industry in the country failed to be reinvested in the nation, since the control over capital was exercised from outside. For the most part, reinvestment of profits in tin mining and other competitive primary goods elsewhere drove down the economic position of Bolivia's mines even further. The failure of industry to create other centers of production in the country means that Bolivia's labor force is not absorbed at a level wherein the demand and consequently the wage it can command increases. On the contrary, unemployment has increased over the past two decades and labor has not been able to hold on to the gains it made in the fifties. Added to that, the willingness of military regimes since Barrientos to massacre workers when any protest movement starts, has resulted in a constantly deteriorating position for labor in the country.

Bolivia exhibits those characteristics of dependency and underdevelopment summarized by Sunkel (1973:134) as low income; slow growth; regional disequilibrium; instability; inequality; unemployment; dependence on foreign countries; specialization in the production of raw materials and primary crops; and economic, social, political, and cultural marginality to a degree more extreme than that of any other Latin American country. As a result, the policies of the government are responsive to outside interests, and there is no self-correction possible within the present system. The crisis came in 1962 when, in response to the Triangular Plan, the unions tried to maintain the position labor had won in the early days of the revolution and to offset the reduction of the labor force threatened by capital intensive investment planning required under the plan. The resulting strike, described in chapter 8, marked the end of their control when it was broken.

The growing imbalance in the position of management and labor is especially acute in Bolivia because of its dependency position and the repressive political regimes which have come to control the nation. Labor's attempts to reverse this situation and the ideological transformations that accompanied them are described in the following chapter.

Chapter 8
◈◆◈
Labor Conflict and Unionization

◈THE LABOR MOVEMENT was emerging from one of the worst periods of repression in its history when I arrived in Bolivia in 1969. Unemployment was at a peak in the mines, as capital was being transferred to oil in Santa Cruz and to agriculture. In the restructuring of the labor movement that I witnessed in 1970, a mood of anxiety was present, but the prevailing sentiment was a resolve to pull the organization together and fight for survival. As one of the FSTMB delegates put it, "If the dog [union] dies, the fleas [workers] die with it."

The Bolivian trade union movement reflects the conditions of those Latin American countries with small pockets of industrialization, high unemployment, and impoverished sectors of the middle class. In these situations, the elite of full-time employed workers have often supported the business sector against populist movements. However, the Bolivian miners, because of the strong community identification, turned to an alliance with segments of the marginally employed who would otherwise be their competitors. Hence the unemployed and pensioned workers are represented in the union and send delegates to the Congress of the Federation of Mine Workers Unions (FSTMB). In addition, salaried office workers are integrated in the FSTMB along with those who work below ground. However, they often earn less than the contract workers, and their partial entry into the middle class did not seem to determine their ideological outlook. Among those who were leaders in the miners union, one was the Revolutionary Left Nationalist party (PRIN), one was a Communist Party of Bolivia (PCB) member, and another was a former Trotskyist now unaligned. Unlike the Bolivian Workers Central (COB), where members in the progressive and commercial sectors seized control of the leadership, the FSTMB was firmly grounded in the working class.

When I first tried to analyze the relationship between the union and the government as I observed it during my stay in Oruro in 1969, 1970, and briefly in 1971, I concluded that the rhetoric of revolution had become a substitute for revolutionary action. The level of skepticism, doubt about their leaders, and ambivalence toward undertaking any action in the tumultuous political changes from 1967 to 1970 made me question their potential for revolutionary action. However, when I placed the events I had observed in the context of a long history of violence and repression with intermittent reversals of power relationships, I could see that 1969–70 was a period of temporary withdrawal from the battlefield with the demands for revolutionary change persisting because of the failure of the government to bring about economic reforms.

In this chapter I shall review those events from the revolution of 1952 until the military coup of Colonel Hugo Banzer in August 1971, which shaped workers' consciousness at the time of my stay. In summarizing these events I shall question some of the issues posed in the literature on union structure. Among these are what I consider to be the false opposition of economic versus political struggles, and of spontaneous versus bureaucratic organization. Finally I shall consider what bearing the Bolivian case has on the current assumptions about trade unionism in Latin America.

Labor and the National Government

In its relationship with the national government, the Bolivian miners' union underwent four major changes between the revolution of 1952 and the fall of Torres in 1971. In the first period, that of Paz Estenssoro's first presidency (1952–56), the FSTMB operated as a faction supporting the Paz Estenssoro government (Malloy 1970:158). Through the Worker Control, union leaders affected decisions in the day-to-day operation of the mines and even influenced the assignments of superintendents. The second period, 1956–64, brought about the alienation of labor from the MNR. This alienation began with the stabilization plan, passed in 1956 and brought

into effect during the presidency of Siles Zuazo. The breach between labor and the MNR deepened with the introduction in 1960
of the Triangular Plan, which prompted the new MNR position of
decapitalizing the mines and shifting interests to oil and agriculture. In 1963 the labor left turned away from MNR and formed a
new party, the Partido Revolucionario Izquierdo Nacional (PRIN).

The third period began after the Barrientos coup of November
1964. It was one of total repression; union leaders were exiled or
jailed; any remaining activities had to be carried on in secrecy. This
ended in September 1969, when Ovando came to power and "gave
an opening to democracy" which initiated the fourth period of
union reorganization (1969–71). In the following months some of
the exiled leaders returned and the ranks of labor began to re-form.
This led to the Congress of FSTMB and of COB in April and May
1970. These Congresses laid the groundwork for a "General Assembly" of left political and trade union organizations in the following year. I shall now describe these four periods in detail.

Co-government of Workers and Bourgeoisie: 1952–1956

Bolivia's years of co-government are probably the most extended period in which organized labor in a revolutionary period
shared direct political power with an entrenched middle class
movement. According to Zavaleta (1974:88), who compares the Bolivian experience with that of Europe and other Latin American
countries, the failure to move in a socialist direction was a result of
the dominance of the bourgeois ideology in the labor movement
and in government.[1] As the antagonism between classes increased,
nationalization became a substitute for socialism, and the ideology
of nationalism became the crucible for melting down class antagonism.

The economic base for co-government in Bolivia was nationalized industry, its industrial relations were a modified system of
worker control, and its ideological commitment was to nationalism
as the key to solving the differences that inevitably arose between
the two sectors in the government. Their personal commitment to

---

[1] René Zavaleta Mercado (1974) has developed this argument. Lora (1964) points
out that the labor left in the MNR became no more than a medium transmitting
received policy from the government to the masses.

Juan Lechín was the means to weld the two systems, labor and state capitalism, together. In the period of sharp self-criticism within the Federation in the 1970 congress of the FSTMB, all of these aspects of the dual structure were under critical reevaluation.

Three major changes in industrial relations were brought about in the first two years of the MNR government: (1) the consolidation of the labor movement in the Central Obrera Boliviana (COB); (2) the nationalization of the mines; and (3) Worker Control. These will be analyzed below.

Consolidation of labor organizations (1952). After its formation in 1952, leaders within the COB gained political posts at departmental and national levels. Although the COB officially supported the MNR government, it included leaders of the left who took a critical stand. The COB established the position of co-government with the MNR but failed to develop a distinct policy and program for labor. It embraced not only working class organizations such as the FSTMB organization in its early days but also middle class professionals, and entrepreneurs. Armando Morales, a leading organizer of the San José Union from the revolutionary period of 1952 until the military coup of 1965, characterized the organization in the latter days of the MNR government in this way: "You know that formerly the COB was made up of lawyers, even doctors and millers who called themselves bakers, but who never baked a loaf. They said they were union leaders, but they never represented anyone."

Guillermo Lora (1963) summarized the position of the COB as a channel directing the political force of the working class to the support of the bourgeois policies of the MNR. Ultimately it became a block to the formation of a labor party.

The FSTMB, as a product of labor struggles of the thirties and forties, had a stronger rank-and-file base than the COB, which was a creation of co-government, a specific and provisional policy of the MNR. It included clerks and professionals who worked in the mines, but the working class base was dominant. The FSTMB took the lead in the attack on the Stabilization Plan. This reached its peak in 1962 with the strike in Catavi–Siglo XX.

Nationalization of the Tin Mines (October 1952). Anayo (1952) traces nationalization back to 1949 when the Left Revolutionary Party (PIR) called upon the legislature to nationalize mines without indemnification and with a strong worker control. Bedregal (1962; 1963), on the occasion of the tenth anniversary of the nationalization decree, claimed that this act, along with the Agrarian Reform, formed the nucleus of the program of the National Revolutionary Movement (MNR). Lora (1972) traced it to the Thesis of Pulacayo, which he, as leader of the Revolutionary Party of Workers (POR), helped to draft in 1946. These claims to paternity prove one thing: the bastard form of nationalized mines was popular and all parties with a stake in labor claimed to father it.

The hope of nationalization was summarized in the following litany (Anayo 1952:143):

> To liquidate the fifty years of backwardness, of exploitation, of extermination imposed by the great mining companies, we must nationalize the mines.
>
> To destroy the reactionary forces that block progress we must nationalize the mines.
>
> To make possible the economic, social and cultural transformation of the welfare and of the liberty of the Bolivian people we must nationalize the mines.

Nationalization became a reality at a sunrise ceremony at Siglo XX–Catavi six months after the revolution. These six months were time enough for the former owners to return shiploads of capital goods destined for the mines to the country of origin and to cut off further explorations and exploit to the maximum existing shafts. Juan related the meaning of nationalization for underground workers:

> ❖ On the thirty-first of October they signed the act of nationalization in Siglo XX in the Field of Maria Barzola. They declared a day of festivities. All the works were halted, neither factories, nor masonries, nor those who worked in the constructions in the city of Oruro worked that day. We workers gathered together from all the mines for this act in Siglo XX, where they had a huge concentration. They set off some dynamite as if they were in a ferocious combat, a war. When we worked in the companies of the ex-barons of tin, there were no drilling machines nor automatic shovels for the majority of us in Santa Fe. They had compressed air only where there were drills, and this was only in a very few areas. After nationalization they put in pipes in all parts, even into the most oppressive areas where the heat was so intense you could hardly stand it. Before, a worker had to swing a wet burlap in all

directions to drive out the heat into the tunnels or the shafts when they were driving a shaft down to another level. After the revolution they had pipes set up for ventilation.

Before the nationalization of the mines, many workers could not secure a contract. They had to work two years as a peón de la casa at the behest of any work group earning no more than the base wage without a contract. For example, in my case, when the month of May came, I should have been let on the job as a peón for two years, since I had been fired. Instead when I came back to work, the engineer told me, "Listen, Rojas, you cannot continue as a pirkiñero; you have to work as a driller." I was afraid when he said this because never in my life had I worked with a machine, nor did I know anything about the sickness of the miners and how they contracted it. It just scared me to hear, "You are going to work with the drilling machine."

Among the unanticipated consequences of nationalization of the mines was the reinforcement of the economic position of the middle class bureaucrat and technician as well as professionals in the support services of the mines. As political rather than technical criteria prevailed in the top ranks, with generals appointed as directors, the inefficiency in management was reflected in rising losses. This, combined with the denationalization as control was lost to foreign capital interests by the end of the decade, contributed to the disillusionment of the miners with nationalization as a panacea.

COMIBOL was under attack from management, political leaders and labor throughout the decade of the sixties. The US $20 million indemnization paid to the former owners crippled the operation of the enterprise from the start. In the period from 1953 to 1965, the mines lost US $106 million, a figure partly inflated by fiscal manipulation but accurate enough to demoralize the operation of the mines (Arce 1965:17). Labor costs rose from US $0.70 a pound in 1952 to US $1.29 in 1960. American critics such as Stokes (1963) and Zondag (1966) blamed worker inefficiency for the increase in costs. In defense of workers, Canelas (1966:43) pointed to the Ford, Bacon, and Davis report (1956), a study made by a U.S. engineering firm commissioned by COMIBOL, which showed that despite reduction in the overall figures for refined tin exported, there was an increase of 30 percent of gross mineral extracted in the first five years of nationalization. Canelas pointed out that men in Catavi who had turned out 1.22 tons per mita, or work shift, in 1950 were turning out 1.31 tons of ore in 1955, and overall production rose from 1,052,405 tons of crude ore in 1950 to 1,459,389 tons in 1955. The declining production noted by Stokes (1963), who used figures on refined mineral, was due to the fact that it required 10 meters of advance to extract a ton in 1960 in comparison with 1 meter in 1950. The failure to explore new tunnels and declining administrative efficiency were blamed for this by the union.

Other adverse conditions affected the newly nationalized industry. According to Norman Gall (1974), the industry "had been sustained for more than twenty years by the efforts of the first three decades of the century." The existing shafts were nearly exhausted and there was limited mechanization. In all but the largest centers, such as Siglo XX and Catavi, the pirkiñero system was still in operation.

Federico Escobar, the Secretary General of Siglo XX–Catavi's union and head of Worker Control in 1962, attacked the administration for having benefited Patiño more than the workers in the course of nationalization. Bedregal, then president of COMIBOL, countered the attack by claiming that COMIBOL was crippled by world market prices which had dropped severely in the post-Korean period. The United States had, he said, taken advantage of the nationalization of mines to break its contracts with the former companies, which were pegged at the high wartime price of US $1.83 per pound of refined tin and reset their price at US $0.90. He tried to enlist the support of labor with the statement, "Nationalization of the mines does not have as an object only the betterment of the conditions of work and the life of the miner, but also the entire transformation of the economic and social conditions of the Bolivian nation" (1959:14).

Both sides in the attack on COMIBOL used the Ford, Bacon, and Davis report to bolster their claims. However, the conclusions point out both low worker productivity and technicians' failure, but with the cause for these failures being managerial inefficiency. Arce, an engineer in Patiño mines, pointed to the nub of the technological problem in nationalized mines, stating that "a fiscal administration cannot carry out risks of long range exploration" since they are constantly subjected to criticism and review, often by military men with little or no knowledge of mining (1965:15). The resulting policy in the mines was one of intensive exploitation of existing reserves, a point most of the workers made to me on the basis of their immediate experience. Arce's recommendation was that there should be holding companies of Sociedades Anonimos which would be decentralized, with managing boards including workers to "create a spirit of belonging between workers and employers that would reinforce efficiency and production with healthy and constructive competition."

Despite the attack from both management and labor on the policies of COMIBOL both sides were dedicated to vindicate the process of nationalization and prevent the mines from falling back into private ownership. In part this was due to self-interest. The union leadership had benefited in the 1952 populist period, when unions had a greater recognition and opportunity to benefit financially under nationalized restraints which were more subject to populist pressures and more willing to invest in cooptation funds. Management benefited in the very positions they occupied in replacing previous foreign incumbents at technical and managerial levels. These vested interests made nationalization an irreversible process. Neither the government nor the military attacked COMIBOL because they were, as one miner said in the Congress in 1970, using it as their own private purse.

In view of these vested interests, the attack was limited to "false nationalization," not the process in general. The thesis worked out by the Political Commission at Siglo XX–Catavi in 1970 pointed to the fact that COMIBOL, "as inheritor of the rosca, has constituted a true super-state over the blood of the workers, limiting the role of the workers to produce and obey." However, it attributed this failure to a false nationalization in which the middle class maintained control of the decisionmaking apparatus and continued subservient to the international private capitalists. The union "line" became one of splitting the economic and political consequences of nationalization. This was expressed by an aspiring candidate for union office at the San José union meeting:

❖ I believe that nationalization of mines and of Gulf is a positive
step for the Bolivian people and for the liberation of Latin American countries, but it is a negative step economically because the
world market is controlled now by imperialism. . . . Who fixes the

prices? It is no one else than the imperialists who are the great monopolists. . . . Nationalizations are positive from a political point of view, but from an economic point of view, we do not control the world market.

This point of view was expressed even more sharply by another aspirant for union leadership:

❖ The nationalization of the mines put the Bolivian pueblo to sleep, changing only the name. The mines now belong to international private capital. Williams Harvey [the British smelting concern] controls everything, all the mineral production of the country. . . . The program of agrarian reform, of the universal vote and of the nationalization of the mines, cannot be advanced, why? because those who are interested in that, the pro-imperialist petite-bourgeoisie, can never raise it to nationalization of a socialist type, using simply the term nationalization instead of the practice. The only one interested in acquiring the social transformation of the people is the working class. The only thing that *Lechinismo* has served is to teach us by experience, not to act any longer in this way.[2]

He went on to analyze the nationalization of Gulf as a fiction in that Hispanoil, a Gulf subsidiary, was engaged to sell Bolivian oil not only from their former holdings, but also from YPFB.

As for the internal effect of nationalized industries, an economist in the University of Oruro demonstrated that they reinforced the position of the middle class who entered into the inflated bureaucracy along with the retired generals.[3] Their capital reserves were drained by the nationalized bank's policy of charging heavy tariffs for the dollar exchange—COMIBOL sold bolivianos for dollars at a higher rate (13 to 1 instead of 10 to 1) and bought them at a lower rate (8 to 1) than was possible in the open market, and as a government industry, was forced to do so. This made their overall position look even worse than otherwise. Furthermore, they were more subject to political pressures in hiring personnel. The workers in particular were critical of the decline in efficiency in technicians

[2] This aspiring leader was trained in the leadership school of Organizacion Regional Interamericano de Trabajadores (ORIT). His attack on imperialism may have been a ruse to overcome workers' suspicions as to his position. In focusing on Williams Harvey and ignoring the large share of Bolivia's tin that went to Dallas, he may have spoken from ignorance or guile.

[3] Talk given in Sindicato Training School, Oruro.

and managers after nationalization. This could have been excused on the basis of the difficulty in transition in the early period, but it got even worse in the second decade of the nationalization. Finally there was the destruction of small private mines, which limited employment opportunities for workers. Although small private mines persisted, they were uncertain as to how much they could sell, since COMIBOL had priority to sell under the national quota. The investment of foreign capital was in the reworking of the slag pile. This was a capital intensive operation which did not employ much labor.

Worker Control. A major innovation in industrial relations was the initiation of Control Obrero, Worker Control, with workers having the right to veto managerial action. This plan was drafted by the FSTMB and the COB and passed as a presidential decree on December 15, 1953. Juan summarized the effect of the decree from his perspective:

> After the Control Obrero was organized, the secretary general of the Federation declared that the administrators of the nationalized mines were taking advantage of their position in the cashier's office, the head office of personnel, the supply office, the heads of the encampment and of welfare. In the personnel office there was a list of workers called *maquipuras* [irregular, nonsupervised workers], who were not people who worked but only appeared as names on the pay ledger, and the chief received their pay.
>
> As a result of these irregularities, the secretaries general in the nationalized mines asked that COMIBOL organize the management which would serve as a base to control each company. They wanted to form a Worker Control with the right to veto. The government of Víctor Paz Estenssoro prevented the organization of this group. With great effort, the miners organized it but without the right to a veto. Without this, nothing had any worth. The workers of Siglo XX took a stronger position than the other mines. They wanted to enter into a strike, the first threat during the time of Víctor Paz Estenssoro. Paz Estenssoro did not want any problem in this period of office, and he gave in to their demand. After that they did not have these kinds of arbitrary acts that were happening in the other nationalized mines. They had more earning than ever because every receipt had the signature of the men in charge of Control Obrero. No one had the right to issue any drug, any work material in any part, no matter how urgent it was, without passing through the office of Control Obrero.

In Santa Fe mine we did not know what the Control Obrero was and for what it served, since our company wasn't nationalized in the year 1953. We only knew that the Control Obrero had to interfere in all kinds of arbitrary acts that existed in the breast of the company. In the year 1954 our company was nationalized as well as the Japo mines. We immediately organized the Control Obrero with the right to veto. The first secretary general was Víctor Carrasco, who was secretary of the union organization in the Federation of Miners. He apprehended various employees who had misappropriated the earnings of the company. For example, Señor Manuel had built a house in Oruro by collecting materials from the company. He came in person to Oruro to collect materials in Santa Fe, saying that he needed pipes, wood, all kinds of fixings for the construction of housing. They discovered it when the Control Obrero looked over a mountain of receipts from the year 1952. He was transferred to another post. Also they discovered a Señor Minaya, chief of the offices. He was a Paraguayan who stole B $30,000. Another chief of the offices, a Chilean, took B $25,000 to his country, but they couldn't get it back. The Control Obrero is the one which put a quota on everything and made things more rational.

The decree establishing Worker Control called for worker representatives to take part in planning for the future as well as to exercise vigilance over supervisors and disciplining personnel (Ruiz Gonzalez 1965:275). However, the worker quoted above reveals that the main activity of Worker Control was an attack on the administration, which took for granted that the managers were the owners of the house and the workers were the outsiders. The very function of being a watchdog was at odds with entering into the administrative functions as partners. The aggressive stance taken by miners in the Worker Control prevented the assimilation of their outlook to that of administrators'; a common weakness of such systems, but it also severely limited their managerial functions.[4]

The experience with worker control and participation in industry reveals some of the same contradictions that were observed in the nationalization process of which it was a part. Many of the Worker Control representatives rose to the occasion and gained

[4] Selser (1970) has spelled out the major problems encountered in the Argentine experience as follows: (1) difficulties in the exchange of information with the base; (2) workers dedicate more energy to salary and welfare than to management of enterprise; and (3) workers assimilate to the point of view of managers. These problems point to the need for continued surveillance of trade unions independent of the Worker Control group outside of the particular enterprise.

enough entry into the administrative process so as to shake up the bureaucratic apparatus. For the first time they challenged the premise of production geared to meeting external demands. By gaining some access to information, they were able to question the basic premises for the allocation of resources and the distribution of gains.

For the most part, however, the Worker Control functioned as a watchdog over the disbursment of funds; they never had a sense of participation in decisionmaking. This limitation of function had a structural base in the failure to take a position independent of the union. Even after worker councils are formed and operating smoothly, it is important to retain a strong union organization that operates in the capacity of watchdog over both managerial and worker representatives and that oversees the problems of salary and welfare that Worker Control councils often get bogged down in. In the case of Bolivian mine workers, there never developed a clear-cut separation of functions. The FSTMB controlled the selection of Worker Control representatives, more often than not with the secretary general acting both as Worker Control representative and head of the union capacities; and the union deciding on the issues. The ever-present fear of the rank and file that their representatives were becoming an elite corps was exacerbated as they entered into managerial functions.

Another structural weakness was the fact that there was only one worker representative on each management board. As Ruiz Gonzalez (1965:272 et seq.) said, "A lone representative trying to carry out the functions of control and effective intervention in the administration as the decree provides is like a shipwrecked sailor hanging from a log on the high seas."

As a result of these functional ambiguities and structural inadequacies in defining lines of jurisdiction between Worker Control and the union, workers failed to gain a sense of participation, and this increased their sense of frustration. A cooperative relationship between labor and management was never worked out. To the technicians and management, Worker Control meant anarchy in the mines. I spoke about this to a mine inspector who was one of the first Bolivians to graduate from the national engineering school. He commented:

◆ The sindicatos would come to the engineers and say about a certain tunnel that they had planned to excavate, "There is nothing in there. You have to leave that work. It's not worth spending money on it." And so they suspended the work, even though everything was prepared to go ahead.

I am very much in favor of Worker Control, but with limited power. [What kind of limitations? I asked.] Well, there would be times when some materials were ordered, and the letter circulated to Worker Control for their signature, and they would not sign it. It was a kind of super-authority over the superintendent. That is the kind of thing that can't continue if the operations are to proceed.

The rapid changes in the structural relationships between the labor movement and the national government in this first period responded to the vacillating policy by which the government tried in vain to balance the internal interests of the labor force and the external demands of foreign creditors. The impossibility of balancing the diametrically opposed interests led to polarized political situations and a constant series of coups. The labor movement relied on the charismatic leadership of Juan Lechín to hold together the ideologically split labor ranks, but in the political arena there was no solidifying force. I shall spell out the impact of these changes as interpreted by miners.

The Alienation of Labor from the MNR: 1957–1963

The conflict between the various parties and class interests embraced by the MNR that surfaced in Siles Zuazo's presidency had its roots in the act granting indemnity to former mine owners in 1953. Although labor conducted a battle against this move, they accommodated to it. The conflict intensified with the Stabilization Plan, a wage-price freeze to overcome inflation decreed in December 1956 which put the burden on the wage-workers. When the San José union opposed the Stabilization Plan from 1957 on, the national administration of COMIBOL tried to have the mine closed (see chapter 7), but the opposition of businessmen and engineers of the community acting in the Bloque Oruro prevented this setback.

As the conflict between labor and the bureaucracy sharpened after 1957, the government tried to appeal to patriotism and nationalism to overcome the differences in nationalized enterprises as well as in the political area. Bedregal sums up the appeal to patriotism and nationalism as he tried in the latter part of the fifties to overcome the developing class antagonism in the mine (1959:14):

> In the natural order of political priorities, first is the country, and then unionism; first is the national liberation, then the liberation of the working classes. If one insists on altering this nationalist order of priorities, on the premise that the union can earn when the nation is losing, then this will put the interests of the workers in opposition to the interests of the nation as a community, a weak and irresponsible position. It would put new forces of the proletariat with the old forces of the counter revolution.

But the workers were disillusioned with the appeals to patriotism after the Stabilization Plan.

Their disillusionment deepened when management of COMIBOL broke the strike in Siglo XX–Catavi. Any lingering sense that the government represented national interests ended with the "Revolución Restaurada" of Barrientos in 1964. This disillusionment was best symbolized for me at a fiesta celebrating the Day of the Virgin of Candalaria, which coincided with the Day of Independence. Two miners transposed the meaning of nationalism when I asked what the colors of the national flag signified. One miner played straight man and said, "Red for the blood of the heroes of the Chaco War." The other interposed, "For the blood of the miners killed by the military dictatorship." "Green for the Bolivian agriculture," said the first. "For the vegetable products no longer grown by the campesinos," interposed the second. "Yellow for the gold in our hills," persisted the first. "For the wealth of the mines that we lose to foreign powers," the second rejoined. I was told that, during the fifties, the miners had marched proudly in the Independence Day parades, wearing new helmets with battery torches and the yellow slickers that COMIBOL had issued, some carrying the rifles and machine guns they had seized from the army in the days of the revolution. But in the demonstration I watched in August 1969, only the administrators and technicians of COMIBOL marched; there were no men from inside the mine.

Union power, and with it, the participation of workers in the management of the mines, had begun to decline with the Stabilization Act, and reached its lowest point with the Triangular Plan and the strike of Siglo XX–Catavi in 1963. The Triangular Plan, promoted by the Bank for Interamerican Development (BID), West Germany, and the United States, required "labor discipline" and mass layoffs as a condition for a US $38 million loan for recapitalizing the mines.

When Paz Estenssoro signed the Triangular Plan in 1960, he lost his base with the mine workers. During this period, Lechín, alerted by the leaders working in the mines, returned from Rome, where he had been sent as an ambassador. He warned the workers of the increasingly anti-labor moves of Paz Estenssoro. The Miners Federation organized the National Left Revolutionary Party (PRIN). A leader in the Oruro union commented to me on this period:

❖ In the period of 1962–63 the workers left the MNR and joined the PRIN, formed by the farthest left elements in the party. We were in the same conditions as we were before 1952: we had low wages, and there was little to buy in the pulperías and there was repression of workers. The government of Paz Estenssoro wanted to liquidate the gains of the revolution. The new economic base was the Yacimientos Petroliferos Fiscales Bolivianos [YPFB] in Santa Cruz. The program of the new party was anti-imperialist. This caused splits in the working class. The new petroleum code of 1963 gave many concessions to foreign companies and there was an increase in the army. In the period from 1960 to 1962 Paz Estenssoro lost his popularity and relied more and more on the army.

The fight against the Triangular Plan was centered in Catavi–Siglo XX, which was the first mine to be hit by the plan. The union leaders were fired and 1,000 workers were threatened with layoffs. The company formulated plans to send 2,000 Catavi miners to the Yungas jungle. In August 1963 the union retaliated, calling for a strike. The workers, who still had the rifles seized in the 1952 revolution, sealed the town and declared themselves in revolt. However, one of the San José leaders of that period told me the strike was no longer an effective weapon, since COMIBOL received credits from the United States to tide them over.

The army was increased from 10,000 (*Newsweek,* August 19, 1963:48) in August to 15,000 in December. In addition, an armed militia of 60,000 peasants supported Paz (*Newsweek,* December 23, 1963:35–36). In December the leaders of the FSTMB in the Catavi mines were jailed when they left the mine center to rally workers of other mines. The miners in Siglo XX seized United States government representatives and foreign technicians as hostages in order to ransom their leaders. The union was in control of the encampment and maintained a kind of military discipline. However, not all unions in the FSTMB supported the workers of Siglo XX–Catavi. There was no national direction to bring about unity, since Lechín was still in Rome, serving as ambassador. Armando Morales, the secretary general in San José who had pulled the workers out of the strike after supporting it at first, defended his position to me as follows:

> In the year 1963 the miners of Siglo XX–Catavi initiated the general strike, but those of San José did not enter because the administration of COMIBOL was introducing the Triangular Plan. This was the agreement for a loan between Germany, North America, and the Bank of Inter-American Development. Then the Communists of Siglo XX struck. Since Catavi was losing money, the managers reduced the work force by twelve hundred. Many people realized what was happening and did not strike. Paz Estenssoro sent troops and surrounded Siglo XX and Catavi. As a consequence of this, the Federation of Miners had to declare a general strike in solidarity with the members of Siglo XX and Catavi. And they carried this out with the exception of the San José mine. We did not enter the strike because they were in the process of reducing the work force by fifty percent. It would have been irresponsible because we would have been playing with extremists and we would have forced COMIBOL to do what they did in Catavi. There, as a consequence of the strike, they sent in troops. Instead of the strike being a triumph for the working class, it was a triumph for COMIBOL. They fired many workers and took their bonus.

The breakdown in the solidarity of the mine workers marked the union's loss of control of the sites of production. The 1963 strike reveals a shift in the balance of power from the 1946–47 crisis. The strike in August 1963 quickly escalated into revolt when the workers, still armed with the weapons they had seized from the army in 1952, sealed the mine in December. Their reversal of power relations was quickly defeated as Paz turned to U.S. aid in armamemts to forestall a revolution. In addition, Paz tried to build up a popular base of support with the peasants: he rapidly turned over titles to land and enlisted their aid in peasant militia. The union tried to counter this force with the tactic of taking hostages as a means of gaining time. Their strategy might have succeeded had the unions not been split by internal disunity fomented by trade union leaders, some of whom were trained in the Organization Regional Inter-Americano de Trabajadores (ORIT) school promoted by the United States.

The strike of 1963 also revealed the increased politicization of miners and their redefinition of their role in national politics. The immediate issue was jobs and the fact that the Triangular Plan would mean unemployment for many. But the larger issue was the denationalization of the mines through external capital financing. The union fought the loss of the control over production that they had gained in the nationalization process. While *Newsweek* (December 23, 1963:35–36) presented the case as simple recalcitrance on the part of workers ("the miners invariably react to our proposal designed to increase the efficiency of the mines by staging crippling strikes"), the trade union leaders and rank and file saw the problem as the loss of control over the enterprise by nationals with the penetration of foreign capital.

One of the most negative consequences of the period of co-government, which ended with the breaking of the strike in 1963, was the breakdown in confidence in union leaders at local and national levels. In the first period (1952–56) the support given to unions had been a matter of internal redistribution, with the politics of popularism reinforced with handouts from high government officials or party leaders to union leaders from the base. A former union leader told me that when a commission went to La Paz, President Paz Estenssoro used to hand them money out of his pockets. In the second period, after the penetration of a great deal of U.S. aid and agencies in 1957 and especially after 1962, the handouts came from beyond the national borders, and there was a diffusion of the responsibility that happens as the redistribution process goes beyond national leaders. When Ben Stephansky, who rose to leadership in the U.S. labor movement, was ambassador to Bolivia, he gave surplus food and clothing directly to the union leaders. The temptation was too great to resist and some union leaders succumbed. A classic example of the corruption resulting from such direct gifts was that of a shipload of Air Force jackets shipped from Korean battle fronts and donated by Stephansky to the union leaders, who allegedly sold them in the company stores. Rank-and-file members of San José mines are still accusing union leaders of making a personal profit from the "bloodstained trophies of imperialist wars," as one worker said in a union meeting.

Armando Morales, the union leader quoted above on the strike, gave me a specific appraisal of the United States AID program:

> Speaking generally on the problem of Food for Peace and handing over edibles, I can show that here in Oruro I was one of the first who asked for this kind of aid in agreement with the attaché of labor, Señor Thomas Martin, of the embassy of the United States in 1962. We set up this program in San José with the food that was sent, and it had magnificent results because it was a really planned program. There were many unemployed, some three hundred families. They couldn't get work and they had the lowest income. And so we gave this food out weekly. I saw the results of this. However, this program of Señor Martin, for motives that we do not know anything about, was changed by the American ambassador. Afterwards, here in Oruro, they created a regional committee and some of the food fell into the hands of buyers and did not reach the people who needed it. They made a business out of it, as we proved. We saw AID goods from the United States being sold that were prohibited for this, because we were not in control.
>
> So this is a small problem that we have in the American aid program in my country: In practice it did not benefit the popular sectors nor was it a question of who needed this help. It was used more as a program of a political type and in accord with the government in power. They help their people, and the people who are not of the government are not helped. I believe that the government of the United States really wants to cooperate in economic aid here. It ought to have some planning, but the form becomes political as it is carried out. We want a type of aid without any conditions, only that it is for overcoming underdevelopment. We really need help to overcome underdevelopment. The type of aid which any country offers, in extending the hand, has to merit our respect always, and our cooperation. But our governments make *chataques* of a political type. Then the food goes to the peddlers or to the bureaucrats high up in the hierarchy. Whatever the reasons for the aid, it is possible that the United States heard that the Soviet government was giving help, and thinking that it was the truth, added to the aid without contemplating really what the help was used for.

Armando went on to tell me that he was sure that Bolivians were not Communists, having the impression, I think, that I might have some influence with the embassy or even be in a position to offer aid. The statement from this pro-American leader reveals the kind of undermining of local groups that drew upon the aid. When it stopped, they were subject to criticism and suspicion that they were taking advantage of the materials. The undermining of the national wheat program by surplus wheat, given away or sold at prices under the cost of production in Bolivia, is an often cited example of the dependencies created in the ties with the United States (Burke 1972).

The Repression of the Labor Movement: 1964–1969

The workers' fear over the effect of the Triangular Plan was justified in the following months. Teachers joined with students and trade unionists to protest increasingly anti-labor policies of the government. On October 26, 1964, students were massacred by the military when they demonstrated against the government of Paz Estenssoro in Oruro. The reaction to this violence spread to Potosí, Cochabamba, and Santa Cruz. The FSTMB protested the massacre, but the government responded by sending troops into San José mines. As students, teachers, and workers staged a protest in the city of Oruro, the army attacked the mining community. Domingo, a mechanic in Itos mines and a delegate to the union, who complained of insomnia since the event, told me of the resistance in the Oruro mines:

> On the third of November the regiments came to Itos and San José. In San José there was a lot of killing. They even entered into houses of families and took people out, forcing people into the streets in their underwear and killing them. We miners in Itos tried to defend the mines. We put up a fierce resistance with dynamite and armaments that we had taken from the regiment here in 1952. The Ranger regiment was in San José and the Chichas regiment was in Itos. They didn't let us leave. We made a cordon and stayed awake all night from eight until dawn.
>
> The attack on San José began at three in the afternoon. Two miners fell in the road from Oruro to San José where the shrine of Corazón de Jesus is. From there, we crossed by the hill of San Felipe and we returned at seven at night, just when the regiment was coming. They fired at us with mortars and we ran. We came here and the Camacho regiment was already here. There were about two hundred or two hundred fifty miners fighting. Then a

miner fell prisoner and we had to go out to save our companion. Then they took us, and the whole army entered and occupied positions in all the hills. They kept us well guarded so we couldn't go fight. And then they disarmed us, and from that day they have treated us like slaves.

Ever since then, the whole situation of the workers changed. They began by lowering our salaries and increasing the prices of some of the articles in the pulpería, and they lowered our overtime that we won in 1952 with the revolution of the ninth of April. The encampment was full at that time, There wasn't a single house unoccupied. And now you can see how it is up there. Everything is dead. There are only a few working there. And the mine is only used up on the upper levels. Beneath there are still great riches.

General René Barrientos, a member of the military group that supported the MNR in their bid for power in 1952, took advantage of the conflict to install himself in power in 1964, promising the workers improvement in their working conditions and pay. Shortly after he came to power, his promises were revoked. Many workers were fired and their union leaders put in jail, not only in the mine area of the highlands, but also in the oil area of Santa Cruz. Domingo, the worker in Itos quoted above, told me of his experiences following the coup:

❖ They put me in the prison for three days, in the Camacho regiment. The government said it was a precaution to hold us. They thought that we were going to try a counter-coup, and so they put twenty-six of us leaders in prison. All of us were of the Left, some were of the Communist party, both the Peking and Moscow branches, and others were of the MNR and the PRIN. And afterward they let us free. They didn't give us back our jobs, however.

Soon after, there was a strike in the city of La Paz of those who were fired for political and union motives in the period of Barrientos. Ovando [who was Barrientos' cohort in the coup] had said that it was a revolutionary government that was going to correct the injustices that his predecessor had committed. According to a revolutionary mandate of the armed forces on the day that he made the coup, he promised to return the salaries to the workers who were fired and to reinstate them. But then he did not carry this out. Many of us who were fired went to La Paz and declared a hunger strike with the help of the university students.

The government proceeded to destroy systematically labor organization. There were massive layoffs and some killings in the offices and work places of COMIBOL, the National Council of Social Security (Consejo Nacional de Seguridad Social; CNSS), and Bolivian Oil Refineries (YPFB). Economic depression combined with political repression destroyed the basis for reorganization of the unions.

In May 1965 the FSTMB tried to recover its position by declaring a general strike in the mines. In response, the army invaded the encampments of Colquiri, Milluni, Catavi, Siglo XX, and San José. Domingo told me about the encounter in San José mines:

❖ In May two thousand men, women, and chilren went out into the fields of Hilbo in a demonstration to free Lechin, who was jailed on May twelfth. Colquiri miners were coming to join us. Then came the assault of the Rangers on the twenty-fourth of May. The radio of Buenas Verdes was destroyed and on the field of Hilbo, seventeen to eighteen men and women died, shot down by American bazookas. The people were corralled in. We tried to organize them in ranks, we tried to save them. But the soldiers were well armed and we had nothing. Later in Sora Sora, twenty died. The army sent in men with machine guns, but the leaders had sold out. If the leaders had organized the rank and file, the miners would not have gone down. But the army of Barrientos had given money to them. Because of the union leaders we are suffering in our flesh. Twenty-five percent of the directors have fought for the workers, but they [the army] have terrified the workers with so many massacres we are not yet able to act.

Another miner reiterated this position:

❖ In May we knew there was going to be trouble; we workers along with the university students called for a reaction to the military. The secretary general of the union answered that we shouldn't worry. They had a signed document from the commander of the Second Division that these military men would not enter the mines. "You ought not to be armed," he said. "Better go home, be calm, rest." But the workers cannot have confidence in the military. At that moment, they were on the way to take the mine. Our radio was seized, our encampment destroyed. But our leaders told us not to be paranoiac. If we hadn't let ourselves be deceived, San José would not have been turned over to the military. It would have resisted. I was a member of the mine militia. I had a rifle and we would have fought if the union leaders who came in after the secretary general had not tied our hands.

It is difficult to judge whether the outcome would have been different if an all-out campaign had been launched. A professor of economics in the Oruro University stated, in a lecture to aspiring union organizers of 1970, that Sora Sora destroyed the myth of the strength of the miners' militia. The strong and well-equipped army that was reorganized in the last days of the Paz period and was reinforced in the Barrientos coup was not the same army that the miners had faced in 1952. However, many workers retained faith in their armed strength and blamed failure of the 1965 campaign on their leaders.

Following the defeat of the mines, the principal leaders were exiled and the armed forces moved into the encampment. Armando Morales, who all his life had supported reformist measures and was of the PRIN, was exiled in this period: "We had to leave our syndicalist role behind and enter into the political fight. In a word, we looked for a new regime to carry on the fight and guarantee the rights won in the thirteen years of struggle. The benefits had to be won by fighting; it is never given as a gift." This leader, like many of those in the PRIN, still defined the role of labor as that of a dependent supporter of some bourgeois reform regime, undefined, which would guarantee their legal rights, but he recognized that the existing governments failed to carry out their minimal support of labor. After his exile in the Barrientos period, he returned to San José mines and tried to reinstate Juan Lechín as leader of the FSTMB.

A campaign to destroy confidence in the leaders was systematically carried out by Barrientos with the aid of the military police squad and the Departmento de Investigaciones Criminales (DIC). These agents found that it was cheaper to spread rumor that a union leader had been paid off than to try to bribe him directly. The labor movement identified with the ORIT began to penetrate the ranks of labor organizations at all levels after the entry of Barrientos.

Despite the presence of the military in all of the mines with military police and spies, and garrisons armed with the latest weapons from the United States, the miners of Huanuni attempted to recoup their forces. In 1966, after the government tried to replace the leadership with officials favorable to the government, the workers defended the principles of union independence but the government refused to recognize the new leadership. At the end of the year, when the union presented a petition on wages and contract prices, the management rejected any proposals. The following year, when a protest demonstration against the lowered wages and imprisoned union leaders was planned at Oruro on June 6, Barrientos lost no time in calling a state of seige. Homes of miners were searched as the army went on alert in Playa Verde, Sora Sora, and Oruro. The leaders of the union suspended the march, pointing out that "we ought not to break the military encirclement because the government is waiting precisely for this in order to massacre us" (Reyes 1967). Union leaders refused an invitation by Barrientos to join him in a round table in the governmental palace and instead planned a large meeting at Siglo XX for June 24 and 25.

The delegates began to arrive in Llallagua, the town adjacent to Siglo XX mine, on the eve of San Juan, June 23. The music of bands greeted the visitors, who joined the workers of Siglo XX in the traditional fiesta of San Juan, when fires were lit to warm the Pachamama on the coldest night of the year. Simon Reyes (1967), one of the union leaders of Siglo XX, described the evening's festivities:

> The enthusiasm for the night of San Juan was linked with the welcome to the delegates, demonstrating in everything a spirit serene and confident for the outcome of the meeting. The enthusiasm was prolonged until 4:30 in the morning, when the people returned to their homes while some workers prepared to go to work.

It was at that moment that the military force, along with the national guard, armed with machine guns, mortars, and hand grenades, entered the encampment and fired at people who were still dancing on the streets. They fired machine guns and threw grenades into the houses with their sleeping occupants. In the streets everything that moved was fired on, even dogs, as one miner told me—"And what kind of politics does a dog have?" he added.

News of the horrors of the massacre seeped out slowly. *La Patria*, the daily newspaper of Oruro, reported on the following day, June 25, 1967, that there were 16 dead and 171 wounded, and that the operation had been carried out by the mining police, the Department of Criminal Investigation (DIC) and the Rangers with airplanes circulating overhead. Colonel Prudencia, in charge of the operation, announced that the army had occupied the mine centers of Siglo XX and Huanuni with the object of capturing the pro-guerrillas in the encampment that were stirring up the union leaders. Later the papers revealed that at least 87 were killed, including men, women, and children, and there were many wounded. An eyewitness at the funeral assured me there were many more; he told me that the number of caskets he saw going by looked like a stream of ants, and that there were burials in common ditches of bodies so destroyed by bazookas that they were no longer intact. The ovens that were used formerly to dispose of the dead after such massacres were no longer in operation with the new technology of the sink-and-float plant, and so there was no longer an efficient way of disposing of the evidence of the terror.

The massacre of San Juan was more destructive than any previous terror let loose in the mines. The tactic seemed to be to inspire fear in the mining community, where the buildup of resentment against Barrientos was the greatest, at a time when Che Guevara was still operating in Santa Cruz. It was in no way a selective operation to eliminate guerrilla sympathizers, as the colonel in charge of the opposition claimed, nor an attempt to rid the community of labor "agitators," but rather a total class attack to break resistance or rebellion.

While the miners had emerged from the repression and massacres of the forties strengthened and prepared to fight at a broader national level, after the conflict of the sixties the workers were demoralized and without faith in any leadership, even in those who had gone to prison or into exile. Only the dead were heroes, and the very fact that some survived was proof to the workers that they had sold out. A worker expressed the sentiment most felt in the aftermath of Barrientos:

❖ Many workers were dismissed for the calumnies that were spread in the streets. They were thrown out of their work at the moment that General Barrientos rose to power because he decreed other laws. They were pursued by Barrientos who destroyed the mine under the military boots. And so the slavery of the workers was complete. They disarmed us in Milluni, in San José, Siglo XX, Catavi, and Huanuni. The workers saw with their own eyes their wives, children, and friends die. They were demoralized. They no longer kept this revolutionary spirit. It did not exist because there were no guarantees; there was no justice. There exists a great deal of injustice.

The era of populism ended with Barrientos, and along with it the hope for reform measures to draw the workers into national development.[5] As negative as the miners' sentiments were toward Paz Estenssoro in his later days, they recognized that his regime did not commit massacres, but selectively picked off leaders. As Almaraz (1969) points out, Paz slowed down the penetration of foreign interests and put obstacles in the path of their control. Barrientos was not only favored by the United States, he was aided by U.S. military advisors. Following his entry into the presidency, the character of the American presence changed. Instead of development advisors there were military advisors and CIA personnel, sometimes operating within the Agency for International Development (AID). Expressing the sense of the "progress" that had been made in the military occupation of the mines, Zondag, an American economist working in Bolivia during this period, commented that "the military government, after a short period of vacillation, showed a remarkable courage in facing the lack of labor discipline" (1966:78). He went on to say that President Barrientos issued decrees which permitted COMIBOL to "make a more rational use of labor, to use disciplinary measures, to hire, dismiss or transfer workers, to prohibit firearms and to exile political figures and labor bosses who

[5] Reformist politics and the tactic of cooptation were an explicit part of government policy from the early years of the Independence, although promises were rarely backed up by a program that could effectively channel the revolutionary forces. Belzu's statement of reformist strategy could almost have been written by Paz Estenssoro one hundred years later:

"The popular masses, excluded from all representation, object of the scorn of governments and always victims in the political changes, have made their voice heard and have performed their role spontaneously: they have suppressed revolutions and fought for the Constitutional Government. The advent of this formidable power is a social fact of transcendent importance. A profound revolution has consumed itself among us under the influence of civilization, and that which in this respect causes the terror and preparation of certain classes which pretend to claim the title of privileges, makes for the satisfaction of men of faith and heart.

It is certain that this innovation has been signaled by some catastrophe, but no social revolution is complete without them. To the wisdom of the governments, one is moved to avoid them, putting those at the head of a moral and political movement in order to direct it and normalize it. Otherwise this torrent breaks the dikes, opens a way and inundates without any remedy to the society. *Do the necessary reforms, gentlemen, for yourselves if you do not want the people to make revolutions in their own way.*" (Belzu 1970: my translation and italics)

kept the miners stirred up" (Zondag 1966:233). The technique of North American analysis to translate political-revolutionary issues into questions of efficiency and profit predetermined the judgment of events in this tumultuous period in Bolivia's history. Revolution and even reform were bad for business and hence were luxuries which could not be tolerated.

Reorganization of the Labor Movement

The repression of the trade union movement that Barrientos had exerted until his death in an airplane crash in May 1969 continued unabated with his vice president, Siles, throughout the months of June, July, and August 1969, the first year of my stay in Oruro. Over 280 leaders were in exile, 30 of them from San José. The active rank-and-file members were unemployed, some of them scratching out a living panning metal or entering abandoned shafts in the night. The local union was described by the miners as a "yellow union," headed by a man who reportedly spied on the workers to discover if there were any remaining militants.

What was left of the union movement met in secrecy, maintaining vigilance since the lives and jobs of the workers were in jeopardy. What concerned them was the fear for their families if the breadwinner should be lost. Women showed the strength of generations of miners, taking the leadership in household management when their husbands were in hiding or in jail. All of their skills in marketing were drawn upon as they supported their families, buying vegetables and fruits in Cochabamba or the Yungas, or manufacturing goods in La Paz and selling the products for a few cents' profit in Oruro. The most daring bought illegally mined minerals from the jucos, those who scavenged for minerals in the abandoned shafts, and sold them at less than half the legal price at the back door of the Banco Minero. Their capacious shawls and petticoats provided the camouflage for carrying several pounds of metal on their trips from Huanuni or Siglo XX to the commercial center of Oruro. One of my comadres kept her three children and her husband (who was in hiding because of union activities) alive with these sales, along with the profit eked out from a small store she operated in her house. Cut off from the labor force, these women made the most of the marginal commercial operations available to them.

When I went to Oruro in the summer of 1969, the repression was still on. After Che Guevara's guerrilla troops had been liquidated Bolivia was like an armed camp. A strong military force existed in all of the barracks stationed near the mines. The tactical force, called Boines Verdes (Green Berets) after the anti-guerrilla force in Vietnam, were well trained by officers who had received their training from U.S. officers withdrawn from the Asian battlefields and stationed in Panama. The army was visible everywhere: a sentry was on guard at the main entrance of the mining community. Their marching band was a reminder of their presence in the plaza, where they played concerts on Thursdays and Saturdays. They were well equipped and well armed, and, much to my dismay (I was one of the few North Americans left in the city), they did not bother to erase the insignia "US Army" from the equipment. It would clearly have been suicide for the labor movement to act at that moment in history on the revolutionary premises they espoused.

With the repression of union activities, the student movement became the most vocal opponent of repression and the most vocal support of workers, since the university's autonomy permitted some freedom of speech. When I first visited Oruro University in 1969, the students had just carried out an election campaign for student leader. I was amazed at the attack on the military and support for the defunct guerrilla movement, considering the complete repression within the mines. Posters of Che Guevara were the main billing for almost all of the student groups.

I spoke with one of the university student leaders about the movement in these times. He told me that, following the massacre in Siglo XX, a pact was signed between university students and miners calling for the reinstatement of wages as of 1964, for the right to speak, for the return of the radio and withdrawal of the army. Their broader demands were phrased as a call for the autonomy of the university, liberation of Bolivia from imperialist controls, and the political and economic rights of citizens. The miners were the first to denounce Barrientos as a traitor of the working class, he said. He added:

❖ You can't say all the workers are Communists. The advanced sectors are, but it isn't rare for miners to be Falangists, although the Falangists are a party against miners. However, those who support the Falangists do so because of their low level of political understanding. They don't always know. That is always a problem. But now all the working class is against the government because of the low salary. That is general and that is what determines things.

I asked him what was happening then in the movement, and he continued:

❖ They are taking the first steps to reorganize. The clandestine movement has risen in Siglo XX, a short time ago, and the people work in secrecy. They are always afraid that they will be thrown out of work and that there will be nothing to eat in the house. But they are making the first moves, and that is positive. And in the forefront of the working class movement are the miners, before the railroad workers and the factory workers. The others vacillated, while the only ones who fought were the miners, and they remain the tonic of the working class.

There were many natural bases for students and workers to meet and reinforce left-wing political activities. In the first place, Oruro University was attended by some children of miners, and some wanted to continue as technicians in the mines. Their continuing ties to the home and family provided a link to working class origins that is perhaps the strongest identifying factor. Second, many students worked in the mines and the contacts were significant enough so that the superintendent forbade the hiring of students in the recent past, because, as one worker said, "They were afraid the students were coming to agitate the people, to give them a head, to start meetings and give ideas to the workers in order that the workers begin to make demands or something."

In August 1969 the election campaign for president was launched. The major contenders were Luís Adolfo Siles, the incumbent, Ovando, and Escobar, mayor of La Paz. I asked Morales, the San José mine leader who had returned from exile, what he thought about labor's role in the campaign. He replied:

❖ The Falange Socialista Boliviana has a left wing within the party which supports Lechín and is the most progressive group. In the same organization are fascists and also university students. The MNR was a bourgeois party, prior to the alliance with labor in the forties. When they repudiated labor support, the PRIN split off and is attracting some of the forces which left the MNR because of its treason.

I asked him if labor was going to support any of the candidates, and he replied:

❖ The elections won't solve the problems of the workers. We are preparing an insurrection. There is a program of unification of the unions which began at Sieta Suyos about a hundred kilometers from Oruro with representatives from Siglo XX, Catavi, and other mines. These unions have not been recognized by COMIBOL and they act in secrecy.

There were no elections held that fall, since Ovando seized the presidency in a coup on September 26. Because he had little popular support, he was forced to make a dramatic statement of his intentions in the presidency immediately on his arrival in the Burned Palace. His strategy was to nationalize the Gulf holdings in Santa Cruz, a move precipitated by political rather than economic considerations, since the difficulty of finding markets and the lack of a pipeline to Argentina's market made it impossible to take advantage of the move. However, he did find some support with labor, and he tried to reinforce this by permitting some opening for the union reorganization on a legal basis. Other leaders returned from exile, and in the spring local unions were reelecting new leaders by voice vote. The union in Oruro met in the open for the first time since 1965 in March 1970 and elected as secretary general a man who was a member of the PCB.

By April 1970 the FSTMB was sufficiently reorganized so they could hold their 14th Congress in Siglo XX–Catavi mines. The Congress, which I attended, struck some very important notes. First, the rentistas, or pensioners, were represented along with the non-contracted workers on the slag piles and in the panning areas. Second, women called for and gained a small part in the proceedings, but the strength of their position had a greater impact than the time allotted to them would have suggested. Third, workers made a strong plea for a higher institution of technical learning in their centers so that the children of miners could be assured of a better future than their parents. Finally, the political program called for the fight for socialism and a rejection of reformist politics of co-goverment.

ANTHROPOLOGIST ATTENDS PLENARY UNION MEETING.

The delegates who formed a political commission summarized in the Thesis of Siglo XX–Catavi the experiences learned in the eighteen years of co-government and nationalization under the MNR and the military regimes that succeeded it. The following conclusions were drawn:

1. Workers must intervene in the political life of the country, and in their role as vanguard of the revolution, they must not forget that the Bolivian tragedy is nothing less than the absence of strong workers' organizations, because we are the only ones who

can really save Bolivia from her backwardness and dependency in order to accomplish our historic mission.

2. The accumulated experience of the cruel methods of repression employed by the enemies of the class teaches us the necessity of being prepared for the employment of all forms of struggle, including the use of revolutionary violence.

3. The tactic of the working class is to involve us in the final strategy of socialism. Our objective is socialism and our method to arrive at this goal is the social revolution that will permit us to transform the nationalistic process into a socialistic process.

The political commission rejected the policy of co-government, or working within bourgeois parliamentary forms that "closed the road of the proletariat to the conquest of its own power." The weakness of a limited democracy consists, the authors said, in that Bolivia does not have an independent bourgeoisie and as a result light industry is no more than "an appendix and an integral part of imperialist domination in the country." As a result of this, they concluded, "the congenital limitations of the bourgeoisie forces them always to capitulate to the desire of the country to the North." They attacked the nationalized mines as "a superstate built on the blood of mine workers," limiting the role of the workers to producing and obeying.

In the months following the Congress, the FSTMB carried out a disciplined program of gaining back the pay cuts made in 1965 by Barrientos. Workers did not, as many opponents of labor claimed, resort to strike in an irresponsible way. In the year I lived in Oruro, I saw only two strikes. One was a sitdown strike declared because workers did not have the tools to produce, and only inadequate water and power lines which constantly broke down, causing them losses in their contracts. The bourgeoisie failed them not only in the "democratic task" of destroying precapitalist forms of labor contracts and property relationships, but also in maintaining capital equipment. The other strike was, incongruously, that of the unemployed rentistas. It was a hunger strike, the ultimate protest when one can no longer threaten to withdraw labor power, but to destroy life itself. The pensioners were well organized and employed an agent who argued their cause for them.

Ovando failed to follow up what appeared to be a pro-labor position in the early days of his coup with an economic program to answer the demands labor made following the Congress. It was evident to the union leaders in June that Ovando was moving to the right. He replaced the few leftist ministers with military commanders, including General Rogelio Miranda, right-hand man of Barrientos, who had planned massacres in the mine. Ovando refused to respond to any of the labor demands presented after the Congress. Morales, who was trying to reorganize the PRIN movement, spoke at a union meeting in San José shortly after the Congress:

> When this government, on the twenty-sixth of September [Ovando's 1969 coup], made a revolutionary kind of movement of the country, they promised the Bolivian people to reinstate all their economic rights and the conquests of labor that they had lost under Barrientos. "I am going to give back liberty to the people of Bolivia." That was what Ovando said on the twenty-sixth of September. And on the following day, the twenty-seventh of September, this president, who possibly had good intentions on the twenty-sixth of September, made a trip to the Corporación Minera de Bolivia and said, "The Corporation is bankrupt," and instead of giving us back our wages, he froze them just at a time when the cost of living is going up. This is the first contradiction of a government that claims to be revolutionary.

When the break came in September, it was precipitated by the extreme right-wing military leaders, led by General Rogelio Miranda. When he failed to muster support even from the army, a succession of military claimants to power resulted finally in the backing of Juan José Torres, general of the air force. When he appeared at San José mine in November, the workers gave tentative support to him. Because they remembered the betrayals of the revolutionary promises made by Barrientos and Ovando when they came to power, the workers' main demand was for arms. In his speech, Torres called for labor peace and a relinquishing of the guerrilla stance, saying that the revolution would come through peaceful measures and promised restitution of wages. He finally made good his promise on the Day of the Miners, December 21. However, some sectors of the work force were disappointed to find a reduction in contract payments which was not fully offset by increases in the base pay. In addition, the "incentive pay" for working full time without missing a single day of work was reduced.

GENERAL JUAN JOSÉ TORRES VISITED ORURO MINES SHORTLY
AFTER BECOMING PRESIDENT IN OCTOBER 1970 TO ANNOUNCE
THAT HIS GOVERNMENT WOULD RAISE WAGES.

In short, relations with the national government were never
stabilized in what one might consider a structural form, guarantee-
ing some continuity. The miners' ideological opposition to co-
government and to the rule by the military was constant, but the
relationships they established with the *presidentes de torno,* or
gyrating presidents, were dictated by expedience rather than
theory. Gregorio, a Marxist theoretician who worked in the administrative office of COMIBOL and who was a master of union rhetoric, expressed this distrust of the military leadership which made
claims for union support at a union meeting in June 1970:

> In the year 1952, comrades, the fight was: revolution and counter-
> revolution, and from that rose two other words, two other sen-
> timents, the left and the right, anti-imperialism and reaction. Gen-
> eral Barrientos also was an anti-imperialist, as he put it, he was
> against the right, he was a leftist. However, comrades, time has
> shown in this same regime of General Barrientos what relation ex-

isted between him and imperialism. General Ovando compromised his government, by taking away the wages of the workers. And so, comrades, North American imperialism has made an advance in Bolivia ever since the days of October [1969], producing a reactionary movement in the country and playing its cards as it plays them in all the countries of Latin America which have made military coups and then makes them appear like military of the left. The military is set up for one purpose, to use weapons. A comrade driller is also specialized for one purpose, to know how to manage the drill and he knows how to do it, but not how to be president. But when he came into power, Ovando gave a democratic opening and that opening was the result of the efforts of Che Guevara and of many people who spilled their blood. [Applause from the audience; speaker asked for a moment of silence in their memory, then continued.] I don't want you to think I am a guerrillero, comrades. I am going to ask you to analyze this problem: Given that Ovando, after his coup of October 26 when he made these promises to the working class, turned to the same measures as Doctor Siles [the interim president who had served as vice-president to Barrientos] and General Barrientos, I am sure that General Ovando is no more in power than they were. In these reformist thrusts into power that those military men proposed, their only intention was to arrive in the presidency, not only in this country, but also in the other countries of Latin America. The general has no other post than to be president, as this ought to be the only ambition, comrades. And so, comrades, if we are revolutionaries, as we say we are, we ought to make a front against the common enemy, which is at this moment North American imperialism, which is manipulating the present government like airplanes.

In the eleven months that Torres was in power, labor continued to try to gain back the pay cuts made by Barrientos. Shortly after the increases were granted, Hugo Banzer made his first unsuccessful bid to take over the presidency in January 1971. Labor supported President Torres and the rebels were defeated.

The labor movement, along with left-wing political parties, tried to consolidate their gains in the Popular Assembly organized in May 1971. The Popular Assembly included representatives of most of the organized segments of labor except for the peasants, whose representatives were considered either entrepreneurs or government-controlled. Despite sharp ideological differences, there was cooperation between the Workers Revolutionary Party (POR), the Communist Party of Bolivia (PCE, Moscow line), the Party of the Revolutionary Left Movement (MIR), the Christian Revolutionary Democrats (DCR), and the National Revolutionary Movement (MNR).

In a move to gain greater worker contribution to production, Torres proposed a plan for co-participation in nationalized industries. In theory, co-participation was to mean a "replacement of exclusive authority of the employer by the collective authority of all those who take part in production." However, the degree of entry by workers was not explicitly stated (*Presencia* May 8, 1970). The Bolivian Petroleum Company (YPFB) and the National Housing cooperatives (CONAVI) accepted the proposal as presented immediately. The FSTMB made it a central point for discussion in the Popular Assembly that opened on May 1, 1971. The proposal was designed to gain greater cooperation from the workers in raising production, but since they lacked the veto, the miners considered it a company ploy.

When the issue of co-participation in management was brought up in the Popular Assembly in 1971, it was supported by a wide range of politically differentiated labor representatives attending the sessions. The FSTMB representatives contrasted the co-participation proposed by the Popular Assembly in 1971 with Control Obrero of the MNR period in that they proposed to work "from below to above rather than the reverse" as had occurred in the early years of nationalization, when only top leaders entered into the councils. They demanded that a majority of the representation in the council of workers and managers should be labor, and insisted that the president of COMIBOL should be chosen by the directors of COMIBOL from a list made up by representatives of the FSTMB. COMIBOL rejected these two proposals and called for the president to be named by the executive power in a council of ministers from a list presented by COMIBOL. The ultimate aim of co-participation as envisioned in the Assembly was "the social ownership of the means of production" (*Presencia* May 8, 1970).

The duties of the worker representative as drawn up by the FSTMB and presented to the Popular Assembly were more specific than those included in the 1953 decree for Worker Control, especially with regard to the workers informing themselves about all aspects relating to activities of the company, such as plans and projects for exploitation of minerals, reforms of administrative structures, costs, accounting, commercialization, financing, evaluation, and control of growth in the enterprise. If this set of provisions had been implemented, it could have reversed the imbalance in labor-management relations caused by the control over information by the latter.

Lora (1972:84) summed up the contrast between Control Obrero and co-participation, stating that, while the first was individual and bureaucratic, co-participation was collective and exercised by the working class itself. The contradiction in function between that of being a vigilance body over the operation of management and participating in the administration as co-equals, referred to above, was not made explicit. No direct provisions were made to ensure that the theory of *ocupación de abajo* instead of *de arriba*, or occupation of posts in worker control councils by the rank and file instead of the top leaders of the union, would be realized (Zavaleta 1971:6).

The left was divided on the importance of the assembly and its major proposal for co-participation. While some called it "a symphony of the left" (*Presencia*, August 8, 1971) others accused it of being reformist in orientation and goals. Lora (1972:16) summarized the divergent trends in an article published after the coup.

The Banzer coup in August 1971 makes any speculation as to how co-participation would have worked out an academic issue. However, the reaction of the rank and file that I witnessed in the period when the plan was still being discussed in July 1971 revealed a lack of confidence in the labor leadership and a fear of the resurgence of the elitism and growth of the union bureaucracy that had characterized the labor movement in the MNR period. Rank-and-file workers in San José mine broke up a meeting scheduled for a discussion of the plan when I visited that center in July 1971. They resented the fact that their motivation for implementing the plan before many of the concrete problems of contract prices and wages had been ironed out. The heritage of corruption from the period of cooptation had born its harvest of mistrust.

Following Banzer's coup, labor leaders were sent into exile, and all opposition from the left was imprisoned or exiled.

In summing up the changes after the 1952 revolution, we can

see how the labor movement turned from a strategy of participation in a reformist, middle-class government to one of rebellion in the defense of class interests. What this transformation reveals about trade union problems is analyzed below.

The FSTMB and the Problems
of Trade Unionism

Three problem areas recur in the analyses dealing with trade unions. The first is the question of spontaneity versus organized, institutionally based, centralized control in the labor movement. The second is economic versus political issues as the focus of labor action. Finally, there is the relationship between ideology and practice. I shall try to assess here what Bolivia's experience indicates about labor's role in the world market in which it participates.

Spontaneous Action versus Trade Unionism

Spontaneous rank-and-file action is often posed as a contradiction to trade union organization with a bureaucratic leadership. Rosa Luxemburg extolled the strength of a movement made up of rank-and-file activisits, because of the counter-revolutionary tendencies implied in centralized control by an elite leadership of a trade union. Trotsky shared her view that the consciousness of the proletariat, acting directly, could provide the necessary challenge to capitalist society without the delegation of their historical functions to trade union leaders. Lenin recognized that spontaneity was often evidence of "consciousness in an embryonic form" (2:52) but asserted that the consciousness of the irreconcilable antagonism of the workers' interests to the whole of modern political and social systems must be brought from without. In an often quoted statement he elaborates this thesis:

> The history of all countries shows that the working class, exclusively of its own efforts, is able to develop only trade union consciousness, i.e. it may itself realize the necessity for combining in unions, for fighting against the employers and for striving to compel the government to pass necessary labour legislation, etc. The theory of socialism, however, grew out of the philosophical, historical and economic theories that were elaborated by the educated representatives of propertied classes, the intellectuals.

Although Lenin recognized that the "spontaneous rising of the masses often moves ahead of the leaders" (1947 2:73,121) he reiterates that the organization is even more necessary with the broadening mass entry since it would otherwise inevitably fall into trade unionism.

When we look at these propositions in the light of a half century of labor struggle in Latin America, we must question some of the basic assumptions in both Luxemburg's and Lenin's position that the spontaneity of the rank and file must be conceived of as opposed to organization in the trade union. The character of the work force as well as that of the capital-owning group negate the basic assumptions in each position.

On the one hand, Lenin's assumptions that the rank and file are incapable of carrying out any more than trade union issues has changed because of two important factors which are inextricably linked: the spread of mass education combined with the inability of the modernizing sector in most underdeveloped countries to absorb even the "talented tenth" of the mobile population. Mass education by itself reinforces bourgeois tendencies when the absorption into technical and professional ranks is assured, especially since the basic orientation of the Latin American schools serves to alienate students who go to higher education from their working class base. But when this group is cut off from the gains of mobility and falls back into the ranks of workers, or becomes conscious of the process and rejects the careers that might be available, a potent leadership can develop. This happens in the Bolivian mines, as many students are forced to leave schools because of economic necessity. The need for ever-increasing levels of education to enter higher employment possibilities limits the mobility aspiration of many. Clerical help is paid at lower levels than interior work in the mines, and consequently the educated office workers who have access to information are active and vocal elements in the trade union. This radicalization because of "status inconsistency" (Ossowski 1963:53) causes some to identify with workers and provides educated leaders for the labor movement.

On the other hand, the assumption that the workers can seize power without organized and institutionalized training grounds for revolution, made by those who champion spontaneity, has to be reviewed in the light of the increased centralization and control of their opponent. The dependent capitalists of the Third World countries are not in themselves mobilized and integrated, but the capitalists associated with the export market have behind them the highly integrated world market, which can rapidly reinforce them with capital or arms. Spontaneous action is ineffective if not disasterous in encounters such as those in Hilbo, Sora Sora, and San José, where the army is prepared to use massive force against poorly armed or unarmed workers. Furthermore, in the ordinary course of events short of major crises, the union serves to raise the consciousness of members of their position in the wider society. It is an arena where they learn to formulate their problems and test them out on an audience of peers. Men often came to my house to listen to their dialogue in the tapes made of union meetings in order to assess and try to improve their delivery.

In a recent paper analyzing spontaneous mass mobilization in events occurring in Mexico in 1958, Brazil in 1968, and Argentina in 1969, Jelin (1973) points to the following common factors: (1) all started with simple wage demands that were not being handled by the union bureaucracy, (2) this raised the issue of the legitimacy of the union, (3) which went on to question the distribution of power and the class status and (4) led to the high participation of base activity with absence of regular leadership. Granted that such events reveal the advances rank-and-file workers can make in periods of stress, the question should not then be whether trade unions should be supported, but rather how to maintain the channels to leadership open to emergent forms of protest and action within the existing structure. Even when the trade union fails in the crisis to advance at the pace the membership is prepared to, it has often been the base in which the workers first became conscious of what collective action is capable of doing and how to phrase the subconscious yearnings in demands that can be socially articulated. If it serves only as a spark plug to set off action which goes beyond its control, the trade union performs an important function. Workers may criticize the particular action of a specific union at a certain time, but they rarely carry their criticism to the point of questioning whether there should be unions, as a theoretician free of collective responsibility might do.

While Bolivia's history of labor mobilization indicates that communication between leaders and the rank and file breaks down, especially in times of successful trade union operation, there are in the mine workers' unions significant contrary tendencies to promote high involvement of the rank and file over sustained periods, a constant reference to long-range ends even while the members are preoccupied with immediate goals of wages, hours, and conditions of work, and a constant running critique of the leaders in power. During times of repression when the union organization is underground there is no opposition between leadership and rank-and-file sentiment. The opportunistic leaders are self-eliminated or ensconced in the "yellow unions" promoted by the company. Those who are dedicated to advancing the cause of the workers are supported by their working comrades, who shelter them when they are being sought by the police and who endeavor to share their food and income with the families of the leaders in hiding. It is at these moments in Bolivia's history that workers are closest to the university students; in the periods 1946–51 and 1965–69 they worked closely with students in the underground.

Miners are very aware of the problem of cooptation of leadership and opportunism, and after the 14th congress they tried to counter the tendencies toward bureaucracy on the part of the leadership and toward apathy on the part of the masses by the following means: (1) stimulate criticism and self-criticism within the union; (2) overcome the mental isolation of the workers and broaden the base for leadership; and (3) minimize the concentration of control through charismatic leadership or bureaucracy. I shall describe those efforts that I observed in 1970.

Attempts to stimulate criticism of leadership. Leaders were under constant surveillance. I learned after I was under attack as a CIA agent that I was constantly watched, as well as the superintendent of the mines. The visits made by the secretary general of the union to the house of the superintendent were reported along with the fact that only workers came to my house. This information was generally known at the time the secretary general attacked me, and he received no support from the men. It taught me that, at least at a local level, consensual opinion was well informed.

This censoring of the leadership went on in the day-to-day

operation of the union activities even though the rank and file accepted a specialization of leadership function. The workers spoke of leaders who "have earned the right to speak for us," and very few spoke at the union meeting. The accepted leaders and those who were aspiring to be leaders carried out long discourses, while the majority of the membership limited themselves to uttering a kind of chorus of catcalls and boos, at worst throwing stones at the podium, or even in agreement, to applause and cheers. Although this kind of participation by rank and file was somewhat diffuse, it was nonetheless effective in eliminating those leaders who had lost their base. Men who had betrayed the movement remained silent or did not attend meetings.

After the 14th congress, this informal level of surveillance and criticism was raised to a more explicit level. During the congress, the sessions of "criticism and self-criticism" were impressive, especially since the press and foreign visitors such as myself were present. Comparable behavior on the part of management would be unthinkable. The congress of the COB following in May proposed the organization of a tribunal of rank-and-file members to raise criticism to a more explicit level. The 1971 coup interrupted carrying out this program.

Development of leadership. Workers told me of the early days of the revolution, when there was a kind of ferment that broke the mental isolation in which miners had lived. One of the most important factors in this was the radio run by the unions in all of the major mines. This brought news, dramatizations of novels such as *El precio de estaña,* and bulletins from the other mines daily from 6:00 A.M., when the program *Los dormilones* (Sleepyheads) roused the family to begin the day, to midnight. It was an opportunity for developing expression and a collective consciousness. Although often controlled by the top leadership of the union, it nonetheless developed a strong sense of the community of miners that went beyond the individual encampment. It was one of the first targets of the army, which seized or destroyed all of the radios operating in the mines in 1965. It became the medium by which the national federation leaders communicated directly with the base, and although the reverse communication of the base with the leadership was minimal, it was not absent. Children's programs allowed some development of amateur talent, and as one mother of six said, it helped the children overcome a sense of inferiority that some felt when they left the mining center.

Following the reorganization of the FSTMB, courses taught by economists and sociologists from universities in La Paz and Oruro were presented in Siglo XX and Oruro. The subject matter went far beyond simple trade unionism into the questions of socialism, communism, dependency relations in imperialism, and the analysis of class relations. Most of the speakers were left of center, but there was a wide range of ideological differences among the theorists, both in and outside of the university. There was intense involvement of the rank-and-file members who attended the meeting. Questions from the floor were often cast in terms relating the theoretical positions to the specific conditions in the mines and in Bolivia. The ferment of intellectual interest in which these workers were caught up seemed more comparable to the nineteenth century than to twentieth century industrial centers. These workers had not learned to be ignorant of the major social and economic crises of which they were a part, as have workers whom I have worked with in U.S. factories.

Overcoming charisma and bureaucratization. Contradictory tendencies of bureaucratization in the administration of the trade union combined with charismatic leadership limited the involvement of the rank and file in the labor movement. Lora (1960:32) pointed to some of the attempts to avoid such problems through the alternation of jobs in the union and the power to revoke leaders when the workers lose confidence in them. The main effort is toward strengthening the power of decisions made by the delegates in the congresses of the organization. This requires a certain amount of prescience on the part of the leaders and the base representatives in bringing up issues that are liable to require action in future months so that the leadership can be guided by prior decisions.

"Lechinismo" was the short-cut solution to the ever-present problems of operating a mass organization with insufficient funds to mobilize the decisionmaking group. One attempt to overcome the rule by charismatic leadership was mentioned above. The problem goes farther than the organization, since the difficulty is not just in curbing the individual leader but in changing the orientation of the press, which tends to turn the publicly known figures and quote their personal opinions as representative of "labor" or some such fictive entity.

To force a choice between spontaneity and institutionalized control as the basis for labor action is to ignore the daily concerns and the long-range perspective of trade unionism. Workers need organizations to defend their rights against a highly organized opposing force. The spontaneous rising of the rank and file in periods of crisis when the leadership fails to respond to the needs of the masses is both an index to the breakdown in communication as well as an assertion that they are the prevailing historical force. And in order to sustain the spontaneous move, even greater organizational efforts must be made.

Economic versus Political Issues

In periods of repression, the distinction between economic and political goals is obliterated because the struggle for a living wage requires opposition to the political representatives of an entrenched class. However, in the moment-to-moment struggle, there is often a lag in consciousness as to whether an economic or a political slant should be emphasized, and it is only the most profound hindsight that can disclose this. There are four periods surveyed in chapter 2 and this chapter that have bearing on this. The first was the strike in Uncía in 1923, when the workers stuck very closely to trade union demands and the government, by refusing to negotiate, precipitated the struggle into the political arena. Only the constant presence of military forces constrained the people of Uncía and the adjacent encampments of Siglo XX and Catavi from a full-scale rebellion. While the government insisted that the massacre they carried out was provoked by revolutionaries, the historical record (Lora 1969; Rivera 1967) indicates that it was conducted on strict trade union principles of legitimizing the union and negotiating a contract. In this situation, the resistance of the company, backed by President Saavedra's order to send the troops into the encampment, turned an economic into a political struggle, but there was no chance of counter-resistance by the workers. Deluded by the populist stance President Saavedra had taken in his election campaign, the union was proceeding on strictly trade union principles to establish a union and carry on a wages and hours negotiation. The massacre was planned at the moment the delegation arrived in La Paz.

The second instance of an economic struggle being transformed into a political one came in 1947, when the resistance of the workers to smashing of the unions in Patiño mines evoked another massive use of armed forces ordered by President Enrique Hertzog. Like Saavedra, Hertzog had run on a reformist platform, but he used national resources to protect private-capital interests against the pressure for popular reform. The recognition of the government's willingness to use massive opposition served to politicize the workers and led to their support of the MNR uprising in the succeeding years. When the trade union movement was forced to go underground in the intervening years up to 1952, trade unionism as a policy was in abeyance and the political bid for power was the basis for mobilization.

The third instance of politicization of the confrontation between the union and the nationalized mine bureaucracy occurred in 1963. The basis for the confrontation from the beginning was defined in political terms: the opposition to the Triangular Plan and the intervention in the nationalized management of the mines by externally controlled capital interests. The split between the mines, with the Oruro union assessing what was in fact a political rebellion in purely trade union terms of avoiding a confrontation that would possibly mean the loss of jobs, meant that the unity of the labor movement was broken and the repression of the trade unions made possible.

The final instance occurred during the year I lived in Oruro, in 1970. In July the union leaders were fully aware that an internal coup within the Ovando government had occurred in which all the labor supporters in ministries such as Bailey and Quiroga Santa Cruz were relieved of their posts and replaced by military leaders such as Rogelio Miranda, who had carried out the 1967 San Juan massacre. While the students responded to this by mobilization of guerrilla activities in Teoponte in July, the trade union leaders vacillated as to whether they should support the movement. Some of the leaders in San José argued that the guerrilla activity under the

Ejercito Liberacíon Nacional (ELN) forces left over from the Che Guevara siege was counter-productive to their winning an agreement from the government for the statement of demands drawn up by the FSTMB and presented to President Ovando. One speaker argued:

> The guerrillas are a pretext for using military forces to deal with the petition for higher wages. They want to use the ELN as a means of declaring the state of siege. We have to join the ELN as their allies. The *foco* in Teoponte is a means of fighting against imperialism. We have to go out in the streets to fight imperialism. We must remember how Barrientos used the guerrillas to make a concentration camp of the mines.

Another responded:

> I am against the guerrilla; this attack is made by the university students. It is not the time to support them. The problem of the state of siege has to be understood not as a reaction to the guerrillas but to the statement of union demands.

Another countered:

> The guerrillas give their lives to make us aware of conditions while the working class has to liberate the country. We have to support them. It is the opportune moment to overcome the demoralization and call for a movement of workers, campesinos, and intellectuals of the left.

But while the rank and file on the whole expressed sympathy for the guerrillas, indicating this by cheering when these forces were mentioned, there was no decision made that the workers should participate. It was not until after the guerrilla leaders were killed and the movement routed by the army that labor mobilized in a march of protest in September. The general reaction against Ovando's mismanagement of the event precipitated the coup that brought Torres to power. Thus in this first concrete opportunity to act on certain of the principles promoted in the Congress supporting the revolution for socialism and the linking of political and economic strategies, the union evaded taking a definite position and consequently opted for economic ends—promoting the petition—in the absence of a political struggle.

In all of these cases, presidents who promised some democratic rights to workers betrayed the promise that brought them to power and supported the anti-labor measures of the mine operators, whether private or nationalized. In all except possibly the 1963 strike, the workers phrased their demands in limited economic terms. The fact that the struggle was translated into political terms by management's resistance to labor's demands indicates that the choice of economic versus political focus is limited by a combination of historical conditions and cannot be framed as a theoretical choice made on the basis of an a priori theory, even if correct. Perhaps the only point at which theoretical choice made the difference was in 1963, when the unity of the trade union was broken by the "economist" approach of San José union. By cutting off support of the Siglo XX–Catavi strike when they were advancing toward a position of determining extra-national alliances, they cut off the trend toward self-determination in the labor movement. It was at this point in history that the union "tried to bring economics and politics together into the true synthesis of proletarian praxis," in the words of Lukacs (1971), and thus "reconcile the dialectical conflict between immediate interest and ultimate goal." And it was at this very moment that ideological differences within the federation made a significant difference.

The Relation between Ideology and Practice

From its early days, the Federation included in its leadership and ranks leaders with strong ideological differences. In 1944 the MNR forces predominated but did not overshadow the leadership aligned with the Trotskyist Revolutionary Workers Party (Partido Obrero Revolucionario; POR), which raised the reformist, nationalistic orientation of the MNR to international issues of the working class (Klein 1969:376). Given the ideological differences, the question is, how was unity achieved?

In the MNR period the Federation relied on the unity achieved under the charismatic leadership of Juan Lechín. It was no coincidence that during his absence the differences between the Communist leadership of Siglo XX and the MNR leadership of Oruro broke the solidarity of the workers in the crucial strike of 1963. His charisma began when Juan Lechín was a goalie for the soccer team at Siglo XX and became known throughout the mining community. It was crystallized in the forties when he joined with the workers' to form the basis for the FSTMB and its link with the MNR. Although not a pure Bolivian since he was of Arabic descent, he was born in Bolivia and the attempt by his enemies to brand him as a Chilean failed. Domingo, a worker in Itos, spoke almost with reverence of this early period, and the mystical identification was heightened by the cadences of his attachment to the Pentecostal cult:

> ❖ Juan Lechín Oquendo was always the principal leader of the workers of the mine. In 1945 he was a leader who fought along with the workers. In 1949 he was in the Siglo XX mine. Watchmen waited with arms to catch him and take away his life. He entered the mine dressed as a campesino. We were going into the mine at five in the morning, and we saw him enter the union hall with three Indians. We were curious and went in. And there we saw him, Juan Lechín Oquendo, dressed as an Indian and accompanied by the Indians. Then he showed himself to us, saying at that moment, "Come, let us have a general meeting." Then all went out to round up the people for a general meeting.
>
> And this is the way Juan Lechín Oquendo manifested himself to us. Then he was young. Perhaps because of the suffering he has endured, for all the education that he had, as the mines fell and as the military regime educated us as to what it was, he has changed, but he was always occupied with problems of the workers. He was a very combative leader, with much revolutionary faith. In 1949 the vigilantes put him in prison. Three nations guaranteed his life, and so they did not kill him. In the regime of Barrientos, they called him a chileño. He was a Bolivian, born in Coro Coro, and he could prove it with his documents. He was the principal leader of the miners and he was known by many nations.

Lechin embodied the aspirations of the workers. He was the mediator between the workers and the MNR government in the early days of the revolution (Lora 1964; Zavaleta 1974). However, as Paz Estenssoro established his mass base with the campesinos, whose syndicates linked themselves directly to the patron, the support of the miners became less important and Lechín's role was diminished to the point that he was eventually expelled from the MNR (Lora 1964:42). His failure to develop a rallying point for all workers in the ten years from 1952 to 1962 meant that, when the miners moved into rebellion against the state in 1963, they had little support from other working class bases or from the campesinos.

The latter, in fact, were mobilized by the MNR against the miners in their campaign to implement the Triangular Plan.

At the local level, personality and performances of the leaders prevailed over ideological positions. In the first period of the MNR government, Oruro had the reputation of being one of the most militant sectors of the mine industries owing to the strong leadership of Armando Morales, an MNR leader who had risen in the ranks of the movement when it was underground. As a nurse in the mine hospital infirmary, he occupied a notch above that of the underground workers in the social hierarchy. However his dedication to the working calss came from his father's experience; blinded by an explosion in the metallurgical plant, he was thrown out of work without compensation. By working cooperatively with his brothers,

UNION MEETINGS STIMULATE THE RHETORIC OF UNDERGROUND WORKERS.

TALKS AT UNION MEETINGS COVER WORLD SITUATIONS AS WELL
AS LOCAL.

Armando gained an education which he used to advance the cause
of workers. Because of the opposition to the Stabilization Plan that
he led in San José, the national administration of COMIBOL tried to
have the mine closed (see chapter 7), but the opposition of the
businessmen and engineers of the community acting in the Bloque
Oruro prevented this setback. He solidified his position in the
union by working closely with his brothers, and by reinforcing his
relationship with aspiring new leaders in the compadrazgo bond, a
familiar strategy pursued with campesino union leaders as well as
industrial unions (cf. Dandler 1977).

Union leadership became a stepladder to political success, and,
just as on the national scene, there was a replication of posts held
by the same person at the local level. The secretary general of the
union was, in addition to this post, the director of the radio station,
a delegate to the FSTMB, and later on, a senator. While this tactic of
proliferating the roles of the top leaders served to consolidate
power, it minimized the spread and succession into leadership of

young men. It also defeated a politics of confrontation within the ranks that would prepare the organization for developing problems. When the issue of support for the Catavi–Siglo XX strike of 1963 came up, the word of the leader was enough to reject a policy of unity with the workers of Siglo XX in repudiation of the Triangular Plan. The unity of the Federation and even the local began to disintegrate from that point. The kind of unity achieved within this structure was sufficient for carrying out the day-to-day work of syndicalism. It was not, however, capable of meeting the crises that came with the Triangular Plan and the military repression.

When Ovando permitted the return of exiled labor leaders and the reorganization of the unions as a move to find a mass base after the September 1969 coup that brought him to power, the diverse political forces within the Federation were able to find unity among the top leaders from the POR, Filomen Escobar, the PCB, Simon Reyes, the PRIN, Juan Lechín Oquendo along with Secretary General Lopez, all of whom shared power in the national leadership of the FSTMB. The leadership pursued a policy of concentrating on basic issues of wages and contract payments. In the particular historic circumstance of a polarized class situation, these bread-and-butter issues were revolutionary concerns, since the state bureaucracy was not following through on its promises to labor. The POR and PCB leaders curbed the tendency toward the reemergence of Lechinism by insisting on policy approval by the elected representatives of the federation rather than unilateral statements by the head. For example, in a statement to *Presencia* (July 1, 1970) they asserted that certain declarations of the former "principal leader" were not officially endorsed positions of the FSTMB.

It is at those moments in the history of Bolivia's labor movement, when the transformation of economic into political action occurs, that the real issues of "theory and practice" come into play. Only when the concatentation of economic interests come into conflict with a given political reality can the transformation of particular differentiated ends of the working class into the collective ends of an advancing society become realized.

Within the local union there was a tendency to treat the issue of theory and practice not as a dialectic that each individual must confront, but rather as a separation of tasks, with "theoreticians" and "practitioners" as specialities in the revolution. This defeats the attempt to overcome intellectual versus practical activities characteristic of the European socialist movement. This habit of thought, inherited from the colonial period, threatened the very basis for overcoming the contradictions and conflicts that plague the trade union.

Bolivia's experience brings into question the duality between spontaneous action and organized trade unionism, of political mobilization versus economism, and of the theory and practice. The line between such positions is rubbed out in moments of crisis, and Bolivia was living in a constant state of crisis because of the repression of the revolutionary process. Those who linked theory and practice in such a period risked ending up dead or in exile as long as the existing power structure remained. However, those who failed to draw the conclusion of the need for structural change lost their base in the union.

Critics of trade unionism often attribute the characteristics of cooptation of leadership, of the separation of leader and rank and file, of the exclusion of long-range ends in the interest of short-range—or opportunism—as dangers inherent in the syndical organization. Judged from a historical perspective, these characteristics are not structural features per se but organizational features that appear in certain kinds of historical settings. For Bolivia, the set of circumstances that promoted them was the structural duality in the cogovernment period. The MNR succeeded in demoralizing the union movement far more than the half century of labor repression preceding it.

When we replace the tired dualities and the stereotyped categories with an analysis which views history as a process of unfolding potential, the characteristics attributed to the unions can be seen as adaptive mechanisms of all institutions that emerge in specific circumstances. Opportunism, co-optation, "economism" are more significant features of trade unions, since the only power of the organization lies in the strength of collective support. The miners are aware of the problems inherent in their trade unions, but they never question the necessity for this only defense against the massive opposition they confront for their very survival.

The history of the labor movement in Bolivia brings into question some of the commonly held notions about Latin American unions. Alexander (1965:11), generalizing for Latin America, explains the "violence of the movements" on the basis that unions at first make really excessive demands which are impossible for employers to meet, and do so not as bargaining devices but as a precipitant to violence. We have seen that violence was consistently introduced by management, both by the earlier foreign-controlled firms and later by the nationalized mining enterprise, which persuaded the governments to send in the army, and the deaths were always on the side of labor. Before the revolution of 1952, the union struggles were cast in strictly economic terms. But when the demands for housing, a minimal wage, and an eight-hour day were consistently rejected by the companies, which did not recognize the right to organize and were not prepared to negotiate, their demands became more revolutionary. Following the revolution, the unions held control at the mine site, but they failed to win the struggle to assert decision-making control at the national level. Their power was broken with the military invasion of the mines during the Barrientos regime in 1965. The massacres carried out in the conquest and annihilation of the mine workers following his entry exceeded all previous attacks on the miners.

The second generalization about the Latin American trade union movement concerns the revolutionary character of labor leaders and the rank and file. Landsberger (1967) has raised the question in terms of the character of the leadership and the thrust of labor ideology, but his discussion of these in relation to the behavior of labor in the strikes fails to show the evolution from economic demands to political positions of a more global nature as the repressive action is escalated. Each of the strike actions taken by labor in Bolivia began with a statement of bread-and-butter issues. Within the framework of a dependency relation to the external market, even reformist governments were not able to respond to their demands with reformist measures. The question is not whether the labor movement is revolutionary but whether conditions provoke revolutionary solutions. In Bolivia this had become increasingly so, and only massive military repression prevents an outbreak of these tendencies.

The backwardness of the company contributes to the politicization of the unions as Millen (1963:59) and Alexander (1972:376) point out, but a more important factor revolutionizing the movement arises in the very imbalance of the struggle. As the unions became politicized, they made their alliances outside of the working population and with the marginally employed and the unemployed. Lora (1969:25) shows the strategic importance of this in giving syndicalism a much wider meaning just because the proletariat is so small. It incorporates the masses in general including campesinos, artisans, and even clerks in the lower middle class.

The kind of adaptations unions have made to this set of conditions in Bolivia may indicate the innovative capacity that labor in industrial centers might well adopt. Instead of turning against the unemployed or partially employed as a competitive threat, trade unions in Bolivia have incorporated them in their ranks and raised the right to work as an issue in their congresses. Their failure to realize the goals they have set themselves is due not to the tactics and strategy of the unions but to a failing economy, especially in the mining sector, and the continuous pressure exerted on it by outside interests.

Another lesson labor has learned in the marginally producing areas is the need to link economic demands with political gains. Lacking the basic framework for redressive action in labor conflict, workers are aware that their only hope to gain advances is by seizing political power. Bolivian workers have no illusions about the impartiality of courts or the representativeness of the bourgeois governments that have pretended to represent them. They have learned that without arms thay are the prey of mercenary troops as the presidents they vote in succumb to foreign pressures. However, if the struggle against control by foreign capital interests is limited to a nationalistic idiom, the Bolivian workers will lose the thrust of their attack on international capitalism.

Bolivia's experience as one of the nations most exploited by foreign capital in Latin America has cultivated the political consciousness of its working class. With the country devastated by decapitalization of its only productive base, and with the reform policies of its populist leaders destroyed by lack of growth, workers have been massacred when they attempt to carry out minimal organizational tasks. As a result they are the most enlightened, although perhaps the least rewarded labor force in Latin America. Labor in the industrial centers is just beginning to grasp the implications for its own position of the threat of unemployment as more and more of the capital it generates is shipped abroad in the search for lower income earning labor and lower taxes. The kinds of alliances labor is forced to make in the marginally producing areas of the world may be the index to a future policy for survival in the centers.

The lessons workers have learned in the Bolivian labor movement are summarized in the words of a delegate to the 14th congress of the FSTMB in April 1970, which I taped in one of the sessions: "The accumulated experience of the cruel methods of repression employed by the enemies of the working class teaches us the necessity to be prepared for the use of all forms of battle, including that of revolutionary violence."

The strength of the labor movement draws upon the community that enables workers to resist the most oppressive conditions and the most aggressive attacks. In the following chapter the relationship between community and class consciousness will be summarized.

Chapter 9

◈◇◈

COMMUNITY AND CLASS CONSCIOUSNESS

◇THE ASSUMPTIONS underlying most analyses of the working class consistently underestimate the capacity for understanding and responding adaptively that exist among the people in less developed countries where industrialization has occurred late. The opposition of "traditional" and "modern" or "rational," of "heteronomy" and "autonomy,"[1] deny the potential for reinterpretation and growth in a cultural idiom different from that of the developed centers of the world but nonetheless capable of generating new understandings and adaptations, sometimes far in advance of the models we have from industrialized societies.

Eurocentric categories as to what constitutes rational behavior or what conduces to autonomy have little meaning for a marginal labor force in a dependent economy. The special characteristics of the work force in underdeveloped countries derive from the structural position of workers in the world economy as well as from ethnic differences defining the internal and external relationships. Bolivian miners are an extreme case of a work force linked to the international market and conscious of their role as producers in the global exchange system at the same time that they retain strong identification with prehispanic sources of cultural identity. As a result, their class consciousness is intrinsically tied to an awareness

---

[1] See, for example, a discussion of Weber's uses of concepts "traditional" and "rational" in H. H. Gerth and C. Wright Mills (1946:56). Alan Touraine and Daniel Pécaut reject the old dichotomies, but construct their own in the opposition of "heteronomy" and "autonomy." The so-called autonomy of the modern industrial working class is won at the expense of the semi-subsistent household production base. Given its condition of alienation from the means of production, the proletariat is even more dependent on capitalist enterprise and conditions of work over which they have little control.

of the world division of labor, in which they feel themselves to be exploited not only as a working class in opposition to a managerial elite, but also as nationals of a dependent economy subject to domination by developed centers. As a class, they are more aware of international relations than are their counterparts in the United States. As a cultural enclave they are less alienated than the majority of the working class of industrial nations, since they are not cut off from the base of self-identification and communication that is still generated in the mining communities. The alienation of the working class takes on a more concentrated meaning in the tin mining community since it is related to the work scene, not to community or to self.[2] In this chapter I shall attempt to weave together some of the themes that I have touched on in relation to the problems of consciousness and ideology.

The Cultural Roots
of Working-Class Identity

The culture of transition in the industrial setting is that of the cholo. In studying such transitional cultures we discover that culture is not only something transmitted from the past to present and future generations. It is the generative base for adapting to conditions as well as for transforming those conditions. When we conceive of culture in this historical structural framework, it becomes a tool for analyzing processes of change rather than an ideology for confirming the status quo.

Miners are, as a group, very mobile, and many chose to go to the mines, since it was the only place where there were schools and the wages opened up at least the illusion of a better standard of living. However, becoming a cholo offered only a partial entry into the culture of the dominant Spanish-speaking group; it held the promise, but not the full admission, into the national society. Cholos speak Spanish but are not always functionally literate. They wear an adaptation of the early Independence style of clothing, but the pol-

---

[2]D. Lockwood (1968:100–101) asserts that industries which concentrate workers in single-industry communities reinforce "proletarian traditionalism" and polarized class patterns. This view is supported by C. Kerr and A. Siegel (1954) and N. Dennis, F. Henriques, and C. Slaughter (1956).

lera, or voluminous skirt, worn by women, even when made of
synthetics, is distinctly different from modern dress, and the derby
hat is an emblem of ethnic identity. The cholos learn to despise the
"ignorance and backwardness" of their Indian origins, but not to
participate fully in the dominant culture. Women who have more
than a primary school education often reject wearing the pollera
that identifies them as cholas. Within the same family, sisters will
often have different styles of dress and identify with an entirely different segment of the national culture because of educational differences. Children of the same parents may be labeled differently
on their birth certificates as "blanco," "mestizo," or even "indio."[3]

The chola culture is, then, heterogeneous. Laymen and even
social scientists often repeat the platitude that Bolivia's social problems result from its cultural and linguistic heterogeneity. However,
when you have a sense of how the community functions, you realize that its strength derives from its ability to deal with differences
not by suppressing them but by incorporating them. The miners
are recruited from both Quechua- and Aymara-speaking communities as well as from mestizo populations of the altiplano and the
Cochabamba valley. Since many are third-generation mine workers, they are often indirectly tied to a campesino background. Often
parents are of different language groups and Spanish is the language of the home. Even when both parents speak the same Indian
language, Spanish may be preferred in order to advance the children's opportunities. Quechua is more frequently spoken than Aymara, which is always combined with Quechua words. Language is
not a basis for tribal identification, and whatever conflicts once existed have been worked out within family and neighborhood primary groups.

A gross measurement of the acculturation to a national pattern
can be seen in the language used in the household. In sixty-one
families for which we have language information in the household
survey we found that in the households with parents between the
ages of 21 and 30, Spanish was the only language spoken by the
children, with only one adult speaking Quechua. In the remaining
four cases with younger parents, the children were too young or
their language was not recorded. In the household where the

[3] For an interesting discussion of Indian and chola subcultures see Harris and
Albó (1975).

parents were from 31 to 40 years of age, the proportion was nearly even, with the children speaking an Indian language as well as Spanish in eleven cases compared to thirteen. In twenty-four households in which parents were from 41 to 50 years of age, the generation difference between older and younger children emerged, with six families in which older children spoke the Indian language and the younger spoke only Spanish. In one of these families, children spoke only Spanish. Finally, in the five households of the age group of parents 51 and over, in all but one case the children spoke the Indian language as well as Spanish.

For the most part, men have a higher acculturation rate than women, and this is reinfored by a specificity of tasks within the household. Women take responsibility for the old traditions with the house rituals to the Pachamama that give a sense of meaning and security to the men, while men bear the honor of the family, the root of which is providing with their wages the means of sustenance. If the family requires a loan or a favor of any kind, it is the woman who makes the approach in order to preserve her husband's honor. All the requests that I receive for loans or to become madrina of a cake for a birthday party, or a ring for a graduation ceremony (in effect a nonreciprocal loan, since the balance was maintained by the honor I received) were made by women. Men are typically more generous, and their wives limit this in the interest of the family. Thus the men have a stronger front and greater solidarity in the community, while the women have to preserve, out of a sense of family survival, what little resource base they have.

While men may be the primary modernizing agent, as Inkeles (1969), Kahl (1968), and others maintain, their position often depends on the strength of women who maintain the traditions that make life seem worthwhile and may even ensure survival. Women balance the tensions of penetrating into the modernizing sector of the society in a partial way, where the wage is insufficient to cover the new demands of living at a standard that is always beyond their family means, and where the modern health services are inadequate to their culturally felt needs, which were satisfied in the old system. They may maintain productive activities in the semi-subsistence areas of the economy that sustain the family in times of industrial layoffs and strikes.

As a result of this intrafamilial fragmentation of the culture, there is ambivalence about the chola/Indian identity, particularly in the first generation of transition. Basilia, a woman of 58 who worked inside the mines during the Chaco War, still retained the sense of contradiction between rural Indian and national chola cultures. She told me in Quechua:

❖ I understand Spanish, only I don't speak it. If I could speak at all clearly, I would have had another fate. If I knew how to read, if I understood the paper, I would have had another destiny. I would have taught them [the government agents from whom she was trying to get her pension] how to respect people.

She chose gente de vestido as padrinos for her children, and when her daughters grew up, they were de vestido.

❖ None of my children are chola. They wear only European dress, because people have more respect for such. For the cholas there is no respect. Whenever they want us, they just yell at us. They do not have the cross in their mouth [Quechua expression for Christian speech]. They don't have the standard that this brings. If one is a chola and doesn't know how to read, niñita, they don't have a good word. "The cholas don't know anything," they say. "They speak only ten words of Spanish."

Cholos often deprecate the Indians, even those who are their relatives. Manuel, who went into the mines to escape the poverty of his parents' home, says:

❖ My father was no more than an Indian with little capacity intellectually and with little vision. He was ignorant, my father, and I have tried to correct all that he did not have. And so have all my brothers and sisters who live tried to correct the errors and insufficiencies that our parents had.

Often the differential acculturation rates between husband and wife cause conflict in the home. Generally the man is the first to move away from the Indian or cholo culture. Petrona's mother was more acculturated than her father. She said:

❖ My mother fought a great deal so that I could go to school. My father was a brute who didn't understand. He didn't want it. "Why go to school? What is a woman going to learn in school?" he would ask. He fought that way with my mother. He didn't understand letters. He never went to school. He learned to speak Spanish when he went to work in the mines in Chile. My mother used to

say, "Your father is an Indian and doesn't understand anything."
My mother was well read, and she understood. She said that she
was de vestido when she was young, but when she went to live
with my papa she put on the pollera, because my father insisted
on it. She cried when she changed her dress.

Men feel that they can control the mobility of their wives if they
continue to wear the clothing that identifies them as cholas.

Becoming a chola is a continuous process of penetration into
national culture stimulated by educational advance and increasing
consumption dependency. It was this process of becoming someone
more advanced that kept the cholos tied to the mine and to the
wage that gave them the promise if not the actuality of a better life.
The tensions generated in this mobile strata are somewhat overcome in the family, work groups, and neighborhood compounds of
the mining community. The homogeneous housing and life style
limit the constant threat of invidious display that cannot be
matched. While some think of the encampment as a trap, it offers
some compensation in the communal sharing that overcomes the
envy and divisiveness of other cholo subcultures. The mobility aspirations of the individual miner contradicts the ethic of communal
sharing cultivated in the encampment. What shifts the balance in
favor of solidarity in the class struggle is the inability of a flagging
economy to permit social or economic advances for the vast majority of workers.

Within the chola culture of the mines, there is also a dialectical
tension between egalitarianism and paternalism. The search for a
patron is institutionalized in the compadrazgo relationship and in
the fiestas given to saints. Saints have varying degrees of luck that
can be exploited by the lavishness of the fiestas offered to them.
Since saints, like people, feel envy if one is not loyal to them, people tend to cultivate a single saint. Cholos often say of saints that
they are "very evil," but this is taken as a sign of power, and people feel that this can be manipulated to one's advantage.

The chola culture in Bolivia differs from that of Peru and from
the rota culture of Chile. Bourricaud (1970:79 et seq.) speaks of the
cunning and violence of the cholos in Peru. He quotes José María
Arguedas on the cholo who "no longer lives or belongs to the ayllu
but he is constantly reminded of the fact that he comes from it" to

capture the marginality of the cholo (Bourricaud 1970:71). Cotler (1969:68 et seq.) sees the cholo culture as a more positive product of the dislocation and migration that serves to break the monopoly of the mestizos in their control over Indian communities. By providing alternative sources of goods and services, the cholos open up new centers of social identity.

The difference in the Bolivian culture, at least in the mining community, is that cholos are the central figures here, not intermediaries between a subordinated Indian group and a superordinate *ladino* group. In their "centers of social identity" they have found a basis for social solidarity and collective action. This is based not on homogeneity, but on a cultivated ability to weave together the different cultural strands in the context of family and community.

The myths and rituals of the pre-conquest were an important means of transcending the culture shock of the Indian population that entered into the mines in the colonial period. The sense of fear that came with the violation of the earth and descending into the domain of Huari, the spirit of the hills, is dealt with explicitly in the myth set forth in chapter 1. The mythic time encompassed in this legend can be related to the Inca invasion merging into the Spanish conquest. The first invasion brought to an end the Garden of Eden, when the Uru Uru were pastorialists and agriculturalists, as the people turned from agriculture to work in the mines. They were delivered from the plagues brought upon them because of their indolence and vice by the Inca virgin, Ñusta. The return of the four plagues can be related to the Spanish conquest. This threat was overcome by the introduction of the Christian faith, symbolized by the church erected at the sites of the slain monsters. Each of the catastrophic events in the lives of the Indians was reworked into a thanksgiving for the merciful protection of the Ñusta, later identified with the Virgin of the Mine, who made it possible for life to go on. The Spaniards applied the term devil to the power of Huari, but this distorts the concept of this force as a potentially benevolent source of riches.

The ch'alla for the Tío, or devil, inside the mines reenacts the strategy of appeasement and restoration. In the first place, the offering of blood and the palpitating heart of a sacrificed llama to the Tío satisfies his appetite and keeps him from unleashing destructive forces. Second, the offering of life is felt to restore the equilibrium of productive forces upset by mining. The foreign technicians were tolerant of these customs, but the national technicians, who replaced them after the nationalization of the mines, rejected them, possibly because of their own alienation and desire to separate themselves from the traditional culture. As one miner told me at a ch'alla I attended:

❖ Today the jefes that we have are nationals, and they are inattentive to the rituals. They believe themselves to be great señoritos who do not want to mix into the beliefs of the pueblo or of the workers. And because of this, the mines are declining. There is not as much production today.

Most of the miners feel that these beliefs are in no sense contradictory to the modernization and industrialization processes of which they are such an integral part of the country. A young miner who had completed his secondary school education said:

❖ The ch'alla this year was better than ever before. The miners are modernizing this kind of ch'alla; now the worker automatically goes to work on Tuesday, or Friday, prepares his coca, his cigarettes, his alcohol, his liquor, and whatever else he uses and makes his offering to the Tío.

In his view, this systematization of the ritual as part of an automatic work habit was the modernizing element and he saw no contradiction with the past. It reminded me of the Taylor principle in work process, where the modernizing aspect is the automatic performance regardless of content or whether the segmentation of the task structure actually means greater efficiency.

The cult of the Tío reinforces the solidarity of the work group. In the prenationalization days when the team operated collectively and was paid in proportion to its output, the inner solidarity of the cuadrilla was in opposition to the other work groups. The ch'alla was performed to wheedle more output from the devil, as each group competed with other cuadrillas. After nationalization, the individual worker was paid a basic wage regardless of the mineral produced, and solidarity included not only the entire work force of the mine but all nationalized mines. The ch'alla was more a recreation than a basis for solidarity in the productive work group. However, following the military takeover of the mines in 1965, the ch'alla was repressed along with unions and Worker Control. Workers continued to perform the ritual in secret, and these sessions become a focus for discussing the problems and struggles of the workers. Just as other pre-conquest rituals, such as the warming of the earth ceremonies at the fiesta of San Juan, became more explicitly the ritual expression of the desire to live, to multiply, and to enhance the reproductive and productive sources of life, so did the ch'alla. The resistance to military repression by men and women of the mining community came from these deep wells of cultural identity that gave them a sense of worth and the will to survive when they recognized the genocidal power of the Barrientos regime.

The separation of the indigenous customs in time and space from those of the Catholic religion imposed on the people gave a greater viability to the traditions in comparison to those cultures of Latin America where syncretism characterizes the relationship between Catholic and indigenous rituals. With the Virgin assigned to her niche in the church, the saints in their neon-lit boxes at level zero, the Supay could maintain his dominion more effectively below ground and the Pachamama her identification with the earth and the riches thereof. The chola culture maintained this anchorage for the industrial workers who were only partially admitted into the industrial era.

Carnival remains the pinnacle in the yearly cycle of rituals that vindicate the chola culture and their means of dealing with their conditions of life. It is a dramatization of the occupational and ethnic roles into which Indians, blacks, and mestizos were thrust—llameras, morenadas, negritos, tobas, diablos—the polymorphous and perverse dance combinations where whites play blacks, men play women, and all the contradictions of their lot in life are transformed into their opposite and transcended. Weaving in and around the dance figures are the condors, bears, hedgehogs—the totem of Oruro—which remind people that these enchanted figures can still make all their dreams come true.

Chola culture is an adaptive mode for adjusting to an industrial scene, but it does not provide a basis for changing the scenario. The fluid social ties, the coca chewing, the stress on commercialization are adjustive mechanisms to maintain humanity in inhuman working and living conditions. Even the mobility striving for self-improvement is adjustive, since it provides limited entry to a few top positions of influence in the dominant society and, by co-opting the talented tenth, cuts off leaders from the masses of cholas. In the adjustment to the new, the technique of complementary distribution permitted cholos to retain elements of the old Indian culture that gave them the strength to resist the alienating effects of the industrial setting and to survive in the harsh physical and social environment of the mines. Instead of confronting the power structure that made the conditions of exploitation, it provided the myths that justified the polarized wealth and cultivated a desire on the part of workers to become a part of that dominant group. On the other hand, it is the milieu in which cholos become conscious of their class position and identify their frustrated mobility with a common understanding of their problems. Thus the chola culture stimulates the aspirations and desires that cannot be met for any but a small minority, and it is out of these frustrations that a class awareness is developed.

In the writing of political economists of the industrial age, there is a mystique about alienation as the human condition. This rests on the assumption that the sale of labor power universally results in estrangement culturally and socially because of the reification of the will and activity involved in work controlled by the owners of capital. Certainly industrialization does set the conditions for such alienation. But little has been said of the workers' resistance to that inner estrangement that reflects the social conditions imposed on them. Hobsbawm touched on it in *Primitive Rebels* (1959), when he saw in religion not just a pacifying illusion but the vindication of the self that was denied workers on the job. Anthony Wallace and others who have written about revitalization movements of colonized people touched by the industrialization process have captured some of the essential characteristics of such resistance. My experience living in mining communities taught me more than anything else, how a people totally involved in the most exploitative, dehumanizing form of industrialization managed to resist alienation. They did this in both a political and a religious idiom. For most miners, these were not contradictory expressions of commitment to proletarian struggle, although leaders of the institutions which promoted religious or political goals preached or polemicized that the aims and means of each sphere were dissonant. Huari, the devil, the Pachamama, Christ, and the Virgin Mary inhabited a unified world view where separate spheres of activity and timing enabled the miners to respond appropriately to each and all of these figures. Most miners did not oppose them to Marxist and Maoist teachings. What gave coherence to these pre-Hispanic, Christian, and modern ideologies was a sense of self as members of a community sharing the sustenance offered by the Pachamama and occasionally taking advantage of the riches controlled by Huari. The ritual of the ch'alla—from the simplest reference to it in sprinkling liquor on the earth to the sacrifice of a llama in the k'araku—are a part of communal gatherings that collectively enable the miners to overcome the alienation in their lives.

Class Consciousness

The class consciousness of the industrial worker postdated the factory system of production by over a century, emerging in explicit form about 1830–40 (Hobsbawm 1971:7). The time period for the development of class consciousness in Bolivia was telescoped into two decades following the industrial mining in Patiño's mines beginning about 1886. The shortening of this incubation period was in part due to the transplanting of anarcho-syndicalist and socialist conceptions of society by European emigrant workers from Argentina and Chile coming into Bolivia about 1910 (Alexander 1963, 1965; Lora 1969), as well as the opening up of communication and contact with other regions of Bolivia. Shortly after the Russian revolution, class consciousness was carried into organized syndical activity. The strikes from 1918 on and peaking in the massacre of Uncía in 1923 established the modern industrialized consciousness of the miners.

The distinction that Marx drew between a class in itself, or a group which has not as yet formulated a consciousness of its identity in opposition to the capital-owning class, and a class for itself, or one that has developed a theory about its place in society and a program to change it, established the basis for understandings and assessing consciousness in working class movements. Lukacs further distinguished the actual ideas men form about class and ascribed class consciousness, or the theoretical constructs which could be derived from objective conditions (Lukacs 1971; Hobsbawn 1971).

Most discussions about class are meta-theories of the second category; that is, they put the conditions observed in a set of propositions the theoreticians would derive if they were experiencing those conditions. This does not always (or perhaps ever) coincide with the ontological propositions of the men and women in the work setting. Even notions of poverty, of excessive labor, of insufficient nutrition are relative to a theory of what the worker should get if he were justly compensated. In the case of the cholo miners, the very fact that they are mobile makes them assess their condition in life in terms relative to the Indian culture from which they came and to the national culture to which they aspire. The contradiction between the mobility drives cultivated in a context of bourgeois identification with the limitation set on those mobility drives forces an identification with the community in which they live. When they accept the fact that their mobility depends on that of the class as a whole, there is a basis for a class-conscious movement. In order to gain a hold on some of those elusive concepts, I shall take four themes that bulk large in the theoretical literature on class consciousness: identity as a class, alienation, and their corollaries, dependency and exploitation, and try to sort out the ideas which men and women in the mining encampments form about their class condition.

Identity as a Class

If we take Gramsci's formulation of the three stages of ideological transformation from (1) economic corporative, or one trader with another, to (2) solidarity of all members in a social group defined in the economic field, and (3) awareness that one's own corporative interests transcend the narrowly defined group and can become the consciousness of other subordinated members (Gramsci 1973:169), the cutting edge of a collective movement comes in transforming the sentiments developed in stage (2) to those of stage (3). As an example of this, I shall take the frequently expressed anger and frustration against technicians and show how this gripe is transformed into protest in the rhetoric of trade union organizers. In the three positions taken below, one can see the transformation from stage one to stage three.

As a self-selected group with high mobility drives, miners, when they feel themselves or their children to be blocked in gaining access to middle class posts in the technical or administrative ranks, often turn against this intermediate level in the bureaucracy, where the contrast in power and privilege is accentuated by a pay scale that tries to maintain engineers' salaries comparable to world market prices while depressing labor's rate of return to below subsistence levels. "The jefes," as one miner told me, "earn B $4,000 and we earn B $400, a little less than enough to earn our daily bread."

One worker who interrupted his studies in the Oruro University to help support his family carried this same complaint one step further toward defining the condition of the miner:

❖ The president of the company earns twenty-three thousand pesos [about US $195] a month, but a worker gets only three hundred [US $25]. They only earn big salaries in the bureaucratic section of the administration—some in dollars and another part in Bolivian bills. And the ones who bear the burden of the work are the workers, whose contribution ought to be recognized. They ought to be paid one hundred percent of what they earn, not the miserable two or three hundred pesos they get . . . and there are technicians who never show their aptitude, any special knowledge or ability. They come into the mine rarely and only say, "Here, hurry up!" This does not demonstrate technical capacity. . . . This bureaucracy is a calamity! . . . They should know our suffering. . . . I want to make them know the reality of the miner. I am the son of a miner, and now I am working in the mines, and I am going to do what I can to help them. They are the subsistence base of the community, but they are the class that suffers most.

The use of the term "they" reveals the distance this man puts between himself and his co-workers, perhaps because of his university education. In contrast, the rhetoric of trade union leaders is the inclusive "we," as the speech of one of the candidates for secretary general of the union reveals, summing up the essence of the miners' discontent and relating it to a more global statement of the problem.

❖ The engineers earn in dollars and they produce less than we do. The workers earn less and produce more. We have to earn for the engineers, the lawyers, and the colonels and we pay for their errors. Our mechanics know better than the theoreticians the problems inside the mine. The workers always have to work for the rest. For every three hundred workers there are twenty engineers. There are technicians of oil, technicians of designs, all are useless. When they travel to other mines, they receive one hundred pesos a day. This comes from the ribs of those workers. When we receive a bonus, they receive the same percentage, but they have higher salaries. Our capitalists do not help their country. They save their money in foreign banks. The miners are maintaining the country.

Here the labor union leader transforms the complaints of the workers into a theory about the relationship of the exploited underground worker to the managerial bureaucracy and the expropriation of surplus value by a capitalist state. In his final statement he even pushes classical Marxist theory into the understanding of dependency relations and the uneven development of world capitalism in pointing out that the capitalists of Bolivia do not even carry out their fiction of primitive accumulation of capital within the country.

Another aspiring leader at the forum went on to attack not only the bureaucratic state apparatus but the penetration of monopoly capital from abroad:

❖ Monopolistic state capitalism [referring to COMIBOL] is nothing but the administrator of foreign monopolies. We want the deepening of the revolution and we are going to ask for it with the workers themselves because they are the ones who have decreed the deepening of the revolution in Bolivia. We comrades are the ones who have won the democratic conquests and the civil liberties of our country. No government has given them to the others. This is the reason we must go out in the streets and demonstrate to the feudal reactionaries, comrades, in the United States of America and give them an injection and put on a poultice of *ulupica* [herbal medicine] to take out the blindness to real life. I believe, comrades, that imperialism in this time in our country is acting like a dog making circles chasing his tail. It is necessary to point out, comrades, this initiative role of the working class to the other labor sectors and unite their revolutionary forces in order to show North American imperialism and those who put themselves up in this country without permission of the working class.

These three statements point to different programs for transforming the position of the working class. The first looks toward gaining a greater share for workers of the surplus generated within the system. The second, the position of a PRIN political activist, points to a kind of worker control or participation in management whereby the workers gain a greater role in the organization of work. The third, spoken by a political leader of the Fourth International or Trotskyist orientation, relates the nationalized enterprise to the external market control systems and attacks imperialism. The fact that the second speaker won the election in the union says more about the particular historical circumstances in which the workers were operating than it does about the level or weight of opinion. The mining communities had only recently emerged from some of the most brutally repressive actions carried out by Barrientos.

Most miners attributed the massacres from 1965 to 1967 to the penetration of U.S. imperialism exercised through its agent, Barrientos, in the interest of carrying out the prescription of the Triangular Plan. However, they were not willing to risk a confrontation at this point, since they were still in a stage of recuperation. Their wages were the primary point of reference for making demands on the system, and the memory of the confrontation with an army well-equipped with M-1s and bazookas on the fields of Hilbo and Sora Sora was too fresh for them to want to link their trade union demands to an attack on imperialism. There was no less consciousness of class in 1970 than in 1961, when the miners of Siglo XX–Catavi elected Federico Escobar, the PCB leader who was the "most combative," as the workers said, of the leaders running that year.

I want to emphasize that the term "leaders" is not an absolute category. The moment men and women of the encampment moved from private statements of discontent to an analysis of what this means in a wider framework and began to organize others around this, often in opposition to the official leaders, they become recognized as "people who have earned the right to speak for us." Leaders in office who become spokespersons for the government or COMIBOL are soon recognized as *oficialistas* who no longer represent the sentiments of the community. This process is as true of the women in the encampment as it is of the underground workers. Domitila spoke of this process among the women in the 1961 strike:

❖ When they stopped sending in food to the encampment and cut off the payment of wages, then the idea rose among those women whose husbands were imprisoned and they saw the necessity of organizing. The wife of Escobar went to ask for the freedom of her husband and did not gain it on her part alone, and the wife of Pimentel went alone on her part and failed. Then they saw the necessity of unifying the women in a front to go ask the freedom of their union leaders and at the same time to demand provisions in the pulpería, which they had cut off for a month. We had nothing to give for food; there was not even wages with which to buy food. They had even cut off the water. Then the committee organized a delegation to go to La Paz and there they declared a hunger strike.

This identification of the housewives with the workers during the strike reinforced the class solidarity based in the community. It was at that point that massive military force was mobilized to overcome the growing unity in the protest.

Alienation

Marx pointed to the sources of alienation in capitalist society as (1) separation of the producers from the product, or the alienation of surplus value; (2) separation of the producers from the means of production, which forces them to become dependent on the owners of capital in order to make a living; and (3) separation of the producers from the sense of meaningful self-involvement in the work process. The final source of alienation is the separation of the worker from the sense of identity with a community. Marx did not develop this source of alienation, since he assumed that the solidarity of workers in the factory would be the basis for their vanguard action. However, workers in industrial centers have been deprived of that identity with community which provides the moral basis for human action that goes beyond self-interest.

When the process of alienation of labor is complete in all spheres, there is probably little basis for rebellion and revolution. The sense of the self being denied comes from some reinforcement of what this means, either within the work process or in the community. The quality of life in the mining community, by virtue of retaining roots of cultural identity, defies the process of reification

(Lukacs 1971:91) that arises when a society learns to satisfy all of its needs in terms of commodity exchange.

In the Bolivian tin mines, the process by which the worker is cut off from control over the work process and the distribution of rewards has been on the increase. Nationalization of the mines increased the alienation, contrary to the expectations of the workers. The repression of the trade unions under Barrientos and later under Banzer confirmed the separation of the workers from the organization of the work. The only sphere in which a modicum of control remains is in the community, where the politicization of the people continues to grow. I shall summarize this process, which has been touched on in preceding chapters, in each of these spheres.

1. Alienation from the rewards of work is the basis for exploitation. The returns from productivity are doubly expropriated in dependent economies: first from the workers, who are paid less than the value of their marginal productivity or whatever other rationale is used to calculate the wage, and second from a nation selling raw materials or semi-processed goods in a market over which the nation has little or no control. Tin has fluctuated between being 42 to 75 percent of the exports of the balance of trade in the twentieth century. When private companies expropriated the profits of the mines, they could control the politics of the country. Paradoxically, after nationalization of the mines, the MNR government became increasingly dependent on foreign aid. The debts tied Bolivia to heavy interest obligations and required that imports come from the United States even when some of the needed tools and supplies could have been purchased more cheaply in other countries.

The wealth of the mines, which in colonial days enriched the merchants and kings of Spain, in the days of Patiño enabled him to expand competitive production in Malaya and in the nationalization period enabled the government to build up the oil industry in Santa Cruz. Very little remained in the mining centers.

This sense of double expropriation is sharply felt in the mining community and is expressed in both the denunciation of the COMIBOL bureaucracy as well as in anti-imperialism. The attack on U.S. imperialism is a constant and never-ending theme of all the workers as well as the leaders. All of the candidates for the office of secretary general of the union in 1970 ran on an anti-imperialist platform. The PRIN candidate stated it in this way: "Bolivia's economy is set in a field of simple, primary materials. . . . Its economic, social, and institutional structures are conditioned by the needs and pressures of the imperialist countries." He proposed a revolutionary plan of anti-imperialism, opposed to occupation by external economic forces, the Bank for Interamerican Development and other "opponents to socialism." The Communist party leader stated his anti-imperialism in opposition to the MNR and its offshoot, the PRIN, stating, "It is necessary to have a vanguard party that is of the working class, but you cannot find this in a party that has betrayed the workers since 1952." The Fourth International contender was more specific in his attack on imperialism: "We must prevent a restructuring of unions on the basis of 'free unionism' or 'yellow unionism' [a reference to the U.S.-based ORIT school], which just atomizes the union movement," and he called for the expulsion of the CIA and an end to the alienation of national resources as well as stopping indemnity to Gulf Oil Corporation.

Anti-imperialism was a unifying slogan to draw support from sectors of the middle class and students as well as workers, since nationalization provided work for technicians and professionals who replaced foreigners, but the level of worker gains declined, especially in the second decade after the revolution. Both Ovando and Torres attacked imperialism in their speeches, but their inability to overcome the dependency relations with the United States crippled their ability to make their nationalistic programs work. When Torres appeared to be succeeding in attracting capital from the Soviet orbit in 1971, he was no longer tolerable to the United States.

2. Alienation from the means of production implies dependency on the jobs provided by capital owners. By reviewing the changing mode of production in the history of Bolivian mining, we can perhaps gain a sense of the causal relationship between forms of ownership and control over the labor force.

In colonial mining the technological input was minimal and consequently the amount of capital needed to enter mining was minor. The hand mallet and drill, the carbon lamp, leather bags and helmets were made at low cost by local craftsmen. The only thing that prevented a large number of small contractors going into the mines for their own profit was ownership of the mine site in the major centers combined with a coercive labor system in the mita. With industrial mining at the turn of the twentieth century, metal carts, lifts, and later mechanized drills raised the capital required to enter into competitive production. The need for a coerced labor force not only lessened as the capital requirements lessened the competition of small independent entrepreneurs, but it became counter-productive as the risks to expensive capital goods from worker sabotage increased. Workers were tied to the job through consumer dependency cultivated in the pulperías. This was further reinforced by the kind of paternalistic dependencies that developed in mining communities where the company supplied not only the main food stocks but the dwelling place, hospital, and schooling for workers. Whenever the workers developed a strong united front to fight for wages the managers responded by closing the pulpería. If a strike persisted, they followed this up with a lockout. The lack of alternative employment means that the workers must rely on the mines as the source of their life.

3. Alienation from the work process is the focus of much of the sociological literature on industrial relations which concentrates on "social isolation," "powerlessness," "meaninglessness," "self-estrangement," and "normlessness," to use Seeman's (1959) categories. Most often, studies are made without reference to other forms of alienation or to the framework in which it is cultivated. Control over the means of production has become increasingly concentrated with the growing complexity of the technology of production. Dependence of Third World countries on technology from industrial centers has, as Harry Magdoff points out (1976:7), cultivated a lack of self-confidence and reliance on foreign expertise. The work process is defined in terms of technological imperatives which may or may not be required for efficient operation, but which are often not questioned.

The organization of work in Bolivian mines has eroded the autonomy of the work group and reinforced the authority of the technicians. Scientific and safe exploitation of the mines obviously requires sound engineering principles to control the advance in the pits. However, this has not been followed up by training workers to enable them to enter into management. In the pirkiñero system favored by the rosca, the worker was paid for the mineral content of what he produced. He was highly motivated to use all his ingenuity and senses to work the veins. Miners used their skill, exploiting their bodies and their souls, which they "sold" to the devil in their desire to find the metal. Some would work up to twenty hours at a stretch and even sleep inside the mine when they got caught up in the quest. Although the payment in relation to brute loads introduced after the revolution may have been a fairer system from an overall industrial perspective, it negated that intelligent involvement of the workers' faculties. Worker Control failed to cultivate the abilities workers had developed in the old system of production. Instead, it served to heighten the conflict between workers and management and technicians by serving as a brake on supervisors without implementing worker initiative in production.

The Triangular Plan was a further step toward controlling the workers in the plans for nationalization of the work force. In addition to cutting down the number of workers, it attempted to com-

AFTER FIFTY YEARS IN THE MINES, A WORKER'S FACE REFLECTS WEARINESS AND BITTERNESS IN HIS SMILE DURING A BREAK IN THE DAY'S WORK.

bine a speedup with reduced contract payments. The increased alienation was expressed in the series of strikes carried out between 1961 and 1963.

4. Alienation from the community is counterproductive to collective action. Turner (1974:45), following Znaniecki and Thomas (1963: ch. 3), develops the meaning of community (or *communitas* as he prefers to call it) as "consciousness and willingness, in so far as they exist, [that] constitute a social bond uniting these people over and above any formal social bonds which are due to the existence of regulated social relations and organized social groups." As Turner develops the idea (1974:47) he shows how communitas emerges in periods of anti-structure when the society is in a stage of liminality. This threshold condition, in which the usual structural processes are in abeyance, is a period when "undifferentiated, equalitarian, direct, nonrational (though not irrational) behavior is manifested."

To the extent that the community has these generative bonds of new growth, the people can sustain the most brutal attacks. The mining community has demonstrated the strength of these sentiments that carry it through such periods. It provides the resistance against alienation that is the essence of the work system in industrial centers. When the company recognized this, they tried to destroy it by firing or sending into exile the husbands of those women who focused on the sentiments of communitas therby breaking the primal base of solidarity. The rituals in the mine, the ch'alla to the Pachamama, and the offerings to the enchanted spirits are all reminders in normal periods of the root sources of communitas.

Dependency and Exploitation

The sense of alienation from the means of production creates a feeling of dependency in the owners and managers of capital goods. This consciousness, which is endemic in the mining population, is in dialectical opposition to the feeling of exploitation which comes from alienation from the distribution of rewards. The lowering of wages and control of workers in the organization of tasks in the nationalized mines, especially after 1965, could continue only because the lack of alternative employment possibilities compelled the workers to remain on the job. Management played on this fear of losing their only basis of subsistence in the labor conflicts of 1946–51, and after nationalization from 1961 on, when they carried out the masacres blancas, or mass layoffs. When resistance persisted, they used masacres rojas, or the bloodbaths, to end the conflict, especially in the years 1949–51 and 1965–67.

The fear of layoffs inhibits the militant action of a class fully conscious of the exploitation they endure. Francisca, who had worked on the slag pile since she was 12 years old, expresses the workers' fear:

❖ The Second World War ended in 1945. In 1946 and 1947 there was not much need for this part of Latin America to take out tin. Then we were not well off. There was no need for our tin. There was no need for hands to continue working. Then the mines began to decline and there was unemployment. The unemployment rose. [Here she used *flotar*, floated, like the scum of nonusable ores in the flotation process of the preconcentration plants.]

I worked since I was twelve collecting mineral from the slag pile. There were pirkiñeros in this time and we used to produce two or three pounds or even four pounds each day. Sometimes they cut us off from that and we went without eating up to two days, chewing coca. My father was dead. I had an older brother who went to Potosí. My sister was still small. My mother knew how to work, breaking up the mineral for our daily bread. They used to pay us ten bills for a pound of mineral. We worked all day from early morning. We worked like a man with a shovel. Sometimes we went into the mines to take out the mineral. We had to work or we wouldn't have been able to eat.

When the workers developed a strong union, the managers often responded by threatening to close the mines. This woman's husband commented on the management's threat to close San José in 1957, when the union was at the peak of its success in gaining worker control:

❖ It is a threat that puts fear in the workers. It is like a weapon for them to threaten us. A worker knows more than they do about where the mineral is. They frankly do not know the mine. Itos has plenty if the technicians wanted to prepare it and develop it. If they only want to "eat" from one place, that gives out. They ought to search elsewhere.

The decision to close the mine was blocked by engineers and government officials who recognized the threat to the basic economy of Oruro. But such threats were always present and served to tame the workers' protest.

Dependency feelings cultivate a sense of the need for a patron in order to gain some security in a threatening situation. In the mines this was countered by the strong egalitarian tendencies and communal exchanges existing in the encampment, but it survived as a strategy. These patron-client relationships, usually institutionalized in the compadrazgo relationship, reinforced the sense of dependency and the super- and subordination that undermine the drive toward self-determination. It entered into and defined some of the relationships within the union. The potential leaders as well as those elected to office were the most vulnerable to paternalistic cooptation, since management worked directly on them to limit protest action. Those leaders who were vulnerable became the only beneficiaries of paternalism, whereas formerly it was more diffuse. Their own dependency on management and political leaders limited the development of a worker-directed organization.

In contrast to the U.S. labor movement, alienation in the Bolivian working class is derived more from the exploitation inherent in the global productive relations than from the work process itself. This is a corollary of the position of the country in the world market system. In advanced industrial centers, redistribution of profits is a stimulus to the economy by enabling workers to become consumers and buy the goods produced. When Henry Ford raised his workers' wages, he did it so that they would buy the cars he was able to produce cheaply and plentifully on the newly introduced assembly lines. In Bolivia, the process of redistribution begun in the MNR period was interrupted by the Stabilization Act of 1956. The government moved from a policy of setting minimum wage laws to one of freezing wages but without stopping the runaway inflation of consumer goods prices. Thus the dependency relation between an underdeveloped country and the center limits the ability of working class organizations to affect the flow of capital even more than in the developed centers. In the United States, the greater return to labor reduces their awareness of exploitation. Their trade union activities are directed toward limiting work output on the job. In contrast, Bolivian trade unions phrase their resistance in more global political statements. The fact that U.S. intervention supporting anti-

A RETIRED MINER WITH HIS WIFE POSE IN THEIR TOWNHOUSE.
HE IS ONE OF THE FORTUNATE BUT FEW MINERS WHO SURVIVED
THE HAZARDOUS WORKING CONDITIONS IN THE MINE THAT LIMIT
MOST WORKERS' WORKING SPAN TO AN AVERAGE OF SIX YEARS.

labor governments negated their only weapon in the strike sharpened their anti-imperialist sentiments in all ranks of the labor
force.

The opposition between consciousness of exploitation, which
stems from alienation from the rewards of one's work, and consciousness of dependency, which stems from alienation from the
means of production, has not been adequately treated in theory or
practice. The assumption is that the two forms of alienation reinforce each other in the creation of a revolutionary movement. In
fact, they tend to negate each other, since consciousness of dependency leads to a search for security and the cultivation of patron-
client relations. By rejecting not only the tactics springing from this
dependency, but even the existence of such consciousness in the

working class, theorists have failed to deal directly with the kinds of relationships in which dependency is cultivated. However, it is possible to counter the pernicious effects of dependency, played upon by management in periods of economic crisis, by raising it to the level of consciousness that the union has done with the sense of exploitation and at the same time cultivate the kind of support system the women developed during the strike of 1963. Women are very aware of the vulnerability of the household with a single wage earner and do everything in their power to acquire another income or cut living costs by buying directly from farmers. As yet, their efforts have not been given official support by the unions.

Despite the fact that Third World countries like Bolivia are doubly dependent—as workers within the capitalist enterprises in their countries, and as a nation in a world market over which they have no control—their working class movements are potentially more militant than those of the developed centers. First, as the victims of the exploitation of nations as well as of class, they are more aware of the implications of a world market than are their counterparts in developed centers. Second, as the "bastard child of imperialism," as they say, they have neither the illusions about the ability of their own bourgeoisie to bring democratic reform to their country nor the benefit from the surplus value expropriated from the workers of other countries. They are, as a consequence, more at liberty to define their own future.

Appendix

◈THE FOLLOWING observations were made in a six-hour observation period in the John F. Kennedy school in the San José mining barrio.

Because of the stress on school facilities, there are two shifts for pupils, one in the morning and the other in the afternoon. Each classroom has between 30 and 40 students. In addition to 13 regular teachers there are special teachers in religion, physics, manual labor, and music.

The classrooms are not overcrowded, with two students to a double desk and no overflow. Boys sat in segregated rows. Although it was a new school, the walls were marked with writing and the newspapers at the window to block the sun were shredded and tattered. The classroom turned into a demonstration when we entered. The teacher asked the students to volunteer sentences and selected others to go to the board to write them. She helped one slow child by reiterating the syllables slowly. She turned to me and made excuses for the class, saying in a tone the children could hear, that they are children of parents who do not take care of them and who have no interest in and do not cooperate with the school program. This was negated by the neat and clean appearance of the majority of the children.

In the second classroom I visited, the teacher had more personality and a better rapport with her class, but she too made excuses for the children. We asked her to proceed with the class as though we were not there, and we sat at the back of the room. She wrote the vowels on the board and combined them with consonants. The lesson was a distinction between small and capital, or what she called "papa" letters. She asked the children to volunteer proper names with the consonants she pointed to, and then selected a child to go to the board and write. The children as a group were then asked to sound out the consonants and told to write in their notebooks. She said that she used the "empirical" method of teaching the children to read, starting with sounds familiar to all such as the grunting of a pig, the mooing of a cow, etc., and associating the sound with the sign. Some students had come without their own notebooks and she lent them some partially used copies. She said to me, "We cannot obligate the parents to buy materials as they do in the private school."

Detail in observation of teaching technique in use of capital letters:

Teacher asked children to name names with A. "Ace" said one. She said, "Who is called that?" "Anna" said another. She went to board and wrote it. Class spelled it out. Teacher uttered sounds as child performed at board in a kind of prompting. Many of the children wore their coats and hats in school because of the cold. The teacher then said, "Ahora vamos a pasar a otra letra," and wrote R r on the Board. She told the children to write it in their notebooks. She helped some find the blank pages and walked around checking to see that each one was following out her order. One boy finished and came up to show it, saying proudly, "Alli está, señorita." (Here it is, señorita). She gently ushered him back to his seat without comment. The children sounded out R and were told to gesture it as though writing on their desks. Most of the children followed the teacher's orders. They then sounded out vowels with the consonants. She asked them if the capital R appeared like the small r. The children said no. She asked for names beginning with R. Rosa, Raul, and Rita were volunteered, and the children proceeded to take turns writing on the board. The principal came in and called the children to attention. She seemed more concerned about classroom decorum than with learning.

There are no sanitary facilities in the school because of the lack of water. The children squatted in ditches in the yard during recess.

The teacher began to get the idea that we might be going to help the school, and started volunteering what was needed. She said first of all they needed a fence around the schoolyard because of the danger of thieves. (It was hard to think what they might steal aside from the children since there was nothing at all in the schoolrooms except benches. She expresses the usual cultural paranoia about theft which has little to do with reality.)

The teacher of the fourth grade was a well-dressed young man who had the class well focused on a lesson in multiplication with two multipliers. Many children raised their hands when he asked for solutions. When one child voluntered the product 24 to 6 x 4, the other children laughed. I sat in the back of the room and saw no signs of sabotage to what was going on in front. He wrote the products on the board as the children volunteered answers. The children stood as they responded. The teacher then taught them a method of checking their answers. After each example, he told the children to write the solutions in their notebooks.

From this behavioral data, one senses a lack of congruence between the teachers' statements about the unresponsiveness of the children of the working-class parents and the classroom interaction. Their own attempts to put distance between themselves and their role in commenting on the backwardness of the children and the uncooperative attitudes of the parents did not seem to be corroborated by any signs of alienation in class.

References

Abegglen, James C.
1958   *The Japanese Factory: Aspects of Its Social Organization.* Glencoe, Ill.: Free Press.
Ad Hoc Committee on Mines of the Alliance for Progress
1963   "Measures Designed to Speed Economic Development in Bolivia under the Alliance for Progress." Memo to the Government of Bolivia. Mimeo.
Aguirre Zeballos, Julio
1959   *El mito del agotamiento de la mina San José.* Oruro: Comisión Técnica de la Universidad Técnica de Oruro.
Alessandri, Arturo Z.
1968   "Facetas de 'la morenada,' un ensayo." In *Ensayo de interpretación del Carnaval Orureno: Leyendas, tradiciones, costumbres.* Oruro: Instituto de Filosofía Indígena Oruro.
Alexander, Robert J.
1963   "Organized Labor and the Bolivian National Revolution." In E. M. Kassalow, ed., *National Labor Movements in the Postwar World.* Evanston, Ill.: Northwestern University Press.
1965   *Organized Labor in Latin America.* New York: Free Press.
1972   "The Politicization of Organized Labor." In S. and P. Liss, eds., *Man, State, and Society,* pp. 374–83. New York: Praeger.
Almaraz Paz, Sergio
1969   *Requiem para una republica.* La Paz: Universidad Mayor de San Andrés.
Ames, Michael M.
1973   "Structural Dimensions of Family Life in the Steel City of Jamshedput." In Milton Singer, ed., *Entrepreneurship and*

Modernization of Occupational Cultures in South Asia. Durham, N.C.: Duke University Program in Comparative Studies in Southern Asia. Monograph No. 12.

Anayo, Ricardo
1952 *Nacionalización de las minas de Bolivia*. Cochabamba: Universal.

Andrade, Carlos
1956 *Bolivia: Problems and Promise*. Washington, D.C.

Anti-Slavery Society
1977 "Report on a Visit to Investigate Allegations of Slavery." London, England. Mimeo.

Aquino, Estanislao
1968 "Ensayo de interpretación del Carnaval Oruro." In *Ensayo de interpretación del Carnaval Oruro: Leyendas, tradiciones, costumbres*. Oruro: Instituto de Filosofía Indígena Oruro.

Arce, Roberto
1965 *Recommendaciones para le rehabilitación de la industría minera*. La Paz.
1969 "Ubicación histórica y económica de la explotación del estaña en Bolivia. Política minera." In *El estaño en Bolivia*, pp. 1–17. La Paz: Instituto Boliviano de Estudio y Acción Social.

Archivo de la Municipalidad
1606 *Historia de Oruro*. Oruro.

Barrios de Chungara, Domitila and Moema Viezzer
1977 *"Si me permiten hablar": Testimonio de Domitila, una mujer de las minas de Bolivia*. Mexico, D. F.: Siglo XX.

Barrios Zilla, Erasmo
1966 *Historia sindical de Bolivia*. Oruro: Imprenta Universitaria.

Bedregal, Guillermo
1959 *La nacionalicación minera y la responsabilidad del sindicalismo*. La Paz.
1962 *La Revolución boliviana*. La Paz.
1963 *COMIBOL: Una verdad sin escandalo*. La Paz: Departamento de Relaciones Pública de COMIBOL.

Beltrán Herédia, B. Augusto
1962 *Carnaval de Oruro y proceso ideologica e historia de los grupos folkloricos*. Oruro: Edición del Comité Departmental de Folklore.

Belzu, Manuel Isidor
1970 "Las masas populares hacen oir su voz." In Guillermo Lora, ed., *Documentos politicos de Bolivia*. La Paz.

Blanco, P. A.
1910 *Monografía de la industría minera en Bolivia.* La Paz.
Bourricaud, Francois
1970 *Power and Society in Contemporary Peru.* New York: Praeger.
British Mineworkers Union
1977 "Report on Bolivian Miners." Mimeo.
Burke, Melvin
1972 "Del populismo nacional al corporativismo nacional: El caso de Bolivia 1952–70," *Aportes* (October), 26:66–96.
1974 "Combined International Assistance to a National Industry: A Case Study of the Corporación Minera de Bolivia." Mimeo.
1976 "El desaparecimiento de COMIBOL: La última fase de la larga historia de la explotación del minero boliviano." Paper read in Lima, Peru, 1976.
Canelas, O., Amado
1966 *Mito y realidad de la Corporación Minera de Bolivia.* La Paz: Editorial Los Amigos del Libro.
CEP (Centro de Estudios y Publicaciones) America Latina
1976 *Bolivia 1971–1976. Pueblo, estado y iglesia: Testimonios de Christianos.* Lima.
Comisión Economica para América Latina.
1964 "El financiamento esterna de América Latina." Mimeo.
Comptroller General of the United States
1975 "Report to the Congress: Bolivia: An Assessment of U.S. Policies and Programs." January 30. Mimeo.
Cotler, Julio
1969 "Actuales Pautas de cambio en la sociedad peruana: Una perspectiva configuracional." In José Matos Mar et al, eds., *Dominación y cambios en el Peru rural,* pp. 23–59. Lima: Instituto de Estudios Peruanos.
Crespo R., Alberto
1967 "Fundación de la villa de San Felipe de Austria," *Revista Historica* 29:3–25.
Dandler, Jorge
1977 " 'Los Classness' or Wavering Populism? A Peasant Movement in Bolivia, 1952–1953." In June Nash, Juan Corradi, and Hobart Spalding, eds. *Idiology and Social Change in Latin America,* pp. 142–73. New York: Gordon Breach.
Dennis, N., F. Henriques, and C. Slaughter
1956 *Coal Is Our Life.* London: Eyre.

Dubois, Cora
1944   *The People of Alor.* New York: Harper Torchbooks.
Economic Commission for Latin America
1970   *Economic Survey of Latin America.* New York: United Nations.
Eder, George Jackson
1968   *Inflation and Development in Latin America: A Case History of Inflation and Stabilization in Bolivia.* Ann Arbor: University of Michigan Program in International Business, Graduate School of Business Administration. Michigan International Business Studies 8.
Ford, Bacon, and Davis, Inc.
1956   *Mining Industry of Bolivia: A Report to the Bolivian Ministry of Mines and Petroleum,* vols. 1–9. New York.
Gall, Norman
1974   "The Price of Tin," *West Coast South American Series* 21:1–2. Hanover, N.H.: American Field Staff 37.
Gerth, H. H. and C. Wright Mills, trans. and eds.
1946   *From Max Weber: Essays in Sociology.* New York: Oxford University Press.
Godoy, Richard
1985   "Mining: Anthropological Perspectives," *Annual Review of Anthropology* 14:199–218. Palo Alto, Calif.
Gonzalez, Nancie L.
1969   *Black Carib Household Structure: A Study of Migration and Modernization.* Seattle: University of Washington Press.
Goode, William
1963   *World Revolution and Family Patterns.* New York: Free Press.
Gramsci, Antonio
1973   *Selections from the Prison Notebooks.* New York: International Publishers.
Hanke, Lewis
1956   *The Imperial City of Potosí.* The Hague: Nijhoff.
Harris, Olivia and Javier Albó
1975   *Monteras y guardatojos; Campesinos y mineros en el norte de Potosí.* La Paz, Bolivia: Centro de Investigación y Promoción del Campesinado (CIPCA).
Herédia, Luis Edmundo
1966   *Sociología de la ciudad latino Americana.* La Paz.
Hobsbawm, Eric J.
1959   *Primitive Rebels: Studies in Archaic Forms of Social Movements in the Nineteenth and Twentieth Centuries.* New York: Norton.

1971　"Class Consciousness in History." In Estéban Mészaros, ed., *Aspects of History and Class Consciousness*. New York: Herder and Herder.

1977　"Ideology and Social Change in Colombia." In June Nash, Juan Corradi, and Hobart Spalding, eds., *Ideology and Social Change in Latin America*, pp. 185–99. New York: Gordon Breach Co.

Ibañez C., Donaciano
1943　*Historia mineral de Bolivia*. Antofagasta: MacFarlane.

Inkeles, Alex
1969　"Making Men Modern: On the Causes and Consequences of Individual Change in Developing Countries," *American Journal of Sociology* (September), 75:208–25.

International Labour Office
1947　"Informe al gobierno de Bolivia." Geneva. Mimeo.
1964　*Informe al gobierno de Bolivia*. Geneva.

International Work Group on Indigenous Affairs
1978a　*The Indian Liberation and Social Rights Movement in Kollasuyu* (Bolivia), No. 30. Copenhagen.
1978b　*Colonization Program for White Settlers* (Bolivia), No. 31. Copenhagen.

Investigación del Estaño en Bolivia
1935　La Paz.

Jelin, Elizabeth
1973　"Spontaneidad y organización en el movimiento obrero." Ms.

Justice and Peace Commission, Catholic Church
1974　"The Massacre of the Valley." Ms.

Kahl, Joseph A.
1968　*The Measurement of Modernism: A Study of Values in Brazil and Mexico*. Austin: University of Texas Press.

Kardiner, Abraham
1939　*The Individual and His Society: The Psychodynamics of Primitive Social Organization*. New York: Columbia University Press.

Kerr, Clark and Abraham Siegel
1954　"The Industrial Propensity to Strike: An International Comparison." In A. Kornhauser, R. Dubin, and A. Ross, eds., *Industrial Conflict*, pp. 189–212. New York: McGraw-Hill.

Klein, Herbert S.
1969　*Parties and Political Change in Bolivia 1880–1952*. Cambridge: Cambridge University Press.

Kyne, M.
1943 "Trouble in Bolivia," *Commonweal* (June), pp. 198–202.
Landsberger, Henry A.
1967 "The Labor Elite: Is It Revolutionary?" In S. Lipset and A. Solari, eds., *Elites in Latin America*, pp. 256–300. New York: Oxford University Press.
Latin American Political Report
1978 Vol. 12, no. 28. July 21, 1978.
1978 Vol. 12, no. 34, September 1, 1978.
Lenin, V. I.
1947 *Selected Works*. Moscow: Foreign Languages Publishing House. Vols. 1 and 2.
Letter to Terence Todman of U.S. State Department
1977 Drafted by a group of American citizens. April.
Lipset, Seymour
1963 *Political Man: The Social Bases of Politics*. New York: Doubleday.
Lockwood, D.
1968 "Sources of Variation in Working Class Images of Society." In J. Kahl, ed., *Comparative Perspectives on Stratification*, pp. 100–101. Boston: Little, Brown.
Lora, Guillermo
1960 *Sindicatos y revolución*. La Paz: Editorial Masas.
1963 *Lá revolución boliviana*. La Paz: Difusión SRL.
1964 *Perspectivas de la revolución boliviana: La politica reaccionaria de la junta militar conduce a la guerra civil*. La Paz: Editorial Masas.
1965 *Abajo la bota militar: Analysis de la situación politica*. La Paz: Editorial Masas.
1967 *Historia del movimiento obrero boliviano, 1848–1900*. Cochabamba: Los Amigos del LIBRO.
1969 *Historia del movimiento obrero boliviano, 1901–1922*. Cochabamba: Los Amigos del Libro.
1970a *Documentos politicos de Bolivia*. La Paz: Los Amigos del Libro.
1970b *Historia del movimiento obrero boliviano 1923–1933*. Cochabamba: Los Amigos del Libro.
1972 *Bolivia: De la asamblea popular al golpe fascista*. Santiago, Chile: Industria Impresora Bio-Bio.
Lukacs, Georg
1971 *History and Class Consciousness: Studies in Marxist Dialectics*. London: Merlin Press.

Magdoff, Harry
1976 "Capital, Technology, and Development," *Monthly Review* (January), 27(8):1–11.
Malloy, James
1970 *Bolivia: The Unfinished Revolution.* Pittsburgh: Pittsburgh University Press.
Mannheim, Karl
1936 *Ideology and Utopia.* New York: Harcourt, Brace and World.
Marof, Tristan
1934 *La tragedia del altiplano.* Buenos Aires: Editorial Claridad.
Marx, Karl
1906 *Capital: A Critique of Political Economy.* Vol. 1. Chicago: Charles Kerr.
1969 "Wages, Price and Profit." In *Karl Marx, Frederick Engels: Selected Works,* pp. 186–229. New York: World Paperback.
1971 *The Grundrisse,* ed. and trans. by David McLellan. New York: Harper and Row.
Matos Mar, José
1968 "Idea y diagnostico del Peru. El pluralismo de situaciones sociales y culturales." In *Péru problema.* Lima: Francisco Moncloa.
1969 "El pluralismo y la dominación en la sociedad peruana: una perspectiva configuaracional." In *Dominación y cambio en el Peru rural,* pp. 23–59. Lima: Instituto de Estudios Peruanos.
Medinacelli, Carlos
1935 *Chaskañawi: novela de costumbres bolivianos.* La Paz: Libreria y Editorial "Juventud."
Millan Mauri, José
1968 *Minero y otros relatos de la Paz.* La Paz: Librería "Renovación."
Millen, B. H.
1963 *The Political Role of Labor in Developing Countries.* Washington, D.C.: Brooking Institution.
Murillo Vacareza, Josermo
1969 "El diablo de Oruro y la supervivencia de un anhelo," *Fraternidad Revista Cultural,* pp. 7–9. Oruro.
Nash, June
1970 *In the Eyes of the Ancestors: Belief and Behavior in a Maya Community.* New Haven: Yale University Press.
1972 Devils, Witches and Sudden Death," *Natural History Magazine* (Spring).

Nash, June and Manuel María Rocca
  1976 *Dos mujeres indígenas: Basilia; Facundina.* Mexico, D. F.: Insti-
        tuto Indigenista Interamericano.
Nash, June
  1988 "Mobilization of Women in the Bolivian Debt Crisis," In
        Barbara A. Gutek, ed., *Women and Work*, pp. 67–86. Beverly
        Hills: Sage Press.
Nash, June with Juan Rojas
  1976 *He agotado mi vida en la mina: Autobiografía de un minero bo-
        liviano.* Buenos Aires: Nueva Visión.
Nash, June
  1989 "Cultural Resistance and Class Consciousness in Bolivian
        Tin-Mining Communities." In Susan Eckstein, ed., *Power
        and Popular Protest.* Berkeley: University of California Press.
Nash, June
  1992 "Interpreting Social Movements: Bolivian Tin Miners' Re-
        sponse to the IMF Restructuring of the Economy in the Debt
        Crisis," *American Ethnologist*, vol. 94, no. 2.
Ossowski, Stanislaw
  1963 *Class Structure in the Social Consciousness.* New York: Free
        Press.
Page, Janet
  1991 "Beyond Economics: ADAM and Sweater Knitting in Bo-
        livia." Paper read at the Northeastern Conference of Latin
        American Studies, Smith College, October.
Patch, Richard W.
  1960 "U.S. Assistance in a Revolutionary Setting." In R. Adams,
        C. Lewis, J. P. Gillen, R. W. Patch, A. R. Holmberg, and
        C. Wagley, *Social Change in Latin America Today: Its Impor-
        tance for U.S. Policy*, pp. 108–76. New York: Vintage.
Patiño Mines and Co.
  1948 *Los conflictos sociales en 1947: I. Documentos; II: Notas Finales,*
        por el Dr. José Rivera. La Paz.
Peacock, James L.
  1968 *Rites of Modernization: Symbolic and Social Aspects of Indonesian
        Proletarian Drama.* Chicago: University of Chicago Press.
Peñaloza, L.
  1953 *Historia economica de Bolivia.* 2 vols. La Paz: n.p.
Platt, Tristan
  1983 "Conciencia andina y consciencia proletaria: Qhuyaruna y
        allyu en el norte de Potosí," *Revista Latinoamericana Historia
        Económica y Social*, 2:47–73.

Redfield, Robert
1947 "The Folk Society," *American Journal of Sociology* 52(2): 282–308.
1953 *The Primitive World and its Transformations.* Ithaca, N.Y.: Cornell University Press.
Reyes, Simón
1967 *La masacre de San Juan.* Oruro.
Rivera L., Gumercindo
1967 *La masacre de Uncía.* La Paz.
Rojas, Juan and June Nash
1976 *He agotado mi vida en la mina.* Argentina: Nueva Visión.
Ruiz Gonzalez, René
1965 *La administración empirica de las minas nacionalizadas.* La Paz.
Salamanca, Alberto.
1950 *Tierra del Chaantaca.* Oruro.
Salazar Bondy, Augusto
1968 "La cultura de la dominación," in *Peru problema,* pp. 57–82. Lima: Francisca Moncloa.
Sanjek, Roger, ed.
1989 *Fieldnotes: The Makings of Anthropology.* Ithaca: Cornell University Press.
Secretariado Nacional de Estudios Sociales
1969 "Informe sobre la situación de las minas de Bolivia: Sondeo sobre las condiciones sociales." La Paz. Mimeo.
Seeman, M.
1959 "On the Meaning of Alienation," *American Sociological Review* (July), 24:783–91.
Selser, Jorge.
1970 *Participación de los trabajadores en la gestión economica.* Buenos Aires: Ediciones Librero.
Singer, Milton, ed.
1973 *Entrepreneurship and Modernization of Occupational Cultures in South Asia.* Durham, N.C.: Duke University Program in Comparative Studies of Southern Asia.
Stokes, William S.
1963 "The *contraproducente* Consequences of the Foreign Aid Program in Bolivia." In Helmut Schoeck and James Wiggins, eds., *The New Argument in Economics: The Public vs. The Private Sector.* New York: Van Nostrand.
Sunkel, Oswaldo
1973 "Transnational Capitalism and National Disintegration in Latin America," *Social and Economic Studies* 22(1):132–71.

Taboada, Nestor
1960   *El précio de estaña*. La Paz: Escuela Gráfica Salesiana "Don Bosco."
Taussig, Michael
1980   *The Devil and Commodity Fetishism in South America*. Chapel Hill: University of North Carolina Press.
Tax, Sol
1941   "World View and Social Relations in Guatemala," *American Anthropologist* 43(1):27–42.
Thompson, Eric
1963   *The Making of the English Working Class*. New York: Vintage.
Thompson, Eric
1978   *The Poverty of Theory and Other Essays*. New York: Monthly Review Press.
Touraine, A. and D. Pécaut
1970   "Working-Class Consciousness and Economic Development in Latin America." In I. Horowitz, ed., *Masses in Latin America*. New York: Oxford University Press.
Troncoso, Moises Poblete and Ben G. Burnett
1960   *The Rise of the Latin American Labor Movement*. New Haven: Connecticut College and University Press.
Turner, Victor
1957   *Schism and Continuity in an African Society*. Manchester: Manchester University Press.
1969   *The Ritual Process: Structure and Anti-Structure*. Chicago: University of Chicago Press.
1974   *Dramas, Fields, and Metaphors: Symbolic Action in Human Society*. Ithaca, N.Y.: Cornell University Press.
United Nations
1964   *América en cifras*. Washington, D.C.: Organization of American States.
1968   *Yearbook of International Trade*. New York.
1970   *Yearbook of International Trade*. New York.
1970   *Statistical Bulletin for Latin America*, vol. 7, no. 2. New York.
United States Agency for International Development (AID).
1965   *Latin American Trends in Growth Rates*. Washington, D.C.
1969   "Background Data." Mimeo.
1970   *GNP Growth Rate and Trend Data by Region and Country*. Washington, D.C., April 30.
Valdiviesa, Rafael, Marcelo Sanjines, and Jack Brown
1965   *Estudio de ingresos y dieta, Empresa Minera Colquiri*. Ithaca, N.Y.: Programa Cornell-Bolivia.

Velasco, S. José Miguel
1964 *Mito y realidad de las fundiciones en Bolivia.* La Paz.
Wallace, Anthony F. C.
1964 *Culture and Personality.* New York: Random House.
Widerkehr, Doris
1975 *Bolivia's Nationalized Mines: A Comparison of a Cooperative and a State Managed Community.* Ann Arbor: University Microfilms Ltd.
Wilkie, James W.
1969 *The Bolivian Revolution and U.S. Aid since 1952.* Los Angeles: University of California Press, Latin American Center.
1977 *Statistical Abstract of Latin America,* vol. 18. Los Angeles: University of California Press, Latin American Center.
Wilkie, James W. and Peter Reich, eds.
1977 *Statistical Abstract of Latin America.* Los Angeles: University of California, Latin American Center.
Zavaleta Mercado, René
1963 "Soberania, significa industria pesada: Hay que derrota el atraso en las fundiciones nacional." Ph.D. dissertation, Technical University of Oruro.
1971 *Porque cayó Bolivia en manos del fascismo?* Santiago de Chile: Punto Final No. 144.
1974 *El poder dual en América Latina: Estudio de los casos de Bolivia y Chile.* Mexico: Siglo XXI.
Zeitlan, Maurice and James Petras
1968 *Latin America, Reform or Revolution?* Greenwich, Conn.: Fawcett.
Znaniecki, Florian and W. I. Thomas
1963 *The Polish Peasant in Europe and America.* New York: Dover.
Zondag, Cornelius H.
1966 *The Bolivian Economy, 1952–1965: The Revolution and Its Aftermath.* New York: Praeger.
Zulawski, Ann
1990 "Social Differentiation, Gender, and Ethnicity: Urban Indian Women in Colonial Bolivia, 1640–1725," *Latin American Research Review* 25:93–113.

Index